Framing Nature

AMERICA'S PUBLIC LANDS

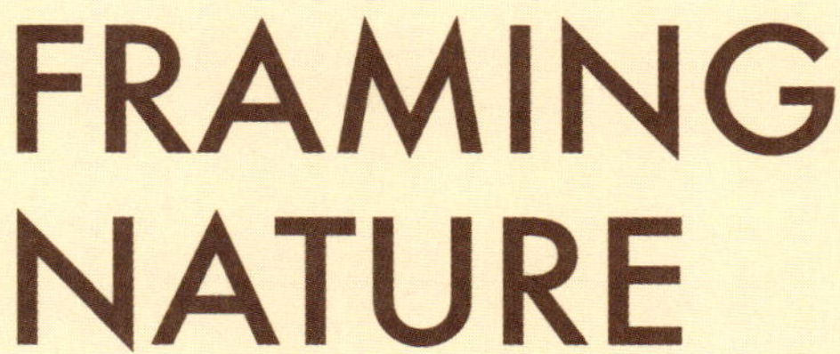

FRAMING NATURE

The Creation of an American Icon at the Grand Canyon

YOLONDA YOUNGS

University of Nebraska Press Lincoln

The University of Nebraska Press is part of a land-grant institution with campuses and programs on the past, present, and future homelands of the Pawnee, Ponca, Otoe-Missouria, Omaha, Dakota, Lakota, Kaw, Cheyenne, and Arapaho Peoples, as well as those of the relocated Ho-Chunk, Sac and Fox, and Iowa Peoples.

Publication of this volume was assisted by a grant from the Charles Redd Center for Western Studies at Brigham Young University and by a grant from the Office of Academic Research and College of Social and Behavioral Sciences at California State University San Bernardino.

Library of Congress Cataloging-in-Publication Data
Names: Youngs, Yolonda, author.
Title: Framing nature: the creation of an American icon at the Grand Canyon / Yolonda Youngs.
Other titles: Creation of an American icon at the Grand Canyon
Description: Lincoln: University of Nebraska Press, [2023] | Includes bibliographical references and index.
Identifiers: LCCN 2023013601
ISBN 9781496202185 (paperback)
ISBN 9781496238351 (epub)
ISBN 9781496238368 (pdf)
Subjects: LCSH: Grand Canyon National Park (Ariz.)—In mass media.
Classification: LCC F788 .Y65 2023 | DDC 979.1/32—dc23/eng/20231023
LC record available at https://lccn.loc.gov/2023013601

Designed and set in Minion Pro by L. Welch.

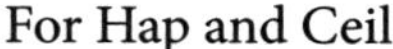
For Hap and Ceil

Contents

Illustrations

Acknowledgments

The book in your hands is the product of fifteen years of archival and library research, writing, analysis, and extensive field reconnaissance at the Grand Canyon and in the Southwest. Although writing is a solitary task much of the time, I could not have finished this project without the inspiration, research assistance, and support of many people over the years. The seed for this work started while I was a student at Arizona State University. Daniel D. Arreola provided encouragement and guidance at key times as my advisor and mentor. I will not forget our many enjoyable discussions during afternoon coffee breaks, as he tirelessly pushed me to establish my voice and style. I benefit greatly from his keen insights into the postcard production process, his passion for geographic scholarship and field studies, and his love of the Southwest. I deeply appreciate his mentorship and introduction to historic postcard analysis. I also am indebted to Paul Hirt, Anthony Brazel, and Stephen Pyne. Paul Hirt was wonderfully enthusiastic as this project developed. He informed my thinking about wilderness, environmental history, and the Grand Canyon and he was a patient guide and leader with a National Endowment for the Humanities grant that supported the early stages of this project. This project would not be the same without the influence of Anthony Brazel, who I thank for his zeal for physical geography, fieldwork guidance, and good humor. I also owe hearty gratitude to Stephen Pyne, whose extensive work in environmental history and eloquent wordsmithing inspire me. I am grateful for the fine lessons and gentle but structured guidance he shared in his nonfiction writing seminar, which will stay with me for many years. Other key scholars guided and nurtured my research abilities and opportunities along the way at Arizona State University (ASU), including David White and Patricia Gober, whose work on desert cities and the demands of balancing limited water supplies continue to shape my thinking and scholarship on the subject.

The research and publication of this book are made possible with the assistance of multiple funding sources. I appreciate the generous support of the Grand Canyon Association (now the Grand Canyon Conservancy) and a National Endowment for the Humanities "We the People" grant, for providing support for my early field reconnaissance and research that started this project. I am grateful to Idaho State University's College of Arts and Letters and the Department of Global Studies and Languages, for a sabbatical to complete various research stages of this project and the encouragement of faculty and students along the way. The University of New Mexico's Center for Regional Studies Scholar-in-Residence award provided valuable time to live in New Mexico for a semester and complete regional forays into field, library, and archives of the Southwest. The University of New Mexico's Department of Geography and Environmental Studies and Maria Lane generously hosted me with office space and provided much-appreciated comradery during my stay. Special thanks go to Gabriel Melendez, Benjamin Warner, Joni Palmer, Joe Rivera, and John Fleck, for their insightful comments, invigorating conversations, and perspectives on cultural heritage, hydropolitics, and water resources of the Southwest. I am deeply thankful to my current academic home of California State University, San Bernardino for a Summer Research Fellowship to support the final stages of preparing this book for publication and my fellow faculty in the Department of Geography and Environmental Studies, for their enthusiasm for this project and enduring collegiality. I am deeply honored by a publication grant from the Charles Redd Center for Western Studies, which supplied key funding to the University of Nebraska Press to help offset the costs of publishing this book.

This project draws on many hours of archival and library research at sites around the United States. I thank the archivists, librarians, and support staffs for their expert assistance in locating and accessing historical collections. Special thanks to Colleen Hyde at the U.S. National Park Service Grand Canyon National Park Library and Archives in Arizona; to Debra Gust at the Curt Teich Postcard Archives; to Illinois Digital Archives photography editor Jeff Kida at *Arizona Highways* magazine; to Allan Lagumbay, Bruce Guter, and Henry Golas, for their help with Frasher Foto postcards at the City of Pomona Public Library in California; to Colleen Curry and Kim Besom at the National Park Service Grand Canyon National Park Museum Collection in Arizona; to Christine Marin at the Arizona State University Special Collections and Luhrs Reading Room; and to Tomas Jaehn and the archive and library staff at the University of New Mexico's Center for Southwest Research.

Writing scholarly books and conducting library researching has transformed during the digital age. I am deeply thankful for the investment and work behind digital and online archives creation, management, and maintenance. Through digital archives I was able to complete some of the archival research for this project and saved valuable travel time and budgets. Many thanks to the Arizona State Library and the Arizona Memory Project for the *Arizona Highways* online digital collections; the Benson Ford Research Center; the David Rumsey Map Collection; the New York Public Library; and the Library of Congress. The massive collection of over 360,000 images was transferred from Lake County Historical Museum to the Newberry Library in 2016 and now rests in the Newberry's highly capable and diligent hands. I had the pleasure of working with both the Lake County and Newberry collections staffs, who were generous with their time and patience with my inquires. Through the Newberry's digitization efforts, access to the CTC and DPC collections has been amplified as an enduring resource for researchers and scholars of visual media.

The best ideas are sometimes formulated during extended conversations and correspondence with colleagues and friends. William Wyckoff has been and continues to be an outstanding mentor, colleague, and friend, sharing many delightful conversations about the Grand Canyon and the American West over the years, comparing our photographs and field stories, helping me sort through ideas and conceptual approaches, and guiding me along the book publishing trail. At the Grand Canyon, Mike Anderson always took time out of his busy schedule to point me in the right direction for documents and resources during my field reconnaissance and research in the canyon. He generously shared his extensive knowledge and experience of the Grand Canyon with me, often acting as a sounding board for my ideas. At ASU, I thank Mark Klett for his interest in this project, his inspiring projects, and the fine conversations about repeat photography and visual history. Jeremy Rowe generously shared his well-honed Arizona postcard knowledge with me and shaped my ideas about postcard production. Donald Worster provided me with many insights over the years through his research and writing, a shared environmental history conference paper session, and ongoing conversations about the cultural meanings and history of the Grand Canyon.

I thank the people who read various parts and versions of this manuscript over the years, including William Wyckoff, Terrence Young, Lary Dilsaver,

Judith Meyer, Kevin Blake, and Geoffrey Buckley, along with two anonymous reviewers. Their thoughtful comments and insights made this work more accurate and improved the manuscript tremendously. Robert M. Edsall deserves special thanks for creating the maps for this book. His refined cartographic skills transformed my sketches into crisp maps. I am grateful to the University of Nebraska Press, especially the unwavering support and skilled editorial guidance of Bridget Barry. Bridget embodies the very best of editors. Through the years she remained dedicated to the project, showed encouragement through the twists and turns of project development, and contributed expert reading and suggestions that improved the manuscript in innumerable ways. I am also deeply grateful to series editor Char Miller, for his enthusiasm and expert feedback on the project and for including this volume in the America's Public Lands series.

The support and encouragement of family and friends sustained me through the years of this project. Valerie and Kevin, my patron saints of geography, thank you for seeing me through Arizona monsoons, record heat waves, and other calamities with love and good humor. Rob, your love and zeal for long road trips, hikes, and visits to obscure viewpoints in the canyon is the heart of this book. I owe an eternal thanks to my parents, for introducing me to national parks on our annual summer road trips. Their gifts of travel, curiosity, love, and tenacity fuel my work and passions to this day.

Abbreviations

AH	Arizona Highways
CCC	Civilian Conservation Corps
CTC	Curt Teich Company
DPC	Detroit Publishing Company
FFPC	Frasher Foto Postcard Company
FHC	Fred Harvey Company
GGCR	Greater Grand Canyon Region
GRCA	Grand Canyon National Park
NPS	United States National Park Service
USFS	United States Forest Service

A Selected Chronology of Grand Canyon National Park

1893	Grand Canyon Forest Reserve
1906	Grand Canyon Game Preserve
1908	Grand Canyon National Monument
1919	Grand Canyon National Park
1975	Grand Canyon National Park Enlargement Act
1979	Designated a World Heritage Site by the United Nations Educational, Scientific, and Cultural Organization (UNESCO)
2019	Designated an International Dark Sky Park (IDSP) by the International Dark-Sky Association

Framing Nature

Introduction

A View from the Rim

> The most famous national parks have come to resemble television shows or photography books—controlled or static sequences of scenery and sights. Tourists see and remember with visual aids.
>
> —Lucy R. Lippard, *On the Beaten Track*

When I started this project as a student living just a few hours south of the Grand Canyon in Tempe, Arizona, I often asked friends and colleagues about their impressions of the Grand Canyon. What struck me most from these conversations is that most people quickly conjured a distinct visual image of the Grand Canyon, even if they had never visited it. They summoned a very specific place in mind: the South Rim. Almost every conversation turned to their memories (or their imagination) of standing *on* the rim, staring *down* into the vast depths of the canyon and seeing the Colorado River at its base. They also held specific colors in mind for the canyon: red, orange, and pink tones for the canyon walls; robin-egg blue for the sky; and bright white for the few clouds that dotted the horizon. This amazed me. For about a decade, I worked as a commercial river rafting and kayak guide, often spending weeks deep in the wilderness settings of national parks in the American West. I mostly knew the Grand Canyon from my experiences looking *up at the rim* from the perspective of the Colorado River and along the trails along the canyon's walls. My perspective, I quickly discovered during those early years in Arizona, was in the minority. The dominant visual of the Grand Canyon was a view from the rim. What lead people to this very specific geography? And why was it so common? That was part of my inspiration in pursuing this research and ultimately writing this book.

The cultural context for the Grand Canyon draws on a deep visual and cultural archive. How did this canyon become so iconic? What images, experiences, and visitor accounts built its reputation as the "one great sight that every American should see," as Theodore Roosevelt once proclaimed. What specific locations did photographers and other image makers select, within the vast realm of the canyon and its neighboring lands, to represent the canyon? And how did this visual archive influence environmental management, cultural heritage preservation, and tourism experiences throughout history in ways that shape our present understanding of this place? These are some of the questions that *Framing Nature* will explore.

What Makes This Canyon So Grand?

There are many "grand" canyons. In the United States the Grand Canyon of the Yellowstone River in Wyoming gained national notoriety through explorers' accounts and artistic representations well before its Arizona cousin. Internationally, Mexico's Copper Canyon or Barranca del Cobre is "grander"—both larger and deeper—than its neighbor to the north (Sylvester 2019). Indeed, given the geologic and geographic patterns around the globe, many countries claim a local grand canyon. Yet this one canyon, in northern Arizona, has become *the* Grand Canyon, the one to which all others are compared.

The Grand Canyon is a national and international icon. It is one of the most recognized and frequented national parks and protected areas in the world; it is a UNESCO World Heritage Site and one of the seven natural wonders of the world, hosting over six million visitors each year.

The Grand Canyon is an important place of national discourse about evolving ideas and practices of environmental management, public lands policy, and ecological change. It has often been at the center of debates about rivers and dams, water resource use and management in the arid West, invasive species, wildlife management, and climate change. It is the one of the most extensive canyons on earth at over 277 miles long with many places 10 miles wide and a mile deep. It is an important source of scientific discovery and theoretical development. In the field of geology, it contains some of the oldest exposed rock on the earth, Precambrian Vishnu schist formed 1.7 billion years ago.

It is also a place of strong cultural identities and traditions. Southwestern American Indian tribes trace their lineage to the canyon for thousands of years. It is home to the Ancestral Puebloans and the Hopi, Hualapai, Havasupai, Paiute, and Navajo who now live across the states of Arizona, New Mexico, Utah, and Nevada. Recent initiatives, such as the revitalization of historic murals and cultural demonstration programs at the Desert View Watchtower, are strengthening ties between the National Park Service

(NPS) and the eleven Traditionally Associate Tribes of the Grand Canyon. Although this is a positive sign of potential collaboration and renewed respect of tribal agency and cultural heritage, there is a history of American Indian land dispossession that underlies national park origins. Many of the U.S. national parks, including Grand Canyon National Park (GRCA), were used by American Indians for seasonal hunting and gathering, spiritual ceremonies and traditions, and as homes before the U.S. federal government forcibly removed them from their traditional homelands throughout the late nineteenth and early twentieth centuries. Today that contested history fosters a complex mix of human geographies and environmental management legacies.

The Grand Canyon is an important source of iconic imagery of America. It is through popular visual representations of the canyon that many people first "see" the Grand Canyon. Tourists memorialize their trips with postcards, photographs, paintings, and films; railroad and hospitality companies publicized the canyon through thousands of postcards and photographs; magazines and newspapers print photographs; films situate their action here; and federal agencies such as the National Park Service create guidebooks and imagery to interpret the canyon for visitors from around the world. The canyon draws people because of its scenic beauty and its important role as a source of potent ideas and meanings.

People seek out the Grand Canyon, perhaps more than any other national park or popular tourist destination in the United States, to simply look at the scenery. Hiking, rafting, and camping are popular to be sure. But for many people, just *seeing* the Grand Canyon is high on their bucket list. More than that, the Grand Canyon is also a place where national debates play out about environmental management, public lands policies, water resource use and management, American Indian land rights and cultural heritage, tourism impacts, and wildlife conservation. Imagery play a key role in shaping popular ideas and emotions about the Grand Canyon that can influence lasting policy decisions.

Framing Nature at the Grand Canyon

Close your eyes for a moment and think of the Grand Canyon. If you have visited the canyon, then recall those memories. Where did you go? What did you see? If you have not been there, then stop for a moment in your reading and consider what images or feelings come to mind.

Fig. 1. A view from the rim. Scenic viewpoint and tourists at the South Rim of the Grand Canyon. Photograph by the author.

I will guess that when you open your eyes, the image that resonates in your mind looks something like this (fig. 1). You are standing on the rim of the canyon, feeling dwarfed by the immensity of the scene before you. Your viewpoint allows you to look across the vast gorge to the rim on the other side, the blue sky above, and into the canyon with its dizzying array of internal contours marked by deep orange and red rock color variations. You are perhaps standing with friends or family along with you on the journey or alone in a small crowd gathered at this scenic viewpoint along the rim.

Your imagination is not alone in this visual recollection of the Grand Canyon. Before making the journey to the canyon, most tourists have seen images of it in a magazine, a film, or an advertisement. The Grand Canyon is as visually ubiquitous and as readily recognized in American popular culture as Yellowstone's geysers or the Statue of Liberty. But the Grand Canyon "is more than a view," as the NPS intones in several of its short *Grand Canyon in Depth* videos (Grand Canyon National Park 2021). Images of these places embedded in popular media often serve as the primary source of information about the park for visitors.

In *Framing Nature* I trace an iconographic arc of more than 150 years of Grand Canyon popular imagery (1869–2020) as an instrument to tell the broader cultural, political, and social story about how people construct ideas and meanings about nature through visual representations and how that process shapes decision-making, use, and management at the canyon over time and at multiple scales. This narrative recognizes the fundamental intertwining of human and environmental geographies and how interactions of the past shape the present day. The politics of scientific and geographical knowledge production, visual representation, and narratives about the canyon intermingle in this book. Considering how the canyon is visually represented, by whom, and for what purpose are primary considerations. As noted nineteenth-century explorer, scholar, and writer John Wesley Powell observed in 1909, the canyon's visual presence is powerful. "The wonders of the Grand Canyon cannot be adequately represented in symbols of speech, nor by speech itself. The resources of the graphic art are taxed beyond their powers in attempting to portray its features. Language and illustration combined must fail" (1909, 32). Vision is not merely a recording of facts from the physical scene; it is an act that involves both the physical component of seeing, as well as the intellectual process of viewing and interpreting the scene through a cultural lens. Analyzing this imagery arc offers insight into the ways that different cultural conceptions of nature shape the world around us and inform environmental policies, interactions, and expectations. Nature is not a passive player in this storyline. The natural processes of the Grand Canyon are pivotal components of its history, revealing the canyon as an active player that shaped and sometimes stymied the intentions of concessionaires, park management agencies, and an array of other human actors.

There are numerous books written about the Grand Canyon; *Framing Nature* differs in several significant ways. Few previous studies of the canyon combine the methods, interdisciplinary literature, extensive archival and library sources, multiple visual mediums, and extensive field research found in this book. I present and analyze images that are rarely seen by the public and often overlooked by other scholars. My findings are grounded in a visual content analysis and interpretation of the 1,473 postcards and photographs of the Grand Canyon. The postcards draw on the imagery found in public archives of three of the largest and most prolific manufacturers of their day—Detroit Publishing Company (DPC), Curt Teich Company (CTC), and Frasher Foto Postcard Company (FFPC). But this book also goes beyond the interiors of a library. I cross-checked what I found in the archives and historical primary sources against the landscape itself. Over the course of several years, I took copies of archival postcards, photographs, and maps with me into the field as I traveled to various locations along the rims, the trails, and the Colorado River of the Greater Grand Canyon Region (GGCR). Once I reached these sites, I would take repeat photographs of the historic imagery and check archival map accuracies against contemporary readings and locations.

My intent in *Framing Nature* is not to provide a comprehensive history of the Grand Canyon, followed as a strict linear chronology, nor is it a comprehensive and exhaustive analysis of every photograph and postcard of the canyon and the technological process of creating this imagery. Instead, I offer vignettes of the Grand Canyon's past that provide windows into larger conversations about how these select historical moments and images may influence the present and future of the Greater Grand Canyon Region.

My goals are: 1) to systematically cross-examine visual representations of the Grand Canyon in multiple sources of popular media over one hundred years; 2) offer an interpretation of the processes behind the creation, production, distribution, and consumption of these images; and 3) connect these images and their makers with the impact they had on the changing tourist experience, environmental management, and public lands policy in the Greater Grand Canyon Region historically and how those impacts may be traced to contemporary issues and problems in the region.

My thesis is that producers, distributors, and manufacturers of visual representations created a visual and cultural narrative that transformed what we know, understand, and value about the Grand Canyon. They favored a selective and repetitive inventory of park features, subjects, and locations. They altered this visual catalog in the production process through slight edits of framing, color, and content. These viewmakers also created a spatial bias in their imagery by focusing their locations on a relatively narrow set of canyon scenes. As other geographers have found with detailed visual content analysis of popular imagery sets, not all subjects or places are represented equally (Wyckoff and Dilsaver 1997). People, animals, plants, cars—almost any object—could be removed, edited, or altered with each postcard printing or framed out of the view of photographs.

Findings from this study reveal that through a process of manipulation and commodification, image manufacturers created a visual code that equated select ideas, values, and meanings about nature with certain Grand Canyon locations. To understand this process better, I go behind the scenes of postcards and photographs to better understand who created, produced, and distributed these images. I reconstruct the social, technical, and spatial process of representing the Grand Canyon temporally and spatially through a content analysis of the subjects and locations found in historical imagery and cross-reference those images and my findings with the records of their creation found in production notes, field survey reports, and other records.

Scope and Intent

My intent in *Framing Nature* is not an exhaustive analysis of all images ever created of the Grand Canyon. That imagery set would be enormous and well beyond the scope of this work. Based on years of archival and library research for this book, I suspect that the total number of Grand Canyon imagery exceeds hundreds of thousands of images, especially if we expand the list to include all postcards, photographs, films, maps, tourist snapshots, railroad brochures and posters, stamps, internet ads and websites, NPS brochures, survey sketches, and other ways that people have depicted the canyon throughout history.

The scope of my interpretations of the themes and trends discussed in this book draws on my analysis of select imagery sets, their subject matter, and geographic locations. I chose the postcards, photographs, and maps for this book based on their broad popularity at the time of publication and distribution, their density of Grand Canyon imagery, and their availability to me today (ruling out private collections). I focus on a series of images of the Grand Canyon, created for a popular audience, widely distributed around the United States and the world, inexpensive, and manufactured by the most prolific image makers of their day. Within these guidelines, I selected manufacturers who consistently published imagery of the Grand Canyon during their manufacturing activity without long breaks between production years.

From an extensive analysis of these imagery sets, I developed a thematic and geographic list of the most common scenes and places shown. This provided a basis for my comparison across time and development of my broader arguments about what is at stake for the canyon's present and future. Note that for additional details, I discuss my methods in this introduction and in appendix B. The postcard and photograph selection and manufacturing process is discussed in chapter 2 and 5.

A Conceptual Approach

Visual representations are images such as photographs, postcards, advertisements, films, maps, and other visual media that depict a scene. They can take many forms and circulate in a variety of outlets. An exploration of seeing nature through a visual and cultural lens can enhance an understanding of how places become inscribed with meaning—how they are produced, consumed, and negotiated over time. My conceptual approach for this book weaves together an interdisciplinary mix of theoretical approaches from geography, environmental studies, visual culture, and media studies to create an innovative framework for exploring environmental management, tourism, and cultural heritage in an iconic national park and protected area. There are four main conceptual pillars to this framework.

The first and central conceptual pillar for this book is the notion of an iconographic arc. The concept is borrowed from a long tradition of visual arts and culture scholarship that seeks to trace the roots of what makes an image, scene, or city an iconic symbol by cataloging its visual elements, tracing their sources, and exploring their thematic development. Cultural geographer Arthur Krim applied this method in his book *Route 66: Iconography of the American Highway* as he explored the origins of the highway and its rise to pop culture prominence from roughly 1830 to 2000. He asserts that there is "nothing random or haphazard about the process by which powerful symbols such as Route 66 arise form the background noise of human activity and communication to generate novels movies, songs, and television shows" (2005, 4). To test this claim, he traces Route 66's iconographic arc from the idea of a proposed Pacific Railway along the thirty-fifth parallel, to a concrete fact as a transcontinental auto highway constructed in the early twentieth century, to an abstract symbol referenced in novels, song lyrics, films, pop art, and television shows. Krim's clever and award-winning book combines a classic cultural landscape reconstruction of Route 66 with a visual and pop culture analysis to reveal larger ideas and meanings attached to the road. "At each step the evolving icon fused all the accumulated imagery existing at the previous stage with new purpose, melding idea, fact, and symbol into an increasingly powerful image" (5). I take a similar approach to Krim's method by tracing the Grand Canyon's transition from "fact" to "symbol," yet no other study has applied the combination of elements that I bring together in *Framing Nature* for a study of a U.S. national park or a geographic region. My approach is an iconographic arc study, combined with the detailed visual content analysis of multiple types of imagery sets taken from different but contemporary creators and applied to the context of the cultural and environmental landscape of the Grand Canyon.

Visual media and culture are vital to understanding iconographic arcs. This book builds on and expands the work of scholars who explore national parks or other protected areas through the lens of popular visual culture and environmental perception. Popular visual representations are images printed or produced in widely circulated and distributed sources and are easily accessible for a broad public audience. Standout examples of these studies investigate how visual culture and popular geographic imagination intermingle in Niagara Falls (McGreevy 1994); Yosemite, Yellowstone, and Grand Canyon (Grusin 2004); and Hoover Dam (Arrigo 2014). Environmental historian Finis Dunaway crafts an engaging dive into photographs, films, and Sierra Club coffee table books to better understand the modern conversation movement and environmental perceptions in *Natural Visions: The Power of Images in American Environmental Reform* (2005). Visual arts scholar J. Keri Cronin's *Manufacturing National Park Nature: Photography, Ecology, and the Wilderness Industry of Jasper* (2011) explores Jasper National Park and the historical tourism industry there. Her critical and perceptive study unravels complex ideas about how images such as postcards and photographs can shape environmental policy and management. But my approach takes a different direction in that I am systematically tracing the iconic rise of the Grand Canyon as both a national park and the core of a larger Greater Grand Canyon Region, using an extensive visual content analysis of multiple forms of visual media, combining this with in-depth fieldwork and reconnaissance, and connecting the insights gained from this work with environmental management and tourism use trends. This work reveals shifting ideas and meanings attached to the canyon and cultural landscape transformations that may escape other visual studies that lack the fieldwork to pinpoint exact locations of landscape change, the regional approach to place the work in a larger geographic setting beyond park borders, and the systematic content analysis to reveal small visual changes over time that accumulate into larger iconographic arcs.

The second pillar of this book is the exploration of new and innovative approaches to visual cultural analysis. Geographer Steven D. Hoelscher's

Picturing Indians: Photographic Encounters and Tourist Fantasies in H. H. Bennett's Wisconsin Dells (2008) provides a guiding light for my approach both in terms of visual cultural studies and deconstructing ideas and meanings associated with American Indian representations. Although there is a growing literature of studies that ground their work in visual culture and media, the approaches to organizing, selecting, and analyzing these images varies greatly. I adhere to Hoelscher's assertion that new insights may be revealed when we juxtapose a primary set of photographs with those of other photographers, especially if their timelines of production overlap. I pursue a similar line of methodology by comparing the postcards of three different manufacturers—Detroit Publishing Company, Curt Teich Company, and Frasher Foto Postcard Company—all with some historical overlap with each other. Also, from Hoelscher's methodology, I look behind the scenes of these images to the people who created them—the photographers and postcard manufacturers. I take an additional step in comparing multiple *types* of visual media, in this case contemporary postcards and photographs.

Building on Hoelscher's work and others, *Framing Nature* adds to a growing body of scholarship that recognizes historic visual representations of landscapes as valuable sources of information. They are not just as tourist ephemera, data from federal scientific surveys, or documents in industry archives. While I delve into these media types and topics in more detail in the following chapters, it is worth mentioning here that this study joins a cadre of works that critically analyze visual media for environmental and geographical themes including photographs (McCloud 1993; Sandweiss 2002; Schwartz and Ryan 2003; Buckley 2004; Berger 2008; Wyckoff 2014; Rose 2016), photographs and the geographical imagination (Nye 2003; Schwartz and Ryan 2003; Schwartz 2014), film (Dunaway 2005; Mitman 2013; Jenkins 2016); visual culture and tourism (Crouch and Lubbren 2003), advertisements and mixed media (Starrs 1988; Wilson 1992; Lane 2013), and magazine imagery (Lutz and Collins 1993). There has been a recent explosion in popular books featuring historic postcards, but many of these volumes treat the images superficially. However, more scholars are taking a serious look at this medium as a rich visual archive of cities, landscapes, and people (Jakle 2003; Arreola 2013, 2017; Larson and Swanbrow 2006; Rowe 2006; Sawyer and Butler 2006; Thornbush 2008; DeBres and Sowers 2009; Jackson 2013; Cronin 2011; Francesconi 2011). Throughout *Framing Nature*, I cite and discuss cartographic representations of the Grand Canyon. Although

I do not critically deconstruct these maps, the scholarship of other writers informs my analysis of these images and their role as sources of geographic knowledge and information (Piper 2002; Schulten 2001, 2012; Hanna and Del Casino 2003; Pickles 2004; Monmonier 2018).

The third pillar of my conceptual model focuses on cultural landscape studies. It builds from a humanistic tradition in geographic scholarship and theoretical works that critically evaluate culture, place, and landscape. The bedrock of my research for this book is scholarship produced by geographers Donald W. Meinig, Yi-Fu Tuan, Richard Francaviglia (1994 and 2005), J. B. Jackson (1972), Michael Conzen (1990), Wilbur Zelinsky (1973), Pierce F. Lewis (1979), and David Lowenthal (1975 and 2015). D. W. Meinig's classic volume *The Interpretation of Ordinary Landscapes* (1979), along with essays from Lewis's "Axioms for Reading the Landscape" and Meinig's "Symbolic Landscapes," sparked my passion for understanding and interpreting cultural landscapes. Yi-Fu Tuan's verdant meditations on perception in *Space and Place: The Perspective of Experience* (1977 and reprinted in 2001) and *Topophilia: A Study of Environmental Perception, Attitudes, and Values* (1974) opened doors to explore the art and science behind our experiences in and representations of diverse environments.

Critical approaches to landscape studies also shape this book's narrative. Denis Cosgrove and Stephen Daniels's *The Iconography of Landscape: Essays on the Symbolic Representation, Design and Use of Past Environments* (1988) and Denis Cosgrove's *Geography and Vision: Seeing, Imaging, and Representing the World* (2008) present compelling examples of how ideology, power, place, and landscape are interwoven. In these works, the idea of landscape is reformulated. "A landscape is a cultural image, a pictorial way of representing, structuring or symbolising surroundings. This is not to say the landscapes are immaterial. They may be represented in a variety of materials and on many surfaces—in paint on canvas, in writing on paper, in earth, stone, water and vegetation on the ground" (Cosgrove and Daniels 1988, 1). In the case of the Grand Canyon, then, the canyon is represented in the materials of stratified and eroded rock layers, stands of ponderosa pines, and the Colorado River. It is also represented by postcards and photographs, the words in tourists' journals, and the sketches and maps of nineteenth-century survey artists. Richard Schein's "The Place of Landscape: A Conceptual Framework for Interpreting an American Scene" (1997) explores how a cultural landscape is the "tangible, visible articulation of numerous discourses" that are "reflective and symbolic of individual activity and cultural ideas as they simultaneously are central to the constitution and reinforcement of those activities and ideals" (660). I apply this approach at the Grand Canyon to better understand how cultural landscapes, such as Grand Canyon Village on the South Rim, are articulations of discourses about tourism development, environmental management, cultural heritage, and the NPS preservation mission, for example. Schein's work also paves a way to understanding how visual representations of landscapes, such as postcards of El Tovar Hotel, are also portals to better understand the social and cultural processes that shape the landscapes they present. They are "not just innocent documents of the built environment," instead they are "constructed images of constructed places" that convey the cultural ideals and changing values of the society that creates and propagates these images (Schein 1993, 8).

In terms of visual culture approaches to the Grand Canyon, a major influence on my work comes from environmental historian Stephen Pyne's *How the Canyon Became Grand: A Short History* (1998). His masterful tour through the Grand Canyon's environmental and cultural history traces how major U.S. events, movements, and ideologies influenced the interpretation about the canyon's meaning while also reflecting broader cultural and intellectual trends in American society from the sixteenth to the early twenty-first century. Like the elegant but robust suspension bridge that it resembles, the book spans across three primary structural beams: the cultural canyon, the populist canyon, and the environmentalist canyon. Each of these marks a shift in the history of the canyon and its place in American intellectual scenes, from European American exploration and first contact with the canyon creating its initial cultural context in American society, to tourism booms and wide recognition intellectually and visually to the post–World War II conservation movement and outdoor recreation boom that fueled a renewed focus on the Colorado River, whitewater rafting, and environmental management. Pyne traces the roots of the cultural canyon through art, literature, scientific field surveys, geology, and fluctuating visitor numbers to forward the argument that, starting with tentative Spanish conquistadors and missionary explorations of the canyon's edges in the sixteenth century and then with each succeeding encounter across generations, the "Grand Canyon was not so much revealed as created" (xiii). In other words, the ideas and meanings attached to the canyon—in popular writing, journals, newspaper articles, and photographs—had real consequences in creating an idea of the Grand Canyon that permeated American society. With each era a new layer was added to the popular geographic imagination about the canyon so today's Grand Canyon is a product of this process and a relic of its creation.

Pyne's work inspires the structure of *Framing Nature*—in three parts as Finding the Grand Canyon, Creating the Grand Canyon, and Framing the View—but I also diverge from it. I take a more explicit visual and geographic approach to excavating the canyon's intellectual, cultural, and visual history. I trace popular ideas about and experiences at the Grand Canyon with a different visual sample set than Pyne by using photographs and postcards, interwoven with historic maps. Additionally, I expand on the stories of the people and companies behind the scenes of these images to better understand the technical and social process in their making and distribution. Finally, I trace many of the historical images that I discuss in this book to their contemporary physical contexts in the canyon with extensive personal fieldwork on the Colorado River and along the canyon's trails and rims, employing repeat photography techniques to recapture images and compare them across time.

The fourth pillar of my approach explores the concept of hybrid places at the Grand Canyon, situating it as an interdependency of human-environment relationships (Cresswell 2013; Havlick 2018; Lane 2018). I join the cadre of scholars who see nature and culture not as separate entities, but as interwoven and mutually constituted elements. The environment is not a passive background for human actions and development (Gumprecht 2001; Cronon 1996; Callicott and Nelson 1998; Feldman 2011). There is a healthy scholarly discussion underway across contemporary geography and other disciplines about the meaning and usage of the terms *nature* and *culture*. A wave of recent work suggests moving beyond dualisms of nature or culture to instead focus on connections in a more-than-human geography. I recognize and value this debate. However, I chose to use the words *nature*, *environment*, *society*, and *culture* in this book because they are recognizable to both interdisciplinary scholarly and public audiences. Throughout this study, I hope to shed light on the multiplicity of views and break down simple nature-culture dualisms, especially in my assertion that there are many Grand Canyons embodied in its diverse cultures, environments, and potential experiences. The Grand Canyon that I discuss in this book is very much a series of interconnected hybrid places, where humans, other animals, birds, trees, rocks, and all elements of the environment have agency. Examples abound: the Colorado River's floods confound dam engineers, elk migrate out of the national park boundaries into adjacent U.S. Forest Service lands and different management schemes, vegetation planted by Civilian Conservation Corps laborers in the 1930s dissipates in the canyon's summer heat or self-seeds in nearby parking lots. *Framing Nature* offers an opportunity to explore and better understand national parks and protected areas as hybrid places.

Changes in Representations Over Time

Even before its establishment in 1919 as a national park, photographers, painters, and other illustrators produced visual representations of the Grand Canyon. These images did not stay in their hands long. Some of them, especially images printed as popular media such as postcards or magazine photographs, were replicated in mass as copies and distributed widely. Travelers purchased postcards as souvenirs and then circulated them as correspondence to friends and family back home. Magazine images reached audiences around the country and the world through their subscribers. *Framing Nature* mines this vast visual archive of popular imagery. Tracing the evolution of these images and their production narrates the story of the canyon's cultural metamorphosis from a place once known as an "altogether valueless" location (Ives 1861, 110) to a national park that attracts from four to six million visitors a year. Over the course of this book, I explore how the subject matter in this imagery and the locations represented and visited changed over time and analyze those imagery sets for common themes and patterns about who, where, and what was represented. This analysis reveals that not all locations and subject matter at the Grand Canyon were presented equally. For example, scenic landscape images featuring the southeast rim of the Grand Canyon, especially around Grand Canyon Village, were the most common theme and location in both the postcards and photographs in the early twentieth century.

This geographic and thematic bias is significant for several reasons. Consider the accumulated effect of this imagery over time; repetitive and widely distributed as thousands upon thousands of postcards and photographs, these images effectively flooded the popular geographic imagination with a fairly limited set of options for what the canyon looked like, what you could do there, and who visited this place. Scenic views of the canyon from the South Rim, featuring red and orange canyon walls, deep side canyons, blue sky, and the occasional stand of juniper bushes—an image recreated over and over again in the postcards from the late nineteenth century onward—effectively became the dominant visual narrative. It was the establishing shot for all other canyon images afterward, but it left so much out. Fern grottos, scores of animals and birds, cottonwood groves along the Colorado River's banks, Hualapai family farms along the river bottom in the western canyon, Havasupai camps at the southeastern rim, mines, and so much more—all missing. Postcards of the north or east sections of the canyon are also rare. Only a few locations at the Grand Canyon make appearances, yet these select images of select locations came to represent *all* places of the Grand Canyon, especially for those who have never visited the area but only knew it through their postcard collections or the pages of a magazine.

In *Framing Nature*, I trace the Greater Grand Canyon Region's iconographic arc (fig. 2) over more than 150 years. My diagram is conceptually based on Krim's iconographic arc of Route 66 but adapted and revised for this study of the Grand Canyon. Specifically, my diagram is a quick visual snapshot of the larger trends in Grand Canyon imagery that are revealed through my analysis of trends and data collected for this project. Following Krim's approach, it traces a historical timeline while considering shifts in the canyon's popular meaning from "idea, to fact, to symbol" and variations on representation style and media type as presented by the specific creators of these images. Later in the book I again present this diagram but with the additions of specific imagery, dates, and image creators as the narrative moves along. For details about the specific data I used to create this diagram and the methods I employed to construct it, see appendixes B and C.

As each era added its imagery to the layers of visual knowledge of the Grand Canyon, the canyon was transformed from an idea roughly conceived (part 1, Finding the Canyon), to a fact with concrete reality grounded in tourism development and traveler experiences (part 2, Creating the Canyon), to a symbol that was easily recognized by a broad public audience and saturated with the previous era's ideas and meanings (part 3, Framing the View). Over the course of this study, I populate the diagram as a way to show how each era of popular visual representations are placed in their social, cultural, political, and environmental context. The core of this work is based in a visual content analysis (discussed in chapters 3 to 8) of the sub-

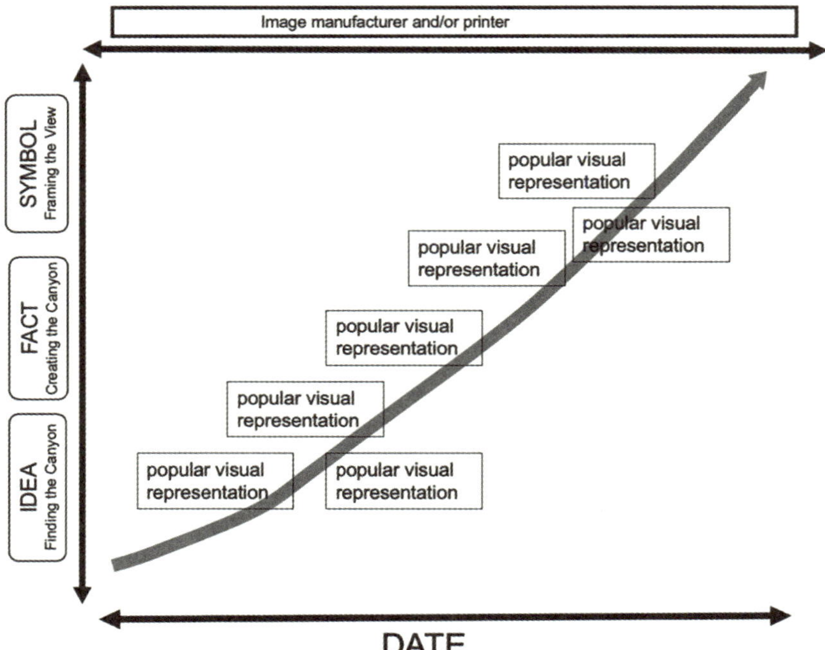

Fig. 2. Conceptual diagram for the iconographic arc of the Greater Grand Canyon Region. Created by Yolonda Youngs. Inspired by Krim 2005.

jects and locations found in 1,473 postcards and photographs manufactured between 1898 and 2009. This includes every postcard of the Grand Canyon manufactured by the Detroit Publishing Company (1898–1932), Curt Teich Company (1898–1978), and Frasher Foto Postcard Company (1920–55) and all photographs of the Grand Canyon found in *Arizona Highways* (1925–70). I bookend this core section of the book first with a brief and less structured discussion of some of the popular imagery and accounts that introduced the Grand Canyon to American and European society from the sixteenth through the late nineteenth century in chapter 1 and then a discussion of a 2009 postcard rack sample from giftshops at the Grand Canyon as a glimpse of contemporary views.

What's at Stake?

Producers, distributors, manufacturers, and consumers of national park imagery favored a selective and repetitive visual inventory of park features, subjects, and locations. Importantly, in the process of creating their imagery catalog, they chose only a few scenes of the canyon's multitude of environments. This geographic and thematic bias favored select locations, features, and viewpoints. Over time and with the power of accumulated imagery, this visual catalog came to represent not just one viewpoint or trail but, instead, *all* of the Grand Canyon. This limited but persistent stream of visual materials created an iconographic arc of imagery that defined what parts and locations of the canyon were important for tourism and environmental conservation and what locations were not. It demarcated who was part of the cultural scene of the canyon and who was left out. Connecting this historic imagery with the influence it exerts upon contemporary policies and debates is an important dimension of this book. Today there are numerous emerging challenges and opportunities that are reshaping and redefining national parks and protected areas around the world. One of my basic arguments is that the visual history of the Grand Canyon is as much as a story about the subjects and locations included in the imagery as it is about who and what was left out. The effects of this geographic and thematic exclusion are extensive.

While four pillars create the conceptual framework of this book, the body of the study is bound by a thematic approach. The first theme that weaves throughout *Framing Nature* is environmental policy and management. My analysis of historic visual imagery reveals shifting approaches to how the canyon's environment was managed and used. For example, many places in the canyon's highly varied and dynamic environment were left out of the picture—literally. Waterfalls, fern-covered grottos, rattlesnakes, squirrels, coyotes, elk, cacti, and ravens are all missing from postcards and photos until well into the late 1970s. If coyotes are missing from Detroit Publishing Company and Curt Teich Company postcards, it is in some ways a reflection of historic and evolving wildlife management and park policies.

Other critical environmental policy and management issues facing the Grand Canyon and much of the southwestern United States are air quality and water resources. Many national parks and protected areas face challenges to air quality and viewshed clarity. At the Grand Canyon, both the postcard imagery and photographs that I encountered during my research show a consistent tendency for clear skies and boundless views across the canyon's rim. Over time, these images serve as accumulated evidence of the pristine quality of the canyon's air and add to tourists' expectations for an unobstructed view into the canyon. But haze, smoke from forest fires, seasonal weather patterns, changing climatic conditions, and air particulates from nearby industries can all act to obscure the canyon. The Grand Canyon is downwind from air pollution caused by many sources. Until 2019 the Navajo Generating Station near Page, Arizona, was a the largest coal-fired power plant in the western United States and in close proximity to the canyon. Haze drifts into the canyon from nearby uranium mining, cities such as Las Vegas and Los Angeles, and output from tourists and residents vehicles. These challenges weave into contemporary debates about how to protect visibility and local air quality. Water resources are paramount to the Grand Canyon's environmental integrity and are vital life lines to communities in the arid Southwest. Hydropolitics—a term used to describe the politics around the transboundary use, management, governance, and allocation of water—reached a heightened tenor over the Colorado River in the Grand Canyon. These tensions are visible in the *Arizona Highways* photographs, where controversies over dam proposals and the construction of massive dam projects—particularly from the 1930s through the 1970s—play out in the images. The Colorado River Storage Project, managed by the U.S. Bureau of Reclamation and initiated in 1956, sought to provide hydroelectric power, flood control, and water storage for states along the upper Colorado River including Arizona, Utah, New Mexico, Colorado, and Wyoming. The project's launch coincided with a peak of postcard manufacturing for the Curt Teich Company, when its catalog of imagery frequently featured the Colorado River.

A second theme is cultural heritage preservation and interpretation. Throughout the images analyzed for this study, there is a consistent (mis) representation of cultural and social groups at the canyon. Two aspects come to mind here. One is for the people missing from the scenes in postcards and photographs. For example, postcards from the Detroit Publishing Company and the Curt Teich Company featured carefully edited versions of locations and people, often at commercial sites built and managed by the Fred Harvey Company and the Santa Fe Railroad with Navajo and Hopi craftspeople as the subjects. But in the process of presenting these places, the postcard manufacturers removed some people, such as the Havasupai, who were living and working there. The effects of this editing carry long-term effects and challenges to understanding the Greater Grand Canyon Region as a multicultural place. The canyon's history reveals a more diverse landscape than the postcards and photographs reveal; it is a historic and contemporary home to many people and groups, including American Indian, Anglo, Mexican, Hispanic, Latinx, African American, and Asian American peoples.

Another aspect of this theme centers on images that are devoid of humans. Not that humans need to be in every image, but the situation is strange when contemplating one of the most visited tourist attractions in the United States. Of course, capturing a photograph that purposefully frames the view to exclude humans is commonplace and, in many ways, not limited to the Grand Canyon. Landscape photographers and tourists alike have created similar images since before the twentieth century. Additionally, Arizona and the western United States, during the nineteenth and twentieth centuries, contained fewer people; population counts were lower than today and settlement patterns were more dispersed. But the effects of this absence of humans in popular imagery call into question larger ideas about who and what constitutes nature and culture and how close, or separate, they may be. Readers more accustomed to contemporary discussions of overcrowding in national parks may be startled by the lack of people in many of the images that were so widely distributed around the world only a few decades ago.

The third theme throughout this book is land management and its influence on tourism impacts, economic development, and sustainability. The story of the Greater Grand Canyon Region is one that includes multiple federal land management agencies—U.S. Forest Service, U.S. National Park Service, U.S. Bureau of Land Management, U.S. Bureau of Reclamation—along with tribal lands, private lands, and other state and city agencies. The evolution of these agencies and their missions has a direct influence on the subjects and places shown in the postcards and photographs of this study. For example, in the 1930s as government contractors and the U.S. Bureau of Reclamation finished construction of Hoover Dam and Lake Mead, *Arizona Highways* editors and photographers focused their efforts on promoting the new tourism potential at the lake through multiple colorful photographs of sailboats and motorboats skimming the lake's surface with joyful vacationers onboard. The development of the southeast and northeast rims of the canyon through U.S. Forest Service and National Park Service management in the early and mid-twentieth century are frequent features of postcards and photographs in this study. But those decisions about where to place tourism development and economic investment carry lasting effects on not only those rim-side tourism service sites but also the surrounding lands. For example, the Grand Canyon Escalade development proposal advanced controversial plans for a gondola, hotels, a golf course, and other tourist services at the bottom of the Grand Canyon near the confluence of the Colorado River and Little Colorado River. The project gathered support from some tribal members and business leaders as it promised thousands of jobs, a road, and new revenue for the Navajo Nation. But Hopi, Zuni, and Navajo peoples consider this land sacred and challenged the proposal, along with environmental protection groups and a vocal national base of Grand Canyon fans. The Navajo Nation Council halted the project through a vote in 2017. Proposals such as this inspire heated debates about cultural identities associated with the canyon, American Indian land ownership and historic treaty rights, transboundary environmental impacts of development, and the future of balanced approaches to sustainable development, tourism management, and cultural heritage protection.

Scholarly Debates about Parks and Protected Areas

While this book discusses places and themes across northern Arizona beyond the boundaries of Grand Canyon National Park, scholarship about national parks and protected areas is an important part of this study. National parks are heavily coded landscapes invested with conflicting meanings of nature and culture in public spaces. In one sense, national parks are wilderness preserves, often viewed as pristine nature, devoid of human cultural marks. This is frequently the dominant view in National Park Service interpretation that casts nature as separate from culture. Since the creation of Yellowstone, established as the first national park in 1872, boosters and the NPS constructed and commodified nature as an artifact of national pride and wilderness monumentalism (Vale 2005; Runte 2010; Keiter 2013). Touting the natural beauty of America's national parks, early promoters and supporters encouraged citizens to "see America first" instead of touring European cultural attractions (Shaffer 2001). These vacations were considered acts of good citizenship and patriotism, as well as pleasure-seeking excursions.

Indeed, national parks are a distinctly American invention—a concoction of nationalism, natural and cultural resource preservation ideology, public lands policy, and Indigenous land dispossession (Spence 1999; Vale 2005; Kantor 2007). Since the creation of Yellowstone National Park, the national park idea has offered exceptional opportunities for natural and cultural resource protection and tourism as well as deeply contested notions of public use, land ownership, class, race, and national identity. One basic tenet of early national park movements in the United States during the late nineteenth century was that these lands, mostly located in the western United States, were uninhabited and "worthless" since their value came from the potential for farming or natural resource extraction (Runte 2010). But this notion was flawed. As historian Mark David Spence argues in *Dispossessing the Wilderness: Indian Removal and the Making of the National Parks*, "uninhabited wilderness had to be created before it could be preserved" (1999, 4). In other words, creating national parks relies on the myth of pristine nature and uninhabited lands. Their creation was prefaced by the removal of American Indians from their traditional homelands and a complex social and political process of casting those lands in new roles as uninhabited wilderness that embodied notions of sublime nature. Woven into this fabric is a persistent egalitarian idea that the national parks are for all Americans, yet the template of the national park model created in the late nineteenth century United States excluded American Indian use and access and promoted a "geography of exclusion" that "transformed class difference into racial difference" (Germic 2001, 9). Adding further complexity to notions of national parks as worthless lands, railroad companies saw potential revenue streams for their passenger lines that connected or passed near national parks. Indeed, major railroad companies vigorously supported many early national parks in the United States (Blodgett 2007).

A more engaging approach beyond traditional views of American exceptionalism is that the national park idea is complex and dynamic, constantly undergoing experimentation, reinterpretation, and revision. The idea of national parks has been exported and reinterpreted by a myriad of countries around the world (Keiter 2013; Young and Dilsaver 2011), adapted to local geographies and cultures (Anthamatten and Hazen 2014), used as a guidepost for resource management and policy decisions, and framed as a laboratory for sustainability practices and studies (Machlis and Tichnell 1985; Smith, Karosic, and Smith 2015). In these global contexts, the national park idea is often challenged by local, Indigenous, or marginalized peoples on the basis of social and environmental injustice issues threaded into the historic core of the national park idea (Dahlberg, Rohde, and Sandell 2010). Part of this complexity draws from national parks as political units and is tied to the inherent political implications of the national park concept (Dilsaver and Wyckoff 2005; Dilsaver 2009). National parks also must be studied within the context of implicit cultural and social ideas of race, class, and gender that transform and shape landscapes (O'Brien and Njambi 2012; Carruthers 2014; Finney 2014; Weber and Sultana 2013). Yet national parks have long served an important role in American nation building and the evolution of wilderness protection and environmental consciousness (Nash 2001).

National parks are also cultural laboratories—they are richly coded landscapes replete with significant themes, ideas, events, individual personalities, and group identities that created the fabric of America as a nation (Nash 2001; Cronon 2003: Frank 2013; Williams 2016; Youngs 2020). In NPS units such as Gettysburg National Military Park or the National Mall and Memorial Parks in Washington DC, interpretation and tours tend to emphasize historical and cultural themes more than environmental ones (Youngs 2018; Benton-Short 2016). However, in many of the national park units—including some of the large national parks of the American West such as the Grand Canyon, Yosemite, and Yellowstone that are typified by vast expanses of forest, large streams, and striking mountain ranges—cultural and historical interpretation plays a minor role. Studies that highlight the complex social, political, and economic contexts of national parks are insightful and growing additions to a national park library (Benton-Short 2016; Watt 2017). Scholars, park managers, and communities are increasingly joining together to discuss and map out the future of national parks in ways that recognize their contested history and their remarkable potential for social change and environmental conservation (Tweed 2010; Machlis and Jarvis 2018; Weber and Harmon 2008).

These scholarly debates about national parks are important to keep in mind when considering the Grand Canyon. Although my focus on Grand Canyon National Park is central to the study, it also considers the larger region surrounding the park. While I hope to expand ideas about the Grand Canyon's landscapes beyond the park boundaries, I also recognize that the national park itself is an iconic symbol. Grand Canyon National Park is one of the crown jewels of the U.S. national park system and is consistently one of the top ten most visited national parks in the United States (National Park Service 2023a). As such and because of so much more, Grand Canyon National Park imposes an influence on NPS policies, federal environmental management of public protected lands, and notions of Southwest culture and heritage that demand attention and further inquiry. In terms of iconic national parks and other protected areas, this book offers a model that can be applied to any park, region, or place that is iconic and documented with a substantial body of popular imagery in the world—Venice's Piazza San Marco, Mount Fuji, the Taj Mahal, the Great Pyramid of Giza, or the Great Wall of China.

Organization of the Book

The book is structured around three parts. Part 1, "Finding the Grand Canyon," sets the stage for exploring the iconographic arc of the Grand Canyon with a baseline of imagery, ideas, and production processes that would later influence the locations and subject matter of popular representations of the canyon for many decades to come. Chapter 1 introduces the Greater Grand Canyon Region (GGCR) as a distinct region and its environmental, social, and cultural context. Chapter 2 focuses on popular imagery that created the visual foundation for introducing the Grand Canyon to European and American society. While this chapter focuses on nineteenth and early twentieth century imagery, it also includes important visual precedents of maps, sketches, and journal reports by sixteenth- and seventeenth-century Spanish missionaries, military scouts, and explorers who played pivotal roles in this era. Chapter 3 explores the processes and people behind the scenes of image production for the three primary postcard manufacturers whose work is featured in this book: Detroit Publishing Company, Curt Teich Company, and Frasher Foto Postcard Company. I describe the technical process of manufacturing postcard imagery and the equally important social and cultural process as photographers and postcard manufacturers selected locations and subject matter for their images. In subsequent chapters I expand on this and place it in the context of the era and technical process of each of the postcard manufacturers.

Part 2, "Creating the Grand Canyon," follows the canyon's iconographic rise from 1893 to 1935 as it shifts from a place on the periphery of American society to a readily recognized landscape in the center of a burgeoning tourism industry. This is a key transition time for the expansion of popular ideas and images of the canyon and a transformative stage for the canyons' formal designation as a federally protected area. Chapter 4 explores postcard imagery from two major manufacturers during the canyon's initial tourism boom—Detroit Publishing Company and Frasher Foto Postcard Company. Chapter 5 shifts the focus to photographs published in *Arizona Highways*, a magazine that began as a highway engineer's trade journal but later shifted to promoting Arizona tourism. As the magazine rose to prominence, so too did

Arizona's investment in massive engineering projects that aimed to harness the state's environment including dams, roads, and bridges that crisscrossed the canyon and aimed to harness the power of the Colorado River.

Part 3, "Framing the View," transitions to a mature stage of the iconographic arc of Grand Canyon imagery from 1936 to 2021. Through this era, the Grand Canyon moves from a well-recognized scene of nature tourism to an icon, a symbol of nature, that is employed and manipulated by a variety of groups including environmental organizations, federal government agencies, and industries. Chapter 6 concentrates on postcards from the Curt Teich Company and Frasher Foto Postcard Company manufactured during the so-called golden age of postcards from 1936 to 1955 (Bassett 2015). Both manufacturers reframed the canyon's environment with every one of their postcards, creating different visual narratives that commodified the canyon into a select set of places, subjects, and experiences that represented the peak of the tourist experience. Chapter 7 builds on the geographic range and visual catalog of places depicted by CTC and FFPC, but in this chapter I narrow the lens for a closer look at the people included as well as excluded from that imagery. This detour into the social landscape of the GGCR allows a deeper exploration of ideas of cultural identity and representation through the lens of ethnicity, tourism, and labor. Chapter 8 continues the focus on mid-twentieth-century popular imagery but adds a comparative angle by looking at *Arizona Highways* photographs from 1936 to 1970. Although set in the same time period at the Curt Teich and Frasher Foto postcards, the magazine photographs tell a different story than the postcards. The photographs highlight engineering and tourism development in the northeast area of the canyon, dam proposals and construction along the Colorado River, and an outdoor recreation boom in river rafting and backpacking following World War II. Chapter 9 brings *Framing Nature* into the twenty-first century with a closer look at imagery sampled from postcard racks at Grand Canyon gift shops. The conclusion presents a summary and assessment of the book's findings and suggests some trends and patterns that may shape the future of the Greater Grand Canyon Region.

A Note on Methods

My mixed-method approach for this book combines quantitative visual content analysis with a qualitative interpretation of themes present in the images. While many scholars work with visual representations and popular culture, few systematically analyze every image in a contiguous data set for subject matter and location information. By contiguous dataset, I mean all visual representations of the Grand Canyon produced year after year by a postcard manufacturer and every photograph of the canyon that appeared in a magazine (as in the case of *Arizona Highways*). Further dataset sorting required specifying the geographic place-name and subject of each image at Grand Canyon, Arizona (thus removing the popular Grand Canyon of the Yellowstone River in Wyoming). With each of the 1,473 images sampled for this study, I conducted a quantitative visual content analysis noting the number of times certain subjects and places were represented in the imagery. I organized this data into a matrix and sorted the findings into a series of common themes found throughout this visual dataset. Here I am following the methodology laid out by William Wyckoff and Lary Dilsaver's "Promotional Imagery of Glacier National Park" (1997) and, as with their work on nineteenth-century photographs of Glacier, I found common themes in the imagery and a geographical bias. In other words, the creators of postcards and photographs of the Grand Canyon favored a select set of locations in and around the GGCR in their imagery.

For readers interested in more details about the specific data that fueled my interpretations and ideas in *Framing Nature*, it will be helpful to refer to the appendix C, which includes a detailed quantitative accounting, organized by chapter, of the specific subjects and locations in the 1,473 postcards and magazine photographs that I sampled, a set that I whittled down from more than 2,000 original images. While my chapters provide the descriptive summaries and my interpretation of the findings, the appendixes provide more details, including annual visitation counts for Grand Canyon National Park and a deeper discussion of my analysis and methods.

Place and space are central to this book. Although I consider locations beyond the contemporary national park boundary, the spatial extent and contours of the canyon are important factors in understanding any interpretation of this place. As a geographer, I am keenly interested in the places and people represented in these images and the reasons viewmakers selected these specific locations from the thousands of possibilities in such an immense landscape as the Grand Canyon. My approach is novel for studies of the Grand Canyon. It raises new research questions that sets this book apart from other studies that rely exclusively on archival and library research or questionnaire survey methods. My method of assessing the locations shown in images expands the dominant spatial narrative about the Grand Canyon beyond the dichotomy of only a rim or river experience.

This book is informed by scholarly research as well as my personal experiences over fifteen years, including field reconnaissance and community engagement. I sought out conversations with people who live, work, and play in the GGCR, including NPS cultural and environmental resource managers, Grand Canyon Conservancy (formerly Grand Canyon Association) educational leaders, commercial river guides, concessionaire managers, and American Indian tribal representatives. I have completed extensive field research trips into the Grand Canyon and throughout the GGCR, including three weeks rafting the Colorado River, multiple trips hiking into and out of the canyon via North and South Rim trails, exploring rim trails and routes via footpaths and the park bus network, visiting the gateway communities that surround the park, and traveling around the Southwest and the United States to visit archives and libraries holding collections relevant to this work. I have lived in seasonal researcher housing at the canyon, camped on its South and North Rim and in the canyon depths along the Colorado River, toured the interior of almost every publicly accessible building on the North and South Rims of Grand Canyon National Park, slept under the stars in the South Rim campground and along the sandy beaches of the inner canyon, plunged through the cold chill of Lava Rapids, and suffered through the searing heat of a July day at Phantom Ranch.

The method of repeat photography is a central aspect to this work, and one that is not underemployed by social scientists and national park scholars. Originally a method honed by physical scientists, repeat photography is a valuable technique that compares images of historic landscapes with the present scene to reveal changes over time (Meagher and Houston 1998; Senf, Pyne, Klett, and Wolfe 2012; Weber 2012; Cole and Maxwell 2019; Klett 2019; Wyckoff 2020). To complete a repeat photograph of a location, I sought out the exact site of the original photograph and then captured another image of the same scene but in contemporary times. These sets of repeat photography images were incredibly helpful as I learned to read the landscape of the canyon. Many of these images are included in this book. This method is part of my research and teaching, yet the Grand Canyon imagery challenged me in ways I had not encountered before. Early on with my fieldwork, I learned to be skeptical of the titles of postcards. I realized that there are hundreds of postcards with the title "at Grand Canyon" or “near El Tovar,” only to also find that this was a shorthand for a general location along the extensive South Rim. “At Grand Canyon” postcards proved even more challenging as they could easily encompass locations anywhere within hundreds of miles of the Greater Grand Canyon Region. It was only through extensive field reconnaissance, years of scouring historic maps and journals, and the important cross-comparison between multiple image makers and producers’ work that I began to find some of the more elusive postcard scenes. I also contended with the fact that the image I was seeking may have been synthetic, that is, not one “real” place but several locations compounded into one image through the postcard production process. As I argue in this book, many of the postcard scenes are highly edited visual documents.

Finally, I recognize that I am a source of knowledge production about the Grand Canyon, with specific cultural and social contexts and personal perceptions shaping my work. The publication of this book, my fieldwork, the visual content analysis, the gathering of postcards and photographs, and the repeat photography series in this book are my additions to the layers of visual and geographic knowledge of the Grand Canyon. I hope that this book inspires new discussions about a transboundary Grand Canyon that strengthens partnerships and collaborations across the multiple federal land management agencies, regional communities, and tribal councils across the Colorado Plateau.

Part 1 Finding the Grand Canyon

Surely no imagination can construct out of its own material any picture having the remotest resemblance to the Grand Canyon. In truth, the first step in attempting a description is to beg the reader to dismiss from his mind, so far as practicable, any preconceived notion of it.

—George Wharton James, *In and Around the Grand Canyon* (1900)

You must have the bird in your heart
before you can find it in the bush.

—John Burroughs, *Leaf and Tendril* (1908)

1 The Greater Grand Canyon Region

The Grand Canyon National Park is centered around an east-west trending gorge in northern Arizona that averages 10 miles across (Grand Canyon National Park 2023). This vast landscape is situated within the Colorado Plateau, a physiographic region at the intersection of Colorado, Utah, New Mexico, and Arizona. The Colorado River bisects the canyon, dropping 2,000 feet in 278 river miles (a measurement that traces the bends of the river as if you were floating in a boat down the stream, instead of in a straight line). An exotic stream is one that has its source in well-watered lands from a drainage system in another region, like the Nile River, but that flows across a desert before reaching the sea. The Colorado River is a classic exotic stream, carrying water from its headwaters high in Colorado's Rocky Mountains across 1,450 miles of arid lands to the Gulf of California on the United States–Mexico borderlands. It is a vital source of water that is paramount to survival and settlement in this region with a consistently dry climate. Over the course of six million years, the river sculpted the Grand Canyon into a chasm laced with a labyrinth of side canyons and punctuated by soaring buttes, expansive mesas, broad plateaus, and sheer cliff faces. The canyon is a geologic marvel featuring textbook examples of sedimentary, igneous, and metamorphic rocks ranging from 270 million years to 1.8 billion years old (Sadler 2018, 14).

Steep and varied vertical terrain, distinct ecological communities, and microclimates are defining characteristics of the canyon. The Colorado River divides the canyon into the North Rim at about 8,000 feet elevation and the South Rim at 7,000 feet. Between the two rims lies the vast depth and stepped plateaus and mesas of the inner canyon. Phantom Ranch, a popular resting spot for mule riders, hikers, and Colorado River rafters, lies at only 2,400 feet. Lake Mead, at the western boundary of the park, is lower still at 1,200 feet (Grand Canyon National Park 2023). To better understand the Grand Canyon's environmental context, it is useful to think of it as an inverted mountain. As a hiker moves up a mountain, the temperature drops, precipitation potential increases, and the dominant vegetation shifts toward conifers and other evergreen trees. But at the Grand Canyon, the highest elevations and coolest temperatures are found along the rims where much of the visitor services are located, such as El Tovar Hotel on the South Rim or the Grand Canyon Lodge on the North Rim. Some of the pathways connecting the rim to river, such as the Bright Angel Trail, are ancient pathways that take advantage of natural faults in the canyon's geology. They have been sculpted over time to descend along the broad plateaus and tabled lands into the hot, arid depths of the inner canyon and Colorado River corridor (Anderson 1998; Hirst 2016). But the river corridor also provides a vital resource, especially around the streams, waterfalls, water seeps, and grottos where perennial—or at least seasonally dependable—sources of water are available.

The combined effects of elevation, light, temperature, slope, aspect, and precipitation create an interconnected system of five biotic communities, or life zones, in and around the canyon (National Park Service n.d.). These communities span from the mixed conifer forest along the higher elevation the North Rim, to the ponderosa pine forests of the South Rim and lower extent of the North Rim. Pinyon-juniper woodlands dot the midcanyon plateaus as one descends into the inner canyon dominated by arid and heat-tolerant desert scrub. In the depths of the canyon, these desert scrub communities are broken by the lush riparian areas along the river corridor with nearby springs, seeps, and streams. Indeed, with 450 bird species, 91 mammal species, 18 fish species, 58 reptiles and amphibian species, and 1,443 invertebrate species, the canyon is thriving and complex environment (Grand Canyon National Park 2023).

The Colorado River corridor, at the bottom of the canyon, feels like a different world compared to the rims. It is sweltering hot in the summer months but a warm retreat in the winter when the rims are covered in snow. Sandy beaches spread out from the canyon walls, offering lizards, snakes, scorpions, bighorn sheep, and other creatures a land-based habitat along the dynamic riverbanks, where varying water levels and flows shape the shoreline environment. Stands of native cottonwood trees provide shade during the summer and stabilize the beaches while thick stands of tamarisk bushes crowd the trees and quickly colonize sandbars. Grottos of various sizes punctuate the walls, from small alcoves to huge overhangs such as Redwall Cavern, that can accommodate hundreds of people. Sinuous side canyons, carved by the erosional forces of seasonal streams and debris, split off from the main river. Over ninety rapids—ranging from small, splashing waves to large maelstroms of whitewater—punctuate the Colorado River's course as it drops over 1,500 feet in the 225 to 280.5 miles of the typical whitewater trips through the Grand Canyon today (Belknap and Belknap Evans 2007; Martin and Whitis 2021; Fedarko 2014a). The contemporary Colorado River is in many ways much different from the historical one that nineteenth- and early twentieth-century river expeditions explored (Staveley 2015; Marston 2014). Once a warm, free-flowing, unpredictably fluctuating, and sediment-laden stream, it is now a river with a controlled flow of cold water shaped by complex hydropolitics and a human geography of water allocation schemes, settlement patterns, and water policies (Graf 1985; Summit 2013). Flows are predictable and managed by the U.S. Bureau of Reclamation as part of the multistate Colorado River Storage Project. The massive Glen Canyon Dam impounds Colorado River water in Lake Powell, where water is released to match the fluctuating demands for hydroelectric power and water use by agriculture, recreation, and urban communities in the western United States (Worster 1985; Carothers and Brown 1991; Reisner 1993; Sneddon 2015; Owen 2017; Gober 2018).

A Multicultural Grand Canyon

The Grand Canyon is also a mosaic of human geography shaped by multicultural societies that have inscribed distinct settlement patterns, land use, travel corridors, customs, and ceremonies. People have been living in and around the Grand Canyon for millennia (Smiley, Downum, and Smiley 2017). As Richard M. Begay, Navajo Traditional scholar, contends, "The story of the Grand Canyon extends well beyond the political and geographic boundaries that are shown on modern maps; we must understand the larger landscape and its histories to truly appreciate the canyon," (qtd. in Hirst 2016, 18). Prehistoric archaeological sites reveal Paleoindian and Archaic hunting and gathering societies in and around the Grand Canyon with substantial evidence of continuous human use and settlement since twelve thousand years ago (Smiley, Downum, and Smiley 2017, 27; Grand Canyon National Park 2023). Other prehistoric cultural groups—

Basketmaker, Ancestral Puebloan, Cohonina, Cerbat, Pai, and Southern Paiute—also left lasting archaeological evidence of their presence (Grand Canyon National Park 2023).

Some contemporary American Indian peoples of the Southwest trace their heritage to these ancestral groups. Today, eleven tribal nations representing eight distinct cultural groups are spread across northern Arizona, New Mexico, Colorado, Utah, Nevada, and California and share a deep and enduring relationship with the land in and around the Grand Canyon as an important cultural, historical, and spiritual home. The National Park Service recognizes these groups as Traditionally Associated Tribes (TAT) that include the Havasupai Tribe, Hopi Tribe, Hualapai Tribe, Kaibab Band of Paiute Indians, Las Vegas Tribe of Paiute Indians, Moapa Band of Paiute Indians, the Navajo Nation, Paiute Indian Tribe of Utah, Pueblo of Zuni, San Juan Southern Paiute Tribe, and the Yavapai-Apache Nation (Grand Canyon National Park 2023). Three of the TAT share a boundary with Grand Canyon National Park: the Navajo Nation, the Hualapai Tribe, and the Havasupai Tribe. As tribal representatives maintain, "We have been here since time immemorial, we are still here, and we will always be here" (Hirst 2016, v). Although the tribes come together for TAT collaborations and tribal consultations with the NPS, the tribal perspective is not uniform; there is variation between individuals' values, ideas, and beliefs, and this is often influenced by their geography. Some tribes, such as the Hopi, are dispersed across vast areas. For example, there over thirty Hopi clans living across three mesas and thirteen villages (Balenquah 2016, 2).

It is important to keep in mind the evolution of the relationship between the federal government and American Indian tribes to better understand the Grand Canyon's broader context. The creation of the first U.S. national parks in the late 1800s coincides with the development of the Indian reservation system that sought to restrict Indigenous peoples' movements, assimilate them into Anglo-American society, and remove them from traditional homelands (Morehouse 1996; Spence 1999; Kantor 2007; Wilson 2020). When looking at a map of the region around the Grand Canyon and the locations of American Indian reservations with ties to the canyon, it is essential to keep in mind that the spatial distribution of modern-day reservations and tribal nation lands are a testament, in part, to historical efforts by the federal government to reorganize and remove American Indians from their traditional homelands. This relationship influences not only federal lands policy and management across the American West. It connects directly to the findings and arguments herein. The popular imagery discussed in this book is a visual archive of how this contested history played out at the Grand Canyon. Who was included in the retelling of the canyon's history through the tourism lens? How were each of the tribes represented in the imagery? Who was left out? How were social and cultural processes such as assimilation and ideas of exotic reinscribed into the Grand Canyon landscape and leveraged to fuel a tourism industry?

These questions are significant for the arguments presented in this book. Many of the tribes affiliated with the Grand Canyon today consider it a sacred space and carry memories of a recent history of living within and around the canyon (Smiley, Downum, and Smiley 2017, 16–17). There are many excellent books, first-person narratives, and scholarly studies that explore the depths and contours of American Indian experiences at and around the Grand Canyon and the history of the Indian reservation system in the United States. Although a detailed discussion of that literature is beyond the scope of this book, it is important to recognize the conflicted relationship of the tribes with the federal government and how this influences the context of the Grand Canyon.

The Grand Canyon is part of a multicultural Southwest. The Southwest is what geographers call a vernacular region—a cultural region perceived as a distinct place by its inhabitants and recognized by people outside of the region in the popular geographic imagination. Geographer Donald W. Meinig, in his landmark study *Southwest: Three Peoples in Geographical Change 1600–1970*, asserts that this region is a "distinctive place to the American mind but a somewhat blurred place on American maps, which is to say that everyone knows that there is a Southwest but there is little agreement as to just where it is" (1971, 3). Meinig observes that while the region has distinct ecological zones of high plateau country and dry climate, it is the diverse cultures that truly give shape to the region. Blends of American Indian, Hispanic, Mexican, and Euro-American cultures are intrinsic elements. But he also notes that the term "Southwest" is an ethnocentric one: "What is south and west to the Anglo-American was long the north of the Hispano-American" (3). It is shaped by overlapping, historical, colonizing pushes by Anglo-Americans from the Atlantic Seaboard and Hispanic and Mexican from the south. In *The Multicultural Southwest: A Reader*, A. Gabriel Meléndez and M. Jane Young and their coeditors and coauthors add vital texture to today's social and cultural understandings of this complex region, with a collection of first voice narratives, poems, and stories from its inhabitants. They challenge notions of a single, definitive description of the region. "Memory of the Southwest is very often the fuel of human imagination, creativity, and possibility. Often, the southwestern experience sparks powerful, sometimes conflicting memories" (2001, xi). Meléndez, Young, and colleagues bring together a range of voices from American Indian, Hispanic, Mexican, and Euro-American peoples to challenge a simplistic or unexamined view of this region. "For us, a people's memory is the 'deep grammar' of the human story. It is a grammar we need to learn because it brings forth alternative views of the environment, landscape, human social interaction, conquest, dispossession, technological change, and the survival of cultures" (xi).

The history of the Grand Canyon connects to this larger regional story with the shaping of a multicultural Southwest. Although the Grand Canyon has a long legacy of human imprints from multiple cultures, postcards and photographs circulated in tourism economies seldom showed this diversity. Part of unraveling this simplification of the human mosaic at the canyon may be traced to popularized ideas (and images) of *who* was part of the historical American West. Human settlement of the United States was not a simple east to west movement of Anglo-American peoples. Instead, as historian Patricia Limerick asserts in her insightful history of the American West, "humans beings discovered the American landscape from all directions" (2000, 188). The Grand Canyon's human history is a subset of the national story of America.

Spaniards were the first Europeans to set their eyes on the Grand Canyon. From the sixteenth century until the early nineteenth century, the Grand Canyon was part of a vast territory of North America claimed by the Spanish Empire as the Viceroyalty of New Spain. Missionaries, military expeditions, and explorers traced the edges of the canyon during their brief and often ill-informed encounters with the chasm but made few significant travels into it. For almost two hundred years the canyon remained out of the European colonizers' view. But that changed in the nineteenth century as global power and territorial struggles reverberated back to the canyon. In *América: The Epic Story of Spanish North America, 1493–1898*, historian Robert Goodwin surmises that by the early nineteenth century, global struggles and an overextended imperial drive weakened Spain's ability to maintain control of its North American territorial claims (2019).

Mexico gained independence from Spain in 1821 and claimed a vast swath of land to the north renaming part of this territory that included the Grand Canyon, Alta California. However, after the end of the Mexican-American War and the signing of the Treaty of Guadalupe Hidalgo in 1848, Mexico ceded Alta California and its northern territory to the United States. This opened the door to extending American land ownership westward into areas that became the future states of Arizona, New Mexico, Utah, Nevada, and parts of Colorado—all states that are prime components in the environmental and cultural context of the Greater Grand Canyon Region today. After the transition, the area around the Grand Canyon came under the auspices of the Territory of New Mexico, including much of the present-day states of Arizona and New Mexico.

Meanwhile, across the country, debates about natural resource use, ownership, and exploitation increasingly occupied U.S. concerns in the 1860s and soon shaped the western expansion of territory toward the Grand Canyon (Morehouse 1996). But it was not until after the U.S. Civil War that significant efforts pushed European-American and Anglo settlement, commerce, and transportation westward. By the middle of the nineteenth century, exploration and settlement advanced with increasing speed (Lavender 1982; Pyne 1998, 24–25). They built wagon roads and railroad tracks, surveyed natural resources and river corridors, established telegraph and communication routes, and extended Anglo settlement into the Southwest. This came at the expense of American Indians who were forced off their lands and relocated as clashes with Euro-American settlers and the U.S. military fueled the establishment of the Indian Reservation system and cultural assimilation programs. By the mid-nineteenth century Mormon settlers became a major force in the western U.S. territories as they established farms and outposts across what is now northern Arizona and Utah. Trails and wagon roads connected towns and communities to the canyon and to major east-west running corridors. Laws, such as the General Allotment Act of 1887, exacerbated this process of land dispossession and reallocation from American Indian to Anglo hands.

Increasing pressure on and exploitation of the Grand Canyon's natural resources came along with this population expansion. Logging, mining, and ranching were major extractive activities. Prospectors explored the canyon and nearby areas in the late 1870s and 1880s and began mining soon after. They built trails into the canyon, registered mining claims (some of which later became valuable and strategic real estate in the canyon's early tourism boom years), and extracted copper and asbestos with limited success. Ranchers asserted extensive grazing rights on public lands managed by the U.S. Forest Service south and north of the Grand Canyon. They released their cows and sheep to browse the vegetation, which in turn affected soils and streams and displaced native wildlife. Loggers removed trees and forests along the north and South Rim to build the burgeoning towns of Flagstaff and Williams to the south and St. George and Kanab, Utah, to the north (Morehouse 1996). The canyon's forests also fueled the railroad industry's growth into the region with railroad ties, fuel, and building materials.

Tourism Development and Protected Area Evolution

Early development of the Grand Canyon centered on the South and North Rims. The Atlantic and Pacific Railroad arrived south of the Grand Canyon in 1883, connecting the region with the rest of the United States through east-west rail lines. The railroads were aided by federal land grants that extended as far as forty miles north or south of its right-of-way (Morehouse 1996). Plans to build north-south spur lines connecting towns with the Grand Canyon enticed the Santa Fe and Grand Canyon Railroad Company (later the Santa Fe Railroad) to build tracks between Williams and the South Rim village completed in 1901, followed by a Union Pacific Railway spur line to the North Rim.

Although the railroad construction campaigns were fueled by the promise of mining and timber profits at the canyon, tourism ultimately won the day and nudged a turning point in the canyon's social, political, and economic geography. Anglo settlers, miners, and entrepreneurs at the canyon's South Rim hosted the trickle of tourists who made the arduous and expensive journey by train and wagon to the canyon.

During the early twentieth century, settlement and tourism development concentrated on the South Rim, near the present-day Grand Canyon Village, along the North Rim near the present-day North Rim Village at Bright Angle Point, and scattered along inner canyon trails, springs, and a few inner canyon spots near the Colorado River. The social mixture at the canyon was a blend of Anglo settlers, miners, and entrepreneurs and American Indian peoples living at the South Rim and in the inner canyon.

But it was the major corporate partnership of the Santa Fe Railroad and the Fred Harvey Company, a restaurant and hospitality corporate partnership, that truly shifted the tide at the canyon. They formed a symbiotic relationship across the American West with Fred Harvey restaurants and lodges serving passengers at train stations along the Santa Fe's extensive network of routes. Through well-funded and energetic promotional and advertising campaigns, they firmly situated nature-based tourism as a national, if not, patriotic duty and the Grand Canyon as an iconic location in the American geographical imagination (Anderson 2000; Runte 2010). The railroad brought relatively fast and comfortable transportation to the canyon's South Rim and expanded tourism services along with the development of the South Rim Village in the early 1900s. In partnership with the Union Pacific Railroad and the Utah Parks Company, the basic development plan for the North Rim Village was in place by 1929 (Anderson 2000, 19). Together with the U.S. Forest Service, the Santa Fe Railroad and the Fred Harvey Company created a powerful political and economic triumvirate between corporations and the federal government. This arrangement squeezed out individual and family entrepreneurs and the Hualapai people living at the South Rim and midcanyon area of Havasupai Garden (recently renamed from Indian Garden) in favor of corporate organization and development at the canyon (Anderson 2000; Youngs 2019). That corporate and government partnership structure carried over into the next era of federal public lands management of the Grand Canyon as Congress created the National Park Service in 1916 and designated Grand Canyon National Park in 1919.

The imagery presented in *Framing Nature* provides a window into this tourism history as we explore how the canyon's environmental and cultural landscape changed over time. In terms of contemporary tourism, the Grand Canyon now fuels a regional economy. It is still managed by the National Park Service, but there's a different cast of partners at the helm. Local and regional businesses and residents, American Indian tribes, and partnerships with other federal public lands agencies now guide development and use of the GGCR. This mosaic provides opportunities to see and experience the canyon from rim to river: hiking or driving along the rim, rafting the river in the depths of the canyon, hiking or mule riding into the canyon, or touring it all from above by helicopter or small airplane.

Finally, land ownership and management are vital components to understanding the Grand Canyon's context today. A mixture of public, private, and tribal lands surround the canyon. Federal public lands management agencies have a large footprint in this area of northern Arizona. Under the Department of the Interior, the National Park Service manages Grand Canyon National Park at the center of this mix as well as several other nearby units including Lake Mead National Recreation Area. The Bureau of Reclamation (BOR) manages large water resource projects throughout the Southwest, such as Glenn Canyon Dam. The Bureau of Land Management (BLM) oversees lands north of the canyon, including Vermillion Cliffs National Monument and some areas of existing or proposed uranium mines to the northeast. Under the Department of Agriculture, the U.S. Forest Service (USFS) administers the lands to the north and south of the canyon in the Kaibab National Forest stretching across the Kaibab Plateau to the north and the Coconino Plateau to the south. The Navajo Nation (to the east) and the Hualapai Reservation and Havasupai Reservation (to the south), all border Grand Canyon National Park. As noted earlier, there are eight other Traditionally Affiliated Tribes. Although some of these tribes do not all share contemporary borders with the park, they still trace a strong cultural, spiritual, and social connection to the canyon.

It is worth a brief pause here to note that the creation and designation of the Grand Canyon National Park as we know it today is the culmination of boundary changes, different federal public lands agency management schemes, environmental legislation, social and cultural geography, and multiple environmental debates and policy changes. Understanding a basic outline of this evolution is key. Even before Arizona entered statehood in 1912, Indiana senator Benjamin Harrison introduced several bills—in 1882, 1883, and 1886—to Congress to create a national park. All were unsuccessful. But in 1893, as president of the United States, Harrison designated the Grand Canyon Forest Reserve, eventually managed by the Department of the Interior's General Lands Office after 1897 (Anderson 1998, 87). By 1905 the land was transferred to the U.S. Forest Service in the Department of Agriculture. President Theodore Roosevelt invoked the powers of the recently passed Antiquities Act (1906) to create Grand Canyon Game Preserve in 1906 and Grand Canyon National Monument in 1908, both managed by the USFS. Another spate of failed Senate bills for a Grand Canyon National Park followed in 1910 and 1911. But in 1919 park promoters and supporters found success in congressional approval for and President Woodrow Wilson's signature on the Grand Canyon National Park Act. Without a dedicated agency to manage national parks, the U.S. Forest Service administered the new park until President Wilson signed an act in 1916 that created the National Park Service in the Department of the Interior as an agency dedicated to these protected areas. In 1919 Congress approved the establishment of Grand Canyon National Park and transferred the land and its management from USFS to the NPS that year. Within twenty-three years, three different public lands agencies in two different departments of the federal government managed the Grand Canyon.

Other major milestones for the park provide context for the geography of popular imagery locations discussed in this book and suggest the canyon's growing importance of transboundary environmental protections. Although President Lyndon B. Johnson proclaimed Marble Canyon National Monument in 1969, effectively adding federal protected lands status and a buffer to the eastern extension of the physiographic Grand Canyon, the environmental conservation community remained concerned that dam proposals threatened Grand Canyon National Park. In 1975 the park doubled in size with the passage of the Grand Canyon National Park Enlargement Act that added Marble Canyon on the west and Grand Canyon National Monument on the east, securing the protected status of these sections of the canyon from new dam proposals and creating a larger national park unit. This legislation effectively enveloped the area between Glen Canyon and Lake Mead with NPS protected status. In 1979 Grand Canyon's international status as a protected area received a boost with its designation as a UNESCO World Heritage Site. In 2019 Grand Canyon National Park received official International Dark Sky Park certification through a collaborative effort between the NPS and the International Dark Sky Association. This move supported partnerships between the NPS and neighboring communities to boost economic growth through astronomy-based tourism.

In many ways, the Grand Canyon's multiple-stage transition to national park status is typical of the legal and spatial transition (acres, borders) of many crown jewel parks of the western United States, such as Yellowstone and Yosemite (Dilsaver and Wyckoff 2009). Yellowstone National Park is the world's first national park, established in 1872 through an act of Congress and signed into law by President Ulysses S. Grant. However, Yellowstone and other, early national parks had no single, overarching agency to manage them until 1916 and the creation of the National Park Service. Before that time, the care and protection of national parks fells to the U.S. Forest Service, the U.S. Army, or a combination of other agencies. A common misconception about the NPS is that they only manage national parks. In fact, the National Park Service manages over 400 units—areas designated by over twenty different categories. These span from national parks to national battlefields, national seashores, national recreation areas, and a wide cast of other themes and designations. There is a national park unit in in every state. But take a close look at map of public lands in the United States and you will quickly notice a pattern. The spatial distribution of the NPS system is uneven; federally protected public lands managed by the NPS, USFS, and BLM are generally larger in area and more common in in the western United States. This pattern is an inheritance from the distinct historical geography of the United States. Settlement, colonization, treaty-making, wars, resource exploitation, and transportation systems development all shaped the scene for both public lands creation and the shaping of the American West as we know it today.

What Is the Greater Grand Canyon Region?

The Grand Canyon is more than a national park, a colorful scene, or a pop culture meme. It is a symbolic landscape interconnected by the lands, peoples, and environments that surround it. Many scholars, park managers, and American Indian tribes are calling for a new approach to managing large-scale landscapes like the Grand Canyon. Robert Keiter, a legal scholar and the founding director of the Wallace Stegner Center for Land, Resources, and the Environment at the University of Utah, proposes an "ecosystem-scale conservation" approach that considers the myriad of human-environment balances that parks now demand (2013). Gary E. Machlis, the first science advisor of the NPS, and Jonathan B. Jarvis, eighteenth director of the NPS, propose a unified vision for conserving U.S. protected lands in *The Future of Conservation in America: A Chart for Rough Water*. They emphasize that a key to unlocking challenges to transboundary conservation is finding common interests, creating "assemblages" of diverse stakeholders, and recognizing the interconnected concerns of nature protection, historical preservation, sustainability, public health, civil rights, social justice, and science (2018, 70). Other scholars suggest similarly broad regional or geographic boundaries. Geographer Barbara Morehouse explores the history of

American Indian tribes in the "larger domain of the greater Grand Canyon" in *A Place Called Grand Canyon: Contested Geographies* (1996, 6). In *We Call the Canyon Home: American Indians of the Grand Canyon Region*, Navajo Nation Traditional Historic Preservation Officer and scholar Richard M. Begay contends that the "story of the Grand Canyon extends well beyond the political and geographic boundaries that are shown on modern maps; we must understand the larger landscape and its histories to truly appreciate the canyon" (Hirst 2016, 18).

These plans promise an exciting and innovative approach that could facilitate transboundary environmental management and collaborative political, social, and economic policies. In addition, these efforts could decrease tensions between neighboring landowners and users and potentially bring together diverse stakeholders, such as tribal leaders, private landowners, and federal public lands managers for collaborative decision-making that could pave a path forward to managing, visiting, and living in these vast landscapes (Worster 2003; Pyne 1998; Anderson 1998; Morehouse 1996). Examples of this approach already in motion for North America include the Greater Yellowstone Ecosystem, Yellowstone to Yukon Conservation Initiative, and Greater Canyonlands National Monument proposal, to name a few. In *Grand Canyon for Sale*, Stephen Nash argues that consolidating protected areas and prioritizing ecological networks over extractive industries and natural resource harvesting is essential to the health of the Grand Canyon. He cites pressing challenges for the Grand Canyon and its neighboring lands, including limited water resources, development proposals, diminishing wildlife habitat, grazing, air pollution, climate change, noise pollution from helicopter tours, mining, logging, and other concerns. Geologist, environmental educator, and professional river guide Christa Sadler draws on her diverse background in *The Colorado* to suggest that "thinking like a watershed" offers a way forward for managing, using, and conserving the Colorado River on a broad, regional scale that better mitigates climate change and manages regional water supplies (2018, 258). Other scholars and conservation advocates suggest that the networks, exchanges, and biotic communities in and around the Grand Canyon are interconnected, prompting some researchers and environmental scientists to declare the region as the Greater Grand Canyon Ecosystem (Keiter 2013; Alcoze and Hurteau 2001).

During the final weeks of President Barack Obama's term, the Sierra Club and other environmental organizations called for the creation of a

Greater Grand Canyon Heritage National Monument (GGCHNM) to unify and coordinate management of portions Bureau of Land Management and U.S. National Forest areas surrounding Grand Canyon National Park. Although the effort failed, it built on these other precedents around the American West. The effort continues to gain support with an expanding list of supporters that includes American Indian tribes, outdoor recreation companies and organizations, environmental conservation groups, Latinos for Parks, Hispanic Access Foundation, local and state government officials, federal elected officials, and business supporters in Arizona, Colorado, New Mexico, and Nevada (Grand Canyon Trust 2016). I embrace and build upon these ideas for a transboundary approach to national parks and protected areas. But I also see an opportunity to expand the concept based on my analysis, research, and findings for this study, geographic scholarship, and emerging ideas about transboundary environmental and cultural protection.

In *Framing Nature* I propose the Greater Grand Canyon Region as a spatial lens to explore the interwoven environmental, cultural, and visual heritage of the canyon (fig. 3). My concept of the GGCR draws on geographic scholarship that conceives of regions based on shared characteristics and functions of culture. While Grand Canyon National Park is the centerpiece of the region, the GGCR embraces neighboring public, private, and tribal lands, including gateway communities and cities across northern Arizona, southern Utah, and eastern Nevada. The regional boundaries I suggest in this book are not hard demarcations. This not a proposal for a new, designated and demarcated protected area with specific legislation, policies, or territorial claims. Instead, I envision a loose and porous boundary line. The Greater Grand Canyon Region is different from the GGCHNM in its extent—across much of northern Arizona—and it serves a different purpose.

My proposed Greater Grand Canyon Region discussed in this book, goes beyond location-based regional definitions; it offers an opportunity to form new connections between people, places, and landscapes of the American West. For example, connecting NPS programs and geographic scholarship, the NPS Park Cultural Landscapes Program "serves to develop, implement, and oversee an [*sic*] nationwide program of cultural landscape documentation and preservation in national park units" (National Park Service 2021). Under this umbrella, the NPS defines cultural landscapes as "places within U.S. national parks that have significance in American

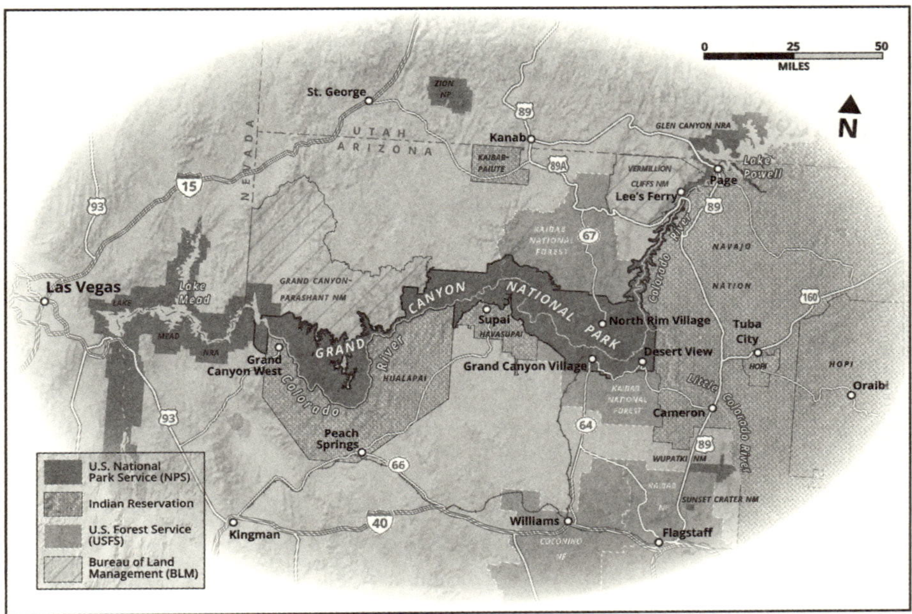

Fig. 3. Map of the Greater Grand Canyon Region. Cartography by Robert M. Edsall. Design by Yolonda Youngs. Based on data from the National Park Service, the U.S. Geological Society, and ESRI.

history and authenticity to a historic time period" (National Park Service 2023). This program overlaps with the field of geography where cultural landscape studies are a robust and long-standing area of scholarship. Unlike the NPS model, however, geographers do not limit cultural landscapes to their significance in history or claims of authenticity. Although some geographers focus their efforts on these aspects of landscapes, the definition is much broader.

Cultural landscapes may be understood through their visible features, but they also play an important role in representing cultural and social elements in the world around us. Geographers Stephen Daniels and Denis Cosgrove contend that a "landscape is a cultural image, a pictorial way of representing, structuring or symbolizing surroundings. This is not to say that landscapes are immaterial. They may be represented in a variety of materials and on many surfaces—in paint, on canvas, in writing on paper, in earth stone, water and vegetation on the ground" (1988, 1). Geographer Richard Schein asserts that cultural landscapes are the "tangible, visible articulation of numerous discourses" and that "U.S. cultural landscapes ultimately are viewed as material phenomena, reflective and symbolic of individual activity and cultural ideas, as they simultaneously are central to the constitution and reinforcement of those activities and ideals" (1997, 660). At the Grand Canyon, Schein's concept of a "discourse materialized" could be understood as how the ongoing discourses and social processes at work in mining claims, trail mapping, and NPS policies shape the look and layout of tourist developments at the South Rim. I carry these geographic concepts of cultural landscape forward in this book by exploring the visual and environmental context of the Grand Canyon through the material landscape elements of hotels, roads, and trails but also through representations of the canyon on the "many surfaces" of postcards, photographs, films, and maps.

My goals in proposing a Greater Grand Canyon Region are twofold: 1) It offers a way to understand the broad geographic range of locations found in more than a thousand postcards, photographs, films, and maps of the Grand Canyon from the eighteenth century to today and my visual content analysis of those images discussed in this book. 2) The GGCR offers a unifying concept that can offer common social, cultural, and environmental issues and themes across the public, private, and tribal lands and the people who share the future of stewardship for this region. My hope is that the GGCR can serve as a framework for organizing new working groups and studies that bring together more inclusive transboundary discussions and shared governance about how to manage, use, and protect the Grand Canyon. This work requires a variety of voices from local and regional stakeholders, such as tribal members and councils, federal lands managers, private landowners, scientists, scholars, visitors, developers, environmental conservation groups, and local businesses to negotiate complex social-ecological interactions.

2 A Great Innovation in Modern Ideas of Scenery

The Emergence of the Grand Canyon on the American Cultural Scene, 1869–1892

> You cannot see the Grand Canyon in one view, as if it were a changeless spectacle from which a curtain might be lifted, but to see it you have to toil from month to month through its labyrinths.
>
> —John Wesley Powell, *The Exploration of the Colorado River and Its Canyons* (1874)

In 1869 the Grand Canyon was not the bustling summer vacation center that we know today. At the time, John Wesley Powell, a veteran of the Civil War and an Illinois college professor with enough curiosity, bravado, and social networking skills to gather funding and support for an extensive field expedition to the desert Southwest, did not imagine its tourist potential. Standing on the banks of the Colorado River, well into four grueling months tracing the course of the river with a handful of men and four heavy wooden boats, he might have been working hard to rein in all the things he *could* imagine about the Grand Canyon. Most of them were not good. "We have an unknown distance yet to run; an unknown river yet to explore. What falls there are, we know not; what rocks beset the channel, we know not; what walls rise over the river, we know not. Ah, well! we [*sic*] may conjecture many things" (Powell 1895, 247). Within that uncertainty, however, lay great potential.

Of course, the Colorado River and the Grand Canyon were not entirely unknown. Paleoindian peoples had inhabited the canyon for more than twelve thousand years (Grand Canyon National Park 2023). Their descendants lived in and around the canyon when Powell and his crew of nine started their epic journey in the spring of 1869. Following the expedition's launch near present-day Green River, Wyoming, they floated past tribal gardens and settlements and hiked to reservation lands to speak to tribal members for information about the canyon's terrain and to send letters to their loved ones and reports back home. American Indians knew the canyon as an everyday place—home, spiritual retreat, workplace, pharmacy, grocery store, meeting ground. The rim and river were part of a seasonal and daily commute. Several tribes—the Havasupai, Hualapai, Navajo, Hopi, and Southern Paiute, to name a few—maintained (as they still do today) ancient cultural and social roots deeply entrenched in the canyon. Their stories of flourishing and floundering in this place extended back for thousands of years to the ancient Puebloan peoples and through each tribe's history. In the process, they constructed ideas and meanings about it through their own stories. Those stories live on in tribal oral traditions, seasonal and annual ceremonies, and family experiences passed on through generations. They animated geographic imaginations with scenes of the canyon's depths and heights.

Powell's 1869 trip followed a different line of experience from American Indian inhabitants of the canyon. The success and a few of the failures of the trip inspired him to lead a second expedition from 1871 to 1872 that produced widely publicized written accounts, maps, and images of the Colorado River through the canyon. But let's take a brief intermission to consider what geographic knowledge and popular ideas about the canyon prefaced his journey. My goal here is not a recounting of imperial or colonial history through the details of every expedition or journey. Instead, I highlight encounters that sought to find the physical limits and contours of the Grand Canyon and, in the process, produced images, maps, and accounts that significantly influenced geographic knowledge and imagination about this region for the American public.

From the mid-sixteenth to the mid-nineteenth centuries, the social context of the Grand Canyon was multicultural and transnational. It blended the experiences and visions of American Indian, Spanish, Mexican, and European-American peoples together. This context framed geopolitical struggles for power, place, and territory in and around the Grand Canyon. Human settlement of the United States was not a simple east to west movement of Anglo-American peoples. Instead, it is a palimpsest of human experience that inscribes layer upon layer of stories. First on the scene were Paleoindians and Ancestral Puebloans. They were followed by their descendants in at least eleven different American Indian tribes who lived, worked, played, and called the canyon home before, during, and after European and later American Anglo settlement and colonization.

In terms of European contact, Spaniards journeyed into the GGCR from the sixteenth century until the early nineteenth century when it was part of the Viceroyalty of New Spain. But their stays were brief and fleeting. Although centrally located in the heart of territory claimed by Spain, the Grand Canyon remained a fuzzy idea in Spanish geographical imaginations due, in part, to its rugged and dry landscape, remoteness from Spanish settlements, misleading or poorly translated terrain descriptions from local guides, and distance from the ocean (where Spanish marine-based exploration excelled) (Pyne 1998).

Within the Greater Grand Canyon Region, Spanish colonization and commodification of North America played out differently than at other southwestern locations. Although they successfully established a network of presidios, missions, and settlement across much of the region, their efforts to concisely survey this land faltered. During what historian Stephen J. Pyne calls the first age of Grand Canyon exploration in his book *How the Canyon Became Grand: A Short History*, Spanish encounters with the canyon and its surrounding landscapes resulted in a few short written descriptions of their experiences and broad caricatures of the landscape on regional maps. Although these maps were foundational documents for expanding European ideas about the proportions and contents of North America, they rarely created any landscape imagery of the canyon, such as paintings or sketches, that reached a broad audience. The reports from missionaries and military explorers grossly misjudged the size of the canyon and discouraged future European travel there based on the steep and rugged terrain, inaccessibility of the Colorado River from the canyon's rim, and the size of chasm. During this early period, from 1540 to 1880, the few visuals created to represent the canyon, nearby plateaus, or the Colorado River were based on brief encounters with the canyon's rim or secondhand accounts or simply left as blank spaces on the map (fig. 4).

How the artists and writers on those exploratory trips depicted the canyon—as a dark and formidable place, as a sublime refuge, or as a region to be avoided—depended greatly on their point of view. As with photographers and postcard manufacturers in later centuries, the view of explorers and the artists in the mid-sixteenth to late nineteenth century was shaped by where they traveled in and around the canyon. These travelers embarked on limited trips, often stymied by the unexpected roughness of the landscape, limited food and supplies, their own curtailed expectations or objectives

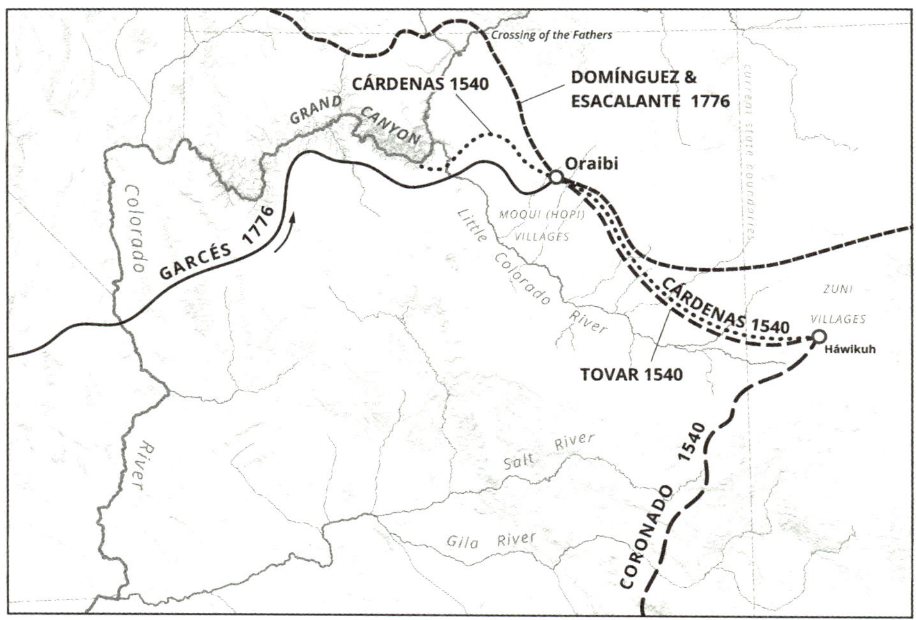

Fig. 4. Map of Spanish explorers' routes in the Greater Grand Canyon Region. Cartography by Robert M. Edsall.

for the trip, or simply inaccurate information about the physical geography of the canyon. Therefore, each group only saw a partial view of the canyon, a slice of the whole. There were no helicopter flights or airplane window seats to expand their views. Theirs was a rim or river choice. This was not a period of midcanyon exploration along trails winding up the canyon walls. The Spanish gathered information from roughly 1540 to 1821 about the GGCR mostly from their experiences in the eastern and northern areas of the canyon and along the rims looking down into the canyon's abyss. The Americans such as Powell and his crew, on the other hand, knew the GGCR from the perspective of the Colorado River, looking up at the rim, during their journeys from 1857 to 1872. It was not until 1882 that Clarence E. Dutton and the artists William H. Holmes and a young Thomas Moran showed American society the Grand Canyon in extraordinary new ways.

Finding the Gran Cañón

Some of the earliest Spanish encounters with the Greater Grand Canyon Region resulted from Francisco Vázquez de Coronado's push into the interior of New Spain from Mexico. Woven into the conquistador's ambitions to seek the fabled cities of gold and to colonize and conquer, he launched a series of scouting groups that gathered insights and geographic knowledge for European audiences. In 1540, using the Zuni pueblo of Hāwikuh as a base (in present-day New Mexico), Coronado sent Captain Pedro Álvarez de Tovar and a small group of men west to the Hopi villages, then known as Moqui to the Spanish and near present-day Oraibi. Through the Hopi, Tovar learned of a large river to the west. He did not venture farther in that direction nor did he see the Grand Canyon. However, later that year and based on Tovar's report, Coronado directed García López de Cárdenas to seek out that river. Again, using the Zuni pueblo as a base, Cárdenas lead a group of men west to the Hopi villages. Then, about three weeks from the villages, Hopi guides led Cárdenas's group to the southeast edge of the Grand Canyon, potentially near present-day Desert View or Moran Point (Weber 1992; Pyne 1998). From that vantage point, they were unable to fathom the canyon's size or scale. Their only comparisons lay back in Europe and their homeland of Spain. A small detachment of Cárdenas's men clambered into the canyon and for three days they attempted to reach the Colorado River. They returned unsuccessful and humbled by the canyon's proportions. They revised their estimates of the river's size—appearing as a small stream from their rim-side perspective—to the girth of the Targus River once they were in the canyon's depths. The boulders and interior buttes of the canyon exceeded the height of the tower of Seville (Goodwin 2019). Cárdenas guessed, correctly, that the width of the canyon was about ten miles, but he sorely misjudged the Colorado River at only six feet wide (McNamee 1997). Clearly the Hopi were familiar the canyon and the region around it as their homeland. But despite the Hopi guides' protests that the river was much larger, Cárdenas insisted on his estimate.

Cárdenas and his men were the first Europeans to see the Grand Canyon, yet they did not record the results of their experiences as sketches or other visual representations that we can revisit now. No artists accompanied them on their journey. Only their words, carrying dire estimations for the immensity and ruggedness of the terrain, reached European audiences. These descriptions discouraged additional Spanish travel and exploration. Over 250 years passed between Cárdenas and next expedition.

A second wave of Spanish exploration of the Greater Grand Canyon Region occurred in the late 1770s, and although these journeys did not result in landscape imagery of the canyon, they did advance the accuracy of European geographic knowledge and maps that influenced popular ideas and perceptions of the area. In 1776 Francisco Tomás Garcés was traveling with Juan Bautista de Anza—a presidio commander and veteran soldier—on his second expedition into the desert interior. Garcés, a Franciscan missionary, attempted to forge a path from the Spanish missions in California to the missions along the Rio Grande. He stands out among Spanish explorers as one of the few to approach the canyon from the west, thereby encountering different places and people than his conquistador predecessors. This ultimately shaped his perceptions of the canyon and provided an alternative assessment.

Garcés started his journey in California and approached the canyon from the southwest. With the help of local guides, he made his way to Havasu Canyon in the central and southern Grand Canyon where he encountered Havasupai settlements (fig. 5). The role of the tribes in Spanish geographic knowledge of the canyon is important. On its eastern side, the first wave of Spanish expeditions into the GGCR launched from the Hopi villages near Oraibi. The Havasupai and Hopi guides also directed what the Spanish saw and where they went through their travels. Garcés continued his journey, moving along the canyon's western rim, but only for a brief time before veering toward the Hopi villages to the east and thereby completely missing a major piece of the Grand Canyon's physical geography: the pronounced bend south in the Colorado River in its east-west flow across the Kaibab Plateau. Despite these experiences, Garcés—like Cárdenas—did not find the Grand Canyon to be sublime or breathtaking. He wrote in his journal that he was "astonished at the roughness of this country, and at the barrier which nature had fixed" as a "prison of cliffs and canyons." He also grossly misunderstood the scale of the canyon and the challenge of accessing the Colorado River from the rim that "to all appearances would not seem to be very great the difficulty of reaching" (qtd. in Pyne 1998, 18–19). From there he continued to travel eastward toward the Hopi villages that were well known to the Spanish by the late eighteenth century. But like Cárdenas, he only saw a partial view of the canyon. Nevertheless, with Garcés's descriptions and maps, the Spanish now had bookends of first-hand experiences, maps, and descriptions of the eastern and western canyon.

Later in 1776, a third major Spanish expedition saw a portion of the Greater Grand Canyon Region. Father Francisco Domínguez and Father

Silvestre Vélez de Escalante led a group of ten men across the Colorado Plateau with the goal of forging an overland route between Santa Fe and the missions and settlements in California. They touched the northern Grand Canyon at a ford across the Colorado River after searching for it for nearly two weeks. It later became known as the Crossing of the Fathers. During their November trip, they traveled across much of northern New Mexico, Arizona, and southern Utah before turning around because of seasonal snows. As with previous Spanish exploration parties, an artist did not accompany Domínguez and Escalante to record their journey. But cartographer Bernardo Miera y Pacheco created an illustrated map in 1778 that moved forward European geographic knowledge of the GGCR. That map did not show the Grand Canyon's rim or many of the other features in the canyon's depths, but it did bring more definition to the locations of the tribes living in the GGCR and the hydrography of the region by featuring the general outline of the Colorado River's course and that of other rivers in the region (fig. 6). On their return trip along a similar route, they chiseled steps into the canyon wall along the north canyon. This is now a lost cultural site, submerged under the waters of the Lake Powell after completion of the Glen Canyon Dam in 1966.

The Spanish were the first Europeans to see the Grand Canyon and move the iconographic arc of the canyon forward in terms of expanding ideas about the canyon to a broad public audience. Their historic legacy is perpetuated through place-names such as El Tovar Hotel in Grand Canyon Village, Conquistador Aisle in the inner gorge, Coronado Butte, Cárdenas Butte, and, of course, the Colorado River. And although some of these names are poorly placed—for example, no evidence exists of conquistadors traveling through the aisles of the canyon's inner gorge where the name is applied on a map—a visitor to the Grand Canyon today would be hard-pressed to find much NPS interpretative materials about the historical Spanish experience at the canyon.

The geopolitics and cultural milieu of the Greater Grand Canyon Region shifted in the early nineteenth century as Mexico became an increasingly important political power in the region. Meanwhile, Spanish colonization and control dissipated in the nineteenth century, as global power struggles reverberated back to the canyon. Global struggles and an overextended imperial drive weakened Spain's ability to maintain control of its North American territorial claims (Goodwin 2019). Mexico gained independence

Fig. 5. Map (*detail*) of Garcés's 1776 exploration of the Greater Grand Canyon Region. The map was created by Friar Pedro Font, another missionary who accompanied Anza on his 1776 exploits in the Southwest. This section of the map shows detail of Garces's route as a dotted line, but the real center stage here is the emphasis on hydrography and ethnography. Thick lines represent the Colorado River and other rivers. Oraibi, the goal of Garces's journey, is marked with a dot and circle in the upper right. The Yabipais (Havasupai) and Moqui (Hopi) tribes' settlements are labeled, along with several other tribes. Spanish Archives Portal (PARES), "Plano que conti[en]e las Provincias de Sonora, Pimerías, Papaguería, Apachería, Rios Gila y Colorado y tierras descubiert[a]s hasta el Puerto de S[a]n Fran[cis]co en la California Septentrional y jasta el Pueblo de Oraybe en la Provincia de el Moqui . . ." (map published in 1778). Ref. no. ES.41091.AGI/MP-MEXICO, 349.

from Spain in 1821 and claimed a vast swath of land to the north, renaming part of this territory Alta California (an area that included the Grand Canyon) (fig. 7). But still, the Grand Canyon remained on the edges of European, and now Mexican, geographical imaginations as a remote and poorly surveyed or understood place for national and international attentions.

Surveying the Scene

The mid- and late nineteenth century brought a major shift for land ownership and geographic knowledge of the Greater Grand Canyon Region. Mexico ceded Alta California and its northern territory to the United States as part of the Treaty of Guadalupe Hidalgo in 1848, signed at the end of the Mexican-American War. The United States expanded into territory that would become Arizona, New Mexico, Utah, Nevada, and part of Colorado—

Fig. 6. Map (*detail*) of the Domínguez and Escalante 1776 exploration. The Crossing of the Fathers, where Domínguez and Escalante crossed the Colorado River in the northern section of the Greater Grand Canyon Region, is marked as *Concepcion* in the upper center of the map. If you look closely in the lower right, Oraibe and other Hopi villages are depicted as distinct pueblos, complete with small ladders, cascading rooflines, and their mesa-top locations. The Rio Colorado prominently cuts across the map in a thick line, although specific and accurate detailing of its course would be well down the line. "Plano geografico de los descubrimientos hechos por Dn. Bernardo Miera y Pacheco y los RRs. Ps. Fr. Francisco Atanasio Dominguez y Fr. Silvestre Veles: S. Felipe Rt. de Chiguagua" (map drawn in 1778). Beinecke Rare Book and Manuscript Library, Yale University. Call number WA MSS S-2856.

all states that are prime components in the environmental and cultural context of the Grand Canyon today. After the transition, much of the GGCR and the present-day states of Arizona and New Mexico were folded into the Territory of Mexico. The Treaty of Guadalupe Hidalgo was significant in opening the Spanish and Mexican borderlands to the purview of an expanding United States; it created new avenues of conquest and knowledge of the Grand Canyon, situating the river as "an American Nile, well within the heartland of Manifest Destiny" (Pyne 1998, 25–26). The underlying ideology of manifest destiny inspired and sanctioned a massive movement of people, technology, American Indian land dispossession, and transportation in the West. From the north, Mormon guides and colonists came seeking new lands to settle. From the east and south, traders sought new markets, while government explorers and scientific expeditions traveled up

Fig. 7. Map (*detail*) of the Mexican West and Grand Canyon, 1847. This map, employed in the negotiations for the Treaty of Guadalupe Hidalgo, depicts the extent of the GGCR claimed by Mexico and the geographic knowledge of the Grand Canyon at that time. The Rio Colorado and Rio Virgin are depicted with more clarity than in earlier Spanish maps but lack additional accuracy about their routes. The Hopi village of Oraibi (Orayha) serves as a key anchoring site for the eastern Greater Grand Canyon Region, although there is still much missing from this map, in terms of both cultural and physical landscape features. "Mapa de los Estados Unidos de Méjico: segun lo organizado y definido por las varias actas del congreso de dicha républica y construido por las mejores autoridades." Map drawn by American cartographer John Disturnell, 1847. Library of Congress Geography and Maps Division. Call number G4410 1847.D5.

the Colorado River to survey this new territory (fig. 8). The Euro-American experiences in the GGCR created the establishing shot of the canyon for the American cultural scene. Later viewmakers were indelibly influenced by these surveyors and scientists.

The Ives Expedition (1857–1858) was the first European or Anglo encounter with the Grand Canyon since Garcés over 250 years earlier. Although Mormon and other Euro-American scouts preceded Ives, their explorations produced few written or visual accounts of the canyon. Army first lieutenant Joseph Christmas Ives of the U.S. Army Corps of Topographical Engineers led the Colorado Exploring Expedition, funded by the federal

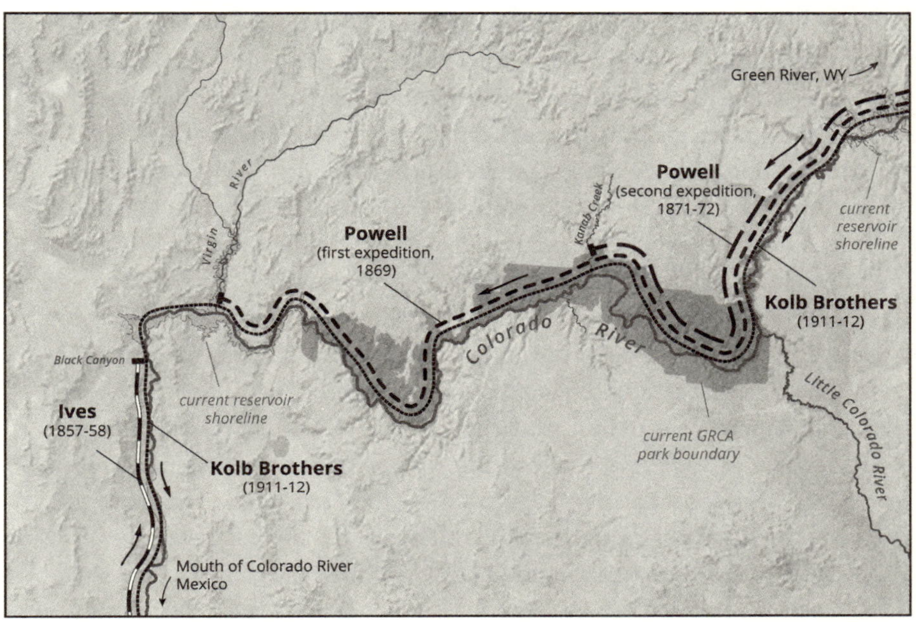

Fig. 8. Map of nineteenth-century U.S. explorers' routes through the Grand Canyon on the Colorado River. Cartography by Robert M. Edsall. Design by Yolonda Youngs.

government, to explore the navigability of the Colorado River, survey and map its course, and prepare a hydrographic survey of tributaries in the region. Starting in December 1857, Ives and his group of twenty-seven men made their way north from the Gulf of California, traveling upstream along the Colorado River on a steamboat as far as Forth Yuma. From there they continued to Black Canyon. But the trip took a bad turn when the steamboat crashed on submerged rocks. From there they continued in a small boat another thirty miles upstream, then continued the journey on foot. With the help of Hualapai guides, they traveled into Diamond Creek (now part of the Hualapai Indian Reservation). After that, they made their way east and descended Havasu Canyon before leaving the canyon and traveling on established trails to Fort Defiance, New Mexico.

The expedition resulted in new geographic information about the canyon and another layer in the iconographic arc of the Grand Cayon. Ives published a voluminous four-hundred-page report of the trip through the western and central canyon. He and his crew traveled farther along the Colorado River into the Grand Canyon than any other European-American to date, but the experience of traveling through the canyon's rough terrain deflated Ives. His report stands as a dour assessment of the Grand Canyon: "The region is, of course, altogether valueless. . . . It can only be approached from the south, and after entering it there is nothing to do but leave. Ours has been the first, and will doubtless be the last, party of whites to visit this profitless locality. It seems intended by nature that the Colorado River, along the greater portion of its lonely and majestic way, shall be forever unvisited and undisturbed" (1861). Contemporary readers might see the folly of Ives's words in the counter data of millions of visitors, profits from the tourism economy, and the powerful symbology of the Grand Canyon as a sacred place for many people. Ives also clearly discounted the experiences and values that American Indians placed on the Grand Canyon. Indeed, his report initially missed public attention even during his time. It was too long and the publication date of 1861 publication date, in the midst of the Civil War, was poorly timed.

Decades later the report's findings hit home, but more for its impressions of the Grand Canyon than its accuracy. It provided the first written descriptions of a rim to river journey in the Grand Canyon via the descent down Diamond Creek and expanded Euro-American knowledge of the west and central canyon. Perhaps an even larger impact came through the sketches and imagery of the canyon, created by the expedition's two artists, H. B. Möllhausen and Friedrich W. von Egloffstein. According to some scholars, they introduced the Grand Canyon to Western art through their sketches (Pyne 1998). The final published report included amazingly detailed maps and sketches by Egloffstein, the survey artist and cartographer, but the cartography was flawed in its representations of the hydrography. The expedition did not travel to the confluence of the Colorado and Little Colorado, so the map misses that vital bend and the confluence in the eastern canyon. It conflated Black Canyon as a part of the main Colorado River canyon (or Big Cañón as the expedition called it), it exaggerated the Little Colorado River as a main branch, and exaggerated Kanab Canyon in the north (Pyne 1998). Egloffstein's final maps in the report, however, represented not only the spatial extent of the expedition but also served as a detailed conceptual blueprint for the Greater Grand Canyon Region, reaching from Los Vegas ("the meadows") on the west and to the Hopi (Moqui) pueblos around Oraibi (Oraybe) on the east. Beyond that, Egloffstein's map elongates to the Zuni settlements as an eastern anchor point, following the cartographic vistas of Coronado, Tovar, and other Spanish explorers (fig. 9).

The sketches inspired American geographic imaginations about the Grand Canyon, but like Ives's descriptions, it dampened any ideas of a sublime or welcoming landscape. Ives wrote that the "sides of the tortuous canyon became loftier, and before long we were hemmed in by walls two thousand feet high . . . imparted an unearthly character to a way that might have resembled the portals of the infernal regions" (1861). Egloffstein's meticulous maps provided an incredible level of detail and clarity to the canyon, yet his sketches are a different story, portraying an impressionistic and exaggerated scene in beautifully detailed but dark and foreboding overtones. They seem to reveal more about Egloffstein and the crews' perceptions of the canyon—shaped by the steamboat crash, the long journey, and the cultural ideas they carried about nature—than about the canyon's physical terrain. For example, in *Big Cañón at the Mouth of the Diamond River*, the canyon's dark walls dominate the image visually and proportionally as they rise in formidable cascades, only parting slightly to reveal a narrow passageway (fig. 10). Egloffstein's sketch and the engraved image that followed employed classic techniques of Romantic artists with light and dark tones in the landscape arranged to create drama—the shimmering river draws the eye toward the center bottom of the image in contrast to the dark canyon walls that surround it. Scale is key here too. Near the river's edge, perched on large boulders are two small figures that almost escape our attention as they are impossibly dwarfed by the grandness of the canyon, of nature, around them.

Scholars and scientists have roundly praised Egloffstein's maps but criticized his sketches as inaccurate and gothic misrepresentations of the canyon. Some clever field reconnaissance by contemporary photographers and journalists—struck by the divergence of Egloffstein's detailed maps from his exaggerated and impressionistic sketches—suggest that the sketches may have been mislabeled and filed. They may have instead depicted the Black Canyon on the Gunnison from another expedition that Egloffstein joined (Miller 2012). Nevertheless, these descriptions and images fed American geographic imaginations with ideas about the Grand Canyon. They added another layer to its iconographic arc, casting it as a dark, desolate, and forbidding environment. Indeed, historian Stephen Pyne contends that *Big Cañón at the Mouth of the Diamond River* is the "first great picture of the Grand Canyon" (Pyne 1998, 46). These images also buttressed dominant European-American ideas in the nineteenth century of wilderness as a formidable place. They knew the Grand Canyon as an inaccessible place—both

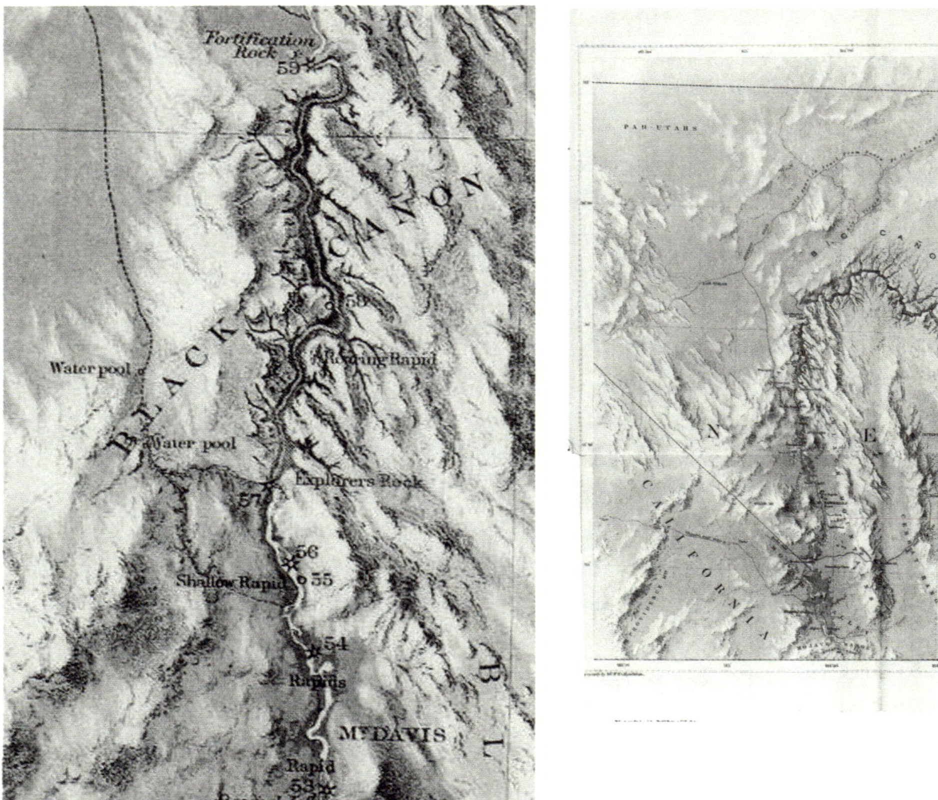

Fig. 9. Map of Friedrich W. von Egloffstein's Rio Colorado of the West, 1858 (*above right*), with a detail of Black Canyon (*above left*). Egloffstein's map may have misrepresented some features of the river and the GGCR, but the detail of the locations the group visited is superb. Note the detail view of the Black Canyon, perhaps the section of the Grand Canyon that the party experienced the most through firsthand river travel and exploration. The map depicts the Colorado River, the topography of the canyon and its surrounding terrain, named rapids, camps, and astronomical observation points. David Rumsey Historical Map Collection, Explorations and Surveys. War Department, Map No. 2, *Rio Colorado of the West, explored by 1st Lieut. Joseph C. Ives, Topl. Engrs . . . 1858*. Drawn by Frhr. F. W. v. Egloffstein, Topographer to the Expedition. Topography by Frhr. F. W. v. Egloffstein. Ruling by Samuel Sartain. Lettering by F. Courtenay. List no. 0341.002.

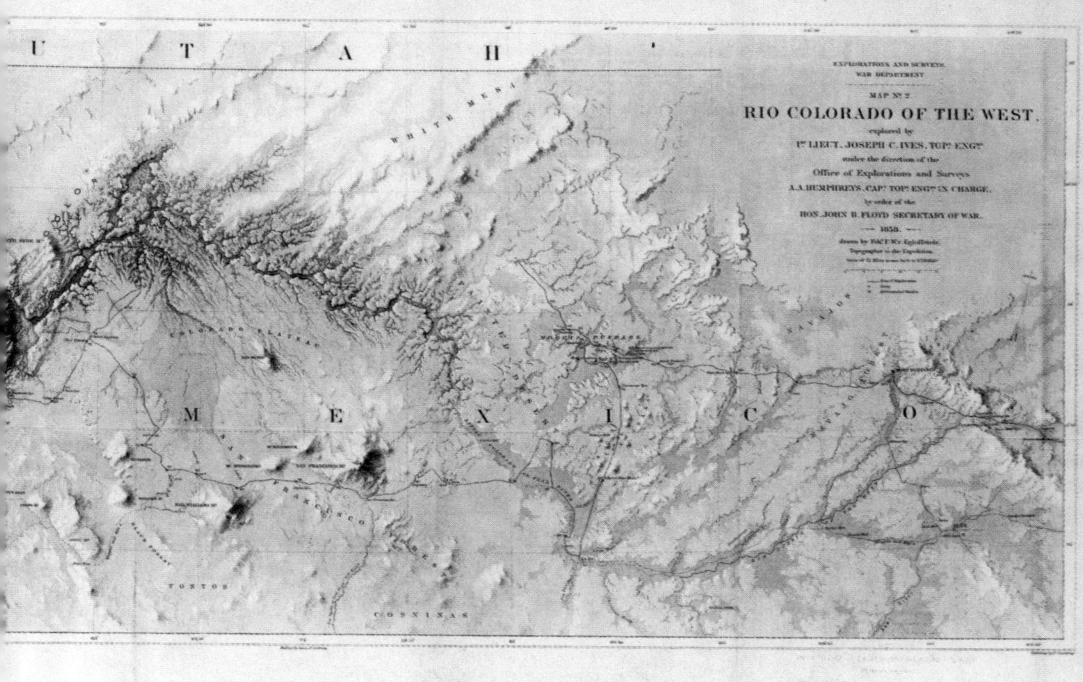

physically and intellectually. Some scholars suggest that the sustained allure of the Grand Canyon well into the present day may even derive from its reputation as a wild and rugged place (Grusin 2004).

In 1869, when John Wesley Powell embarked on his river journey, there was a precedent for the trip but still many unanswered questions about the Grand Canyon. His expedition—a major scientific and exploratory undertaking—was arguably the one that made an impact on American ideas about the canyon, even more so than Ives's journey. Powell and his group of nine men in four boats left Green River Station, Wyoming—near today's Green River, Wyoming—in May and ended the trip near the Virgin River in August of the same year. The river Powell and his men encountered was not the Colorado River we know today—cold water, often green in color, and dam controlled for predictable flows. Powell's experience was on its historic predecessor—muddy warm water, churning through the canyon with erratic and often dangerous force. Unlike Ives, Powell emerged from the canyon with a zeal to return but for quite different reasons. Although

Fig. 10. Friedrich W. von Egloffstein's *Big Cañón at the Mouth of Diamond River* from Ives's 1861 "Report Upon the Colorado River of the West." David Rumsey Historical Map Collection, Big Canyon at Mouth of Diamond River, Colorado Exploring Expedition, General Report, plate VI. J. J. Young, from a sketch by F. W. Egloffstein. List no. 0341.058.

he and his crew survived the ordeal (minus three ill-fated members) and explored the canyon's inner reaches along the Colorado River in more detail and depth than any recorded trip before, the scientific merits of that first trip were negligible. Much of his notes and the expedition's equipment were lost on the trip due to boating accidents in the rapids, fires on the shoreline, and other mishaps. The group emerged from the canyon after months of near starvation as they ran, lined, or portaged their heavy wooden boats down the uncharted and frequent rapids. Powell's desire to lead a more successful scientific recording trip through the canyon was built on his hard-earned experience during those summer months of 1869.

Powell's timing is also significant. In terms of exploration of the American West, the Grand Canyon was well behind other large areas of the region for surveying, mapping, national recognition, and tourism. By comparison, by the 1860s the promotion of Yosemite and Mariposa Grove was in full swing, with stagecoach and rail travel delivering a consistent stream of tourists to the area. The attention led to state park status by 1864 and national park recognition by 1890. Yellowstone was the thoroughfare of trappers, soldiers, early tourists, and several scientific and exploratory expeditions by the 1870s, becoming the first officially designated national park in the world in 1872. But in 1869, fifty years before the Grand Canyon would become a national park, Powell was surveying "The Great Unknown."

To gain support from the political and scientific community for his work, Powell needed more comprehensive and consistent surveying records than the few soggy notes that survived his first trip. He also found new passions in geology and ethnography during his western travels. A bit wiser about trip planning and now hooked on the southwestern landscapes he had encountered in 1869, Powell returned to the canyon. His 1871–72 Geographical and Topographical Survey of the Colorado River was one of the four Great Surveys of the American West focused on mapping and exploring a region in the area west of the Mississippi River. The expedition started in the town of Green River, Wyoming, and ended near Kanab Creek, a tributary of the north and central Grand Canyon. This time he led a trip with more political backing, federal government funding and recognition, support from the Smithsonian, and a more informed plan of action. He also replaced his crew of mountain men, trappers, and Civil War veterans with artists, photographers, and scientists. The artists were carefully chosen and proved instrumental in their contributions to the popular imagery of the canyon. The roster included photographers John Karl Hillers and E. O. Beaman, topographer and artist Frederick S. Dellenbaugh, and noted expedition artist Thomas Moran.

Powell's journey into the Grand Canyon and his ability to emerge alive on the other end were only part of his claim to fame. His efforts in disseminating the *idea* of the canyon to a national audience was equally important, and it started promptly after his first trip. He launched a lecture tour that promoted his recent trip, disseminated his observations and findings about the Colorado River and the Grand Canyon to a national audience, and placed the canyon in the limelight of American popular culture. These endeavors helped to secure the funding, supplies, and political support that he sorely needed for that second expedition (Worster 2001; Stegner 1992).

Powell's published accounts of his trips, though exaggerated at times and often conflating the two trips into one, created new and influential material for the canyon's iconographic arc. His work included published letters and articles in newspapers and magazines, government reports, and books. Importantly, many of these publications included maps and sketches that illustrated his and his crew's journey and served as early visual impressions of the canyon for American popular audiences.

The source and timing of his publications serves as a valuable record of the escalating contributions he created to the canyon's iconography arc. Immediately after his 1869 trip, Powell published descriptions of the journeys in seven letters over three separate issues of the *Chicago Tribune* (Worster 2001, 584). Powell also published two articles as an abbreviated account of his 1869 adventure in the canyon. The first, "The Cañons of the Colorado," appeared in 1875 as a three-part illustrated series in *Scribner's Monthly*. The second was published as a single account in *Scribner's* later that same year (Grusin 2004, 201). His first full recounting of the 1869 expedition appeared as a government report published in 1875 as *Exploration of the Colorado River of the West and its Tributaries*. It was later expanded with maps and illustrations (some from the *Scribner's* articles) in 1895 as *The Canyons of the Colorado* (Grusin 2004, 201; Worster 2001, 584). The book combined Powell's written descriptions of the canyon and the crew's experiences with sketches and prints (Grusin 2004, 201). The expedition was well documented and popularized over a period of several years. Powell also published several books and reports based on his canyon experiences, including *Report on the Geology of the Eastern Portion of the Uinta Mountains* (1876), *Introduction to the Study of Indian Languages* (1877), and *Report on the Lands of the Arid Region of the United States* (1878) (Heacox 2001, 94).

Eventually several of his crew members published all or selections of their journals, but it may be Frederick Dellenbaugh's account of his experiences on Powell's second expedition from 1871 to 1872 that stands out as the best testament to the journey. As a crewmember, Dellenbaugh served multiple roles as field assistant, artist, and oarsman. This gave him a unique and first-person perspective for many of the expedition's encounters. William H. Goetzman, in his foreword to Dellenbaugh's book, noted that—along with Powell's published report of his first trip in 1869—it still served as a "virtual handbook for those modern adventurers who shoot the dangerous rapids of the Colorado" (1962, xvii). Indeed, quotes from both accounts appear in modern river runner guidebooks alongside detailed maps of the rapids and canyon's interior. His engaging recounting of the trip was written almost forty years after the expedition and published in 1908, then reprinted in 1962 and 1984. Dellenbaugh's version is loaded with rich details, insightful observations, and descriptions of rapids and canyon landscapes that make his account more grounded, cohesive, and relatable than Powell's. It is still a great read. For example, as the party floated the Green River on their approach to the Grand Canyon, he recounts that the "river was perfectly smooth, except a small rapid late in the day, with walls on both sides steadily increasing their altitude . . . the Canyon of Desolation pushes its rock walls around one so diplomatically that it is some little time before the traveler realises that he is caught." Later in the trip as the party navigated Marble Canyon, Dellenbaugh vividly remembers his oarsman experiences:

> In the afternoon the walls became greater, the river ran swifter, the descent seemed almost without a break, for rapid followed rapid in such quick succession that was next to impossible to separate them one from another. At times we could barely maintain control of the boats so powerful and uninterrupted was the turbulent sweep of the great narrow flood. At one place as we were being hurled along at a tremendous speed. . . . The Major stood on the middle deck, his life-preserver in place . . . peered into the approach maelstrom. It looked to him like the end for us and he exclaimed calmly, "By God, boys, we're gone!" With terrific impetus we sped into the seething, boiling turmoil, expecting to feel a crash . . . but instead of that result [the boat]

shot through smoothly without a scratch. . . . We had no time to think over this agreeable delivery, for on came the rapids . . . of unending declivity requiring instant and continuous attention. (1962, 221)

The imagery that accompanied Powell's publications about his trips fortified these written accounts and served as a catalyst for propelling an aesthetic idea of the Grand Canyon into a national dialogue. As historian Donald Worster suggests, "each embellishment of Powell's narrative strengthened the impression that here was . . . [a] place that had repelled everyone before him" but was "in fact . . . a place of exquisite color, diversity, light, and form, of natural harmony" (2001, 162). Powell himself often lauded the aesthetic appeal of the canyon in his reports and books. Although he occasionally issued statements that seemed to counter his many efforts to describe and visually grasp the canyon, these sentiments also placed him in a special position as beholder of the scene: "The wonders of the Grand Canyon cannot be adequately represented in symbols of speech, nor by speech itself. The resources of the graphic art are taxed beyond their powers in attempting to portray its features. Language and illustration combined must fail" (Powell 1909, 32).

Thomas Moran was not the only artists in the group, but his social and artistic profile made him a strategic image maker for Powell's second Grand Canyon expedition. By the late nineteenth century, Moran was one of a small cadre of nationally recognized, field-tested expedition and landscape painters in the United States. His reputation blossomed in the early 1870s through his work in national parks of the American West, including Yellowstone and Yosemite. Perhaps it was the strong competition between Ferdinand Hayden, Clarence King, George Wheeler, and Powell—leaders of the four Great Surveys of the West—that inspired Powell to add more illustrations to his account. Both Hayden and King produced their annual reports with images, including woodcuts, line drawings, panoramas, maps, and lithographs (Stegner 1992, 398). Government reports were one way to disseminate the expeditions' findings and imagery. Other routes in the late nineteenth century included popular press and media such as magazine articles, books, stereoview images, and postcards. Powell embraced these supplementary sources to propel the impact of his expeditions to a broad American reading (and viewing) audience.

Two dozen of Moran's wood engravings accompanied Powell's *Scribner's Monthly* articles and thirty of his artworks accompanied Powell's 1895 book-length account of the river trips. These sketches added a view into the expedition's encounters with the Grand Canyon and the Colorado River that appealed to popular tastes and contemporary perceptions of sublime and dangerous nature embedded in ideas of wilderness in the American West. Some critics thought Powell's narrative sorely needed this visual element. Moran echoed these sentiments in a note to Powell, citing the explorer's placid account of his otherwise enthralling expeditions: "You do not once (if I recollect aright) give your sensations even in the most dangerous passages, nor even hint at the terrible & sublime feelings that are stirred in one, as he feels himself in the strong jaws of the monstrous chasms" (qtd. in Worster 2001, 332). While Moran's painting of the Grand Canyon, *Chasm of the Colorado*, is easily recognized by contemporary audiences, in the nineteenth century the painting was primarily available only for an elite audience. The *Scribner's Monthly* articles, sketches, and Powell's book—on the other hand—were far more accessible. Moran's wood engravings are pivotal as an early source of Grand Canyon imagery that superseded Egloffstein's sketches.

Thomas Moran's *Noonday Rest in Marble Canyon* provides a glimpse into his visual style (fig. 11). Here we see the crew of Powell's second expedition relatively early in their Grand Canyon voyage, in the northeast section of Marble Canyon. In some ways, the scene may look familiar to contemporary river runners accustomed to a lunch break during the long days of rowing. The river and beach dominate the foreground, while the canyon's walls rise up along the sides of the image and fade into grayer shades of cascading walls receding upstream and just beyond our view at a river's bend. This is not Egloffstein's dark, gothic canyon; this scene is less intimidating, more of a brief glimpse into a scenic canyon of the southwest and a workaday labor break. A partial view of the sky is visible, just above the canyon's walls, revealing potentially a partly cloudy day. One can imagine the shade from the clouds as a welcome sensation to the crew during those hot summer months.

On the beach, we see two boats, one in the foreground tied to nearby rocks while three of the crew members, in the background, pull the second boat onto the riverbank. A closer look reveals the lessons learned by Powell from his first journey, written into his choice and design of river gear. The boat in the foreground is left akimbo as the crew tends to the second boat. A pile of rope sits on the stern, its two oars are still partially in the water, but a third spare oar is at the ready, tied to the side of the boat. Moran's scene shows us a placid stretch of the river, but Powell's crews lost many

Fig. 11. Thomas Moran's *Noonday Rest in Marble Canyon*. This is one of Moran's wood engravings of the river corridor that appeared in John Wesley Powell's 1875 book-length recounting of the expedition. Similar depictions of the trip created by Moran also appeared in Powell's *Scribner's Monthly* articles in 1869. David Rumsey Historical Map Collection, Noonday rest in Marble Canyon. Thomas Moran, 1895. List no. 0740.068.

oars, crushed in the rapids or washed overboard, as they learned the skills of rowing their heavy wooden boats through the foaming rapids and frequent boulder fields. The crew would suffer trip delays as they replaced this vital piece of equipment, hunting down suitable driftwood or cutting some of the sparse trees to carve another oar. A closer look at the second boat also reveals oars in the water as well as Powell's navigating chair lashed to top of the deck. This odd addition to the expedition was an innovative although cumbersome boat modification that Powell developed based on his earlier experiences on the Colorado River. By 1871 he had explored that "unknown river" he dreaded in 1869 and learned some new tricks. One of the great lessons was the value of an elevated perspective on the rapids. Approaching a rapid, Powell perched in his chair while the two other crew members rowed, their eyes at river level. From his elevated perspective he could see the rapids' pattern ahead, assess its course, and yell rowing directions to the crew. It worked well, mostly, although reading between the lines of his book and the other crew members' journals, one gets the sense that the ride was perilous for Powell and annoying for the rowers as the barked and sometimes erratic commands peppered their muscular pulls on the oars through the rapids.

Although this is a small sample of Moran's vast imagery collections, *Noonday Rest in Marble Canyon* offers some patterns that influence the growing iconographic arc of the Grand Canyon. Comparing Moran's image to Egloffstein's, there is a clear flip in perspective. Both image makers were impressionistic and took some artistic liberties in their portrayals of the canyon. But there are visual clues in the images that hint at broader cultural shifts in American society's view of wilderness, the Southwest, and the Grand Canyon in the fourteen years between Ives's and Powell's trips. In Moran's image we see the river—now a pathway through the canyon instead of a dangerous and unknown foe—take center stage. Egloffstein's, on the other hand is dominated by dark canyon walls while the river is diminished as a sliver of light in the bottom of the image. The people portrayed by Egloffstein are dwarfed by the canyon, almost invisible except to the viewer with an eye for detail. The crew members in Moran's image are still much smaller than the canyon by proportion, but they are larger and more detailed than those in Egloffstein's image, shown in situ at their workplace, their labor in action as they pull the boat onto the beach. They are concrete and relatable, while Egloffstein's are abstract. The Grand Canyon becomes more of a known entity in Moran's image. We can see the sky and trace the detailed contours of the canyon's walls, beach, and boulders. Egloffstein's canyon seems impenetrable and impressionistic in the fuzzy depiction of seemingly endless canyon walls receding into the background of his image.

Although Powell's narrative and Moran's evocative sketches and wood engravings sparked curiosity and scientific exploration of the Grand Canyon, it was Clarence E. Dutton who thoroughly etched the visual canyon into the popular geographic imagination in America. Dutton, a geologist with the U.S. Geological Survey, a Civil War veteran, and a protégé of Powell led a government-sponsored geological expedition into the Grand Canyon from 1880 to 1881. He reported his findings in the *Atlas to Accompany the Monograph on the Tertiary History of the Grand Cañon District* (1882). It was one of the first books dedicated exclusively to the geology of the Grand Canyon and illustrated with "a veritable collage of verbal and visual technologies of aesthetic and scientific representations" (Grusin 2004, 132). Images included those by the expedition photographer Jack Hillers, a few illustrations by Thomas Moran, and twenty-three double-page plates of spectacular, highly detailed chromolithographs by William H. Holmes (fig. 12). Dutton's descriptions "articulated the visual identity of the Canyon forevermore" by "communicating the overwhelming views from the rim" (Trimble 2006, 13). He did this by combining graceful prose describing the scientific merits of the canyon while treating its aesthetics with a nineteenth-century appreciation for the sublime. Dutton placed an empirical description of the canyon into the language and landscape appreciation modes of his day, creating a digestible version of the canyon for literate Americans in the 1880s. In essence, he introduced the Grand Canyon to a non-scientific audience and framed the view for them with his evocative descriptions.

> The Grand Cañon of the Colorado is a great innovation in modern ideas of scenery, and in our conceptions of the grandeur, beauty, and power of nature. As with all great innovations it is not to be comprehended in a day or a week, nor even in a month. It must be dwelt upon and studied, and the study must comprise the slow acquisition of the meaning and spirit of that marvelous scenery which characterizes the Plateau Country, and of which the great chasm is the superlative manifestation. (Dutton 1882, 141)

Historian Wallace Stegner praises Dutton as "almost as much the *genius loci* of the Grand Canyon as Muir is of Yosemite." He wryly observes that

Fig. 12. William H. Holmes's *Panorama from Point Sublime (Part I. Looking East).* This image first appeared in Clarence Dutton's 1882 *Atlas to Accompany the Monograph on the Tertiary History of the Grand Cañon District.* Holmes's view from the rim vividly illustrated Dutton's evocative descriptions of the canyon. David Rumsey Historical Map Collection, Panorama from Point Sublime (Part I. Looking East). William H. Holmes, Atlas Sheets XV. Julius Bien & Co. lith. U.S. Geological Survey, Geology of the Grand Canon District. List no. 4713.016.

"though it is Powell's monument to which the tourists walk after dinner to watch the sunset from the South Rim, it is with Dutton's eyes, as often as not, that they see" (Stegner 1992, 173–74). It is significant that the view that Dutton promoted was from the rim, not the river. Although Powell and others after him floated the Colorado River and publicized their journeys through books, articles, photographs, and films, it was the rim view that tourists sought and artists portrayed in their images. Not until the 1950s was that trend broken with the postwar boom in outdoor recreation and the advent of commercial river rafting. In other words, the "American public connected to the canyon through its overlooks, not its rapids" (Pyne 1998, 71). This river-rim dialectic—a back-and-forth spatial dialogue between these opposing forces of river or rim, looking into the canyon, looking across the canyon, or looking up to the rim from the river—continued to haunt the visual and intellectual history of the canyon well beyond the publications of Powell's or Dutton's reports.

Other explorers and image makers journeyed to the canyon in the late nineteenth century and left their marks through visual records. Photographers such as Timothy O'Sullivan, for example, found himself at an interesting juncture of time and technology where the exploration of the American West coincided with the invention and use of the camera. O'Sullivan created the first photographs of the Grand Canyon while accompanying the 1871 Wheeler Survey in the Grand Canyon (Trimble 2006, 8). His images are amazing for their technical accomplishments; overcoming the challenges of wind, dust, and heat was no small feat for turn-of-the-century photographers who worked with large, heavy equipment and delicate photographic development processes. O'Sullivan's work is praised by photographers today for its ability to capture western landscapes in a way that reveals their beauty, immense proportions, and realism. According to some critics, O'Sullivan's photographs challenged ideas of manifest destiny and American idealism that saw nature as a medium to be controlled, plowed, mined, and colonized (Trimble 2006).

3 The Viewmakers

The People Behind the Scenes of Postcard Manufacturing

"Well I am here at last and a more beautiful sight I ever have seen. Having a fine time." In 1915, Mrs. Buehler wrote this simple note on the back of a postcard and sent it from the Grand Canyon to Mrs. Mary Hieble in Parkersburg, West Virginia. Her sentiments may seem surprising in their brevity (and lack of enthusiasm), but in truth, the handwritten message just barely fits on the back of the postcard of the well-appointed El Tovar Hotel, completed only ten years earlier by the Santa Fe Railroad Company (fig. 13). Mrs. Buehler was part of a small and elite group of tourists who made the slow, expensive, and long railroad journey overland to the relatively new state of Arizona. In sending a postcard she joined a cadre of fellow travelers in the simple act of keeping in touch with friends and family. But she also contributed to the growing global business of the postcard trade.

Although postcards may have faded in today's world of email and social media messaging, they were a standard and highly popular correspondence choice for many canyon visitors. In an era before the internet and telephone, a time when a trip across the country was measured in weeks, not days, and postcards were a means of delivering noteworthy firsthand scenes of floods, fires, earthquakes, and other events; depicting travels to faraway places; or delivering news of a safe trip to relatives and friends back home. Inexpensive, easy to use, and readily accessible, postcards were tough to beat. The sphere of influence for postcards expanded beyond travelers too; many adults and children avidly collected and exchanged postcards as a hobby. Postcards were more than a means of communication, though. They may draw a viewer in with flashy colors or an inexpensive correspondence option, but those images could reveal much more. They were forms of popular media that provided a portal to the ideas and meanings that people associated with the Grand Canyon over time.

This chapter builds upon the intellectual and visual representations of the Grand Canyon promoted by nineteenth-century explorers and artists by adding another layer to the iconographic arc of the Grand Canyon—the

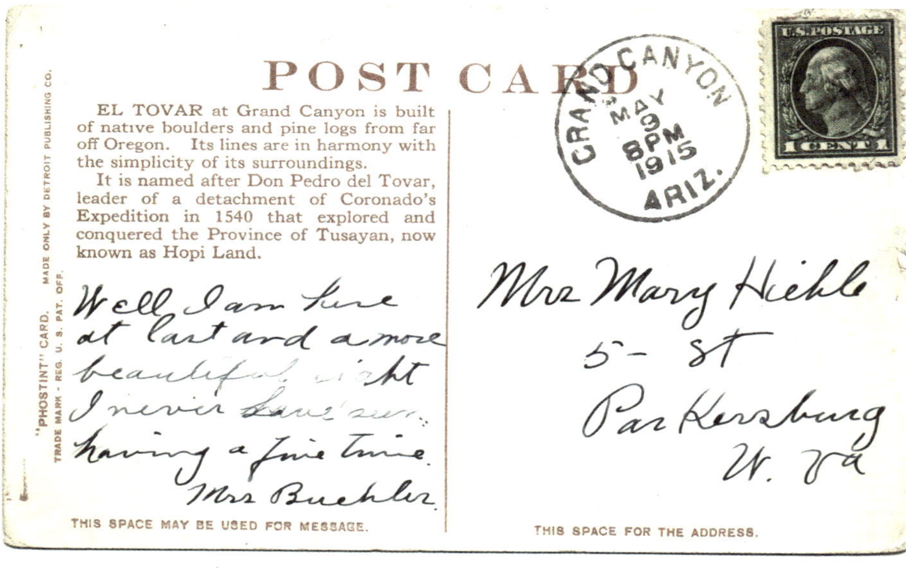

Fig. 13. Front (*top*) and back (*bottom*) of a Detroit Photographic Company postcard, 1915. Note the prominent “Phostint Card” label along the back side of the card, marking one of the DPC’s distinct production styles. Author’s collection.

canyon as a burgeoning tourism hub with commercial value, promotional potential, and aesthetic and emotional worth. Postcards formed a key source of imagery in this new era. But before we explore the early tourism industry at the Grand Canyon and its visual inheritance from Powell and other expeditions, it's important to understand who made these images and how they were created. More than just the nostalgic ephemera of tourism, postcards were a wildly popular form of communication and collectors' item throughout much of the twentieth century.

This chapter describes the technical process of manufacturing postcard imagery from photographs and the equally important social and cultural process of the photographers and postcard manufacturers working behind the scenes to select locations and subject matter in their images. This chapter focuses on the three primary postcard manufacturers whose work is featured in this book: Detroit Publishing Company (DPC), Curt Teich Company (CTC), and Frasher Foto Postcard Company (FFPC). This background lays the groundwork for succeeding chapters and for better understanding of how image makers framed their views of the Grand Canyon and a better appreciation for the social, economic, and political context of their decisions and the impact of their visual representations in the broader social milieu of America.

The Evolution of Postcards as Popular Media

Postcards and photographs share an intimate history. Postcards evolved through many stages to reach their modern form. Their history is intertwined with that of photography, developments in printing processes, and the history of national and international postal standards and services. Postcards are a younger visual medium than photographs, but they are reliant on photographs for their content and share some technical production similarities (Newhall 1982; Arreola 2013, 2017, 2019, 2021). Postcards emerged onto the global stage from their European proving grounds in the 1870s, where they had undergone several format changes and developments over the decades as privately printed trade or advertising cards limited to domestic circulation (Staff 1966; Miller and Miller 1976). However, inexpensive mailing rates and an interest in setting standards for international circulation spurred the development of a new type of card (Staff 1966, 44–54). By the early 1890s, picture postcards filled that demand as Europeans eagerly collected and circulated these postcards, also known as view cards, with an image on one side.

Within a few years, transatlantic communication, innovative new printing technologies, and relaxed postal restrictions and regulations facilitated greater access to postcards as popular visual media. They caught on in the United States after the first souvenir picture postcards were sold commercially at the Columbian Exposition in Chicago in 1893 (Rowe 2006; Meikle 2015). The private postcard printing industry soon boomed with demand for these cards, especially after Congress passed the Private Mailing Card Act in 1898. This legislation allowed private printing companies to manufacture postcards and the U.S. Postal Service to lower the postage rate for them from two cents to one cent. This legislation also required that manufacturers print the phrase "Private Mailing Card" on the back, or verso, of the card. However, postcards did not permit extensive writing or personalization. Format and printing guidelines legally restricted writing on the cards to only a mailing address on the verso of the card and no personalized note. The picture postcards focused on just that—the picture—prominently placed on the front, or recto, of the card. However, senders of these minimalist postcards often circumvented these rules by added a brief note on the front of the card in the blank area around the image.

Oddly enough, it was a small adjustment—printing a slim, vertical line on the back of postcards—that opened a new era for postcards and the travelers who used them. The so-called Divided Back Postcard Era started in the United States in 1907, when Congress passed legislation that allowed privately manufactured postcards to carry a message on the left half of the postcard's back. That little black line divided the back of the card into two sections: the right half for the address, the left half for a note (Staff 1966). This era, from 1907 to 1915, ushered in a so-called golden age of postcards with millions printed, sold, and mailed in the United States (Bassett 2023; Baldwin 1998). Their manufacturing and use skyrocketed with the divided back format change, cheap mailing rate of one cent, and increasingly speedy delivery times.

Postcard fronts also transformed to a more user-friendly and attractive format that marked out three major postcard eras from 1915 to the present day. During the White Border Era, from 1915 to 1930, postcard manufacturers added a frame of white space around the image on the recto of the cards. The crisp, white border added a tidy frame to the image and saved ink costs for the postcard manufacturers. Postcards from this era continued to be printed with a divided back but with a new addition—a description of the image on the front of the card. German printers led the market for early postcard manufacturing, but during World War I, American printers stepped in to fill the gap. U.S. manufacturers did not have the same quality of printing technology as their German counterparts. By 1930, interest in postcards waned.

The Linen Era, from 1930 to 1945, reinvigorated the postcard market with a new printing process that transformed high rag content paper into postcards that had the look and feel of linen fabric. The Curt Teich Company, based in Illinois, was the leading global manufacturer during this era and until 1959. The innovative CTC printing process allowed for faster manufacturing and brighter dyes that created some of the most iconic postcards, many of which continued with the white border around the image on the front of the card.

The third era, the Photochrom (alternatively spelled photochrome or Fotochrom) Era started in 1945 and continues to the present day. These colorful cards quickly moved to the forefront of postcard manufacturing in the 1940s and 1950s (Werther and Mott 2002, 12–37). Photochrom postcards are easily distinguished from white border or linen postcards; the paper is not as textured as the linen cards and does not feature a white border around the front image. They are printed in color and the recto image resembles a photograph. They take advantage of a printing process that produces mechanical prints of photographs in a postcard format. Finally, chrome or photochrom postcards should not be confused with their cousins, real photographic postcards. These postcards were popular in the 1950s. They feature a photo printed on light-sensitive paper through a process that has been around since the early twentieth century (Rowe 2006).

To better understand postcards and their role in the Grand Canyon's iconographic arc, it is helpful to note a few details about the language of postcard culture. I follow the nomenclature guidelines presented by postcard collectors and historians Mark Werther and Lorenzo Mott in *Linen Postcards: Images of the American Dream* (2002). The history of postcard manufacturing, printing, trade, and distribution is complex and long. It is sometimes difficult to discern the specific artist or artists who created images or photographs featured on postcards. The role of each postcard company may be obscured by the assorted and easily confused designations of "publisher, distributor, printer, producer, jobbers, sales representatives, logos, copyrights and trademarks, artists and photographers' names, etc.," information that is often gathered from the back of the card (Werther and Mott 2002, 12–37). To provide consistency about the various actors in this process, I refer to the company that prints a card as the manufacturer. The distributor is the company that "obtained the order from a business, contracted with the manufacturer and distributed the cards."

Postcards as Visual Culture

Postcards are an important source of visual information that shape the way different places are understood and experienced. Studying postcards about past places, cultures, and landscapes is a growing field of scholarly research across geography, visual arts, environmental history, American studies, communication studies, and political science (Arreola 2013, 2017; Arrigo 2014; Blake 2003, 2004, 2014; Cronin 2011; DeBres and Sowers 2009; Dora 2009; Francesconi 2011; Jackson 2013; Jakle 2003; Rowe 2006; and Thornbush 2008). Postcard manufacturers embraced a plethora of visual scenes and subjects—everything from local events, such as a fire in town hall, to main street views, to notable buildings and cityscapes. Postcards were the lingua franca of their day for visually communicating news, events, and impressions of places around the world. Throughout the early to mid-twentieth century, postcards were an incredibly popular medium that people could buy at local shops, such as commercial photographers' studios, postcard company shops, or at tourist sites such as the Grand Canyon. Once purchased, these cards would be circulated through the mail as correspondence or collected in albums common in family homes. Some postcard companies even developed special racks to hold and display their cards in shops.

The process of manufacturing a postcard is fascinating. Understanding it as a combination of social, mechanical, and technical processes is integral to the story of how the Grand Canyon transformed in popular culture from a frontier of Spanish territory to a national icon. Each phase of creation involves individual and group decision-making about the subject matter and locations portrayed in the final postcard product. That decision-making is a social process that provides insights into how much a diverse and sometimes contentious crowd of artists, printmakers, railroad companies, local entrepreneurs, photographers, tourists, shop owners, and public lands managers framed ideas and meanings about the Grand Canyon and how they changed over time. Together they created a composite, idealized, mimetic, and often heavily manipulated visual representation of the canyon that was altered in the postcard manufacturing process by teams of people working to create a marketable product. Their individual and collective decisions—either deliberate or unintentional—shaped where and what people saw of the Grand Canyon. That visual information indelibly shaped geographic imaginations that fueled many a family vacation, but it also influenced environmental policies, cultural heritage preservation and interpretation, public lands management, and tourism development. The three primary postcard manufacturers whose work is featured in this book exerted an impressive force in shaping the Grand Canyon's iconic status.

Viewmakers: The People Behind the Scenes

Detroit Publishing Company

Detroit Publishing Company started in 1895 in Detroit, Michigan, and quickly developed into a major manufacturer, printer, and distributor of picture postcards from 1895 to 1936, with a major bulk of their business before 1924. The business identified as the Detroit Photographic Company until 1905, when it changed its name to the Detroit Publishing Company (Library of Congress n.d.). William A. Livingstone, an engineer, publisher, and wealthy Detroit businessman, formed the company with the photographer Edwin H. Husher. To the mix of their wealth and photographic skills they added the rights to an innovative photolithographic process called Photochrom from the Photoglob Company, based in Zurich, Switzerland. They also seeded their company with skilled draftsmen they hired from Switzerland.

Obtaining the exclusive North American rights to the Swiss Photochrom printing process was a significant coup over their competitors. The process converted black-and-white photographs into high-quality color lithographs through halftone copies pressed onto stone. This process allowed DPC to produce large quantities of color prints that maintained both their photographic look and vibrant colors. After 1907, DPC rebranded Photochrom as "Phostint" and prominently printed its new name on the back of all its postcards. Phostint was a marketing strategy centerpiece that distinguished the company from its rivals and their products (see fig. 13). DPC brochures boasted that "Phostint cards combine truthfulness and delicacy of color, taste in pictorial composition, rare choice of subject and real educational value" through "Nature's Coloring" (Stechschulte 1994, xi). DPC assets also included an enormous inventory of photographic negatives they could mine for new postcard material. Much of that inventory came to the company through the efforts of renowned painter and photographer William Henry Jackson.

One of the most important early acquisitions for the company was Jackson's glass-plate negatives. By the time Jackson joined the company in 1897, he was a well-known landscape photographer with proven field experience in the American West. He traveled with Ferdinand Hayden's 1871 U.S. Geological and Geographical Survey of the Territories as the survey photographer (Endalman 2002). His images, along with those of artist Thomas Moran and the writings of Hayden and others contributed visual and textual impressions that helped to secure Yellowstone's creation in 1872 as the world's first national park. Jackson exerted a tremendous influence on the company; he sold his entire stock of ten thousand glass-plate negatives, including many of the Grand Canyon, to the company in 1897 and joined DPC as president and field photographer in 1898 (fig. 14). These images formed the core of the DPC catalog. Over the duration of his association with the DPC, Jackson traveled widely photographing additional scenes and purchasing other photographers' negative files for use in company stock images (The Henry Ford n.d.; Library of Congress n.d.).

At the apex of its business in the early 1900s, the Detroit Publishing Company had forty staff members; a dozen salesmen; offices in Detroit, New York City, Los Angeles, and Boston; and sold seven million prints a year worldwide (Stechschulte 1994). The DPC produced some of the most influential and widely distributed visual representations of cities, everyday life, transportation, international settings, and scenic landscapes. DPC was a bustling business. Beyond postcards, it sold a range of products including prints, souvenirs, lanternslides, and advertisement card at retail shops and through mail-order across a global distribution network. DPC's success slowed during World War I when the U.S. government categorized the company as a nonessential business. Never quite recovering from this stumbling block and compounded by other challenges that included declining sales of photographs and postcards during the war and competition from other firms that used new and cheaper printing methods, DPC went into receivership in 1924. The company liquidated its assets in 1932 and closed its doors when Robert B. Livingstone, brother of William, died in 1936 (Stechschulte 1994, viii–ix; Endalman 2002; The Henry Ford n.d.; Library of Congress n.d.).

The DPC's process of selecting, manufacturing, and distributing postcard images reveals the social network behind each postcard and the technical

Fig. 14. The View Makers of Detroit Publishing Company. A group of Detroit Publishing Company managers, standing on the steps of the DPC factory in 1910. DPC managers held a strong influence on the site selection, look, and distribution of postcard imagery. The famed western photographer William Henry Jackson (*front center, holding hat*), joined the company and boosted its imagery with his extensive landscape views. "Detroit Publishing Company Managers with William Henry Jackson, Detroit, Michigan, circa 1910." Detroit Publishing Company Collection, from the collection of The Henry Ford, object ID#37.102.107. https://www.thehenryford.org/collections-and-research/digital-collections/artifact/308648#slide=gs-311822.

process of manufacturing a postcard. This process followed the same general steps that many other postcard manufacturers took in the early to mid-twentieth century of direct photographic transfer of an original negative onto a lithographic stone and chromographic printing plates, but each company made their own alterations to create a unique postcard brand. Postcards were big business in the early and mid-twentieth century. Companies guarded their distinct printing processes. You can see the pride (and copyright claim) that each company took in their printing in the brand logos prominently displayed on each postcard, such as DPC's trademark icon—the name Detroit Publishing Co. encircled by an artist's palette. For DPC, the people behind the scenes included a combination of DPC managers who made decisions about what subject matter and locations would be featured in that year's postcard catalogs, sellers who sent DPC requests for postcards of specific scenes or locations, buyers who placed orders for high selling postcards, DPC printers who edited and annotated images, and distributors who sent the postcards to shops and fulfilled mail orders.

The process started when Detroit Publishing Company sent hired photographers to a specific town or scenic attractions, such as the Grand Canyon, with a checklist of locations and subjects to capture in their imagery (figs. 15–20). Those checklists—generated by DPC managers to fit postcard shop distributors' requests and DPC marketing staff decisions—guided the photographers' activities and site selections. For example, a photographer might be sent to the South Rim Village at the Grand Canyon with instructions to capture two photos of El Tovar and one of Hopi House. However, the lists only dictated a general location to photograph. Photographs were still subject to an individual photographer's creative prowess that shaped the final image through framing, angle, and specific site selection. Next in the process, the photographer sent black-and white negatives to the DPC manufacturing factory with written instructions for the printmakers about the colors to add, subjects to include or remove, the framing of the image, and other options. Sometimes photographers wrote these editing instructions directly on the print (also sent to DPC), producing curiously annotated imagery with phrases such as "add more clouds" or "take people out."

Fig. 15. (*opposite top*) The photographers behind the scenes of Detroit Publishing Company postcard manufacturing. DPC, like all postcard manufacturers, acquired its imagery from field photographers. These viewmakers would capture photographs of street scenes or other locations, then send their images back to the postcard factory for processing. In this image, from around 1905, a DPC photographer captures a group of beachgoers in an odd seaside pose of leaning and sitting on a donkey. Library of Congress Prints and Photographs Division, "Photographer taking pictures of group with donkey at crowded beach, Atlantic City, N.J." 1890–1910. Detroit Publishing Company photograph collection, call #LC-D418-30947.

Fig. 16. (*opposite bottom*) Editing and annotating images during the postcard manufacturing process. Look closely at this photograph to see notes scribbled above the buildings and on the street. The image is in the middle of the editing process used to produce a color print from a black-and-white photograph. Photographers would often send notes or write directly on an image to guide the coloring process, such as in this 1904 photograph. "Herald Square, New York City, 1904." Photograph with handwritten production notes, Detroit Publishing Company Collection. From the collection of The Henry Ford, object ID#P.DPC.017236.A.

Red brick
white
cool gray
black
HERALD SQUARE
COPYRIGHT 1904 BY DETROIT PHOTOGRAPHIC CO.

Back at the DPC printing offices, a factory populated with highly skilled and detailed artists and printers translated the photographers' field notes into the final product. They retouched the image, made decisions about the color and hue, and removed (or added) subjects to the scene. The artists' work took hours, days, and sometimes weeks to complete. In this process, the Detroit Publishing Company and other postcard manufacturers effectively altered whole landscapes and social scenes. They removed certain subjects (including people, cars, and animals), changed the colors of buildings or trees, inserted additional subjects, rearranged other subject locations, and generally performed a wide variety of small and large alterations to the original image. Although their actions were intentional, the long-term impressions from those images on American imaginations and environmental perceptions of places like the Grand Canyon created potentially unintended consequences. The postcard manufacturing process hinged on many small decisions—from the photographer in the field to the artists in the DPC factory—that culminated in a new product for next year's postcard racks. Although it may not have been the intention of DPC staff and managers, the postcard production edits transformed the way people saw the Grand Canyon and their expectations of its environment and human geographies.

Keep in mind that postcards were, in a way, a fad and a malleable form of popular visual media. Like many fleeting styles, they were subject to quick changes in the market and fluctuating public expectations. Through the lithographic process, the DPC postcard manufacturers could update their images and sell revised versions of the postcard each year as a new product on the market. The same photographic negative could be used repeatedly

Fig. 17. (*opposite top*) The typical workplace behind the scenes in postcard manufacturing. This stark image shows the muddy street and leafless trees in front of the Detroit Photochrom Company Factory in Detroit, Michigan, between 1900 and 1910. Field photographers would send their images back to factories such as this one to be processed into postcards. Library of Congress Prints and Photographs Division, Detroit Publishing Company Photograph Collection, "Detroit Publishing Company, southeast view, Detroit, Mich." Call #LC-D4-43314, reproduction #LÇ-DIG-det-4a20859.

Fig. 18. (*opposite bottom*) Creating canyon postcards. William Henry Jackson's 1907 *Grand Canyon of Arizona* photograph is shown here in the midst of the color adding and correcting stage of the Phostint process (also known as Photochrom). Library of Congress Prints and Photograph Division, Detroit Publishing Company Collection, "Grand Canyon of Arizona," 1907, Lot 3888, no. 2 (H) [P&P].

Fig. 19. The power of color: A side-by-side comparison of the same William Henry Jackson image of Grand View Point showing a black-and-white glass plate negative of *Grand Canyon of Arizona from Near Bridge at Grand View*, ca. 1906 (*above*), and a 1906 postcard printed from that same image but after cropping and adding color (*opposite*). Jackson photo: Library of Congress Prints and Photographs Division, Detroit Publishing Company Photograph Collection, "Grand Canon [*sic*] of Arizona from near bridge at Grand View Hotel," call#LC-D4-19249, New York Public Library Digital Collections, Miriam and Ira D. Wallach Division of Art, Prints and Photographs, Photography Collection, New York Public Library; DPC postcard: "View from near Bridge, Grand View, Grand Canyon, Ariz," New York Public Library Digital Collections.

10451 GRAND CANYON OF ARIZONA, FROM NEAR BRIDGE AT GRAND VIEW.

Fig. 20. The shops that fueled the distribution network of postcard manufacturing. This image shows the Detroit Publishing Company shop that sold postcards in New York City, ca. 1900. Until 1905 the company identified its distributor shops as Detroit Photographic Company. DPC distributed its postcards through a national and global network of shops, at tourist sites like the Grand Canyon, and through direct mail orders. Library of Congress Prints and Photographs Division, "Detroit Photographic Co., 218 Fifth Avenue, New York, Twenty-Sixth Street front," 1900–1910, Detroit Publishing Company photograph collection, Call #LC-D4-43743.

with certain aspects of the image altered each time to change the resulting print. In this way, a black-and-white negative of Grand View Point, for example, underwent a metamorphosis with each successive printing (see fig. 19). In its first version, the postcard might feature brilliantly colored canyon walls painted in shades of orange and red and framed by the branches of leafy trees and shrubs on the right and left side of the scene. In a second printing, the postcard could be altered to add more greenery depicted as juniper trees along the canyon's plateaus or a lone man standing along the cliff gazing into the canyon. Subjects could also be removed, such as the trees along the left and right sides of the frame from the first printing. Subsequent prints continued this editing process based on a complex mix of factors, including the popularity of the postcard, new orders from distributor shop owners, new buildings or tourist experiences, or photographer's artistic choices.

DPC's early twentieth-century postcards set the stage for subsequent imagery produced by other postcard companies that followed in its wake. DPC imagery was foundational for those who filled the void after DPC shut its doors in the 1930s. Curt Teich, Frasher Foto, and others sought out the same locations and the same subject matter over and over as they built their visual catalog of postcard scenes. Looking at decades of this imagery provides a clearer view of the mimetic quality of postcards throughout much of the twentieth century. Although there were certainly new scenes produced by innovative printing, photographers' artistic license, or new cultural landscape developments, an iconographic arc of the Grand Canyon begins to take shape in the early 1900s as DPC imagery focused on the southeastern canyon with its rim-side viewpoints and roads, midcanyon trails, and growing development.

At the Grand Canyon, two powerful forces joined together when the Fred Harvey Company hired DPC to manufacture and print postcards of canyon overlooks, trails, and lodges. The Fred Harvey Company (FHC) was a major player in the burgeoning mass tourism industry of the early twentieth-century American West with exclusive rights to operate lunch stations and lodges along the extensive Atchison, Topeka & Santa Fe Railway routes. The trains carried thousands of tourists to the Grand Canyon's South Rim depot where they were met by FHC staff as the congenial hospitality counterparts to Santa Fe's transportation network. FHC operated hotels, shops, and restaurants on the Grand Canyon Village on the South Rim. Those shops featured postcard racks full of colorful DPC, and later CTC, postcards to buy as mementos of their journey (Anderson 2000; Fried 2011). The partnership with the railroad and distribution of hotels, shops, and restaurants all along its tracks positioned the Fred Harvey Company as an unmatched force of tourism in the Southwest (Dilworth 2001). Postcards provided tourists a souvenir and served as an influential promotional device for FHC and Santa Fe Railroad's development of the Grand Canyon (Dora 2009).

While business partnerships between DPC and other companies was common practice, sometimes the arrangement can be confusing to untangle, especially when sorting through historic images. For example, as a sign of their partnership, many of the Grand Canyon postcards were printed with the name Detroit Photographic Company or the company's trademark icon of an artist's palette on the front of the card. The Fred Harvey Company name was printed on the back of the card. FHC commissioned these cards, placed orders, and distributed them in their canyon gift shops while Detroit Publishing Company manufactured the postcards and printed them. Fred Harvey Company did not manufacture the postcard or print it; instead, they hired DPC to do that job.

The Curt Teich Company

Following close on the heels of Detroit Publishing Company, Curt Otto Teich founded a printing firm in 1898 in Chicago (Dumbarton Oaks 2023). Teich was born in Germany and worked there as a lithographer until he emigrated to Chicago in 1895. In 1904 he joined his brothers Max and Alfred in incorporating as the American Photochrom Company to import and print postcards. The name formally changed to Curt Teich & Company in 1906 (Meikle 2015, 19). The company used the technique of offset printing starting in 1907 and printed their own postcards starting in 1908. By the 1930s, Teich was manufacturing linen postcards. Scholars use Curt Teich Company when referring to the firm's work, although over the years as the business and their printing methods evolved, the company operated with a variety of credit lines on their postcards, including Curteich-Chicago, C. T. American Art, and C. T. Photocrome (Dumbarton Oaks 2023). Soon after Curt Teich died in 1974, Regensteiner Publishers purchased CTC. They continued to print postcards at the Chicago factory until 1978, when the rights to the company name and process were sold to John Hinde Ltd.

Over his seventy to eighty years of managing the business, Curt Otto Teich leveraged his considerable talents to build CTS into the world's largest printer of postcards (fig. 21). Much of CTC's success can be attributed to the unique skills of its founder. Curt Teich was an entrepreneur, a well-organized manager, a skilled lithographer, and a pioneer of the offset printing process. To reach that point, he had to overcome several hurdles, including finding a way to manufacture a postcard image that was realistic, reproduceable at high volume, and efficiently created while balancing the costs of labor and materials (Meikle 2015, 20).

Teich's knowledge of lithography and offset printing presses played a major role in finding solutions. Lithography is a printing process that uses flat stones to work an image area with a special greasy ink so the ink adheres to the stone while the areas without an image repel the ink. The process allows printing with a wide range of marks and tone areas and makes color printing easier because different colors are applied to individual stones and then printed

Fig. 21. Curt Teich Company postcard factory in Chicago, 1922. CTC boasted that its building was the "world's largest postcard factory in the world." "The Largest Post Card [*sic*] Factory in the World, Curt Teich & Company Plant, 1733–1755, Irving Park Blvd.," 1922, filename A91552. Newberry Library, Curt Teich Postcard Archives Collection.

over each other on the same sheet. Although lithography was invented in eighteenth-century Germany using limestones, Teich developed his own style of lithography and adapted it to American landscapes. He replaced the expensive and heavy litho stones with metal plates that were roughed up by small stones gathered from Lake Michigan, close to Teich's Chicago factory. The original process he devised produced quality results but was complicated. Early on, Teich failed to secure a patent for his process. This left the door open for other competitors. He later developed and patented other offset printing processes that he called C. T. Art Colortone and Curteichcolor. Teich's innovative printing processes helped to secure CTC's place as the largest postcard printer in the market. Curt Teich's factory in Chicago was enormous; it brought the various elements of manufacturing postcards all under one roof, from artistic and photographic processing to printing (fig. 22).

Behind the scenes of Curt Teich's colorful linen postcards was a large, organized, and efficiently managed labor force (fig. 23). Many studies of postcard history often overlook this aspect of manufacturing postcards. The Curt Teich Company excelled beyond all others in the level of organization

Fig. 22. Curt Teich Company factory at work, 1929. This image reveals the daily human labor and machinery behind the scenes of postcard manufacturing, including the large offset printing presses typical of a CTC manufacturing process. Newberry Library, Curt Teich Postcard Archives Collection, "Curt Teich & Company's Factory Floor Showing Offset Presses, 1929," box 7, folder 14.

Fig. 23. Curt Teich Company artists at work, 1930s. This photograph shows the bustling workshop of commercial artists who worked at CTC. They were divided into different departments, each tasked with a separate phase of the postcard production process. Newberry Library, Curt Teich Postcard Archives Collection, "Photo-reprint, Interior of Teich Factory, undated," box 2, folder 1.

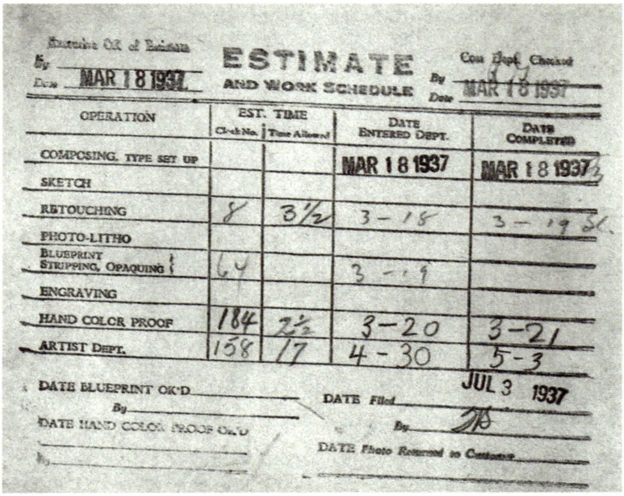
Executive O.K. of Estimate
By
Date MAR 18 1937

ESTIMATE
AND WORK SCHEDULE

Cost Dept. Checked
By
Date MAR 18 1937

OPERATION	EST. TIME Clock No.	Time Allowed	DATE ENTERED DEPT.	DATE COMPLETED
COMPOSING. TYPE SET UP			MAR 18 1937	MAR 18 1937
SKETCH				
RETOUCHING	8	3½	3-18	3-19
PHOTO-LITHO				
BLUEPRINT STRIPPING, OPAQUING	64		3-19	
ENGRAVING				
HAND COLOR PROOF	184	2½	3-20	3-21
ARTIST DEPT.	158	17	4-30	5-3

DATE BLUEPRINT OK'D
By
DATE HAND COLOR PROOF OK'D
By

DATE Filed JUL 3 1937
By
DATE Photo Returned to Customer

Fig. 24. Curt Teich Company Estimate and Work Schedule, 1937. CTC kept meticulous records about each postcard's path through the manufacturing and production process. This particular work order—started on March 18, 1937, and completed on July 3, 1937—provides a valuable window into the time and labor required to manufacture a postcard. This document reflects the typical CTC production line of graphic and visual artists working on listed tasks, such as composing type setup, retouching, photo-litho, blueprint stripping, opaquing, engraving, hand color proofing, and time in the artists department. Newberry Library, Curt Teich Postcard Archives Collection.

and detail of their records, and the sheer number of these records survive to this day, preserved in archives and museums. For example, an Estimate and Work Schedule form accompanied many of the postcards I analyzed for this book (fig. 24). Artists and designers would have this document on their desks as they completed their tasks. Workers were organized into departments based on the tasks they performed (such as sketching or hand coloring) and documented their work and hours on these schedules. These forms provide an intriguing window into the daily lives of artists and postcard illustrators who documented the hours and dates worked while composing, sketching, retouching, engraving, hand coloring, and other tasks.

CTC's diligent organization and management of a large labor force is noteworthy. CTC developed a system that broke down the complex process of manufacturing postcards into a series of logical steps. More than just corporate ephemera, documents such as the Estimate and Work Schedule form provide a valuable source of information that reconstitutes the complex technical and artistic tasks of transforming postcard orders into field photographs and eventually postcards. However, there are shortcomings to this data. While this paper trail that recorded the time, dates, and types of tasks survives in archives and libraries, the names and backgrounds of many of the people who worked in the factories remain undocumented and anonymous.

Finally, Curt Teich Company records provide a valuable perspective into the process of selecting the scenes, subjects, and locations of its postcards. Again, CTC excelled at detailed and well-organized record keeping. Looking closely at the file records of CTC orders for Grand Canyon postcards, for example, reveals the name of the postcard subject and the company that ordered that postcard in two very different examples from the 1920s and 1930s. Both are detailed but rarely seen documents of the postcard production process (figs. 25 and 26). The format for this form changed slightly over time, but each sheet recorded the name of the company that ordered the postcards, such as Verkamps or Fred Harvey Company, and the name of the specific postcard subject they ordered. In this way, CTC kept track of incoming orders while also maintaining a running list of the most popular postcards, measured by the number of orders placed for each scene. A postcard subject or scene that companies frequently reordered or ordered in large numbers, for example "View from El Tovar Hotel," provided data and direction for CTC. The form instructions (see fig. 25, top of image) are to "Kindly state in remarks column, if subject is still a good seller and good for reprints or if changes should be made regarding title, coloring, photo-retouching or new plate. If subject is dead, rule out." If Fred Harvey

Fig. 25. (*opposite top*) Curt Teich Company file records of postcard subjects and orders, 1928. This is one page of a continuing list of Grand Canyon subjects, clients, orders, photography sources, and dates of postcards manufactured by the CTC in 1928. Newberry Library, Curt Teich Postcard Archives Collection.

Fig. 26. (*opposite bottom*) Curt Teich Company register details, 1938. This register shows a finer scale and more clearly organized account than the 1928 version. It is significant for showing the height of CTC's success during the Linen postcard era. The form includes the name of the postcard and subject, the number assigned to it according to the CTC format (such as 8AH854), who ordered the card, the style, and the date. Note the Fred Harvey and Verkamps names in the "ordered by" column. It was common practice for these companies to order and sell postcards manufactured by CTC. Newberry Library, Curt Teich Postcard Archives Collection.

CURT TEICH & CO.—INFORMATION BLANK

Our file record about Grand Canyon of the Colo. Ariz.

Kindly state in remark column, if subject is still a good seller and good for reprints or if changes should be made regarding title, coloring, photo-retouching or new plate. ***If subject is dead, rule out.*** Look in Ariz. Genl. folder for Grand Canyon

No.	Name of Subject	Ordered by	Photo Property	Photo on file	Subject Open	REMARKS—Use this column only.
	Bright Angel Trail, G.C. of the Colo.					
	G.C. of the Colo. from Top of Bright Angel Trail					R Jan. 4, 1928
	G.C. of the Colo. from O'Neils Point					R 1-4-28.
	G.C. of the Colo. " Bright Angel					
16	" " " " Grand View Point					R 1-4-28.
	The Colo. River from the Plateau					
18	G.C. of the Colo. – from Bright Angel Trail					R 1-4-28
19	The Colo. River from the Plateau					
20	Bright Angel Trail					R 1-4-28.
21	Cape Horn, Bright Angel					R 1-4-28
22	The Start of the "					
	From the Picturesque "					
7462	Mooney Falls					J. Johnson Photo only
63	Bridal Veil Falls					Williams Ariz
	Grand Canyon					J. Johnson Photo only
	Grand Canyon Depot	J.H. Verkamp				R 788 45 (folder only) 16-10-19
	El Tovar Hotel					46
	View from El Tovar Hotel					47 [illegible]
	Looking North from Yavapai Point					48
	Grand View Point					49
	Hopi House					789 00 (folder only)
	West from Hopi Point					01
	On Hermit Trail					02

GRAND CANYON NATIONAL PARK, ARIZONA NAME OF SUBJECT	NUMBER	ORDERED BY	STYLE	DATE
Point Imperial, North Rim	8AH 854 D	Utah Parks Co. 6M	Photo Colort	4-12-38
View from Point Sublime	855 D	"	"	"
De Luxe Cabins	856 D	"	"	"
GRAND CANYON AND KAIBAB FOREST	D-5398 D	UTAH PARKS CO. 6M	Lg. Folder Cov.	4-12-38
THE LOOKOUT	8AH 1520 D	VERKAMP'S 6M	ART COLORTONE	7-5-38
EAST FROM HOPI POINT	1521 D	" "	"	"
GRANITE GORGE FROM PLATEAU	1522 D	" "	"	"
ON HERMITS TRAIL	1523 D	" "	"	"
FOOT OF BRIGHT ANGEL TRAIL	1524 D	" "	"	"
GRAND VIEW POINT	1525 D	" "	"	"
Grand Canyon from Moran Point	8AH 1582 D	J. R. Willis 12½M	Art Colortone	7-12-38
Desert view looking north from the Watchtower	1583 D	" "	"	"
Deer and Fawn	1584 D	" "	"	"
Grand canyon in winter	1592 D	" "	"	"
Air views of	1593 D	" "	"	"
Greetings from	1594 D	" "	"	"
The Battleship from El Tovar Hotel	1595 D	" "	"	"
Yaki trail over Kaibab bridge	1596 D	" "	"	"
Zoroaster + Colorado River	1597 D	" "	"	"
El Tovar on the Rim	1598 D	" "	"	"
Navaho Silversmith	8AH 1709 D	Fred Harvey 6M		7-25
Indian Gardens, Bright Angel Trail	8A 307 D	Verkamps 6M	American Art	6-8-38
The Museum	8A 434 D	Verkamp's 6M	Book Views	7-5-38
Indian Watch tower, Desert View	435 D	" "	"	"
Bright Angel Lodge	436 D	" "	"	"
View from El. Tovar Hotel	8AH 2300 D	Verkamp's 6M	Art Colortone	9-16-38
From Breeze Point	2301 D	" "	"	"
Looking North from Yavapai Point	2302 D	" "	"	"

Company sold a lot of the View From El Tovar Hotel postcards but wanted to change their next order to include greener trees or a brighter blue sky in the postcard, it could be done. CTC would reprint this image, maybe making a few adjustments to color or frame, to create a "new" product for the following year.

More broadly, taking a closer look at the file orders for postcards provides another way to better understand the role of those images in forming the iconographic arc of the Grand Canyon. Businesses such as the Fred Harvey Company could drive the selection of locations and subject matter featured in the postcards through their orders. Curt Teich Company would send their photographers into the field to capture these popular scenes, or they would direct their factory artists and designers to recolor existing images to fit the demands in the market. Ultimately, this order fulfillment shaped what subjects and locations people saw of the Grand Canyon through postcards. Less popular views or postcards were not reordered. Popular views were reordered, revised, and reprinted. The relationship between CTC and the Fred Harvey Company paralleled a similar one held earlier by Detroit Publishing Company. Namely, CTC printed postcards ordered by the Fred Harvey Company with the names of both companies on the back of the card. FHC commissioned these cards, placed orders, and distributed them in their canyon gift shops while CTC manufactured the postcards and printed them. (fig. 27) Indeed, soon after DPC closed for business, the Fred Harvey Company opened a large, direct account with Curt Teich Company. CTC manufactured the postcards and FHC distributed them in their shops. This exclusive distribution contract between CTC and FHC, combined with the Fred Harvey Company's presence at the Grand Canyon and all along Santa Fe Railroad's tracks created a powerful combination of distribution networks to willing tourist markets.

Frasher Foto Postcard Company

The third major postcard manufacturing company, Frasher Foto Postcard Company (FFPC), is often overlooked by other studies of the Grand Canyon's visual legacy. FFPC offered an alternative view from other postcard manufacturers of the Grand Canyon in terms of format, style, locations, and business model. Frasher Foto Postcard Company began as a modest photography business initiated by one man's love of photography, western landscapes, and travel. After more than forty years in the commercial photography

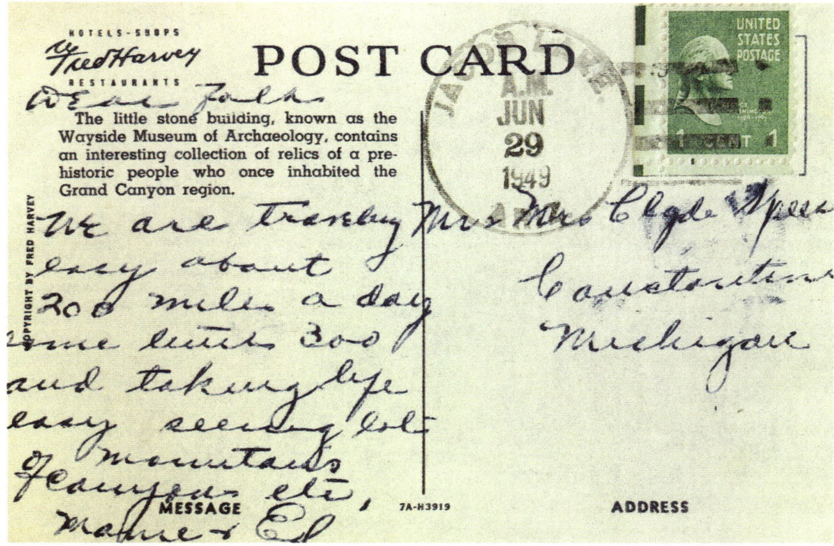

Fig. 27. Postcard partnerships: Curt Teich Company and Fred Harvey Company. CTC manufactured and printed this postcard but Fred Harvey Company distributed it. A close examination of the back of the postcard reveals tell-tale signs of this agreement. The card carries Fred Harvey's logo (*top left*); however a Curt Teich production number (*bottom center, under the dividing back line*) traces the card to Curt Teich. Collection of the author.

business, Burton Frasher Sr. built a visual catalog of over sixty thousand negatives and became the "Southwest's most prolific photographer," selling and producing millions of postcards (Holt 1959, 71).

Frasher grew up in Colorado but left the state in his early teens to travel around the West as an itinerant fruit crate maker. In 1912 he married Josephine Angel and by 1914, they settled in California and opened a commercial photography studio in Lordsburg (now La Verne). In 1921 he moved his studio to Pomona, California, where he sold his photographs, picture postcards, and stationery (Holt 1959). Frasher specialized in southwestern photographs that he captured during his extensive travels through California, Arizona, New Mexico, Colorado, Nevada, and Mexico. Soon after moving to Pomona, his postcards became a major portion of his business. He hired additional photographers who doubled as salesmen, traveling throughout the Southwest taking photographs and selling them along the way. The name of the company varied over time and across logos from Frasher's Fotos to Frashers Fotos and Frasher Foto Postcards (Rowe 2010,

Fig. 28. Burton and Josephine Frasher on the road again. This 1936 business card shows the intrepid couple near a lake in the Sierra Nevada Mountains with their cameras, a car, and the distinct Frasher Fotos logo. Note that the company name changed from Frasher Fotos to Frasher Foto. Courtesy Frasher Foto Collection/HJG and Pomona Public Library, Pomona, California. Frasher Foto Postcard Collection, index #B4364. Title "Frasher Fotos Business Card."

345). (For the purposes of this book, I refer to Frasher Foto Postcards.) By 1948 FFPC had sold 3.5 million postcards across the nation, but the company was ultimately tied to the personality that started it. When Frasher died in 1955, the business faded. His son sold the company in 1959. Later the family donated a collection of over a hundred thousand photographs and postcards to the Pomona Public Library.

Frasher was an entrepreneur, a clever businessman, and a detailed photographer. During his extensive travels, he systematically photographed scenes of everyday America, particularly small towns, gas stations, hotels, and roadside attractions (Rowe 2010). He developed his business by connecting his landscape photography with an expanding national and regional network of roads and auto touring in the 1930s and 1940s. In the process, he documented the increasing popularity of automobile travel, the development of the interstate highways system, and tourism landscapes of the American West in the mid-twentieth century. Early in his career, his photography kit included a large-format 5x7-inch view camera with a tripod and portable

Fig. 29. Frasher's store with a group of employees, 1929. In this holiday photograph Burton Frasher Sr. (*front center*) and his wife, Josephine (*left of Frasher Sr.*), and son, Frasher Jr. (*second row, fifth from right*), and employees pose in front of their storefront at 158 East Second Street, Pomona, California. Courtesy Frasher Foto Collection/HJG and Pomona Public Library, Pomona, California. Frasher Foto Collection, index #8-75. "Our Gang, Holiday Season."

darkroom pack in his motorcycle sidecar. His wife, Josephine, accompanied him on many of these motorcycle trips. By the 1920s Frasher was driving a car for his photography excursions (fig. 28).

Unlike Detroit Publishing Company or Curt Teich Company, Frasher manufactured real photographic postcards with a photograph on the front of the postcard instead of a block print or painted scene. From 1905 to 1920, photographic postcards surged in popularity. Frasher joined a cohort of professional and amateur photographers across the country who produced hundreds of millions of these cards featuring scenes from everyday America. He was a diligent photographer, focused on sharpness and image quality. Although, like CTC and DPC, Frasher could change the way an image appeared in the production and manufacturing process. He printed postcards from larger negatives, a process that allowed alterations to copies of the original, such as cropping the frame of view or changing the exposure or print density. In this way, Frasher could create new batches of postcards in each repetition of printing from the same negative.

Frasher also tapped into an innovative manufacturing and distribution process. He printed his photographs in postcard format, but unlike other manufacturers who used a printing process to create a high volume of cards, he printed in small batches. This process produced postcards with better tonal quality and detailed imagery unmatched by large-scale manufacturers. Frasher manufactured postcards in a small factory with around twenty employees spread across nine departments including developing, film drying, printing, enlarging, postcard printing, washing and drying, retouching and tinting, and reproductions (Rowe 2010, 350). In terms of distribution, Frasher delivered his postcards through traveling salesmen who doubled as photographers. At the same time, he maintained a storefront in Pomona and employed a small staff to sell his photographs, postcards, gifts, and stationery (fig. 29). Although Frasher loved photography and captured many of the images featured in his company's inventory, he also sought out more creative routes to meet the postcard market demands. He copied famous images of historic figures and events but marketed them under the Frasher Foto Postcard imprint. He also loaned cameras to other photographers who provided permission to print their images under the FFPC logo (Rowe 2010, 348).

Finally, like Curt Teich, Frasher was a well-organized businessman. He maintained detailed notebooks and indexes of his photographs, with the image number, title, and notes including the date, camera location, or angle of view (Rowe 2010, 349). He also followed the practice of other contemporary photographic studios by keeping his internal sale catalogs connected to photograph and postcard orders and their negative files. He even produced sample books for sale staff to promote his business.

Part 2 Creating the Grand Canyon

Nature is commonplace.
Imitation is more interesting.

—Gertrude Stein

Bewildered by the wilderness, many Americans are culturally unprepared for its lack of predictability.

— Lucy Lippard, *On the Beaten Track*

4 Nature as Tourism

In his 1900 guidebook *In and Around the Grand Canyon*, George Wharton James warned his readers that "until recently there were few subjects more disappointing to the photographer—professional as well as amateur—than the Grand Canyon." He suggested that its "vastness, its great precipices and wide distances; all covered and filled with a peculiar purple or violet haze, rendered it singularly unaccommodating to the photographer's art. . . . But as in all difficulties capable of scientific solution, persistence, skill, and science at length have overcome the obstacles to excellent picture-making to a great extent and now good photographs at the Grand Canyon may be obtained" (334). In one swift stroke, James issued a pitch-perfect statement of early twentieth-century optimism about human control of nature and shifts from discouraged to hopeful as he connected the travelers' desire for visual mementos of their trip with a solution. Subsequent pages are filled with names of photographers and the canyon viewpoints they captured, along with the endorsement that to "own such pictures as these is to possess those things that are 'a joy forever'" (338).

Later in his book he echoed a perspective expressed by writers before and after him that the Grand Canyon offers sublime experiences and sights: "The Canyon springs upon him with the leap of a panther . . . no reading, no descriptions, no pictures, no warnings can prepare the mind for that one first stupendous, overwhelming impression" (74). Nevertheless, James offers canyon visitors over three hundred pages of descriptions, pictures, and readings about where to go, what to see, and what to do at the Grand Canyon. His guidebook covers routes to and from the canyon, side trips, and excursions that give readers a sense of the early twentieth-century version of touring the Greater Grand Canyon Region. "There are different classes of tourists. Some are anxious to see and know as much of the Canyon as possible but are short of time; others have all the time there is, but merely visit the Canyon as a perfunctory performance" (72). Once at the South Rim and the emerging tourist hub of Grand Canyon Village, James suggests a three-day stay at the minimum with two days in a guided coach touring the South Rim and visiting scenic viewpoints and a third day on a trail down to the Colorado River.

By 1900 tourism development at the Grand Canyon traced faint outlines of its extent in dirt roads and trails, scattered lodges and lunch stops, tent camps, and promoted scenic viewpoints at the South Rim. Tours of the Grand Canyon were available but managed by a patchwork of families and individual entrepreneurs who often moonlighted as tour guides between working their copper or asbestos mining claims. But that all changed in 1901 as the Atchison, Topeka & Santa Fe Railway completed laying tracks from Williams, Arizona, to the South Rim of the canyon. This opened new transportation lines that brought increased tourism and corporate investment into the emerging hub on the South Rim at Grand Canyon Village. The DPC and FFPC imagery offers an opportunity to better understand the Grand Canyon's cultural landscapes, the daily routine of tourists, and the canyon's many environments in the early twentieth century.

In this chapter, I explore some of the earliest postcard representations of the Grand Canyon found in the images manufactured between 1900 and 1935 by the Detroit Publishing Company and Frasher Foto Postcard Company. To start, I discuss the lands management context of the Greater Grand Canyon Region and federal public land agencies shaping the canyon's cultural landscape in the early and mid-twentieth century. I will refer to seven subregions that I have defined in the Greater Canyon Region, based on my fieldwork and the archival image collections. The subregions—Lake Mead Area, West, Midcanyon, North Rim, Havasupai, South Rim, and Northeast—provides a spatial context for the images and a location within the larger region. (fig. 30). Then, I briefly review the most common subjects and locations that I found in the postcards through a content analysis of this imagery. Finally, I discuss the major themes of the postcard imagery and the social context, cultural landscape changes, and environmental management at the GGCR during this time.

Creating Tourism at the Canyon

The DPC and CTC postcards intersect with a pivotal time in public lands management for the GGCR. As more visitors made their way along railroads, in stagecoaches, and by the 1910s, automobiles, they also raised the tenor of support for increased federal protection and management of the Grand Canyon. Its path to national park status was marked by several stages that

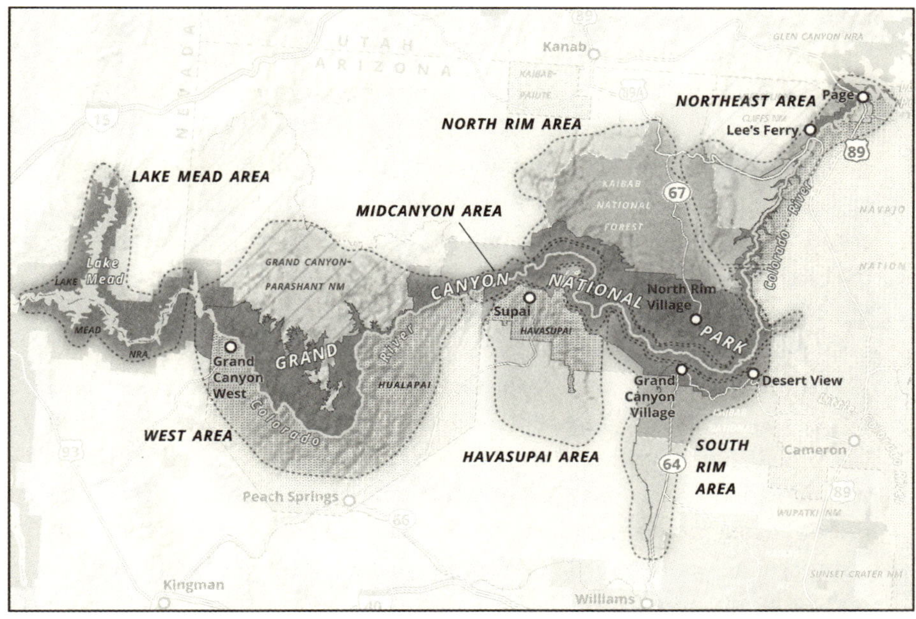

Fig. 30. Map of iconographic subregions of the Greater Grand Canyon Region. Cartography by Robert M. Edsall. Design by Yolonda Youngs. Based on data from the National Park Service, U.S. Geological Survey, ESRI, and author's content analysis results from archival research.

included multiple boundary changes as federal lawmakers divided sections of the Greater Grand Canyon Region into protected areas.

There are three important aspects of environmental and cultural resource management to note about this transition period. First, within twenty-three years, three different public lands agencies—the General Land Office, U.S. Forest Service, and the National Park Service—in two different departments of the federal government—Department of the Interior and Department of Agriculture—managed the Grand Canyon. These agencies operated under very different missions, policies, budgets, and priorities. For example, the General Lands Office was more in the business of disposing of America's public lands to homesteaders, railroad companies, and other landowners than in preserving them. The USFS, on the other hand, operated under a conservation mission with environmental management and forest health as prime concerns. Tourism was secondary to their agenda and difficult to facilitate with limited budgets and staff. At the Grand Canyon, this translated into loose management of canyon development and environmental protections with an array of individual mining claims, business operations, and private land inholdings. A different agency altogether entered the scene with the National Park Service; it brought a new mission of preservation to the Grand Canyon. Tasked by the federal government to manage and protect both the environment and cultural resources of the park, the NPS actively engaged in tourism development and planning. NPS managers encouraged corporate investment from the Atchison, Topeka & Santa Fe Railway and the Fred Harvey Company in the canyon as a way to elevate the quality and quantity of lodging, dining, and activities in the park from the patchwork cast of individual and family operations.

Second, the spatial extent of the Grand Canyon protected and managed by the USFS and NPS only represented a portion of the Greater Grand Canyon Region. In other words, the Grand Canyon National Park that we know today does not encompass the same size and extent as the forest reserve, game preserve, monument, and national park of earlier eras. This is important because the Grand Canyon that we see in the DPC and FFPC postcards encompasses smaller sections of the canyon and was managed by different agencies at an earlier time in their environmental policies and agency evolution. Both the Grand Canyon Forest Reserve and the Grand Canyon Game Preserve were larger units, encompassing more acreage north and south of the canyon's rims than the later monument and park. The Havasupai land in Havasu Canyon and Cataract Creek was an enclave within the Grand Canyon National Park of 1919. Looking closely at a map of Grand Canyon National Monument, the extent of the monument is roughly from Kanab Creek in the west to the confluence of the Colorado River and Little Colorado River on the east, with a north and south boundary that follows the canyon's rims (fig. 31).

Third, with the designation of a national monument and later a park, the Greater Grand Canyon Region, came under renewed interest for tourism and visitation. This attention was particularly heightened for the part national park section of the region. Simply seeing the Grand Canyon became an act of national duty and patriotism. Theodore Roosevelt, during his travels in 1903, asserted that the "Grand Canyon, Arizona has a natural wonder which, so far as I know, is in kind absolutely unparalleled throughout the rest of the world. . . . Leave it as it is. You cannot improve on it; not a bit. The ages have been at work on it, and man can only mar it. What you can do is to keep it for your children, your children's children, and for all who

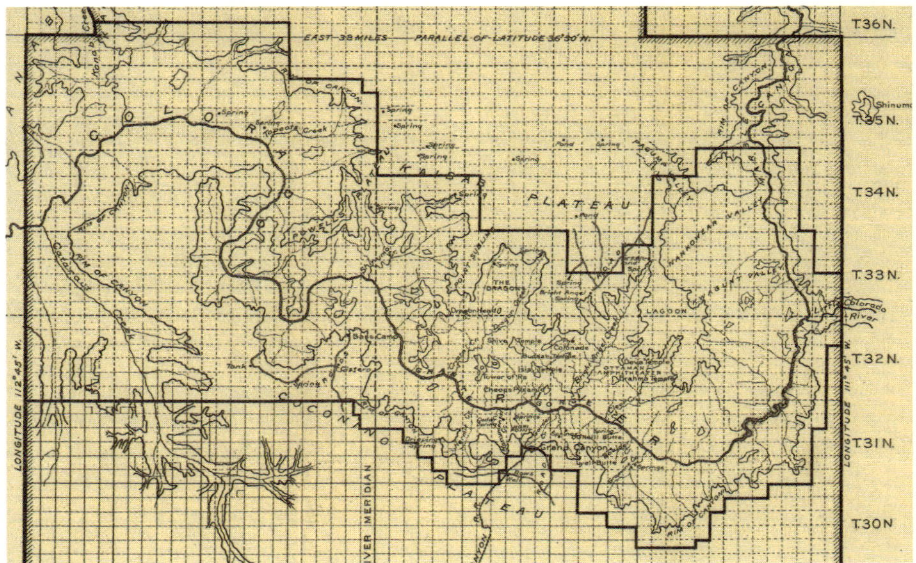

Fig. 31. Detail from map *Grand Canyon National Monument within Grand Canyon National Forest Arizona, 1907*. Library of Congress Geography and Maps Division, call #G4332.G7 1908. U5 TIL.

come after you, as the one great sight which every American . . . should see" (Roosevelt 1903). The comfort of traveling to and staying at the Grand Canyon multiplied over the next decades, too, as tourist services expanded, especially at the South Rim. Visitation steadily increased during these years, from 37,745 people in 1919 to 206,018 in 1935 (National Park Service 2023b).

Detroit Publishing Company closely aligned its imagery to areas that overlapped with the USFS Grand Canyon National Monument and tourism development of trails, lodges, and wagon roads along the South Rim. DPC postcards from 1900 to 1909 not only captured the Grand Canyon before Arizona statehood in 1912; they also captured the USFS-managed landscape at the South Rim before the advent of the National Park Service. This transition period was a relatively short but key era in setting the stage for management and subsequent tourism landscapes that emerged at the canyon. Grand Canyon National Park in 1919 effectively encompassed the lands formerly bound by Grand Canyon National Monument and Grand Canyon Game Preserve (fig. 32). Frasher Foto Postcard Company images from 1929 to 1935 also emphasized the South Rim of the canyon but extended to additional scenes north, beyond the DPC purview.

Fig. 32. *The Grand Canyon National Park Arizona, map, 1919*. Source: Library of Congress Geography and Maps Division, Call # G4332.G7 1919.R3 TIL.

First Glances: Dominant Subjects and Locations in Postcards

Detroit Publishing Company and Frasher Foto Postcard Company manufactured some of the earliest postcard representations of the Grand Canyon from 1900 to 1935. In their choices of locations and subject matter, they set a template for Grand Canyon imagery that other postcard manufacturers and photographers would follow for decades to come. Both manufacturers repeated a selective set of themes and locations and incrementally, postcard by postcard, built a visual lexicon of the canyon's environment for tourist consumption. These images added new layers to the Grand Canyon's iconographic arc by building on established scenes from John Wesley Powell's and Clarence Dutton's descriptions or creating new ones along the canyon's South Rim and midcanyon trails. (Note that I will provide a summary of the most common subjects and locations here, but a brief look at appendixes B and C offers specific counts of all the postcards' content and a detailed discussion of how I selected postcards and analyzed them for this study.)

Analyzing the complete set of all Grand Canyon postcards manufactured by the Detroit Publishing Company between 1900 and 1909 (86 total) and Frasher Foto Postcard Company (65 total), there are some commonalities as well as distinct differences between the subjects and locations shown in the two companies' images. Overall, ten themes of subjects emerged as common to a greater or lesser extent in all of the 1,473 postcards analyzed for *Framing Nature*: scenic views, vegetation, people, buildings, dams, water, animals, automobiles, trails, and roads and bridges. Seven subjects rise to the top as the most frequently represented in both DPC and FFPC image sets from 1900 to 1935: scenic views (with green vegetation), people, buildings, water, animals, trails, and roads. However, the percentage of postcards showing each of these subjects varies between DPC and FFPC. Another major difference between the DPC and FFPC is the format of their postcards. FFPC postcards were exclusively printed as black-and-white images; DPC postcards made ample and strategic use of color and their Phostint process.

Keeping in mind that each postcard sampled could be counted with multiple subjects, there are some commonalities between the DPC and FFPC sets. Scenic views take the top percentage in both DPC (67%) and FFPC (69%) postcards. I assigned the tag of scenic views to images where the primary subject is a vista taken from a rim viewpoint looking across the canyon. Postcards featuring green or abundant vegetation also hold a high percentage of the DPC (44%) and FFPC cards (71%). Buildings were common in both manufacturers' cards, but DPC showed interior and exterior views while FFPC preferred only exterior views. People appeared often in DPC cards but rarely in FFPC images. DPC and FFPC featured water but mostly the Colorado River and only from afar, as seen from the canyon's rim. Mules and horses appeared in DPC postcards but were missing in FFPC images. In terms of transportation and movement, DPC emphasize trails more than roads, while FFPC featured a higher percentage of roads and bridge views but few trails. I will discuss larger trends and the context behind these findings later in this chapter.

In terms of locations represented in the DPC and FFPC postcards, both companies revealed a distinct geographic bias. Detroit Publishing Company postcards featured South Rim locations in 72 percent of their images (fig. 33). Midcanyon locations appeared less often with a small number of unknown locations (that is, the postcards lacked a description of where the scene was

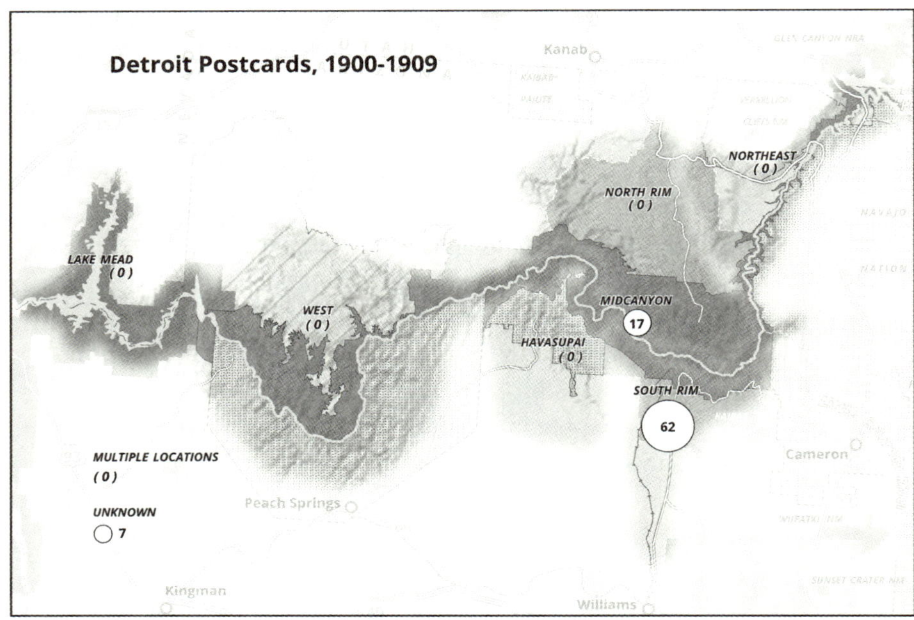

Fig. 33. Map of locations represented in Detroit Publishing Company postcards, 1900–1909. Cartography by Robert M. Edsall. Design by Yolonda Youngs. Based on data from the National Park Service, U.S. Geological Society, and ESRI.

located, and I could not ascertain the location from my field reconnaissance). In terms of vertical positions in the canyon, DPC also favored rim locations in 49 percent of their postcards, while midcanyon, river, and postcards with no distinct vertical position were less common.

This pattern legitimized the centrality, value, and importance of the canyon locations financed and managed by the Santa Fe Railroad and the Fred Harvey Company that were limited to operations on the south side of the canyon, especially at the Grand Canyon Village at the South Rim, the midcanyon trail system, and inner canyon camps along the Colorado River. The postcards also served as a mimetic, naturalizing element that reinforced the spatial organization and the expanding midcentury tourism landscape of the South Rim and Grand Canyon Village. The postcard scenes provided visual evidence to fulfill tourists' expectations of colorful and dramatic canyon views and exciting vacation activities in comfortable proximity to hotels, restaurants, and shops.

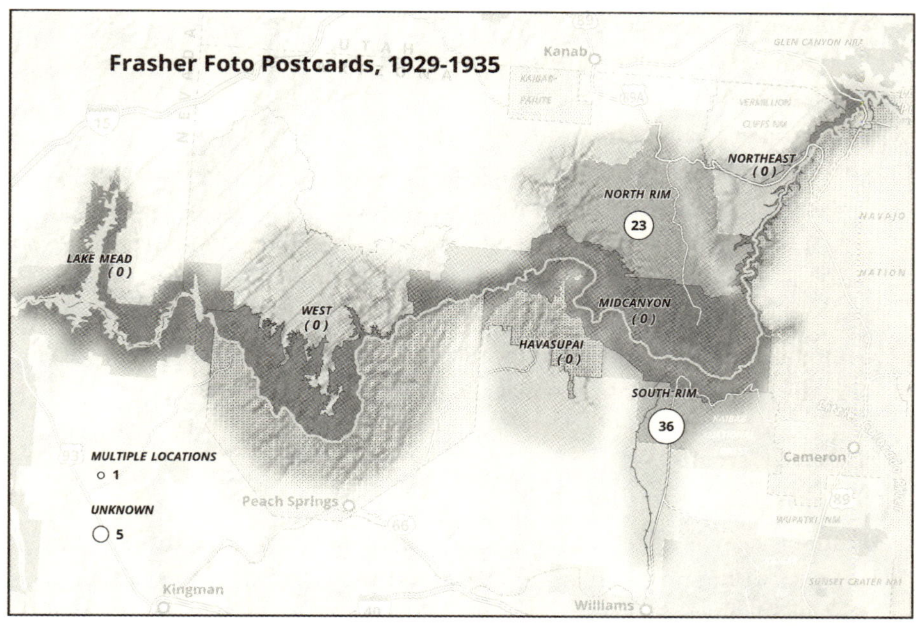

Fig. 34. Locations represented in Frasher Foto postcards, 1929–35. Cartography by Robert M. Edsall. Design by Yolonda Youngs. Based on data from the National Park Service, U.S. Geological Society, ESRI, and author's content analysis results from archival research.

Frasher Foto Postcard Company images, manufactured and distributed between 1929 and 1935, later than DPC, reveal an alternative view of the Grand Canyon (fig. 34). The FFPC images feature primarily South or North rim locations, with only a smattering of other places. DPC did not include North Rim images in their sets while FFPC included twenty-three. This gave FFPC a geographic and potentially commercial leg up on DPC in terms of new content and alternative views of the canyon and opened a new view of the Grand Canyon that was missing from DPC imagery. In FFPC's views, we see locations such as the North Rim, Marble Canyon, and the eastern GGCR, and more roadways and bridges. All of these places are missing in DPC views. Indeed, the FFPC cards portray a regional perspective on the Grand Canyon favoring the view of southern, northern, and eastern parts of this area including the Kaibab Plateau, the Arizona Strip, the Navajo Nation, and Kaibab National Forest. Other FFPC locations included the Vermillion Cliffs, Desert View, El Tovar, Marble Canyon, Bright Angel Point, Hopi

Point, Vishnu Temple and Cape Royal, Point Sublime, Angel's Window, Point Imperial, and the Little Colorado River canyon.

FFPC's photos closely followed the rise of automobile touring culture, the expansion of a national network of reliable roads, and the quickly expanding popularity of western tourism from the 1920s through the 1950s (Rowe 2006). Since FFPC emphasized auto travel and roadside attractions and services, it makes sense that most of the FFPC Foto postcard representations depict rim locations—areas that were easily accessed by auto travelers—as opposed to the trails and footpaths seen in DPC images. At the Grand Canyon, FFPC commonly featured North Rim locations and roads leading toward the park or connecting the park to regional and national auto networks.

Thematic Trends

Scenic Nature as Tourism

Nature is heavily edited and revised in postcard imagery. Postcard makers augmented the non-human inhabitants of the canyon—plants, animals, water, and the geologic stratigraphy—with color, the wholesale removal of people or other subjects from a scene, or other alterations at the hand of the postcard artists. Representations of the canyon from scenic viewpoints, devoid of humans but focused on the canyon's internal stratigraphy, were the bread and butter of both DPC and FFPC. DPC postcards also appropriated and labeled the canyon's extensive rims with named viewpoints hammered into visitor logbooks through repetitive display of these locations in the postcard imagery.

Although a visitor to the Grand Canyon would have a tough time not finding a scenic location along the extensive South or North Rims to view the chasm's inner depths, DPC postcard manufacturers only chose a few locations as representative of scenic beauty (fig. 35). This process of site selection, representation, manufacturing, distribution, and reprinting of cards over and over again helped create a recognizable checklist of named scenic viewpoints for visitors. To see the Grand Canyon was to see it from Hopi Point, Grand View Point, and Hermit Point. Detroit Publishing Company postcard manufacturers established a spatial order out of randomness; where others had seen a vast and unfathomable canyon, a "valueless locale," these viewmakers created order by establishing a linear path of scenic viewpoints of the South Rim (Ives 1861, 110). By representing these sites in postcard imagery, DPC and FFPC constructed what constituted "scenic" at

Fig. 35. Detroit Publishing Company scenic view postcard. This is a typical scenic postcard manufactured by DPC. The company worked with park promoters to make the canyon's landscape legible to tourists. In this image, this goal takes a literal form as side canyons, viewpoints, and prominent peaks are labeled. The image also reinforces the canyon's dramatic stratigraphy through the color choices of red and orange. Courtesy Miriam and Ira D. Wallach Division of Art, Prints and Photographs: Photography Collection, New York Public Library. "Grand Canyon of Arizona, From Hotel El Tovar" (DPC 10925, printing decade 1900–1909). New York Public Library Digital Collections.

the canyon and where one could view this beauty. They also manufactured a desire for tourists to not only see the Grand Canyon but to view it from that specific vantage point. From many field reconnaissance trips along the canyon's hiking trails, down the Colorado River, and along the South Rim trails, I can attest that "scenic" is a relative term at the Grand Canyon. Named viewpoints are not the only locations to see a good sunset or have your breath taken away by the distant expanses of the canyon. Just pick a spot, any spot, along the rim and you'll find scenery galore.

Notably, named and promoted scenic viewpoints were more than pretty photography spots: they were hubs of economic activities, social life, trails in and out of the canyon, and—in the early twentieth century—tourism and mining industries at the Grand Canyon. DPC, and to a certain extent FFPC, were in the business of packaging and commodifying the canyon's scenery for tourist consumption. Postcards were key elements in the creation of a selective and fragmentary view of the Grand Canyon shaped by the tour operators, lodge concessionaires, and railroad company managers who promoted the canyon for its visual qualities and comfortable, modern amenities. Through DPC's partnership, contracts, and postcard orders with the Fred Harvey Company, their imagery often focused on the places that FHC operated. In the early twentieth century, DPC also included images of a few places managed by individual families or local entrepreneurs. It was not uncommon for tour guides, prospectors, and hospitality operators to rename various scenic overlooks and locations according to the proximity of their business to the vantage points or the frequency of their use of these areas. For example, a popular postcard location and named viewpoint was labeled as Rowe's Point in many DPC-era postcards. The same location is now called Hopi Point. DPC and FFPC scenic viewpoints were located close to visitor services and businesses, such as hotels, shops, or restaurants. Although some of these buildings and tourist service centers did not survive beyond the 1930s, the viewpoints—a named site along the rim—often remain as clues to historic locations embedded in the canyon's cultural landscape palimpsest.

A closer inspection of postcards from this era reveals the cultural capital invested in creating and disseminating ideas of scenic viewpoints. In many instances, named viewpoints operated as economic hubs for canyon businesses. This pattern emerged for me after repeated visits to the canyon to capture repeat photographs of DPC and FFPC postcards. Many postcards that appear as simply scenic views from the rim looking across or into a vast canyon landscape of orange and red layers and the blue sky beyond were actually business advertisements. In essence, DPC and later postcard manufacturers commodified scenic beauty of a rim-side location for only a handful of select named viewpoints—especially those with hotels, restaurants, and shops just out of the postcard view. This is a striking pattern when one visits the Grand Canyon and realizes that there are many, many rim locations from which to catch an outstanding canyon view, but only a few of these places were promoted in the postcard imagery. Images such as those captioned "Grand Canyon from Hotel El Tovar" were more direct. Some of these viewpoint names persist today with businesses nearby, such as El Tovar Hotel, but other viewpoint names and the businesses they hosted have faded from memory. Although these viewpoints only represented a fraction of the locations at the Grand Canyon, the creation, production, and distribution of these selective views supported the visual argument of canyon entrepreneurs and railroaders that the canyon was a place worthy of a long trip and offered ample, modern amenities for a comfortable stay.

Independent prospectors and small-scale tourism operators maintained developments at various points along the South Rim, including Rowe's Point (today's Hopi Point) near the Hogan Mine to the west between Hermit's Rest and Grand Canyon Village, Grand View Point and hotel to the east along the East Rim Drive (from 1931 onward), and Hance Ranch farther to the east and also along the East Rim Drive. The Bright Angel Hotel was the first permanent lodging in Grand Canyon Village. From 1901 until 1905, the Santa Fe Railroad was dependent on these canyon pioneers to support tourism. It was not until 1905 that the railroad could boast its own lodging in El Tovar Hotel. By then, the Santa Fe Railroad drew tourism toward the south-central rim of the canyon at what became the Grand Canyon Village with attractions such as El Tovar, Hopi House, and the Bright Angel Hotel, which the Santa Fe Railroad eventually purchased and FHC later operated.

Grand View Point is a premier example of nature commodified as tourism by serving as both a scenic vista and a hub of tourism activity (Youngs 2019). This site along the South Rim was a common scenic view postcard and also the site of one of the earliest hotels on the South Rim—the Grand View Hotel (fig. 36). Canyon pioneers Peter and Martha Berry hosted train and stagecoach visitors here, offering them lodging and dining close to the rim, guided mule trips down the nearby Grand View Trail, and other guest services (Anderson 1998, 71). Over time, the Berrys waged a protracted battle against the Santa Fe Railroad and the Fred Harvey Company for tourist dollars and valuable rim-side real estate. The Berrys eventually sold their property to William Randolph Hearst instead of yielding to their competitor's offers. Hearst demolished the hotel in 1929 and, with spiteful relish after the long legal squabble, left the site undeveloped. El Tovar Hotel and Bright Angel Lodge, several miles to the west but closer to the Santa Fe Railroad station and other Grand Canyon Village services, quickly stepped in as tourist lodging on the South Rim. The location for Grand View Point thus served as a scenic viewpoint, a hotel, and a trailhead (fig. 37). Although the hotel is gone, the trail and viewpoint still remain on tourist maps to this day. Postcards of Grand View Point (with the view looking north toward the inner canyon, not south to the former hotel site) also endure, leaving a connection between past and present Grand Canyon and a visual and cultural legacy of shifting development schemes on the rim.

Fig. 36. Detroit Publishing Company postcard *Grand View Hotel, Grand Canyon, Ariz.* The hotel is perched at the top of the canyon's rim, in the trees (upper right side of image). Courtesy Miriam and Ira D. Wallach Division of Art, Prints and Photographs: Photography Collection, New York Public Library. "Grand View Hotel, Grand Canyon, Ariz." (DPC 11326). New York Public Library Digital Collections.

Fig. 37. Detroit Publishing Company postcard of Grand View, 1906. Many of the DPC cards featured scenic canyon images shown from named viewpoints along the South Rim. Behind this postcard scene was the Grand View Hotel, trail, and other tourist services. Courtesy Miriam and Ira D. Wallach Division of Art, Prints and Photographs: Photography Collection, New York Public Library. "From the 'Outlook,' Grand View. Grand Canyon Arizona," DPC#10452. New York Public Library Digital Collections.

Grand View Point was not the only location treated in this manner. Other viewpoints captured in DPC postcards from 1900 to 1909 include Bright Angel, Cyclorama, Bissell, Hermit, O'Neill's, and Rowe's. Maps of the South Rim from the early twentieth century highlighted scenic viewpoints and their names (fig. 38). Guidebooks, such as George Wharton James's, also identified these viewpoints in their suggestions for tour routes along the canyon's South Rim. Many of these viewpoints that were christened after hotel owners, miners, local guides, or other canyon entrepreneurs, such as Buckey O'Neill in the late nineteenth century, were renamed and reincarnated as these individual entrepreneurs succumbed to the increasing pressure of the Santa Fe Railroad and the Fred Harvey Company to sell their businesses. Postcards tagged as views "from hotel El Tovar" were very common in the DPC imagery and, later in the Curt Teich Company postcards, welding the scenic view with the hotel's location on the South Rim (see figs. 35 and 40). Other named viewpoints, such as Lipan and Desert View, survived with renewed interest as park roads and facilities were built along the rim, extending the Grand Canyon Village's economic and recreational interests to the east and west. FFPC images picked up this thread from the early 1930s showing Desert View Watchtower along the southeast rim and other points easily reached by roads, such as Bright Angel, Point Sublime, Point Imperial, Cape Royal, Lipan, Pima, Yaki, Moran, and Mohave Points (fig. 39). Although not every scenic viewpoint served as an economic hub, the process of commodifying most of these viewpoints was common. Yet it often remains a hidden part of the Grand Canyon's cultural history. The names of scenic viewpoints may have changed and their significance shifted, but tracing the scenic viewpoints at the Grand Canyon over time provides clues for reading the historical cultural landscape at the Grand Canyon back to these early hubs of commerce and tourist activity.

In this sense, scenic postcards of the Grand Canyon featuring canyon vistas were not "innocent documents of the built environment" as geographer Richard Schein notes (1993, 8). These postcards were "constructed images of constructed places" that convey the cultural ideals and changing values of the society that creates and propagates these images (Schein 1993, 8). The postcards of scenic viewpoints were constructed by DPC and FFPC to promote certain locations and tourist services in the Grand Canyon, especially those with postcard orders or contracts with these companies. This is not to say that these rim-side locations are not beautiful or distinct. But behind

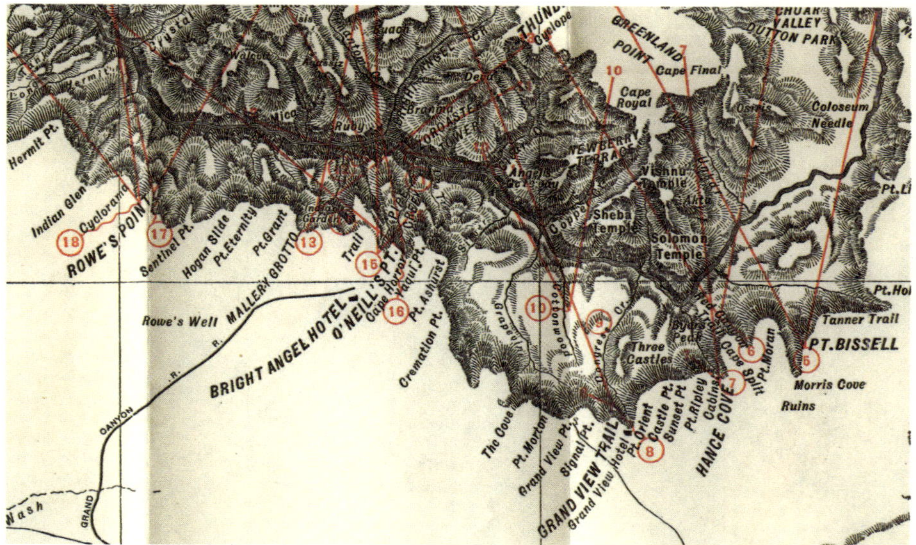

Fig. 38. Map (*detail*) of Grand Canyon named viewpoints, 1904. This detail from a 1904 map created by the stereoscope company Underwood and Underwood reveals the scenic viewpoints depicted in DPC postcards, including (from east to west) Point Bissell, Hance Cove, Grand View, Bright Angel, O'Neill's Point, and Rowe's Point. While the names of some of these viewpoints have changed over time, many of them remain popular tourist sites and connections to historic cultural and economic landscapes including hotels, gift shops, and miners' claims. Underwood and Underwood, "Grand Canyon of the Colorado," 1904. University of New Mexico Center for Southwestern Research.

many of these scenes, alternative ideas of the canyon were in play, ones that often involved attracting tourist dollars. As historian Stephen J. Pyne writes: "At the heart of every Canyon overlook there lies the paradox that while indescribable, the scene is not incomprehensible. It has meaning, and that meaning depends less on the scene's physical geography than on the ideas through which it can be viewed and imagined." He continues that "those ideas are not something added to the Canyon scenery, like a coat of paint. Or taken from it, like a snapshot, any more than the river was something added to a prefabricated gorge. They have actively shaped the Canyon's meaning, without which it could hardly exist as a cultural spectacle" (1998, xiii).

Framing Canyon Vegetation

Both DPC and FFPC framed the canyon's vegetation in new ways. For DPC, that involved the application of color to their postcard images and the ability

Fig. 39. Frasher Foto Postcard Company scenic rim viewpoint from Desert View. Typical FFPC cards featured scenic canyon views mostly along the North Rim, eastern approach roads, or the southeastern rim. These locations, especially along the North and eastern rims, were rarely shown in DPC or CTC postcards, revealing a division of postcard territory by the various companies. Courtesy Frasher Foto Collection/HJG and Pomona Public Library, Pomona, California. Frasher Foto Postcard Collection, index #A-12227. Title: "Grand Canyon of the Colorado River from Desert View Point, Arizona."

to edit their scenes with new colors during each reprinting. Frasher and his photographers angled their cameras to frame views of the canyon in ways that emphasized dense stands of trees and other vegetation. Although each company offered postcards in a different format, color printing versus black-and-white photography, they each made decisions that cast the canyon in appealing views for tourists.

Color was the key ingredient of Detroit Publishing Company postcards. The company liberally applied color to the Grand Canyon's cliffs, trees, water, animals, and buildings to paint a new version of the canyon with each year's printing. With their Phostint process of colorizing the images, DPC postcard manufacturers and artists augmented scenery to emphasize the red and orange tones along the canyon's walls and, at times, a thin veil of green along the inner canyon's plateaus. These scenes created a view of a verdant and vivid Grand Canyon, perhaps caught just after an afternoon rainstorm. Although at times the canyon does indeed glow with renewed freshness of

Fig. 40. A Detroit Publishing Company postcard with an emphasis on color and vegetation near El Tovar Hotel. Note the difference between the right and left sections of this 1905 *Grand Canyon of Arizona—Hotel El Tovar* postcard with the South Rim trail and road. DPC's Phostint process was an early precursor to today's Photoshop, whereby postcard artists could edit color and subjects with the stroke of a brush. Here we see the augmented colors of the canyon as striking shades of red and orange (*right side of image*) and abundant green vegetation (*left side*). This postcard also includes a short message on the front from the sender. In the era before writing on the back of postcards was allowed in sent mail, tourists would often annotate the image or the front of the card with notes. Detroit Publishing Company # DPC8797. Courtesy Miriam and Ira D. Wallach Division of Art, Prints and Photographs: Photography Collection, New York Public Library. "Hotel El Tovar, Grand Canyon, Ariz." New York Public Library Digital Collections.

springtime greenery or a recent storm, this is not the norm. The postcards created a frozen moment in time and season, on that was perpetually verdant. Many DPC card scenic views emphasized and at times enhanced the drought-hardy native vegetation of the Grand Canyon, such as pinyon and juniper woodland, sagebrush, and grasses near the South Rim or along the inner-canyon benches and plateaus. DPC applied vivid shades of green or sketched in additional leafy trees and shrubs to many of their views, when the vegetation would in reality be shades of brown. For example, a DPC postcard featuring a view from El Tovar Hotel is crowded with various shades and sizes of green trees and shrubs (fig. 40). There were very few trees and

Fig. 41. Three views of El Tovar Hotel and cliffs (*above and opposite*). These three views show the striking differences in how postcard manufacturers and artists revised the same canyon imagery through reprintings of an El Tovar Hotel postcard. The image on the far left is a 1905 Detroit postcard *Grand Canyon of Arizona—Hotel El Tovar* that emphasizes the red and orange color of the canyon walls (*above left*). Compare the 1905 postcard of the same image (*above right*), reprinted in 1909 but recolored to emphasize the green vegetation along the cliffs below the hotel and along the rim, a more detailed outline of the hotel and its many windows, and the removal of the water tower to the right of El Tovar. Finally, compare the historic postcards to a contemporary view (*opposite*). Using the two historic postcards as guides to the location and framing used by the original photographer, the author captured a repeat photograph of the image in 2008 from one of the trails along the South Rim near Grand Canyon Village. DPC postcards: Newberry Library, Curt Teich Postcard Archives Collection and Detroit Publishing Company Collection, filename DPC#7999 and DPC#11619; contemporary photograph by the author.

shrubs at El Tovar at this time, but they were there. Repeating the oft-cited pattern in the images, the postcard makers took that flora framework and enhanced the view with more trees, more leaves, more shrubs.

A close look at multiple versions of the same postcard, revised each time DPC printed it, unveils meticulous color applications that emphasize

vegetation. In a view of El Tovar taken from the rim trail just west of the hotel and printed in 1905, the canyon wall below the hotel becomes an eye-popping feature with its saturated orange and red tones (fig. 41). In a 1909 printing of the same postcard, DPC artists reapplied the color to emphasize trees and vegetation along the cliff. This color editing may have been a way to increase the Grand Canyon's appeal to East Coast tourists more comfortable in lakeside and ocean retreats with deciduous trees than the high desert environment of the Southwest. The landscape today is somewhere between these two DPC postcard scenes. The walls of the canyon are not quite as red, the shrubs cling to the wall in a different distribution pattern across the cliffs, and the vegetation is less dense than shown in the 1905 postcard. While some shrubs and grass have likely died or grown in new patterns over time, it is doubtful that this cliff ever was the lush scene that DPC presented.

FFPC provides another perspective on the canyon's verdant nature and alternate locations from DPC imagery. Not all of these views featured rim-side locations. Some postcard scenes included green vegetation around

Fig. 42. *Main Gate, Grand Canyon National Park*, 1930. This poctcard depicts the approach road to the entrance of Grand Canyon National Park, although the exact location of the entrance is not specified on the postcard. Courtesy Frasher Foto Collection/HJG and Pomona Public Library, Pomona, California. Frasher Foto Postcard Collection, index # E737.

buildings and other structures along roadsides. Take, for example, a 1930 FFPC postcard featuring a stone-gated entrance to Grand Canyon National Park (fig. 42). Capturing the park eleven years into its shift from a national monument (1908) to a national park (1919), FFPC places the well-groomed dirt road leading through the historic entrance arch to the park front and center. Like the DPC imagery, the black-and-white FFPC photographic postcards emphasized vegetation at the canyon but without the advantage of color printing. Instead, Frasher used the photographer's toolkit of framing and subject selection to emphasize certain subjects and locations in his imagery. He chose to include the tall ponderosa pines flanking both sides of the entrance arch instead of cropping the image and removing these trees from the scene.

FFPC postcards commonly depicted scenes along the higher elevation North Rim (8,000 feet) as opposed to the South Rim (7,000 feet). The elevation difference, coupled with cooler temperatures, snowpack, deep soils, and more rainfall at the North Rim produces different forest types than that of the South Rim. Dwarf forests of pinyon pine and juniper dominate South

Rim locations and are well adapted to the arid conditions there. Juniper trees have scale-like, wax-coated leaves, but pinyon pines produce short, two-needle clusters that are adapted to conserve water. The North Rim, on the other hand, features hardier, cool temperature species of ponderosa pine, aspen, spruce, and fir trees. The thick forest of ponderosa pines seen in FFPC postcards may be a by-product of his style of image gathering; FFPC preferred to capture auto routes to tourist developments as the North Rim road network was expanding in the 1920s and 1930s along with national road networks. In an arid desert park such as the Grand Canyon, thick, green vegetation is not a common element of the visual scene. Yet in the selection of locations, subjects, and framing of the images, postcard photographers and manufacturers chose to emphasize this element of the landscape. Although we do not have a record of the specific photographers who took these images, the postcard manufacturers' production notes and requests from the companies that ordered these cards provide clues to the motivation for these decisions (figs. 25–26).

The Colorado River from Afar

Forests and shrubs were not the only part of nature revised and edited by the postcard companies; water, especially the Colorado River, was a key element in Detroit Publishing Company's promotional imagery for the Grand Canyon. The DPC postcard manufacturers and creators took liberties with their application of color to water features, particularly the Colorado River. The Colorado River—named by the Spanish for its red color—would have appeared as brown or red until the large dam projects of the 1930s and 1950s changed its flow, temperature, and color. In the era of Detroit Publishing Company imagery, the river was a free flowing, silt-laden, and often brown river. But DPC postcard images present the Colorado River as a brilliant turquoise waterway threading its way through the Grand Canyon.

For a telling example of this revision of nature, take a closer look at a 1902 postcard titled "Granite Gorge from Bright Angel Trail, Grand Canyon of Arizona" (fig. 43). To create the postcard, guided by directions from the field photographer's notes about each image's coloring, artists at the DPC postcard factory used tiny brushes to painstakingly apply color by hand to each subject of the soon-to-be postcard image. For the Granite Gorge postcard, they hand-colored turquoise blue shading to represent the Colorado River's path through the canyon's depths. They painted the alternating red

7059. GRANITE GORGE FROM BRIGHT ANGEL TRAIL, GRAND CANYON OF ARIZONA.

Fig. 43. Detroit Publishing Company's curiously blue Colorado River (*opposite*). The DPC postcards manufacturers and creators took liberties with the color of water, particularly the Colorado River, showing it as a blue stream coursing through the inner canyon. It is doubtful that the Colorado River would appear blue or green at the time of dpc postcard manufacturing of images such as *Granite Gorge from Bright Angel Trail, Grand Canyon of Arizona* (1902). Instead, the river would flow with warm, silt-laden water, especially in an era before the construction of large upstream dams that controlled the flow and held back sediments. Today such silt-laden flows are rare and often follow large rainstorms. A contemporary photograph (*above*) from the author's field reconnaissance hiking and rafting the canyon shows the river churning with silt after a rainstorm. DPC postcard: Newberry Library, Detroit Publishing Company Collection, filename DPC#7059; contemporary photograph by the author.

and orange bands of color on the canyon's walls to represent the rock layers from the Hermit Formation, Supai Group, and Redwall Limestone. The artists even painted a pale blue background and white fill to represent the color of the sky with wisps of clouds hovering just above the canyon's wall.

Water, an essential resource in the arid landscape of the Grand Canyon, was also key to the FFPC subject catalog. As with the DPC cards, the FFPC images showed the Colorado River from a rim-side location looking down into the canyon. Although FFPC postcards did not use color in their images, photographers framed the canyon to emphasize the viewpoints of the river from the rim, especially those locations near a road or highway.

Missing the Wildlife

Selective representation of the Grand Canyon's environment extended to postcard representations of wildlife too. Detroit Publishing Company and Frasher Foto postcard creators chose to omit most of the wild and native species from the visual scene. The list of missing mammals, reptiles, and birds is impressive. Desert bighorn sheep, elk, snakes, lizards, the North Rim Kaibab squirrel and their cross-canyon relative the South Rim Albert's squirrel, wild turkeys, pinyon jays, coyotes, chipmunks, bats, ravens, and condors—all are missing from DPC and FFPC postcards. A contemporary visitor to the Grand Canyon would easily encounter many of these creatures during their visit. It is hard to think that early twentieth-century visitors would have missed a similar array of animals, birds, and reptiles, especially considering the lower visitation at the canyon then with less crowds and cars to deter wildlife. Instead, DPC and FFPC focused their efforts on only a handful of animals: domesticated mules, horses, and the occasional dog.

DPC postcard manufacturers, for example, featured domesticated animals more commonly than wild ones at the canyon. Mules and horses are common subjects of the Detroit Publishing Company cards and always shown in the company of human riders or handlers. A great majority of the DPC postcards that feature animals depict mules on trails carrying riders and supplies into or out of the canyon. An example of this common DPC trail scene is *On the Trail, Grand View* depicting a party of tourists descending Grand View Trail (fig. 44). This was one of DPC's more popular cards. It was reprinted over multiple years with variations on the colors of the rider's clothes, saddlebags, rock walls and trees. Some versions of the postcard included a dog standing near the lead rider's horse, but here we see the dog has been removed. Dogs were a common sight in early twentieth-century miners' camps and tourist service areas at Grand Canyon Village, but surprisingly, this card only occasionally was printed with a canine companion in all the postcard imagery sampled for this study from 1900 to 1935.

This 1906 DPC postcard reveals the meticulous editing and selection of certain wild or domestic animals that DPC manufacturers favored. These decisions—the presence (or lack of) a dog, the inclusion of deer and mules but not bighorn sheep, the omission of ravens and other canyon birdlife—are small, but their cumulative effects on popular ideas of the canyon environment are expansive. With each animal or bird representation, DPC manufacturers were editing the endemic environment of the canyon to create a popular but not altogether realistic view of wildlife. Interestingly, DPC featured more animals in their postcards than did FFPC. Only one FFPC postcard in the sampling of all postcards for this book features a wild animal, and it was a mule deer.

This selective view of animals at the canyon as seen in DPC and FFPC imagery reflects larger issues of wildlife management, predator control policies, and environmental perception in early twentieth-century America. Historian J. Donald Hughes notes that during the 1920s, the "theory of game management in those years maintained that 'good' species such as deer should be protected from 'bad' predators such as wolves and mountain lions" (1978, 107). Indeed, wildlife management policies enacted by the federal government and supported by western ranchers and the public through the late nineteenth and into the twentieth centuries encouraged poisoning, shooting, and trapping coyotes, bears, and other "dangerous" species while protecting game species such as deer and elk. Detroit Publishing Company imagery from 1900 to 1909 overlaps with U.S. Forest Service management of the Grand Canyon (1893–1919) using widely accepted predator control policies. The agency adopted a predator classification scheme from the Bureau of Biological Survey (reorganized in 1940 as part of the U.S. Fish and Wildlife Service) and used it as a guideline to identify which animals were considered harmful predators. Even with the transfer of the Grand Canyon to the National Park Service in 1919 and a slow shift in ideas about wildlife protection and management, early directors Stephen Mather and Horace Albright continued with the biological survey's predator guidelines. They encouraged policies that "clearly" tied "predator reduction to public enjoyment" and the destruction and control of certain animals such as coyotes and mountain lions that they saw as threatening forces to more "desirable" deer and elk, which they argued, were vital for park goals of public enjoyment (Sellars 1997, 72). If coyotes and other predators are missing from postcards but deer are prominently featured, it is—at least in part—a reflection of historic and evolving wildlife management and park policies.

The cumulative effects of these edits to the Grand Canyon's environment—enhancing and adding green vegetation of the canyon, transforming the silt-laden brown waters of the Colorado River into a blue stream, populating the canyon with domesticated mules instead of wildlife—influenced how people

Fig. 44. Detroit Publishing Company's mule-centric postcard. In this DPC postcard from 1906, *On the Trail, Grand View, Grand Canyon, Arizona*, sure-footed mules carried tourists and supplies into and out of the canyon. They were a favored animal in DPC imagery. Detroit Publishing Company, # DPC10450. Courtesy Miriam and Ira D. Wallach Division of Art, Prints and Photographs: Photography Collection, New York Public Library. "On the Trail, Grand View, Grand Canyon, Arizona." New York Public Library Digital Collections.

interacted with the canyon and what they expected of its environment. At the turn of the twentieth century, images of the Grand Canyon trickled into the popular geographical imagination through the works of Powell, Moran, Dutton, and other adventuresome photographers and artists. Although these images served as a foundation for canyon iconography, this visual catalog of canyon themes, subjects, and locations was limited to scenic views of the river, boating on the Colorado River, and a few rim-side viewpoints bereft of humans. The Grand Canyon's potential as a tourism hub and a vast recreational and scenic playground beyond these locations was yet to unfold.

In the early twentieth century, postcard manufacturers, photographers, and other popular viewmakers were well versed in manipulating the thematic and spatial elements of the canyon's physical landscape, thereby reshaping popular perceptions of the Grand Canyon. Through this visual "photoshopping" of nature at the Grand Canyon by adding blue to the Colorado River or cropping the view to emphasize abundant trees, postcard imagery helped transform the alien canyon landscape into a more familiar and appealing environment for affluent American and European tourists. These travelers were more familiar with lake-side retreats, coastal vacations, and lush eastern deciduous forests than the arid, western landscapes they encountered in the Colorado Plateau (Runte 2010; Wyckoff and Dilsaver 1997; Hyde 1990). Nature was commonplace at the canyon but imitation of the environment sold more postcards. DPC viewmakers revised the colors of the canyon's rock layers, the flora and fauna, and the Colorado River that defined this great chasm every year to create a new postcard, a new view, and a new product to sell to eager postcard collectors and senders.

Working and Playing at the Grand Canyon

Plants, animals, and rivers were not the only parts of the Grand Canyon altered at the hands of postcard manufacturers. The people who lived, worked, and played at the canyon were also subject to the viewmakers' editorial decisions. Detroit Publishing Company and Frasher Foto Postcard Company's treatment of people in their postcard imagery raises complex issues about representations of ethnicity, class, and labor. DPC's postcards depicted white adults in fifteen cards, American Indian adults in ten cards, and children—all American Indian—in six cards. FFPC postcards included people as the subject of just two cards. Although his imagery overlaps that of DPC, only white people populate FFPC's postcard images. Detroit Publishing Company postcards, on the other hand, featured white and American Indian people, but they are rarely seen in the same scene. In addition, looking closely at a large set of DPC imagery printed from 1900 to 1909, a distinct pattern becomes evident as to where each group resides, plays, and lives. In DPC imagery, each group is associated with a specific set of places: white people only occupy outdoor scenes, while American Indians frequently are indoors. White people are represented as tourists and guides on mule rides, stagecoach passengers and drivers, or sightseers standing near the rim peering into the canyon's depths.

American Indians in Detroit Publishing Company imagery are represented almost entirely in their homes and workspaces, with rare scenes outdoors. Many of the DPC postcards show life and work at Hopi House, the Santa Fe Railroad, and the Fred Harvey Company building designed by southwestern architect Mary Colter and constructed on the South Rim of the canyon across the road from the El Tovar Hotel. Grand Canyon Village blossomed in 1905 with the construction of Hopi House and El Tovar, only four years after the Santa Fe Railroad extended its tracks fifteen miles to the South Rim (Gratton 1992; Anderson 2001). The tracks terminated at spot that was just a short walk up a series of steps to the breathtaking views across the canyon's rim and, importantly for the railroad's powerful stake in the tourism business, Hopi House and El Tovar. Hopi House served multiple purposes: It provided housing for Hopi artisans and their families and workspace for these highly skilled artists hired by the Santa Fe Railroad to create pots, rugs, jewelry, and other American Indian crafts for sale to tourists. It was also a spectacle where Anglo-American visitors could watch the artisans at work and observe their children and scenes of family life unfolding.

But not all was as it appeared at Hopi House. Although Santa Fe Railroad and the Fred Harvey Company projected an air of authenticity onto Hopi House with its regional pastiche of Southwest culture—pueblo-style exterior, tiered external levels accessed by rustic wooden ladders, adobe walls, unframed doors, and exposed wooden rafters—the scene was an illusion, manufactured for East Coast and European tourists to fulfill their dreams of an authentic but convenient and safe encounter with the wild Southwest (Dilworth 2001). A closer look at Hopi House betrays its apparent fit in the canyon scene. It is perched close to the South Rim, although the location and its proximity to the rim is exaggerated in early DPC postcards (fig. 45).

Fig. 45. Detroit Publishing Company's *The Hopi House, Grand Canyon of Arizona*. In this 1905 DPC postcard the scene of Hopi House is striking in several ways. It is bustling with activity, as if the viewer just happened upon the location and perhaps surprised the group with this image. Adults and children are gathered along the front of the building while others look down from the various rooftops of Hopi House. A woman in the foreground looks directly at the viewer and seems caught midstride as she walks across the plaza; her hair is arranged in traditional Hopi design and she is holding a small child. The Hopi House itself is depicted much closer to the rim of the canyon than in reality but this position provides a visual drama to the scene. The writing on the front of the card, dated April 1907, is necessarily brief for the small space available, but it relates the age-old tourist salutation, "Wish you were here." Detroit Publishing Company #8798. Courtesy Miriam and Ira D. Wallach Division of Art, Prints and Photographs: Photography Collection, New York Public Library. New York Public Library Digital Collections.

Also note the color of Hopi House in this DPC postcard; the artists' paintbrushes are at work with touches of striking color—a whitewash exterior of the building, the pop of color from the red chili peppers hanging on the front of the building, the iridescent green trees, and, of course, the orange and red bands of rock layers in the canyon. The rocks not only add color and frame the rim view to the left of the image but they add a visual affirmation that this is not just any canyon in the Southwest, this is the Grand Canyon.

The postcards of Hopi House fit in with a larger social and political agenda of mainstream white culture in the early twentieth century that intended to sanitize and commodify American Indian livelihoods. During the 1920s, the Santa Fe Railroad in league with the Fred Harvey Company launched their "Indian Detours," a response to automobile competition for the railroad. The railroad arranged for FHC auto tour cars to meet passengers at railroad stops, then take them on journeys of several days to pueblos, ruins, and artists' studios before returning them to the stations to resume their rail excursion (Dilworth 1996, 90–93). Hopi House was yet another piece of Santa Fe Railroad's powerful promotional strategy that fueled and defined a distinct regional identity of the "Great Southwest." Its role in this performance was to present the "Southwest as no longer savage desert" but instead as "salutary, educational, heroic, and finally ludic region" (Weigle 1989, 115). Both Hopi House and the Indian Detours promoted this vision.

But the social context of Hopi House resists easy simplification. In one sense, some Hopi welcomed the opportunity to live and work at Santa Fe Railroad's building. The arrangement offered housing, a good job, and recognition for skilled craftsmanship. But participating in the Hopi House performance was a complex social encounter between Hopi tribal members who held traditional claims to the Greater Grand Canyon Region, tourists, the Santa Fe Railroad, the Fred Harvey Company, and other tribes (Morehouse 1996). Hopi were actors in a larger visual diorama that the railroad and the Fred Harvey Company constructed at the Grand Canyon. This Grand Canyon version of a utopian ideal of a company town took the form of a pueblo settlement populated with skilled and happy workers who willingly displayed their crafts and intimate family life for tourists.

DPC postcards featured American Indian adults (both men and women) crafting a rug, pottery, jewelry, or painting while tending children. Leah Dilworth describes similar scenes across FHC's southwestern tours. "Indians do three things: They make things to sell, they sell things, and they 'lounge' picturesquely" (2001, 149). She argues that "Indian artisans were central to The Fred Harvey Company's display attractions" whereby they either made "objects for tourist consumption" or served "as objects of visual consumption themselves" (2001, 148–49). The same visual culture and social power dynamic of consumer/consumed is evident in postcards. Postcards were a handy medium to carry home as a visual memento of encounters (for white tourists) with an authentic, native Grand Canyon (in the form of American Indian artisans). A closer look at two DPC postcards, *An Indian Living Room* and *Hopi House Grand Canyon of Arizona* (1905) provides an intimate view of an American Indian group tending children, weaving baskets and rugs,

Fig. 46. Two Detroit Publishing Company postcards that reframe the view. Detroit Publishing Company's *An Indian Living Room, Grand Canyon of Arizona*. (*left*): Courtesy Miriam and Ira D. Wallach Division of Art, Prints and Photographs: Photography Collection, New York Public Library Digital Collections, DPC9286. (*above*): Newberry Library, Curt Teich Postcard Archives Collection and Detroit Publishing Company Collection, DPC8930.

Fig. 47. Detroit Publishing Company *A Native Roof Garden Party, Hopi House, Grand Canyon of Arizona*. This view of Hopi House shows Hopi men, women, and children sitting outside on the second-floor rooftop of the building. Detroit Publishing Company. Courtesy Miriam and Ira D. Wallach Division of Art, Prints and Photographs: Photography Collection, New York Public Library. "A Native Roof Garden Party, Hopi House, Grand Canyon of Arizona," DPC 9287. New York Public Library Digital Collections.

and stoking a fireplace (fig. 46). The postcards also reveal DPC's strategies for creating new products from the same or similar photographs and how simple changes, such as cropping an image, can change the context of the view. One version of the postcard represents an interior view of Hopi House with two men, a woman, and children. In a reprinting, a postcard with an identical title and also printed in 1905 is reframed to remove the weaver on the left side of the image and one of the blankets from the far right. This seemingly simple reframing entirely changed the context and meaning of the scene. It shifted the image from a view of domesticity with the family sitting near the fireplace to that of labor and industry (weaving rugs and baskets).

A minority of the DPC postcards feature outdoor scenes. Some cards depicted the exterior of Hopi House with Native American adults and children in small groups standing or sitting together (fig. 47). Another example depicted American Indians, noted in the caption as Navajo, gathered around a large fire near two rounded hogans (fig. 48).

Fig. 48. Detroit Publishing Company, *Navajo Camp Fire, Grand Canyon, Arizona.* Navajo peoples and their homes (hogans) were the subjects of the DPC postcards, usually shown with exterior views of these structures. These hogans may have been some of the replica hogans that were constructed in the Grand Canyon Village near El Tovar Hotel. Detroit Publishing Company Collection. Courtesy Miriam and Ira D. Wallach Division of Art, Prints and Photographs: Photography Collection, New York Public Library. "Navajo Camp Fire, Grand Canyon, Arizona," DPC 11261. New York Public Library Digital Collections.

In the selection of scenes and subjects for these postcards, the creators and manufacturers of these images reveal as much about the social landscape at the canyon as they do the recreational and experiential one. First, by showing white people exclusively engaged in recreational activities in outdoor settings and American Indians in work and home life activities in interior and outdoor settings, the postcard images depict a "visual segregation" (Schwartz and Ryan 2003) at the canyon. In DPC and FFPC postcards, American Indians and white people are never shown in the same image and certainly not doing the same activities. In this sense, these postcard images depicted not only the scenic view of the canyon but also the social organization.

Second, identifying American Indian peoples in these cards as Hopi or Navajo omits other Grand Canyon Indigenous cultures and peoples and oversimplifies the social context of the canyon in the early twentieth century. There are eleven Traditionally Associated Tribes of Grand Canyon

National Park but only Hopi and Navajo peoples are visually included and recognized in postcard titles and back-of-the-card descriptions (Hughes 1978, 70; Hirst 2006; Morehouse 1996). For example, notably missing from the DPC and FFPC postcards views are longtime Grand Canyon residents, the Havasupai and Hualapai peoples (Jacoby 2001). The Havasupai were early guides who led prospectors, miners, and canyon pioneers along the narrow and steep canyon foot trails to precious drinking water and springs and to food sources at the canyon. Havasupai families spent the winter in Havasu Canyon at Supai Village, but some preferred to live near springs throughout the canyon during the summers. In the era of Euro-American canyon settlement, Havasupai families continued to move between Supai Village and Grand Canyon Village on the South Rim.

Indeed, at the turn of the twentieth century, there were Havasupai living in at least three areas that overlapped or were near tourist developments: Indian Gardens, directly north and a few thousand feet below the rim (well within the viewshed of El Tovar guests); Supai Village in Havasu Canyon west of Grand Canyon Village; and Supai Camp on the opposite side of the Santa Fe Railroad tracks from Hopi House (Anderson 2000). Well into the 1930s, Havasupai peoples continued to be a part of the everyday scenes at the central tourist district, working regular jobs at Grand Canyon Village and living in the small community called Supai Camp that was west of Rowe Well Road, the main tourist auto and stagecoach route. However, the Rowe Well community—small and populated by Havasupai workers living in informal shacks—was considered by concessionaires and NPS managers to be an eyesore. Yet the park managers also upheld an informal agreement and encouragement to keep these areas intact. National Park Service managers encouraged the Havasupai to make this transition to wage labor at Grand Canyon Village, even extending preferential treatment and the hiring of tribe members over white laborers (Jacoby 2001, 190). This shift to wage labor drew tribal members away from traditional tribal subsistence of farming and hunting at Supai Village and made them more dependent on the tourist economy at the South Rim, where they performed "much of the off-stage labor necessary to make the park more accessible to tourists" (Jacoby 2001, 190–91).

But tensions grew between the Havasupai who lived in the camps while working in Grand Canyon Village and the National Park Service and concessionaires who increasingly showed less tolerance for these settlements. In the 1930s, the National Park Service razed the camp while the Havasupai were at other destinations. The camp was rebuilt with Civilian Conservation Corps labor and additional funds through the National Park Service's official plans to revitalize the Grand Canyon Village (Anderson 2000, 28). The NPS hoped that the effort would "beautify developed areas by razing old structures" and that the Havasupai workers with regular Grand Canyon Village jobs would move to these newly built cabins (Anderson 2000, 29). Although rarely seen in the postcard imagery from this time period, Havasupai peoples were residing and working in Grand Canyon Village at Supai Camp and at Indian Gardens (Morehouse 1996, 110).

Hopi and Navajo peoples also maintained important associations with the Grand Canyon. After extensive negotiations over treaty rights to land and canyon access, the Hopi and the Navajo were relegated to reservation lands east of the park. However, it was the Hopi who came to represent the face of American Indian communities at the Grand Canyon; the Santa Fe Railroad offered excursion tours to the Hopi reservation for their railway passengers. FHC and SFRR also offered eastward excursions to Topocoba Hilltop and the Hopi Villages (Anderson 2000, 14). After Hopi House was built in 1905, Fred Harvey and the Santa Fe Railroad hired Hopi peoples to live and work in the Hopi House, where their lives were essentially on display for park visitors.

Only two FFPC postcards included people. In both instances they seem to be white and engaged in recreational outdoor activities (fig. 49). Frasher's predilection for unpopulated landscapes scenes may have guided his decision to not include many people in his images. But the reasoning behind his choices may be better explained in the future with new research by biographers who deepen our understanding of Frasher's work and life.

Building Hospitality

Buildings, such as restaurants or hotels, appeared frequently in DPC and FFPC postcard imagery. Although DPC postcards featured interior and exterior building views, FFPC almost exclusively represented the exterior of buildings. The cultural landscape of buildings, roads, and tourist service areas at Grand Canyon Village underwent extensive renovations between 1900 and 1935. European American pioneers at the canyon—miners, ranchers, and entrepreneurs—established a sprawling and disorganized settlement at the South Rim of the canyon that developed into Grand Canyon Village. As the canyon's economic value shifted from mining to tourism, the social landscape of the canyon also shifted as the power of local pioneers and

Fig. 49. Frasher Foto postcard of tourists sitting at rim view, 1929. This card depicts visitors taking in a rim-side scenic view from Yavapai Point, South Rim. Courtesy Frasher Fotos Collection/HJG and Pomona Public Library, Pomona, California. Frasher Foto Collection, index #12229. Title: "Grand Canyon from Yavapai Point."

individual entrepreneurs gave way to a corporate-federal partnership. The material landscape slowly transformed from a patchwork of informal and improved structures to a more standardized and stylized architecture that provided lodging, dining, and service functions for tourists.

In the late 1800s and early 1900s, tourists reached the canyon along transcontinental railroad corridors and regional stagecoach routes. Once at Grand Canyon Village, tourists could find lodging and services (although rather threadbare at this point), join a mule tour into the canyon from the rim, or simply stroll along the rim boardwalk to view the canyon. By 1901, however, the railroad reached the Grand Canyon Village. Railroad entrepreneurs who had long been dissatisfied with local hospitability offered to its passengers now moved forward to several new projects. The Santa Fe Railroad started a wave of construction in a concentrated district near the Bright Angel Trailhead that continued over the next fifty years.

Detroit Publishing Company postcard photographers and manufacturers aligned themselves with the Fred Harvey Company and Santa Fe Railroad interests along the South Rim and inner canyon. Indeed, the DPC postcards added to the corporate trend at the canyon of making SFRR and FHC hotels and buildings into "subsidiary icons" (Nye 2003). Nonetheless buildings such as El Tovar Hotel and Hopi House soon served as a cultural shorthand for authenticity. Thanks to the Santa Fe Railroad and Fred Harvey visual promotional campaigns (including postcard imagery) tourists could easily recognize these buildings.

Many DPC postcards featured interior views of rooms and buildings but without any people. At first glance this seems surprising given that these buildings functioned as gathering centers for tourists. One might expect bustling lodges and busy dining rooms. Indeed, Joseph Ives's prediction that his group would be the first and "doubtless be the last . . . to visit this profitless locality" still lingered in the era of DPC postcards (1861, 110). The DPC postcards of this time featured a number of interior views of buildings, often empty of tourists, workers, and other people. Early twentieth century postcards often followed this trend of depicting vacant interiors as a marketing ploy to appeal to potential visitors. The empty rooms, set tables, and vacant couches were a clever strategy that offered an open door for potential visitors to imagine themselves at the canyon (fig. 50). This approach also offered a chance for the postcard manufacturers, in partnerships with canyon businesses such as Fred Harvey Company, to fill those empty rooms with their ideas about how the Grand Canyon experience unfolded through hospitality, comfort, and relaxation. It was one thing to read in guidebooks or hotel promotions that El Tovar Hotel offered guests running water, electricity, comfortable beds, and ample seating in modern dining rooms. The postcards confirmed these claims in vivid detail.

In a well-executed plan that may have been Frasher's tactic for updating his cards and creating new products, FFPC postcards seem to take advantage of recently constructed buildings and roads at the canyon. This was a timely strategy, as the FFPC cards sampled in this set, drawn from 1929 to 1935, capture canyon scenes during one of the most expansive construction periods for Grand Canyon infrastructure, the early 1930s (Anderson 1998, 28).

The FFPC postcards exclusively featured exterior images of buildings. Most of the structures depicted in FFPC postcards from this era were located at the eastern and northern Grand Canyon, on the periphery of the powerful Santa Fe–Fred Harvey sphere of influence. Many of the FFPC cards depicted the exterior of buildings not found in the DPC set: Grand Canyon Lodge, Yavapai Observation Station, Hermit's Rest, Desert Watchtower, Moqui

Fig. 50. Detroit Publishing Company's El Tovar Hotel lounge postcard. As a grand lodge meant to cater to wealthy foreigners or tourists from the eastern United States, the card features a depopulated interior view of the rooms and facilities at this hotel, making it easy for potential customers to imagine themselves sitting in those rooms and enjoying the comforts of the hotel. Detroit Publishing Company Collection, DPC 7998. Courtesy Miriam and Ira D. Wallach Division of Art, Prints and Photographs: Photography Collection, New York Public Library. "The Rendezvous, Hotel El Tovar, Grand Canyon, Arizona." New York Public Library Digital Collections.

Camp, and Tusayan Ruins. While the DPC cards emphasized imagery of the exterior and interior of buildings in the core of the Grand Canyon Village at the South Rim, the FFPC cards showed an alternative catalog of park structures on the North Rim, such as Grand Canyon Lodge, or on the South Rim, the Hermit's Rest building and Desert View Watchtower.

The most common building shown in FFPC views is Grand Canyon Lodge, built in 1927–28 by the Union Pacific Railroad on the North Rim (fig. 51). Frasher and his photographers may have been taking advantage of the opportunity for "new material" in the always competitive postcard market by using these scenes from locations along the northern and eastern rim. The construction of Grand Canyon Lodge was certainly newsworthy for the auto travelers that Frasher catered to, and FFPC's postcards captured this new feature in the Grand Canyon landscape at its early stages. With more tourists visiting the canyon by car, there is also an increasing number of postcard views of structures along the northern and eastern approach roads to the canyon—Moqui Lodge, Kirby's Camp, and Navajo Hogans near the Vermillion Cliffs (along today's State Route 67). Along the South Rim of the canyon, the FFPC cards depicted many of the recently constructed buildings, including the Tusayan Ruins and Wayside Museum (built in 1932), the Desert View Watchtower (built in 1932 by the Fred Harvey Company) along the East Rim Drive/Navahopi Road/Desert View Drive (today's State Highway 64); the Yavapai Observation Station (built by the NPS in 1928) and Lookout Studio (built by the Fred Harvey Company in 1914) in the core of the Grand Canyon Village; and the Hermit's Rest shelter (built in 1914 by the Fred Harvey Company) at the present-day terminus of Hermit Road (Anderson 2001; Gratton 1992).

Frasher's predilection for auto travel routes and tourist facilities no doubt influenced his choices for his photographs and postcards of the Grand Canyon. In particular, Frasher's business model of engaging small roadside service and motel operations to make custom postcard views may be at work here in the images from this set. FFPC postcards include several view that feature location along the road to the North Rim developed areas, such as Kirby's Camp and Moqui Camp (fig. 52)

Cultural Landscapes of Tourism

Clusters of buildings in tourist service areas evolved into the Grand Canyon's cultural landscapes of tourism. Although between 1900 and 1935 there were multiple enterprises of varying sizes that offered visitor services across the Greater Grand Canyon Region, only a few of these were featured in DPC and FFPC postcards. Indeed, DPC with its Fred Harvey Company contracts and partnerships maintained an affinity to FHC businesses found in Grand Canyon Village and the North Rim Village. Overlapping this visual catalog with the landscapes tourism at the South Rim from this time, we see that the DPC card locations mirrored the three fledging developed areas and access points at the South Rim, but no other places. The DPC cards represent early tourism development at the Grand Canyon, in the transition from stagecoach to railroad and later automobile, from independent miners to large-scale corporations and federal government. The DPC cards from 1900 to 1909 catch the Grand Canyon on the brink of increasing development. These cards favor scenes from three concentrated areas of development at the South Rim, each operated by a different group or individual. The visual

Fig. 51. Frasher Foto postcard, exterior of Grand Canyon Lodge. Exterior scenes of buildings are common in the Frasher postcard imagery from the early 1930s. These images often featured tourist facilities such as the Grand Canyon Lodge and other sites that might be appealing to auto travelers from the north and east approaches to the park. Courtesy Frasher Fotos Collection/HJG and Pomona Public Library, Pomona, California. Frasher Foto Postcard Collection, index #A4819. Title "Grand Canyon Lodge Bright Angel Point, North Rim Kaibab Forest, Arizona."

record provides a way to trace the early locations of tourist facilities as well as access routes to these areas.

The DPC postcards are not complete documents of the canyon's cultural landscape; they present edited versions of it. There were many tourist accommodations, informal structures, and other features of the built landscape (operated by independent contractors) that were excluded from this view of the canyon, such as the Kolb Studio, Bass Camp, Hance Ranch, Ralph Cameron's Hotel, Cameron's post office, and James Thurber and Martin Buggeln's hotels and liveries, to name a few. The canyon was a messy place in the early 1900s. Lack of zoning, sanitation, and an abundance of mules, horses, and humans created a haphazard, odoriferous, and informal residential community by the turn of the century. "As trains steamed slowly up Bright Angel Wash each morning and left in the afternoon, passengers began and ended their vacations by staring through Pullman windows at filth and disorganization permeating the village along the tracks" (Anderson 1998, 98). The village was riddled with workers' tents, wooden shacks, open trash mounds,

Fig. 52. Frasher Foto postcard, exterior of Kirby's Camp at the North Rim. This Frasher Foto card focuses on the gas station and tourist service areas on the North Rim known as Kirby's Camp. Courtesy Frasher Fotos Collection/HJG and Pomona Public Library, Pomona, California. Frasher Foto Postcard Collection, index #E709. Title: Kirby's Camp P.O. Grand Canyon, Arizona Main Entrance, Grand Canyon National Park.

discarded wood stored for cooking, makeshift incinerators that puffed out foul smells, outhouses, and mule stables. These elements are absent from the postcard archive. Detroit Publishing Company manufacturers may have considered this landscape as less appealing or scenic than a view of the inner canyon, but the decisions made by DPC influenced what tourists saw of the canyon and shaped the development of the canyon's tourist services areas, such as Grand Canyon Village. The DPC postcards presented a simplified and sanitized view of the canyon and its cultural landscape. By excluding certain people, buildings, and places from these cultural landscape representations they effectively edited the script of who and what was part of the Grand Canyon scene, leaving out, for example, Havasupai peoples, tent camps, independent or family businesses such as Grand View Hotel, and endemic parts of the environment such as cacti and birds.

Canyon Recreation: Mule Trail Rides and Auto Tours

In terms of recreation and activities, DPC and FFPC showed two different views of the canyon experience. In the DPC imagery, recreational activities at the Grand Canyon featured mule riding on South Rim and midcanyon trails or joining a group stagecoach or auto tour along the South Rim. FFPC represented auto touring as the primary recreation at the Grand Canyon. Although these images rarely included people, they did feature hotels, gas stations, and the expanding network of roads and bridges in the Greater Grand Canyon Region.

Walking paths and mule trails were central to the early Grand Canyon experience (see figure 44). DPC postcards excelled at documenting mule rides into the canyon. Indeed, a great bulk of their cards featured nervous riders, heading into or emerging out of the canyon, perched on the back of a mule and clinging to their saddles as the animals slowly wended their way along the slim trails etched into the canyon's walls. American Indians and their ancestors had long ago carved footpaths throughout the Grand Canyon, often taking advantage of natural fault lines to form a path up the steep canyon walls. Miners and prospectors adopted and later expanded a few of these trails (Anderson 1998, 73–74). For instance, the Bright Angel Trail was originally a Havasupai Indian trail that took advantage of the Bright Angel Fault as an access route to the rim. Later, Ralph Cameron, an early canyon entrepreneur and prospector, redeveloped and extended the trail for his mining claim to the trailhead. Mule and foot trails proliferated along the rim and into the canyon in a haphazard fashion during the early pioneer period from the 1880s to the 1910s and the initial stages of National Park Service management of the canyon. However, only a few of these trails were represented, repetitively, in the DPC postcard sample. The DPC postcards featured Grand View, Bright Angel, and Hance Trails. DPC postcards also used the visual appeal of switchbacks in the trail as an iconic feature, with mule train parties that would take brief breaks along these sections for photographs. Trail builders created switchbacks that eased travel and countered the steep grade of the canyon's walls.

The DPC cards showed more scenes of trails than roads while the FFPC cards—sampled from later in this period—depicted more road and automobile scenes. None of the DPC cards illustrated the journey to the canyon; there were no images of train travel, stagecoach, or horseback trips that were common parts of the journey during this period. The FFPC postcards, on the other hand. represented scenes along access roads to the park including visitor facilities and scenic viewpoints. They heavily featured access routes to the canyon, especially along the Arizona Strip and north canyon area (see figs. 52 and 53). Thus the FFPC cards showed not only recreational opportunities at the canyon but images of what the trip to the canyon might be like for visitors by promoting auto travel to the area.

The FFPC postcards represented scenes along the roadways north of the canyon, near Marble Canyon, and the Marble Canyon Bridge—later renamed Navajo Bridge, site of the future Glen Canyon Dam (fig. 53). This trend supports much of FFPC's work that actively documented the expansion of roads and auto culture throughout the American West into the 1930s. While there was auto traffic in the Grand Canyon in the 1920s, the pace of auto tourism picked up considerably in the 1930s with the completion of roads connecting the park to regional networks. At the Grand Canyon, FFPC's taste for automobile travel may have encouraged Frasher to portray contemporary developments and changes in the roadways during this period. As with postcards of buildings, FFPC postcards also capture newly constructed or realigned roads. For instance, the East Rim Drive (also known as the Fred Harvey–constructed dirt Navahopi Road) connecting Grand Canyon Village to Desert View and Cameron was realigned from 1927 to 1931 and appears in a number of FFPC postcards. In this way, the FFPC cards have the strongest thematic overlap with the *Arizona Highways* images, which also promoted automobile travel to and around the canyon and the northeastern canyon region along U.S. Highway 89 and State Route 67.

Detroit Publishing Company and Frasher Foto Postcard Company manufactured some of the earliest postcard representations of the Grand Canyon from 1900 to 1935. In their choices of locations and subject matter, they set a template for Grand Canyon imagery that other postcard manufacturers and photographers would follow for decades to come. Both manufacturers repeated a selective set of themes and locations and incrementally, postcard by postcard, built a visual lexicon of the canyon's environment for tourist consumption. DPC was particularly influential in setting a template that later postcard manufacturers, such as Curt Teich, would reproduce with fidelity to both subjects and locations. This can partly be understood through the business partnership that both companies shared with Fred Harvey Company and their orders for images that featured their business ventures and tourist activities.

A distinct pattern emerges by overlaying the spatial layout of early tourism development at Grand Canyon Village with the locations represented in the DPC and FFPC postcards. The rim-side locations featured in the

Fig. 53. Frasher Foto postcard, Marble Canyon Bridge over the Colorado River. Postcards of bridges such as this one of the Marble Canyon in the northeastern Grand Canyon reinforce Frasher's emphasis on car culture for touring the Grand Canyon and a preference for north canyon scenes. Courtesy Frasher Foto Collection/HJG and Pomona Public Library, Pomona, California. Frasher Foto Postcard Collection, index #12206. Title: "Grand Canyon Bridge and Vermillion Cliffs at Buck Lowrey's Trading Post, Marble Canyon, Arizona."

FFPC cards tend to track new or realigned roads that terminated at scenic overlooks (Point Sublime, for example) or tourist services (Grand Canyon Lodge or Desert View Watchtower). In contrast, the trailhead of each of the inner canyon mule and foot trails featured in the Detroit Publishing Company postcards (Bright Angel, Grand View, and Hance) doubled as a portal to nearby business ventures. Owners and operators of these businesses stood to profit as gateways to the inner canyon via their rim-side land claims. The repetition of certain trails in postcard representations promoted these trails and nearby rim-side businesses, making them easily recognized landmarks for tourists at the canyon. However, many trails and businesses were excluded from the DPC and FFPC vantage points. Overall, postcard manufacturers such as DPC and FFPC selectively transformed and legitimized certain themes through the subjects and locations of the images they produced, creating powerful place-based symbols that represented a selective and fragmentary ideal of the Grand Canyon.

5 Scenic Drives

Generally speaking, it is not timber, and certainly not agriculture, which is causing the decimation of wilderness areas, but rather the desire to attract tourists.

—Aldo Leopold, 1925, in Callicott and Nelson, *The Great New Wilderness Debate*

Arizona is a big state. It is a beautiful state. It is an interesting state. Its story has been told each month in *Arizona Highways* since April 1925, and it will continue to be told for many years to come. The Arizona story never grows old.

—*Arizona Highways* editor Raymond Carlson, 1951

In 1902 the first automobile traveled to the Grand Canyon from Flagstaff. This was no minor feat. The journey included three days of travel (due to bad roads and several breakdowns). It was not much better than the jostling stagecoach trip of eight hours. Today, drivers can zoom up to the canyon on nearly the same route in about an hour and a half. Increasing the speed of travel blurs many of the scenes out the window of the car, simplifying the view, and focusing attention on travel corridors and roadside attractions. In the case of Grand Canyon, the mode of travel shaped what and where *Arizona Highways* magazine editors and photographers portrayed each month as the "windshield wilderness" (Louter 2006).

Automobile travel has an immense influence on our experiences of nature, wilderness, and the passing landscape (Lippard 1999a; Carr 1999, 2007; Young 2002; Schwantes 2003; Louter 2006). Social observer and scholar Lucy Lippard notes that "as modes of travel changed, so did the act of looking around" (1999b, 136). Alexander Wilson remarks on the "horizon quality" cars impose on landscapes: "The faster we drive the flatter the earth looks . . . distance is experienced as an abstraction. . . . Seen from a plane window the landscape flattens out to something like a map" (qtd. in Lippard 1999b,

136). As road networks and highways connected the Greater Grand Canyon Region in the 1920a and 1930s, a car windshield became the primary frame for visitor experiences at the Grand Canyon.

As tourism promotion reached an increasing national audience and visitation at the canyon expanded, a stereotypical image of the Southwest extended to an entire region, well beyond the boundaries of Grand Canyon National Park. Popular imagery, such as that found in *Arizona Highways* magazine, played an important role in this process. Geographer Richard Francaviglia, in his study of southwestern image making and place identity, noted that artists have shaped popular perceptions by creating "stylized" regional scenery that relies on certain selected natural and cultural features. The process of stylizing the regional imagery of the Southwest is "closely tied to concepts of what belongs and what does not belong in the region." In his article, Francaviglia traces the iconographic arc of southwestern imagery, a process he describes as "stereotyping the landscape." He notes that "viewed statistically, one finds certain elements or scenes overrepresented" and, further, that these representations are connected to the people who create them and their motives. For example, the Santa Fe railway imagery that "promoted a stereotypical image of the Southwest in paintings . . . actually created a romanticized landscape to match the stereotypes, reminding us that art and commerce are interconnected in the region" (1994, 29–30). Francaviglia also reminds us that "portraying the landscape is always a selective process of inclusion, exclusion, and enhancement" (26).

Arizona Highways: Publicity, Tourism, Scenic Drives

Arizona Highways—the Grand Canyon state's equivalent to *National Geographic*—began rolling off the presses in April 15, 1925, five years after women in the United States won the right to vote, eleven years after the completion of the Panama Canal, and four years before the stock market crash that ushered in the Great Depression. It was right around the same time surrealism recast the world of vision into surprise and non sequitur and Charlie Chaplin's gentleman "tramp" charmed the hearts of silent film audiences with *Gold Rush*. It was a time of crisis and uncertainty, when people's lives sorted out after World War I, then fractured once again during the Great Depression. In some ways photography and other artistic endeavors absorbed the ricochet of human suffering, geopolitics, and dislocation from the war and recast it in new angles. The economy in America boomed before it busted. It was in this cultural matrix that *Arizona Highways* got its start. Initially a brochure to promote good roads throughout the state, it transformed and grew into a full magazine format in 1925 as a twenty-six page, 8½x11-inch, black-and-white highway engineer's magazine (fig. 54).

Tracing the magazine back to its roots provides a perspective on its evolution, dramatic change of mission and course, and the editorial and creative decisions made by the magazine's editors, photographers, and writers to carry the magazine forward. The magazine materialized in an era marked by a rising number of independent automobile travelers, free from organized tours, sputtering along the growing network of dirt and paved roads across America. *Arizona Highways* emerged as America (and the Grand Canyon) shifted from horse-drawn carriages to automobiles, a process that involved vast changes to the landscape as roads were rebuilt, abandoned, or created, and motorists explored these avenues of travel.

Americans embraced auto touring and clamored for safer and more extensive road networks and reliable information about the state of these roads. To meet this demand, at least on the engineering side of the equation, the Arizona Highway Department published nine issues of a pamphlet called *Arizona Highways* from 1921 to 1922 in an attempt to follow the lead of other states that were creating similar highway information publications. For several years during this early stage, the magazine served as a discussion board for professional highway engineers to submit images and text describing the products of their craft. Pages were filled with photos of culverts, bridges, freshly graded roadways, and sketches of proposed transportation projects. *Arizona Highways* was a public enterprise from the start: it was created by State of Arizona House Bill 188, managed and published by the Arizona Highway Department, and funded through an initial annual budget of $20,000 (Farrell 1997, 6–7). The monthly publication was supported by taxes, subscription fees (a dollar a year or ten cents a month), and advertising revenue (Carlson 1951). A strong impulse to build and enlarge the state's road networks ran through all of the articles during this time period. The magazine prominently featured the "Highway Engineer's Creed," a sparse but lofty affirmation of the role of transportation in "civilization" that is grounded in "the home and productive industry," working in harmony with the automobile manufacturers, and heeding a nationalistic call for the "mission" of highway engineers to do their part in building a highway system for an expanding market of drivers and citizens. Even from these

Fig. 54. Cover of the first edition of *Arizona Highways*, April 1925, featuring an image of a freshly completed roadway. Editors chose to focus on celebrating the work of road engineers and planners during the early years of the magazine. State of Arizona, Arizona Memory Project, *Arizona Highways Magazine*, April 1925, cover page.

earliest days of the magazine, however, the publication was directed toward promoting Arizona tourism and travel. Per House Bill 188, the magazine was created "for the purpose of encouraging tourism travel to and through the state by giving publicity to points and places of historic interest, climatic and recreational advantages, the possibilities of successful pursuits and industrial enterprises . . . to attract visitors to the state" (Farrell 1997, 6).

Throughout the 1930s and under the direction of a succession of editors, *Arizona Highways* gradually shifted away from its engineering roots as it transformed into a "travel and tourism oriented regional magazine that contained only 20 percent highway department information" (Farrell 1997, 13). This transition was accompanied by an increasing number of photographs, sketches, artwork, and travel narratives, all aimed at promoting tourism in the state. The magazine editors created a popular readership during this time by emphasizing three themes: Arizona's physical landscape, ethnic diversity, and southwestern art (Farrell 1997, 14–15). This is notable coming from a magazine that was initially more concerned with concrete than condors. These themes not only sold magazines; they shaped popular environmental perceptions of the Southwest and Arizona in particular. Just as the Santa Fe Railroad promotional brochures featured selected and often repeated subjects that stereotyped the southwestern landscape (Francaviglia 1994), the people that created, edited, and published *Arizona Highways* were motivated to sell Arizona-based travel through place imagery. The Grand Canyon figured prominently into this accounting. Photographer and author Stephen Trimble suggests the powerful influence of the magazine on shaping popular perceptions of the canyon: "The Grand Canyon bound into each new issue of *Arizona Highways* was a wild place domesticated by its capture in the magazine, organized into comfortable predictability by its arrival every month in suburban mailboxes, smoothed into a generic 'magnificent landscape' by hokey captions" (2006, 28).

The 1930s were also important years to the magazine's evolution through changing visual technologies and editorial direction. In 1937 a new editor named Raymond Carlson matched his talents and strong editorial vision with art director George Avery who joined the magazine in 1938. These men reshaped the magazine's content and look, eliminating highway department articles and private advertising while pushing for more photography in the publication, printing the first color photograph in 1938 (Farrell 1997).

Carlson and Avery served in these roles for more than thirty years, guiding *Arizona Highways* and "the world's image of the Grand Canyon" through their selection of photographs, locations, and the use of color photography (Trimble 2006, 21). Indeed, color photographs became a hallmark of the magazine: in 1946 *Arizona Highways* became the first major U.S. magazine to feature four-color separation throughout the publication.

The publisher, managing editor, art director/editor, and eventually photography editor were critical shapers of *Arizona Highways*. From the earliest days of the magazine to the present day, *Arizona Highways* does not employ staff photographers or writers; all of the visual and textual content derives from freelancers (Ensenberger, pers. comm., 2009). This adds a novel ingredient to the push-pull tensions between the consuming readership and audience; the managing editor and art and photography editors; and the image creators, photographers, and artists. As a magazine guided by individuals with strong editorial visions for the publication, *Arizona Highways* reached its climax readership and popularity in 1977 with 507,133 subscribers. Today the magazine is part of the Arizona Department of Transportation (ADOT), but it does not receive state funding (Arizona Department of Transportation Research Center 2020, 9). It gathers revenue from a base of sales in newsstands, bookstores, and other retail outlets and individual, corporate, hotel, and library subscriptions. In addition, the magazine extends its reach through the associated *Arizona Highways Television*, social media pages on Facebook and Instagram, and product sales such as the highly popular calendars. As of 2020, the magazine's monthly circulation of over 136,000 copies reaches readers in all fifty states and around the world through global distribution (Arizona Department of Transportation Research Center 2020, 9).

Arizona Highways's contributing writers and photographers were allowed great leeway in their selection of locations and subjects. This process may be compared to that of postcard photographers who were sent into the field with general instructions from postcard manufacturers (or working independently) to capture notable scenes but not dictated to capture specific locations. In later years, however, *Arizona Highways* editors exerted a greater influence on submissions by releasing a "stock call" (Ensenberger 2009) as a list of themes or locations that editors wanted for feature articles became more common. Raymond Carlson noted with pride that "some subjects are so big they have been approached from many different angles and still their story has not been told" (1951). One of those big subjects was the Grand Canyon, the focus of thirty-one features from 1925 to 1951, second only to features on Navajo Indians (Carlson 1951). From 1925 to 1935, the first decade of *Arizona Highways*, the canyon appeared in increasingly greater frequencies as the magazine exposed its growing readership to a variety of themes and locations throughout the canyon region.

Early Magazine Views

A review of Grand Canyon imagery in *Arizona Highways* from its first decade reveals differences in themes and locations featured in the magazine's photographs. *Arizona Highways* editors and photographers focused on several consistent themes and locations, namely scenic views, building exteriors, and transportation networks along roads and trails. Then, suddenly they shifted their attention after 1935, toward an expanded thematic repertoire. The sample of images used in this analysis is relatively small (thirteen images total), however, these were the early years of the publication, and, for the first five years, no images of the Grand Canyon appeared (refer to appendix C for detailed counts to support the imagery discussion in this and following chapters). After 1930, with an editorial shift toward tourism, there was an increase in Grand Canyon imagery. Notably, for our tour of changing Grand Canyon imagery, early *Arizona Highways* photographs were printed at about the same time as the Frasher Foto postcards, and both were influenced by similar social, political, and cultural trends that shaped the Detroit Publishing Company postcards.

Photographs served as the primary form of visual representations of the canyon in *Arizona Highways*. Occasionally, maps, sketches, and reproductions of paintings also made an appearance between the covers of the magazine. The most common subjects during this early period were scenic views of the canyon and building exteriors. To a lesser degree the other Grand Canyon photographs include a range of subjects, from trails, roads and bridges, and water (specifically the Colorado River) to a lone photograph featuring people peering into the canyon. It's also noteworthy that even the magazine images in *Arizona Highways* reveal a geographical bias. The most common horizontal locations were along the South Rim followed by the North Rim. The only other locations featured were of the northeast and another of the entire canyon (noted as "all canyon" in the appendixes).

Scenic Drives: Creating a Visual Tour

Arizona Highways representations overlap with the Frasher Foto card representations from the 1920s and 1930s in their prominence of scenic views and building exteriors. To a much lesser degree, the Colorado River, trails, roads and bridges, and white people also appear in the images, but the thematic variation of these images seems weak compared to the postcard representations for the same time period. Why is there discontinuity between the two media sources? What events may have influenced and shaped the thematic diversity represented in the magazine? What does this thematic range indicate about popular ideas of the Grand Canyon during the early twentieth century?

In the 1920s and 1930s, national and regional events reshaped the Grand Canyon's cultural, political, and social landscape: fluctuating park visitation, the improvement of park infrastructure and facilities, the expansion of regional and park road networks, and adjustments to park boundaries. The canyon's dynamic environment also changed during this time in some predictable and some unforeseen ways. Years of mining; uneven, opportunistic, and generally unplanned tourism development; increasing visitation; changing management approaches; and boundary disputes also affected the canyon's landscape. The canyon's developed tourism environment was due for a makeover, and the economic boom-and-bust cycles of these interwar years provided the impetus to make some wide-ranging changes to the canyon's landscape.

With a mandate to document and distribute reliable information about Arizona's expanding road network, *Arizona Highways* editors followed the path laid out before them, mile by paved or graded mile. Since most roadways approached the canyon from the rim and followed the course of the canyon and river from this rim-side perch, many of the images showed either a rim, river, and road scenic canyon triumvirate (fig. 55) or a rim view looking across the canyon to the other side (fig. 56). Indeed, of the few images of the Grand Canyon in *Arizona Highways* during this period, most images show the rim and the Colorado River in a consistent formula that echoes the postcard imagery.

But where are the people? In contrast to the stagecoach tourists, mule riders, and Hopi men, women, and children inhabiting the postcard views of Detroit Publishing Company and, to a much smaller extent, the Frasher

Foto postcards, not many people appear in the *Arizona Highways* images from this period. This may be due to fluctuating visitation during these years more than editorial decisions; recall this same issue with the postcard representations (empty rooms for lodging and dining). Visitation at Grand Canyon National Park rose steadily for most of its short history to this point, but it declined during the Great Depression. In 1925, 134,053 people entered the park. Visitation peaked in 1929 at 184,093 visitors, then began a descent throughout the early 1930s, reaching a low of 105,475 people in 1933 (see appendix C).

Building a Village

Buildings are the second most common subject of *Arizona Highways* representations of the canyon, especially exterior views of structures at the South or North Rims of the canyon. The economic meltdown of the early 1930s brought a new and much-needed wave of federal investment in the region through tourism infrastructure improvements. Grand Canyon facilities were shoddy by the 1920s, mostly from overuse, uneven investment and maintenance, and conflicting or nonexistent management by the U.S. Forest Service and then the National Park Service. Roads, trails, and buildings constructed during the pre-park years were now showing wear and tear.

Perhaps one of the greatest impacts that shaped how national parks looked and what visitors experienced was a New Deal federal employment program that created the Civilian Conservation Corps (CCC), which operated from March 1933 to June 1942. Through the influx of labor and funding afforded by the CCC program, national parks received a tremendous upgrade and modernization during the Great Depression. Skilled CCC laborers were placed in camps around the country to complete road and trail building projects, infrastructure improvements, and other additions and renovations. At the Grand Canyon, the CCC efforts had a marked impact on park tourism through roads, buildings, bridges, fences, and communications; CCC workers even fought forest fires (Booth 2005, 78). Six camps and thousands of CCC workers traded places with tourists throughout the canyon.

Grand Canyon Village, however, remained the domain of private business interests during the 1920s. In 1924, Santa Fe Railroad executives drafted the first master plan, or planning and management document, for the Grand Canyon with little guidance from the NPS. Not surprisingly, this document

These tribes cultivated the soil in the little parks surrounded by forests of juniper nearby and broken pieces of their stone hoes can still be found scattered about. Not only were their homes built along the canyon walls, but for defense purposes, five fortresses were located on promontories above the canyon. Geologists find much of interest in the sandy limestone formations of Walnut canyon where valuable fossils have been discovered in the various strata, including some of animal life such as now exists only in tropical seas.

Between Flagstaff and Prescott, to the southwest, stands famous Montezuma's Castle in the face of a cliff overlooking the upper reaches of Beaver Creek. Created a national monument in 1906, it preserves one of the best examples of cliff dwelling in existence. Its remarkable state of preservation has left it practically complete and it stands in haughty grandeur 80 feet above the stream, disdainful of the ravages of time. It was built, undoubtedly, for a fortress and communal house, and must have been the retreat of some war lord who held sway over the surrounding country. Smaller houses surround the main castle which is five stories high and can only be reached with the aid of ladders. Constructed of rocks and cedar timber, a close examination discloses that it was built by many workers as the various rooms show great difference in quality of work and design. From the windows of the castle is a commanding view of the country around where fertile lands were once well populated and farmed. Continued depredations of their more warlike neighbors probably drove these tribes away to safer haunts.

South now, thru the Salt River Valley and up along the colorful Apache Trail are to be found the Tonto Cliff Dwellings, now a national monument. These ruins are well preserved and resemble those further north. They are visited annually by thousands taking the Apache tour.

But west of these mountains, in the now fertile valleys of the Salt and Gila rivers, lived a peace-loving people who through well-planned irrigation systems, raised cotton and corn and attained a high degree of civilization. Around Phoenix there are still traces of the canals they built, some of which were used by modern engineers in planning the irrigation of the Salt River Valley. The best preserved example of their dwellings is to be found near Florence, some 70 miles south of Phoenix, known as Casa Grande or the "great house." This ruin with its four groups of buildings or compounds, reveals an exceptional degree of advancement in the art of building. The compounds were each inclosed in a rectangular wall. The main building in compound A stood four stori high and was probably used as fortress and watch tower, or hon of the chief. Two pretentio apartment houses adjoin it. Dan ing rooms, dining rooms and ceremonial chamber are found compound B, the latter of whi contained a throne or chair pr sumably used for a sick pers during the healing ceremoni Built well of adobe clay, mix with caliche, the walls of the ma building are 3 to 4½ feet in thic ness. Specimens of bone, wo and stone tools have been fou which would indicate that th people lived in the latter Arizo Stone Age. What became of t ten or fifteen thousand people w inhabited this valley can only conjectured, but it is thought t perhaps a long drought and s that was too hard discourag them and they migrated into canyons of the north. Or, const warring with the fierce tribes the hills might have sent them other and safer quarters. As

Above—A solid rock wall on th Grand View Trail. Eleven hun dred feet the blank walls drop sheer from the rim.

Below—A view of the Canyo through blackening storm-cloud that gives it the appearance of terrible, smoky Hell carved out b some divine madman.

Looking out from the walks of El Tovar, the Canyon's principal hotel.

Fig. 55. Excerpted page from *Arizona Highways*, 1930. Images such as these from a page of an early issue of the magazine show the most common location found in the imagery during this time: a view from the South Rim (author fieldwork verifies that these are views from Grand Canyon Village or along the South Rim/Hermit Road) looking across the canyon to the North Rim. State of Arizona, Arizona Memory Project, *Arizona Highways* 5, no. 6 (June 1930): 8.

Fig. 56. Cover of *Arizona Highways*, 1928. Colorado River road and bridge images of the Grand Canyon were common during the 1920s and 1930s. This 1928 cover photo of the northeast canyon near Marble Canyon was part of an issue that highlighted the recently completed Navajo Bridge. State of Arizona, Arizona Memory Project, *Arizona Highways* 4, no. 10 (October 1928).

favored prospering developments at the South Rim, centered on the twenty-acre railroad depot site. Through these early planning stages, the Santa Fe Railroad exerted an uneven influence on the Grand Canyon Village's layout through its investment in roads, trails, and structures to support the growing tourism economy. By pushing out most of the individual pioneers and their business interests and with little to no enforcement or guidance from the park's NPS managers, the Santa Fe Railroad plan had few antagonists. The railroad directed the "location, extent, and character of South Rim developments" (Anderson 2000, 19) toward rim-side commercial services and the areas back from the rim, including auxiliary maintenance and employee housing, still visible today.

By 1935 park use bounced back with a restored sense of economic security. Visitation that year was 206,018, up from 140,220 visitors the year before. As tourism boomed in the years following World War II, these upgrades to the park became vital to its success and ability to accommodate visitors (refer to appendix A).

Connecting the Canyon: Trails and Roads

Importantly for *Arizona Highways*, Grand Canyon National Park's local and regional road network expanded and became more consistent in the later 1920s and early 1930s. The system of informal dirt roads established by canyon entrepreneurs, miners, and cattlemen during the pre-park years served as reasonable pathways to get people, supplies, and water between Grand Canyon Village and southern towns and North Rim development along the Arizona Strip and southern Colorado Plateau. During changes of guard between the Grand Canyon National Game Preserve, Grand Canyon National Forest Preserve, and Grand Canyon National Monument, the U.S. Forest Service paid little attention to improving the road system of the park, leaving this task to canyon residents and railroad interests. Once the National Park Service assumed control in 1919, road building efforts were renewed. The National Park Service built, realigned, or improved several important tourist corridor roads in the canyon during the 1920s and 1930s, including several along the North Rim—North Approach Road, Point Sublime Road, North Entrance Road, Cape Royal Road, and Point Imperial spur—and a few along the southeastern rim—East Approach Road, East Rim Drive, South Approach Road, and West Rim Drive (Anderson 2000, 32). Many of these roads not only provided access to the canyon; they also served as regional connections across the expansive western distances of northern Arizona. *Arizona Highways* was there to eagerly document this expansion and improvement of the state's road system.

Space and Place in Magazine Imagery

Arizona Highways representations during the 1920s and early 1930s focused on the eastern regions of the canyon (fig. 57), primarily along the South Rim (69% of the imagery). A few locations along the North Rim and the northeast parts of the canyon also figured into this total. Vertical views of the canyon presented by *Arizona Highways* during this time included mostly rim locations (68%), although aerial views and midcanyon or trail corridors into and out of the canyon also appeared between the magazine's covers. The rim view of the canyon, popularized throughout canyon cultural history, starting with images created by Clarence Dutton and William Henry Holmes, then postcard manufacturers such as Detroit Publishing Company and Frasher Foto Cards, is once again repeated and confirmed as the dominant view of this vast landscape in the first ten years of *Arizona Highways* magazine representations.

Although the Colorado River appears in several scenic representations of the canyon from the rim looking into the canyon, none are taken at river level. The explanation for this may lie in the fact that there were few roads to the river level at this time, so *Arizona Highways*, a magazine charged with going where every motorist should go, found little appeal in off-road adventures. Although seemingly irrelevant at the time, the importance of what locations Arizona Highways profiled in its photographs and essays becomes more obvious in later years of the publication as the magazine went beyond paved surfaces. In the 1950s and onward, *Arizona Highways* photographers increasingly selected locations that were on dirt and back roads or even places without roads, such as the Colorado River for raft trips, Lake Mead for motorboat excursions, and the canyon's many trails for mule rides and hiking trips. Perhaps the photographers and magazine editors were adapting the publication to popular tastes that increasingly sought outdoor recreation beyond the road's end or maybe they were seeking new ways to promote tourism in Arizona.

As the story of the Grand Canyon's iconographic arc unfolds, it becomes apparent that the locations featured in visual representations of the canyon depended on where and what was defined as the Grand Canyon. As odd as

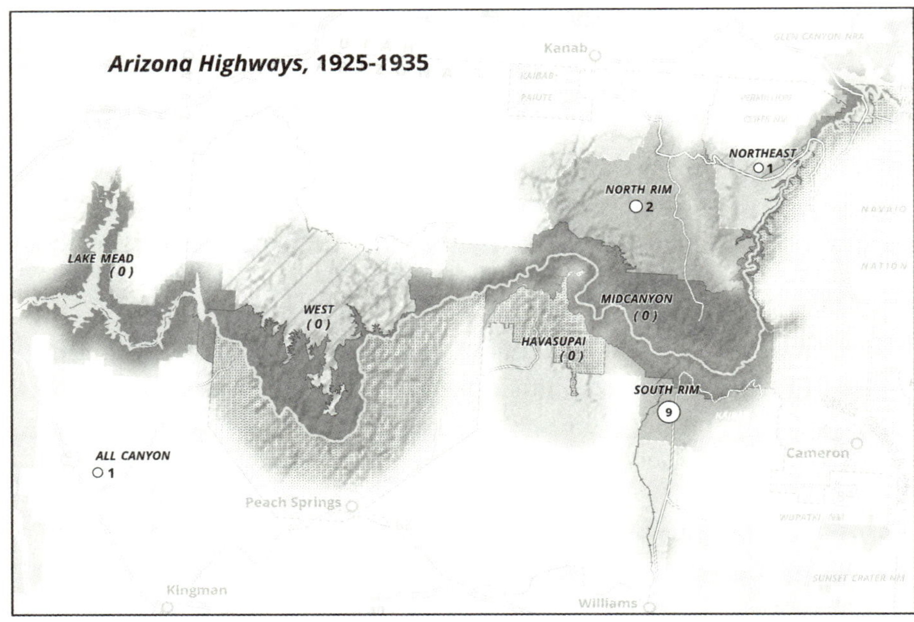

Fig. 57. Map of Grand Canyon photograph locations in *Arizona Highways*, 1925–35. Most images showed locations at the South Rim, with only a few images representing the North Rim and northeast views. Cartography by Robert M. Edsall. Design by Yolonda Youngs. Based on data from the National Park Service, U.S. Geological Society, ESRI, and author's content analysis results from archival research.

this suggestion may be at first, consider this: the declaration of a protected and reserved (not yet *pre*served) Grand Canyon brought about more than just a few lines on a map. A proclamation that sets aside a selected area of the Grand Canyon protected this space from certain uses, creating a boundary between public and private, triggering certain perceptions and expectations about what this place would look like, what activities you could do there, and what parts of this landscape were valued highly enough to be worthy of this special classification. This process involved a number of decisions, made by individuals and groups, predicated on the notion that the river and rim were sublime beauty and worthless for all economic ventures outside of tourism (Runte 1997).

In 1908, Grand Canyon National Monument was carved out of several other protected areas, notably the Grand Canyon National Forest created in 1893, the Grand Canyon Game Preserve created in 1906, and lands in the public domain that were unclaimed by white settlers during this era (Anderson 2000, x). Each of these land ownership and management changes reserved or withheld part of the Greater Grand Canyon Region from certain uses, a move that signaled a transition from private space to national public space. With the declaration of monument status for a section of the Grand Canyon, however, this area was moved to another level of protection. Selected locations and landforms of the canyon were privileged over others, namely rim-side developments and the central river corridor between the confluence of the Little Colorado River and Kanab Creek. The definition of the rim of the canyon served to guide mapping and surveying the boundaries of Grand Canyon National Monument. For example, in a 1908 map, the "RIM OF THE CANYON" is clearly marked all along the monument's boundaries, cutting close to Grand Canyon Village (marked as "GRAND CANYON" on the map) and Bright Angel Point and the few roads near that area (see figure 31). The monument protects and delineates a section of the canyon as a core area on the east side of the canyon. The west canyon is largely left out of this formula and, by extension, excluded from expectations about what and where the "real" Grand Canyon is located. In addition, Grand Canyon National Monument closely followed the rim of the canyon, protecting the central river corridor (called midcanyon region in this study) but just barely the emerging Grand Canyon Village and its smaller sibling tourist landscape emerging along the North Rim near Bright Angel Point.

The 1920s and 1930s must have been a busy time for park cartographers with numerous boundary changes, additions, and proposals to the park. This is especially clear if one compares the boundary of Grand Canyon National Monument with the three shifts in boundary status between 1919 and 1928 as well as several proposed additions to the border in 1930. *Arizona Highways* magazine went to press only seven years after the U.S. Congress created Grand Canyon National Park contained in a political and legal boundary that diminished the size of the protected area from its monument days. The Grand Canyon National Monument established in 1908 was 1,279 square miles, but the Grand Canyon National Park of 1919 reduced the size of this protected area to 958 square miles (Anderson 2000, 56), eliminating the western section of the monument from the national park site.

During these earliest days of park boundary making, the Grand Canyon area was a mixed-use and bounded space. The two biggest boundary changes were to the west with the Havasupai Reservation and the north with the Little Park Extension. The Havasupai Reservation was an enclave of the park, and the Grand Canyon Game Preserve coexisted adjacent to this land, as well as the national forest land to the north, south, and east of the park. Indeed, the Havasupai peoples did not gain territory out of the national park service boundaries until the 1975 park expansion.

In 1927 the aptly named Little Park Extension expanded the national park boundary to the north, adding a section of the North Rim that included Walhalla Plateau west to Powell Plateau. In 1930 two park extensions were proposed: The South Park Extension would have added 272 square miles of buffer from Desert View as far as Havasu Canyon to the west. The proposed North Park Extension would have enclosed 348 square miles of additional parklands, nudging the boundary of the park northward to South Canyon (on the east) and Kanab Creek (on the west). In 1932 a separate Grand Canyon National Monument was established west of the national park, enclosing the rim and river corridor from the western park boundary eastward to include Toroweap Valley.

These boundary shifts and proposals to Grand Canyon National Park paired with the expanding road network in and around the park may have influenced the decisions of *Arizona Highways* editors to portray these areas in their magazine. Peter Ensenberger, director of photography for *Arizona Highways*, confirms this assertion:

> After looking at the map, I believe it had mostly to do with the building of roads in those areas. From '25–'55, there were a lot fewer roads around the Canyon than we have today. Back in the day when camera equipment was bulky and heavy, photographers mostly went as far as their vehicles would take them (and their heavy equipment) and that's where they set up to photograph. I suppose horse packers could take them a bit further on the existing trails, but not until equipment improved, becoming smaller and lighter, did photographers venture farther on foot with their gear on their backs. Mobility in the wilderness led to the discovery of new photographic vistas. (Ensenberger May 6, 2009, email correspondence)

Looking at a Grand Canyon National Park map from 1926, one gets a sense of what Ensenberger understood about the formula of camera equipment weight measured against existing roads connecting the canyon to surrounding communities and highways (fig. 58). Extending his argument to the built

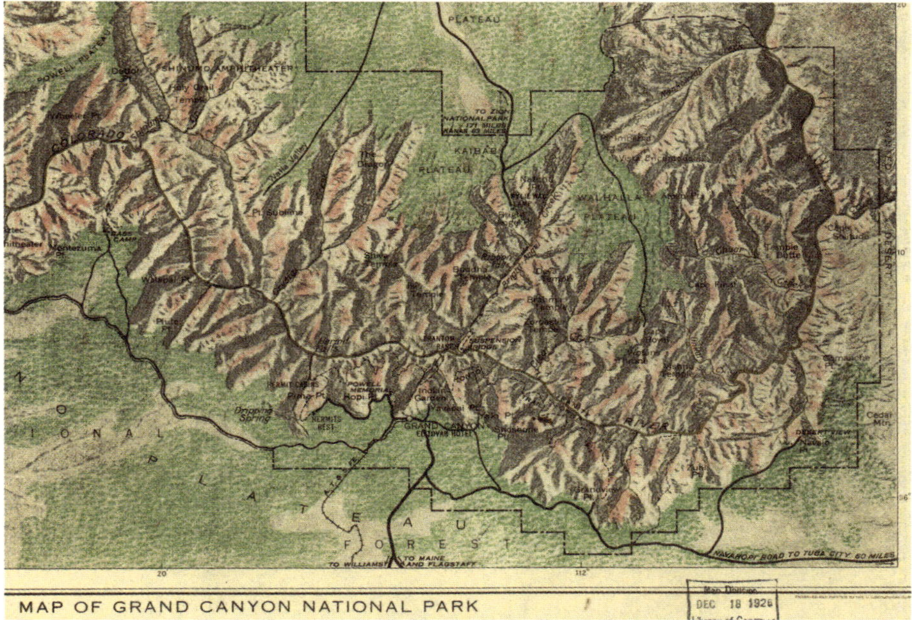

Fig. 58. Detail of 1926 Grand Canyon National Park map. Note the three main arteries of highways that by 1926 connected Grand Canyon's southeast rim and Grand Canyon Village to nearby communities. One main road connects Grand Canyon Village (*lower center*) with the towns of Williams and Flagstaff to the south, while a second spur road connects the village to points east via the "Navahopi Road to Tuba City 60 Miles." A branch of this road leads to Desert View and Navajo Point on the south. Looking west from Grand Canyon Village, a short road terminates at Hermits Rest, while a longer road continues west to Bass Camp and beyond to the Havasupai Indian Reservation. On the North Rim one main road connects the nascent tourism development of the Wylie Way tent camp with the town of Kanab, Utah, 83 miles to the north and Zion National Park 171 miles away. The Walla Valley road branches from this main North Rim route to take visitors to Point Sublime, while a second branch road leads to Cape Royal. Library of Congress, "Map of Grand Canyon National Park," 1925, Call # G4332.G7/ 1926.U5 TIL.

transportation landscape of the 1950s Grand Canyon National Park, the National Park Service made cartographic arguments for the ease of travel and connections at both the North Rim and South Rim tourist villages (fig. 59).

The North Rim, the South Rim, and the northeast area—all featured in *Arizona Highways* representations between 1925 and 1935—also served as the loci of park expansion and proposed boundary changes during this time. By focusing on these areas, *Arizona Highways* editors and photogra-

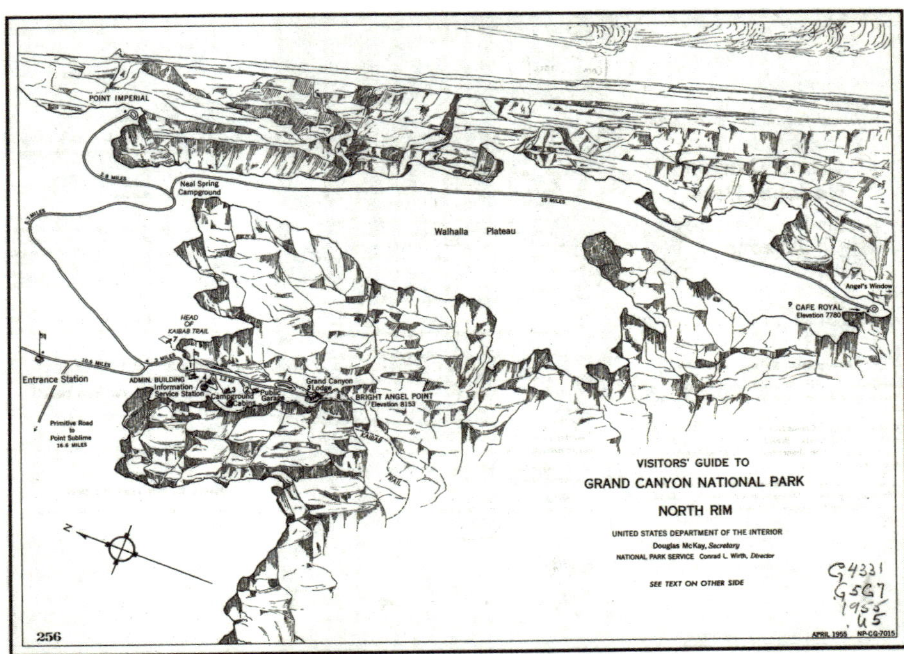

Fig. 59. *Visitors Guide to Grand Canyon National Park, North Rim* (*map*), 1955. Look closely at this map to see the expanding network of roads connecting the North Rim village. Library of Congress, "Visitor's Guide to Grand Canyon National Park, North Rim," 1955, Call #G4332. G7 1955.U5 TIL.

phers presented readers with images of some of the most recent changes to Grand Canyon National Park, showing them an area that was becoming more hospitable to automobile tourists through the addition and expansion of good roads, opening the Grand Canyon to a broader audience. In the process, decisions were made about what parts of the Grand Canyon would be represented, shaping a popular knowledge of what the Grand Canyon looked like, including vast open spaces, rocky cliffs, plunging views into the canyon, broken up by long stretches of newly graded roadway.

Part 3 Framing the View

If the park itself has at times been conceived as an artform, its simulacra ride the information superhighway in search of more lucrative havens. Hyperreality . . . is when constructs become place.

—Lucy Lippard, *On the Beaten Track*

6 Editing Nature

> The new media are not bridges between man and nature; they are nature.
>
> —Marshall McLuhan, *Essential McLuhan*

Writers with the Work Projects Administration (WPA) crafted a dramatic description of the Grand Canyon's first impression for readers of the 1940 *Arizona: A State Guide*. "The dark pines of the Kaibab National Forest conceal the Grand Canyon of the Colorado till its very rim is reached. There, spread out for seemingly endless miles, is an ocean of color." They continued that from "misty blue depths rise gigantic islands of crimson sandstone. Their undulating band of reds and purples grow softer in color and outline toward the horizon where a single firm stroke seems to separate the rosy depths from the sky above. Its immensity is awful; the boldness of its contours overwhelming; its immobility terrifying" (472). The writers employed by the WPA were part of New Deal federal emergency relief programs that employed millions of Americans during the Great Depression. While the country rose out of the economic downturn of the 1930s, visitation to the Grand Canyon increased. The WPA description pairs well with the Curt Teich Company postcards from this era that presented bold, colorful images of the Grand Canyon (fig. 60). The match between words and images, although in the different mediums of books, postcards, tourist brochures, and other sources of information acted in unison, emphasizing the canyon's attractions as bright colors, sublime beauty, and—new in this era—its status as a confirmed tourist destination.

The era from 1936 to 1955 traces the escalating iconographic arc of Grand Canyon imagery and reveals transformations underway in the canyon's social, economic, and cultural landscapes. Media manufacturers, creators, and distributors slowly forged a symbiotic relationship with canyon promoters, corporations, and federal agents who carved a new spatial ordering of tourist experiences at the canyon through a growing network of roads, trails, and visitor service areas. By 1936 as the Detroit Publishing Company faded,

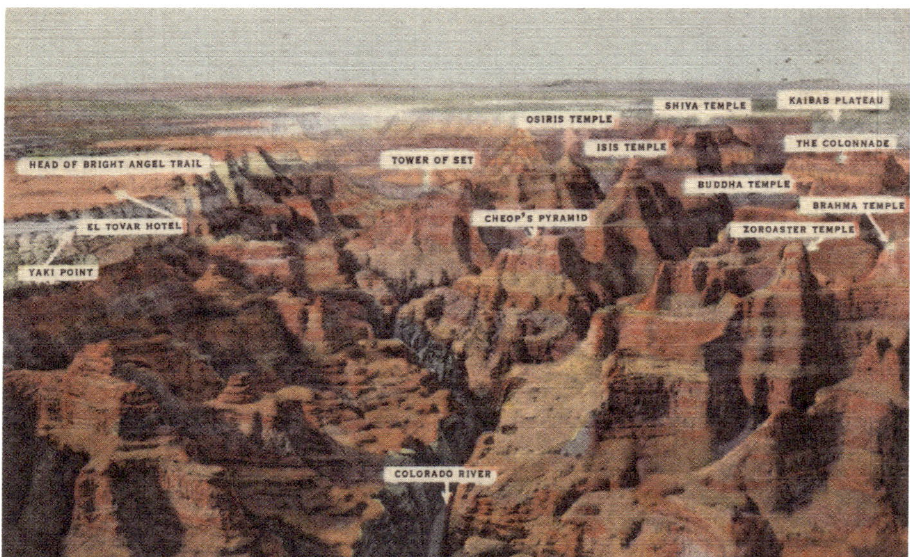

Fig. 60. The Grand Canyon, annotated. Postcard views such as this one promoted the canyon as a colorful and easily recognized feature, annotated with place-names. Curt Teich Company, "Air View of the Grand Canyon, Arizona," CTC, 1938. Author's collection.

the Curt Teich Company took its place as the prime postcard manufacturer with the Fred Harvey Company and other rim-side business contracts. Through these promotional efforts and a growing visual postcard catalog, the Grand Canyon became a scenic commodity and a much-anticipated tourist experience.

Not all locations in the Grand Canyon were used with equal force to make these arguments about human relationships with nature. Increasingly, throughout this era, the Colorado River became an important and potent symbol of nature in America. Along the way, the Grand Canyon firmly shifted from John Wesley Powell's turn-of-the-century "Great Unknown" to a popular tourist destination laced with roads, trails, hotels, restaurants, and gift shops. Looking closely at postcard representations of the canyon's environment from this era, what seems like a large leap—from wilderness on the edge of mainstream American culture and society to a popular and well-known tourism attraction—becomes more legible.

The postcard representations of the canyon in this era obscure massive changes taking place in the environmental, social, and cultural landscape of the Grand Canyon. The Greater Grand Canyon Region, as reflected by the locations of the postcard imagery, focus on a centralized corridor along the South Rim, North Rim, and the inner canyon between these two areas—paralleling the spatial extent of development and planning by NPS civilian contractors, concessionaires, and the Civilian Conservation Corps. Four themes weave throughout the Curt Teich Company and Frasher Foto Postcard Company postcard imagery from this era: 1) a systematic and standardized transformation of the canyon's environment into a scenic commodity; 2) extensive, planned administrative, concessioner, utility, and residential construction projects resulting in a new spatial organization at the Grand Canyon focused on a central corridor of tourism development; 3)shifting social landscape of the class, race, and ethnicity of the canyon's park workers and visitors; and 4) fluctuating NPS environmental management policies that reflected national debates and regional concerns about wildlife management, water supply and distribution, vegetation change, and tourism impacts on the environment.

Dominant Images and Locations

Postcards manufactured by Curt Teich from 1936 to 1955 and Frasher Foto postcards from 1936 to 1937 reveal differences in the themes and postcard scene locations that each manufacturer emphasized in their catalogs (see appendix C). Both manufacturers focused on several themes that formed a frequently repeated set of visual symbols. Those symbols equated certain scenes and views with a growing iconography of the Grand Canyon in popular media.

Following a trend noted in Detroit Publishing Company postcards from 1900 to 1909, the Curt Teich postcards from 1936 to 1955 emphasized scenic views of the canyon followed by views that depicted an abundance of green vegetation. However, in other subject categories, Curt Teich diverged from its predecessor. After scenery, the list of prominent subjects featured in the CTC postcards includes building exteriors, white people, the Colorado River, trails, American Indians, mules with riders, building interiors, roads and bridges, children, miscellaneous, scenery with brown vegetation, automobiles, wildlife and animals, and water (lakes and streams but no waterfalls). Mules and horses are the least common subjects of the CTC postcards from this era.

The Frasher Foto postcards showed a different pattern of subjects and themes from the CTC postcards. Although this was a smaller set of images than the CTC set, the emphasis in subject matter still creates a pattern of preferences. Scenery played a major role in the Frasher representations with canyon vistas being the most common subject followed closely by scenic views emphasizing vegetation. Well behind these counts are representations of building exteriors and the Colorado River. Finally, images of roads and bridges, scenic views featuring sparse vegetation, wild animals, automobiles, and trails appeared throughout this set.

Comparing Curt Teich and Frasher postcards side by side reveals a pattern of subject preferences between the two manufacturers despite the large variation in total number of sample postcards for this study. Overall, the Curt Teich postcards depicted a wider range of subjects than the Frasher postcards. Both sets featured scenery as the most common subject with scenic views topping the counts. Buildings are the next most common subject for both manufacturers, although Curt Teich includes interiors whereas Frasher does not. Curt Teich included white people in some of its postcards; Frasher cards were bereft of people. Both Curt Teich and Frasher included the Colorado River as a common subject. Other less common subjects featured in both sets include roads and bridges, wild animals, automobiles, and trails. The Curt Teich postcards featured subjects that were entirely absent from the Frasher set, including American Indians, mules with riders, building interiors, children, lakes and streams, and mules and horses.

Curt Teich and Frasher postcards also represented a wide and not necessarily overlapping geographical range of places. In terms of horizontal locations, the Curt Teich postcards featured South Rim locations in a majority of its cards (fig. 61). The next most common horizontal locations featured were in the midcanyon (between rim and river) locations, followed by unknown locations, then North Rim, and finally postcards depicting a montage of canyon scenes. Frasher postcards also prominently featured South Rim locations with North Rim and unknown locations less frequently. The Frasher postcards did not feature midcanyon, aerial, river, or multiple-view locations in this set (fig. 62).

The Grand Canyon became a rim-side attraction, at least in visual terms, during this period. With a marked shift from the previous Detroit trends in postcard imagery, that frequently depicted midcanyon scenes such as mule riders along inner canyon trails, CTC postcards favored rim or river (but not midcanyon) vertical locations far more than its predecessor. Curt Teich represented a greater range of locations than Frasher postcards. The CTC

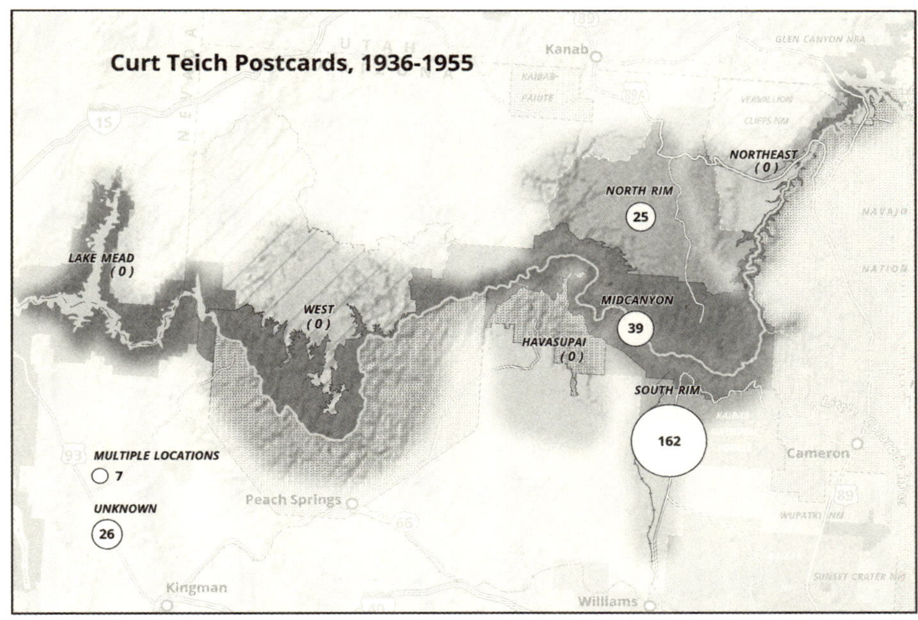

Fig. 61. Map of Curt Teich Company postcards' horizontal locations, 1936–55. The numbers in the circles represent the number of postcards counted in the set for that area of the canyon. For example, twenty-five CTC postcards were located in the North Rim area in the 1936 to 1955 set. Cartography by Robert M. Edsall. Based on data from the U.S. Geological Survey, National Park Service, and author's content analysis results from archival research.

postcards from this era emphasized rim-side locations in a majority of its cards, with Colorado River views the next most common vertical location (see appendix B for horizontal and vertical category descriptions). Other vertical categories included postcards that did not show any view of the canyon, such as scenes that were taken in interior locations without windows. Finally, to a much lesser extent, vertical locations along the trails leading into and out of the canyon—the midcanyon or walls of the chasm—were depicted in a few postcards. Aerial views and postcards featuring multiple locations were also included in this set. Frasher postcards shared Curt Teich's preferences for rim-side locations and a few postcards that show no view or locations well away from the canyon's distinct verticality (e.g., along the Arizona Strip or at the Navajo Reservation).

In this transition between postcard eras, a note should be made about the Fred Harvey Company's increasingly influential force in Grand Canyon

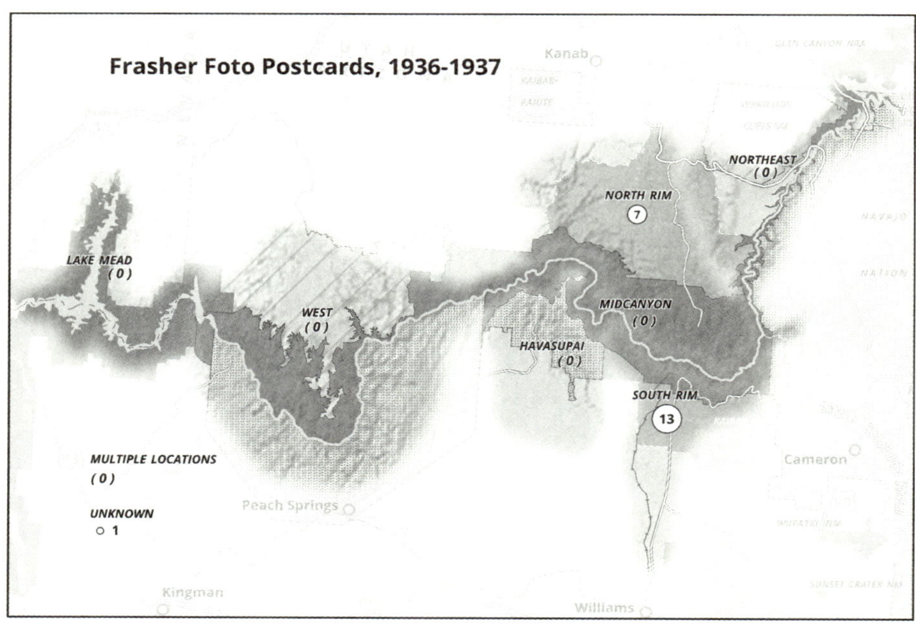

Fig. 62. Map of Frasher Foto postcards' horizontal locations, 1936–37. Cartography by Robert M. Edsall. Based on data from the U.S. Geological Survey, National Park Service, and author's content analysis results from archival research.

postcard publishing and distribution. Founded in 1876 as a restaurant in a railroad depot in Topeka, Kansas, the Fred Harvey Company grew into a sprawling and powerful national chain of restaurants and shops tied to the railroad corridors and depot sites of its business partner, the Atchison, Topeka & Santa Fe Railroad. From 1901 until the the Detroit Publishing Company folded in 1936, DPC manufactured postcards for the Fred Harvey Company, which acted as the publisher and distributor of the cards. Consumers of the postcards may be confused about this arrangement, however, since some postcards manufactured by Detroit Publishing Company carry the distinctive DPC stamp and a Fred Harvey credit line while others only credit the Fred Harvey Company. This arrangement (and potential confusion) continued beyond the Detroit Publishing years as CTC manufactured postcards for the Fred Harvey Company through the 1950s. Frasher Foto Postcard Company did not have a relationship with FHC, instead Frasher only manufactured his and his photographer's images into postcards. In addition, FHC operated in a relatively narrow band of Grand Canyon territory—primarily along the South Rim at Grand Canyon Village and at a few smaller visitor services sites at the bottom of the canyon, connected by foot and mule trails to the South Rim. So Curt Teich Company's primary customer at the Grand Canyon—Fred Harvey Company—maintained a vested interest in promoting their hotels, restaurants, and activities at the South Rim through postcards of these locations.

Framing an Inexhaustible Scenic Commodity

Postcard manufacturers developed a set of visual standards that codified the Grand Canyon's environment into an easily recognized and profitable tourist commodity. Tremendous changes in the canyon's cultural landscape and tourism development went hand in hand with this process, resulting in NPS and concessionaire management of the Grand Canyon as "an inexhaustible scenic commodity" (Anderson 2000, 40). Looking closely at CTC and FFPC postcards and their manufacturing provides more details about how this process unfolded.

For Curt Teich Company, this system of scenic commodification relied upon an editing process that allowed the postcard manufacturer to adjust and alter images, including their colors. CTC framed the Grand Canyon through a fixed set of color bands representing the canyon's geologic strata as red, orange, and brown with emerald green vegetation, and a sapphire blue Colorado River. The sky was also a major point of active image editing. A majority of the postcards present the view from the rim, looking across the canyon to a sunny or at least clear blue-sky day with a few billowing clouds. Although some of these patterns of representation mimic or follow Detroit Publishing Company's path, in this era we Curt Teich and Frasher Foto changing this by systematically standardizing certain scenes of the canyon, then replicating them over and over. We can access this process through the postcard manufacturers' records, especially those of CTC.

Influenced by contemporary art movements, postcard manufacturers, introduced new styles for depicting the Grand Canyon. Curt Teich postcards from the 1930s mirrored an art deco aesthetic in its landscapes, simplifying and reducing color and emphasizing geometric shapes. All of the care taken in earlier eras to depict a detailed view of the canyon's stratigraphy is gone. Canyon walls etched in precise pen strokes by William Henry Holmes were blurred and merged together in the 1930s as a shift to a new artistic ideal came to light. While postcard creators drew on some of the representational practices from preceding eras, they also diverged from this path and forged a new standard, one that allowed more liberties with the canyon's physical depiction.

Curt Teich manufactured postcards that tethered the idea of the Grand Canyon to its physical reality by combining images of the canyon with superimposed titles and names for the scenery it depicted. The distinctive white border allowed the space for text to accompany the image on the front of the card. Many of the postcards could now carry a short title or caption under the image describing the location or scene, such as "North from Pima Point." Some cards, especially in the 1940s and 1950s, inscribed the title "Grand Canyon" over a an expansive scenic view from the south or North Rim. This style of depicting the Grand Canyon with named viewpoints that could be recalled, collected, and consumed by the armchair traveler affirms how the CTC postcards anchored place to memory.

A prominent example of labeling the landscape is evident in a 1938 postcard that shows an aerial view of the canyon looking west (see figure 60). In the "Air View of Grand Canyon," the scenic landscape of the canyon is vertically exaggerated so the canyon's buttes and plateaus appear to be mountains and spires rather than the flat-topped rim and plateaus. The coloring of the canyon is decidedly red, tan, and orange; absent from the representation are clusters of green vegetation so common in other contemporary views of the canyon from this postcard manufacturer. The canyon scenery is tagged with labels and arrows locating and naming selected features, including high points such as the Tower of Set as well as the Bright Angel Trail, El Tovar Hotel, Yaki Point, and the Colorado River. In this manner, the postcard viewer's experience of the landscape is heightened, while the landscape becomes a commodity with named points of interest that can be collected, marked, and claimed as part of the touristic experience at the canyon.

Curt Teich also excelled at creating postcards that featured the names of towns or other notable places with colorful, large letters spelling out the name of the location. Indeed, these postcards became iconic, stylized images for CTC as a company. A "Greetings from Grand Canyon, Ariz." postcard is an ideal example of this style (fig. 63). Inside each letter of the word "Grand Canyon," there is a slice of the canyon in miniature view. The *G* reveals a view of Lookout Studio, the first *N* of Canyon shows Desert View Watchtower, and the other letters show various scenes of canyon ledges and scenic views. This style of postcard offered the added bonus of featuring multiple sites

Fig. 63. A Curt Teich Company Grand Canyon postcard showing multiple locations. This postcard was highly popular in CTC's catalog, reprinted multiple times between 1938 to at least 1948. Curt Teich Postcard, "Untitled," 1938. Author's collection.

through a pastiche of scenes. The Fred Harvey Company and the Santa Fe Railroad ensured this worked to their advantage by mixing images of their buildings with images of the canyon's environment.

The process of editing in CTC imagery can be traced through the company's detailed records. Curt Teich Company commercial artists retouched postcards to create new images from the same base photo for next year's printing. Color was key. CTC updated and reprinted high selling postcard as new products each year by changing their subject matter and colors. As an example of this color editing we can look at a black-and-white photograph that served as the base for the postcard titled "Sheer Wall on Desert View Drive, Grand Canyon National Park, Arizona." It reveals the tell-tale signs of the retouching process starting with a handwritten note of "original photo" at the bottom (fig. 64).

A photo ticket from March 10, 1937, from Curt Teich and Company reveals additional clues to this color editing process (fig. 65). The ticket outlines the specific requests of the customer including a color description section that stipulates "CARD 4A357 SHOWS TOO MUCH GREEN AND YELLOW. THERE SHOULD BE MORE RED SHOWN." CTC imagery prescribed a specific color

Fig. 64. Creating a 1937 canyon view. This is the original photo that accompanied the work order for the postcard *Sheer Wall on Desert View Drive, Grand Canyon National Park, Arizona*. The back of the photo shows several handwritten notes, including "From Desert View Road 1932" and the directive to recolor the image to emphasize less green and yellow to more red. The documentation reveals the details of reusing older photos for newer products, as is the case with this 1932 photo edited and republished in 1937. Newberry Library, Curt Teich Postcard Archives, production #4A-357.

palette for the Grand Canyon and reinforced this even when the canyon itself provided a counternarrative of green and yellow. At the bottom right of the card, a circle drawn around the "yes" "handcol[ored] proof" confirms the careful work required of CTC artists to recast the postcard colors by hand. The process of transforming this request into a new postcard product while simultaneously recasting the colors and look of the Grand Canyon involved the labor of hundreds of postcard artists and printers at the CTC factory and the network of sales crew, photographers, and marketers that linked CTC and, in the case of the Grand Canyon, the Fred Harvey Company.

This photo ticket was a standard form that directed and documented the work of CTC's extensive postcard factory. The top of the ticket notes CTC's customer, in this case the Fred Harvey Company. The number at the upper right of the form is the postcard manufacturing number. This is a clever numbering system specific to CTC that the company developed to quickly

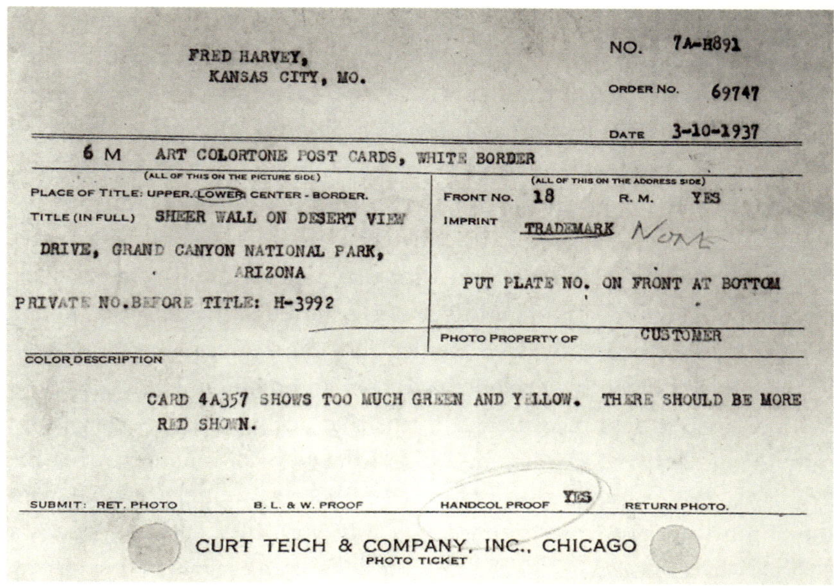
FRED HARVEY,
KANSAS CITY, MO.

NO. 7A-H891

ORDER NO. 69747

DATE 3-10-1937

6 M ART COLORTONE POST CARDS, WHITE BORDER

(ALL OF THIS ON THE PICTURE SIDE)

PLACE OF TITLE: UPPER. LOWER. CENTER - BORDER.

TITLE (IN FULL) SHEER WALL ON DESERT VIEW DRIVE, GRAND CANYON NATIONAL PARK, ARIZONA

PRIVATE NO. BEFORE TITLE: H-3992

(ALL OF THIS ON THE ADDRESS SIDE)

FRONT NO. 18 R. M. YES

IMPRINT ~~TRADEMARK~~ None

PUT PLATE NO. ON FRONT AT BOTTOM

PHOTO PROPERTY OF CUSTOMER

COLOR DESCRIPTION

CARD 4A357 SHOWS TOO MUCH GREEN AND YELLOW. THERE SHOULD BE MORE RED SHOWN.

SUBMIT: RET. PHOTO B. L. & W. PROOF HANDCOL PROOF YES RETURN PHOTO.

CURT TEICH & COMPANY, INC., CHICAGO
PHOTO TICKET

Fig. 65. Anatomy of postcard color editing. Photo ticket from March 10, 1937, for "Sheer Wall on Desert View Drive, Grand Canyon National Park, Arizona." Newberry Library, Curt Teich Postcard Archives, production #4A-357.

identify elements of the postcard. It is a code that unlocks many details about CTC postcards and can be found on most CTC cards. The system of letters and numbers evolved and changed over time as CTC developed new printing processes and different card stock. A letter designates the decade (A=1930s, B=1940s, C=1950s, D=1960s, and E=1970s). The number before the letter indicates the year within that decade. The numbering system is highly detailed and extensive covering CTC production from 1900 to the 1970s. For example, in 1931 CTC developed a new printing process that it called C.T. Art Colortone and designated this method with an "H." This process transformed a black-and white photo into a linen-finish paper stock postcard through a five-color printing process. In the 1940s, CTC developed a chrome postcard printing process called Curteichcolor, designated with a "K." With this knowledge in hand, we can glance at this photo ticket and decipher that 7A-H891 was printed using the C.T. Art Colortone method on a linen stock postcard in 1937 (Lake County Discovery Museum n.d.).

CTC imagery excelled at using a select and often repeated set of visual representations of the Grand Canyon's environment as a cue card—a shorthand reminder—to postcard viewers that the scene depicted on the card takes place at the Grand Canyon. In this era, CTC used the image of the canyon's inner depths, stratigraphy of the rock layers, and rim-side views to create a brand name for the canyon as a scenic commodity. One glance at even a small image of the canyon—always depicted in brilliant red, orange, and tan shades and almost always from a rim-side viewpoint—confirmed the authenticity of the image as Grand Canyon based. The power of these images was reinforced through repetition with each postcard reprinting and the consistent but limited geographic locations featured in the images. Looking closely at CTC records provides a detailed view of how this process unfolded.

Curt Teich diligently developed a system and maintained detailed and meticulous business records and forms that accounted for every hour, minute, and activity of work involved in the labor of manufacturing his postcards. For example, a 1937 postcard depicting an interior scene from the South Rim, *A Corner in the Lounge, Bright Angel Lodge*, includes a curious view out the window (fig. 66). The view is an exaggerated, synthetic representation of the canyon created as a pastiche of real canyon scenery displaced from its actual location in the canyon and delicately inserted into the window at an ideal viewing angle. During field reconnaissance to canyon, I compared the postcard window view with that of the actual Bright Angel Lodge window in that same room (now converted to a small Fred Harvey Company museum) and combined this work with some archival sleuthing through the Curt Teich Company postcard archives. My findings: no adjustment of viewing angles or positions will produce a view of the canyon similar to the one seen through that postcard window. The dramatic canyon buttes and ridgelines of the postcard window view are enhanced, magnified, and amplified sections of the canyon lifted from other South Rim viewing locations (Youngs 2012). But for Curt Teich Company postcards in the 1930s, this hardly matters. The window view does not need to be accurate. Instead is functions as a visual cue card for the viewer that confirms the postcard's authentic Grand Canyon location. Visual imagery and marketing of the canyons' scenic qualities in the early twentieth century had already confirmed the vastness, magnificence, and beauty of the Grand Canyon. By the 1930s, these images served a different purpose, in this case to add authenticity and value to the Fred Harvey Company's lodges and businesses at the canyon. The postcard confirms that this cabin is extraordinary. This scene is spectacular. It is the Grand Canyon.

The records of production and the raw imagery for the postcard *A Corner in the Lounge, Bright Angel Lodge* provides a fuller view of the technical process and business contracts behind CTC postcard manufacturing (fig. 67). A photo ticket and work schedule accompanied each photograph and postcard through the production process. The 1937 estimate and work schedule form for the Bright Angel Lodge image records four hours of "retouching," one and half hours of "hand color proof," and the eleven hours in the "artist dept" as well as time with "blueprint stripping and opaquing." The photo ticket "color description" section directs the CTC artists to add a new image to the window frame: "Fake Canyon View In Window As Per Magazine Illustrations Attached." Moving along in the process, a black-and-white photograph with a handwritten "retouched photo" note reveals a raw image in the midst of editing per the photo ticket instructions (fig. 68). A closer look at the window of the log cabin in this photograph shows an odd white border between the canyon view and the window frame. That border is from a magazine image that was the source material for this reimagining of the canyon's environment.

A December 1936 issue of *The Hotel Monthly* attached to the work order provided the layout of the scene replicated in the postcard. The caption for the magazine image of the "Bright Angel Lodge" described the "two huge view windows to either side of the fireplace. These windows are framed by heavy picture frames and give the appearance of two great paintings of the Grand Canyon—except that no painter could ever render the subtly changing marvel of color and form as do these two framed visions." With the work order in place, the production process kicked in. A postcard artist cut the canyon image depicting a more favorable angle and up-close view of the canyon ridges from its original context in the magazine, then pasted that image into the window to replace the more distant view of the South Rim that is the realistic view from that window. Several hours of meticulous work from CTC production artists smoothed over the white border edges of the window frame, added color, and matched the fireplace stones with the canyon view out the window. The scene comes to life for the 1937 version of this postcard scene, reprinted several times over the years.

Frasher Foto Postcard Company imagery provides a striking contrast to the Curt Teich Company's strategies when it comes to representing the Grand Canyon as a scenic commodity. FFPC postcards were black-and-white photographs captured by Frasher or his photographers in the field, then

Fig. 66. *A Corner in the Lounge, Bright Angel Lodge*, Curt Teich Company postcard, 1937. Author's collection.

FRED HARVEY,
KANSAS CITY, MO.

NO. 7A-H895
ORDER NO. 69747
DATE 3-17-1937

6 M ART COLORTONE POST CARDS, WHITE BORDER

(ALL OF THIS ON THE PICTURE SIDE)
PLACE OF TITLE: UPPER, LOWER, CENTER - BORDER.
TITLE (IN FULL) A CORNER IN THE LOUNGE, BRIGHT ANGEL LODGE, GRAND CANYON NATIONAL PARK, ARIZONA
PRIVATE NO. BEFORE TITLE: H-4459

(ALL OF THIS ON THE ADDRESS SIDE)
FRONT NO. 18 R. M. YES
IMPRINT TRADEMARK
PUT PLATE NO. ON FRONT AT BOTTOM
PHOTO PROPERTY OF CUSTOMER

COLOR DESCRIPTION
FAKE CANYON VIEW IN WINDOW AS PER MAGAZINE ILLUSTRATIONS ATTACHED.

SUBMIT: RET. PHOTO B. L. & W. PROOF HANDCOL PROOF YES RETURN PHOTO.

CURT TEICH & COMPANY, INC., CHICAGO
PHOTO TICKET

Executive OK of Estimate
By
Date MAR 18 1937

ESTIMATE
AND WORK SCHEDULE

Cost Dept. Checked
By
Date MAR 19 1937

OPERATION	EST. TIME		DATE ENTERED DEPT.	DATE COMPLETED
COMPOSING, TYPE SET UP				
SKETCH				
RETOUCHING	6	4	3-19	3-19
PHOTO-LITHO				
BLUEPRINT STRIPPING, OPAQUING	65		3-20	3-20
ENGRAVING				
HAND COLOR PROOF	163	1½		3-23
ARTIST DEPT.	34	11	4-9-37	4-12-37 F.W.

DATE BLUEPRINT OK'D
By
DATE HAND COLOR PROOF OK'D
By
DATE Filed JUL 22 1937
By
DATE Photo Returned to Customer

Fig. 67. Photo ticket and estimate and work schedule forms for *A Corner in the Lounge, Bright Angel Lodge*, postcard, 1937. Newberry Library, Curt Teich Postcard Archives, production #H-4499.

Fig. 68. Retouched photo at Bright Angel Lodge, 1937. Newberry Library, Curt Teich Postcard Archives, production #H-4499.

manufactured and printed in postcard format. Their visual appeal draws on the clear, high-quality images and artistic framing of subject matter. FFPC postcards offer stark minimalism compared to CTC's bold colors and linen stock cards, but therein lies a great deal of their attraction. Instead of a factory of artists editing and colorizing his images, Frasher embraced the photographer's toolkit of framing his subject matter, choosing locations accessible along the Greater Grand Canyon Region's expanding road network, and capturing scenes at prime daylight hours with optimal lighting. For example, compare CTC's postcard of Bright Angel Lodge (see fig. 68) with FFPC's *Log Cabins of Grand Canyon Lodge, North Rim Grand Canyon, Arizona* (fig. 69). The Frasher Foto postcard features the cabin exterior as the centerpiece of the image, with tall pine trees flanking the building and a well-manicured lawn with a clearly defined pathway in front. Frasher's view is the inverse of the CTC Bright Angel Lodge scene; there are no people, no cozy fireplace, and no scenic view of the Grand Canyon. Instead, Frasher framed the scene to emphasize the building's exterior. The image focused on the entire extent of this long log building and placed the stone chimney and inviting entrance front and center. The lighting provides excellent definition

Fig. 69. *Log Cabins of Grand Canyon Lodge*, North Rim, 1936. Courtesy Frasher Fotos Collection/HJG and Pomona Public Library, Pomona, California. Frasher Foto Postcard Collection, index #B3928. Title: "Log Cabins of Grand Canyon Lodge, North Rim of Grand Canyon, Arizona."

to the chimney's detailed stonework and the log walls of the structure, but the upper image is overexposed, leaving the treetops fading from view. In this FFPC photo, the canyon's scenic attraction is its hospitality, a rustic retreat set amid a pine grove.

The contrast between FFPC and CTC's visual strategies for framing and commodifying nature at the Grand Canyon is particularly evident in the scenic viewpoint postcards. For example, compare two postcards depicting the same viewpoint—Mojave Point on the South Rim—and manufactured within a year of each other (fig. 70). FFPC's extended descriptive title—*Grand Canyon from Mojave Point, Desert View Showing the Colorado River, Grand Canyon Nat'l Park, Arizona* (1936)—lays claim to the authenticity of the postcard's location, captured at the viewpoint along the west rim drive (now known as Hermit's Road). Framing is key here. FFPC's image provides an expansive view, using the contorts of the canyon to frame the image. The canyon's shaded South Rim darkens the right border of the image in contrast to the left side, which is devoted to the lighter grays of the canyon's plateaus, mesas, and buttes. Mohave Point is one of the few South Rim locations where the Colorado River is visible, including a series of rapids: Salt Creek, Granite, and Hermit. Frasher uses the river's course to his advantage to divide the image in half and draw the viewer's gaze toward the center of the scene. Curt Teich Company's printing of *The Colorado River from Mohave Point* (1937) captures the same view but crops the frame tightly to focus on the bend in the Colorado River and the vertical cliffs just visible in the center of the image. CTC leans heavily on the use of color to amplify the scene through their formulaic applications of brilliant red, orange, and tan shades to represent the canyon's walls and interior. The Colorado River is also a centerpiece, but it captures the viewer's eye by its color—a brilliant pale blue in a sea of electric orange and red—instead of its central position in the image. Note that CTC is carrying on Detroit Publishing Company's visual strategies of representing the Colorado River. Both postcard manufacturers chose to recolor the silt-laden, hazel colored Colorado River of the pre-dam decades into a blue stream as a color for water that would be attractive to East Coast tourists accustomed to the coastal and lakeside retreats more than the high desert of Arizona. Finally, we can see the artist's touch in the sky and canyon rim. Comparing the top portion of each postcard, FFPC's image presents a cloudless gray sky that provides a clear dividing line between the canyon's rim and the distant view beyond. CTC's image also uses the canyon rim as a dividing line in the postcard scene but choses to fill in the narrow band at the top of the image with a cyan blue sky and puffs of clouds rising in the distance.

Both postcards present attractive scenes that build on the Grand Canyon's iconographic arc while adding new strategies to commodify the canyon's scenery. To borrow a phrase from the media and culture theorist Arthur Asa Berger's work on semiotics, these postcards manufacture a desire to see the Grand Canyon from scenic viewpoints (2008). They systematically organize the canyon's geography and orient viewers with named scenic rim viewpoints, create a series of images that provide collectible moments and objects (postcards), and build a catalog of visual representations of the canyon from the same limited set of locations easily reached by roads and trails. FFPC and CTC may diverge on the strategies they employ to represent the canyon's environment, but both companies competed for their viewer's attention by embracing new technical elements (such as CTC's frequent new printing processes and advances in color applications).

Fig. 70. Two views of the Grand Canyon from Mojave Point, Hermit Road, South Rim. A 1936 Frasher Foto postcard representing Mojave Point from the South Rim of the Grand Canyon (*top*) compared to a Curt Teich Company color postcard from 1937 (*bottom*). Courtesy Frasher Foto Collection/HJG and Pomona Public Library, Pomona, California. Frasher Foto Postcard Collection, index #b3858, title "Grand Canyon from Mojave Point Desert View Showing the Colorado River, Grand Canyon National Park, Arizona." Courtesy Grand Canyon National Park Museum Collection, image #GRCA22312.

Finally, both postcard manufacturers emphasized abundant and green vegetation in their views of the canyon. Many of the scenic Curt Teich postcards during this era envisioned the canyon as a verdant place. As Lucy Lippard asserts, "perceptions of nature are constantly being reinvented and often reflect the values and ideas of society itself" (Lippard 2001, 5–6). This certainly seemed to be the case with the Curt Teich postcard imagery from the 1930s through the 1950s when nature was employed as an ornament for the canyon, a benign and attractive decoration festooning the tourist service villages and canyon rim. The canyon's floral communities were some of the most frequently represented and manipulated subjects of the postcards in this vein. These midcentury postcards presented leafy deciduous trees, dense stands of conifers, rounded bushes, and lush green lawns that normalized this view of nature while customizing it to aesthetic norms of the day.

Wishing to lure tourists from the eastern United States more familiar with broad leaf maples than wiry junipers, Curt Teich Company made a visual appeal to these potential customers' sense of scenic beauty by embellishing vegetation in its canyon postcards. Although the South Rim of the canyon does host an intermingling pinyon-juniper woodland with ponderosa pine forest, one would be hard pressed to find the vegetation arrangements and densities represented in the CTC's images at the canyon's arid South Rim. Other postcards employed the native trees and shrubs found in the pinyon-juniper woodland along the South Rim but compensated for their potentially alien or wiry outlines by emphasizing their abundance. A 1937 *Wayside Museum of Archaeology* postcard provides an example of this common representational strategy by framing the view and tilting the angle of the image so that several large juniper trees crowd and nearly obscure the stone museum building featured in the postcard (fig. 71a). NPS administrators built this museum in 1932 on the South Rim as an interpretive site for the nearby eight-hundred-year-old Ancestral Puebloan ruins. A 2019 repeat photograph that I captured near the same location, now known as Tusayan Museum, reveals a less lush juniper tree but a well-preserved stone building (fig. 71b).

Examples of CTC's emphasis on verdant scenes extended to their North Rim postcards as well. In the 1930s printing of *Grand Canyon Lodge, North Rim, Kaibab Forest, Arizona*, the lodge is nestled in an emerald cushion of pine forest so dense that it nearly obscures the building in the upper right corner of the image (fig. 72). Utah Parks Company, a subsidiary of the Union Pacific Railway, assumed visitor services at the North Rim and built the

Fig. 71. Creating a green Grand Canyon at Tusayan Museum. Curt Teich Company *Wayside Museum of Archaeology* postcard, 1932 (*top*) and a 2019 repeat photograph of what is now known as Tusayan Museum (*bottom*). Curt Teich Postcard production #7ah3919, 1937, collection of the author; contemporary photograph by the author.

Grand Canyon Lodge and cottages between 1927 and 1928 near the previous Wylie Way Camp site. As with the South Rim, the early twentieth century and the introduction of the National Park Service to the Grand Canyon area translated into a shift on the North Rim from small, family, and individual businesses such as the Wylie Way Camp to large corporations and railroad companies that could afford the infrastructure and other investments specified by the NPS for all concessionaires (Anderson 2000, 15). A fire destroyed some of these structures, but the lodge was rebuilt and opened in 1937 during a flurry of construction and concessionaire investment at both the North and South Rims (Anderson 2000, 28). Curt Teich postcards may have been employed as colorful advertisements of these rebuilt rustic retreats.

CTC's visual strategies were not limited to the rim-side viewpoints or midcanyon trails; their imagery also extended to the remote depths of the canyon. A 1948 CTC postcard, *Phantom Ranch, Grand Canyon, Arizona*, depicts this Fred Harvey Company development as rustic retreat ensconced in a dense stand of deciduous trees (fig. 73). The site is at the bottom of the Grand Canyon, near the Colorado River and at an intersection of the Bright Angel and Kaibab Trails, two major trails into the canyon. Established in 1903 as a hunting camp, the waning ranch was redeveloped and reimagined by the Fred Harvey Company in 1922 as a modest resort under the direction of the FHC's architect Mary Colter (McNamee 1997). In the 1930s and 1940s, the small oasis became a favorite retreat of movie stars and celebrities. The postcard shows a rare view of water in the canyon that is not the Colorado River. It features a swimming pool built by the Civilian Conservation Corps in front of the main guest services lodge and cantina. Although cottonwood trees are present at this riparian site, the density of the trees and their bright green color are exaggerated. The pool, an extravagant nod toward attracting tourists and providing typical resort amenities, stands out as a rare view of water in the canyon aside from the Colorado River. Its presence in an arid landscape bound by the limits of water and shaped by geopolitics from water access to dam construction projects is particularly striking. Notably, this pool was later filled in and is no longer in use.

Although FFPC did not use color, the photographer could use other visual strategies to emphasize the lush vegetation of the Grand Canyon. In *Footpath to Bright Angel Point, North Rim of Grand Canyon, Arizona* (1936) the image is crowded with the canyon's floral communities (fig. 74). Employing the photographer's strategy of the rule of thirds, the image com-

Fig. 72. (*top*) *Grand Canyon Lodge, North Rim, Kaibab Forest, Arizona*. Author's collection.

Fig. 73. (*bottom*) Inner Canyon, Phantom Ranch lodge and pool. Curt Teich Postcard, production #8bh93, author's collection.

Fig. 74. *Footpath to Bright Angel Point, North Rim of Grand Canyon, Arizona*, 1936. Courtesy Frasher Foto Collection/HJG and Pomona Public Library, Pomona, California. Frasher Foto Postcard Collection, index #B3925.

position is marked by a dense stand of bushes on the right, the footpath dividing the center of the image, and a neat row of stones along the edge of the path and large ponderosa pines standing on the left side of the frame. The ample bushes reach over and obscure the right edge of the trail, adding to the sense of wild, untamed nature and robust flora. Again, we see FFPC using alternative visual strategies such as framing, light, and angle to see the canyon's scenery.

Centralizing Tourism Development

Many building and construction programs started in the 1920s came to fruition in the 1930s, making the 1930s and 1940s pivotal for cultural and social landscape changes at the Grand Canyon. Historian Michael F. Anderson suggests that at the close of the 1920s, the NPS and "its private partners had gone a long way toward recreating Grand Canyon into one of the more popular tourist destinations in the American West." "Opposition presented by pioneer residents had been mostly overcome by a new alliance among federal legislators and bureaucrats, county businessmen, and corporate concessionaires who attracted and satisfied nearly 200,000 annual visitors" (2000, 24). Social and economic networks bolstered by capital investment in the park played a key role in this transformation of the canyon. NPS administrators relied on federal appropriations, marketing and hospitality prowess, and investment by the Santa Fe and Union Pacific Railroads, and "concession agreements that ensured control over millions of dollars in private investments to house, feed, supply, and entertain scenic consumers" (2000, 24).

During this era, extensive, planned administrative, concessioner, utility and residential construction projects resulted in a new spatial organization at the Grand Canyon focusing the central corridor of tourism development between the south and North Rim (fig. 75). These cultural landscape changes intermingled and overlapped with postcard manufacturer's systematic and standardized transformation of the canyon's environment into a scenic commodity. The NPS and concessionaires Fred Harvey Company and the Santa Fe Railroad developed a working partnership of planning and construction that emphasized roads and trails to scenic viewpoints, lodges, and other tourist services along a central north-south corridor in the national park and infrastructure such as water pipelines and power systems to support growing tourism needs. Although the Great Depression and World War II decreased visitation to the park, the midcentury years provided a boom to park construction and redevelopment through New Deal programs. The Civilian Conservation Corps and the Public Works Administration impacted national parks around the country in terms of completing much-needed construction and infrastructure improvements, but they were particularly active and influential in shaping the Grand Canyon's cultural landscape.

Another important element in this socio-economic mixture at the canyon was the development of concessionaire contracts in national parks during the early twentieth century. When visitors come to the Grand Canyon they may think that the NPS operates all the stores, hotels, restaurants, campgrounds, and other facilities in the park, but instead, the U.S. national park model relies on a public-private partnership between the federal government and private businesses, mediated through concession contracts that formalize the economic and legal relationship. It is a complex system, developed over many decades, and present at all park units across the NPS system. The 1918 Lane letter from Secretary of the Interior Franklin K. Lane to the first director of the NPS, Stephen Mather, initiated the concession system. The letter directed the NPS to focus its efforts on natural resource protection but

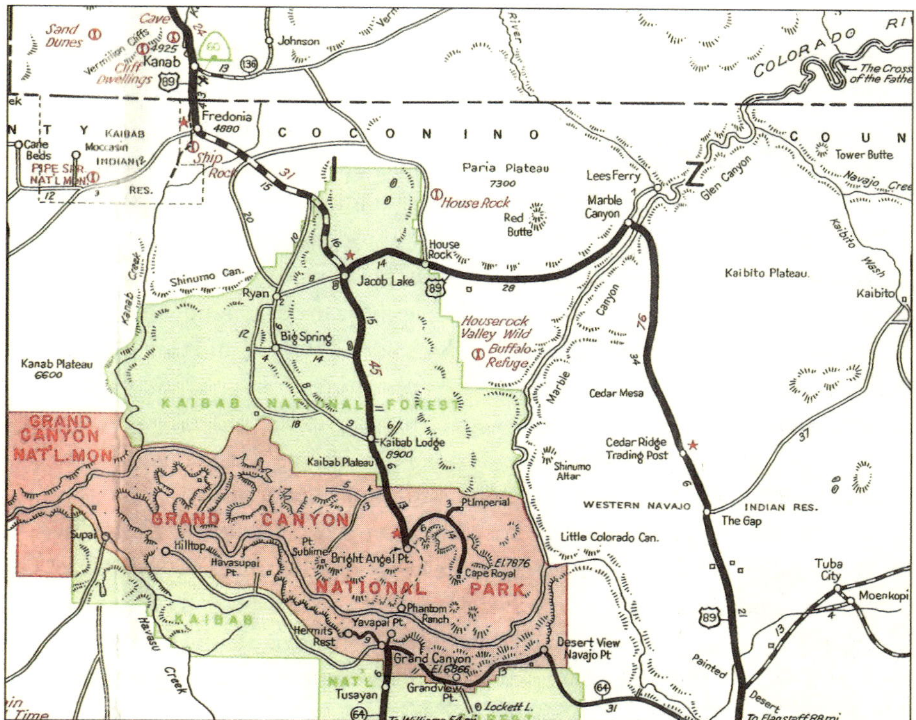

Fig. 75. Detail from 1939 *Road Map of Utah*. This map by the State Road Commission of Utah depicts the Greater Grand Canyon Region in transitional years for NPS management of the area. The map emphasizes the tangle of road networks extending across the region and connecting to the North and South Rims of the canyon. It also shows the Grand Canyon's public federal land ownership divided between Grand Canyon National Park, as a smaller unit before the expansion in the 1970s, and an adjacent Grand Canyon National Monument. Author's collection.

to leave the operation of affordable and reliable tourist services and accommodations to private enterprise (Keiter 2013, 93–95). Mather established a policy that favored corporate concessions over individual or local businesses and treated concessions as regulated monopolies. NPS contracts protected these businesses from competition and guaranteed a return on investment that softened the financial blow of NPS regulated rates on their hospitality services. The evolution of the concessionaire-NPS relationships and the extent of the contract years varies from park to park. At Grand Canyon National Park, Mather's policies encouraged the transition from individual entrepreneurs to corporate interests throughout the early twentieth century as the park grew in popularity and use.

The concession system is an integral but often misunderstood aspect of national park policy and management in the United States and a major influence on cultural landscapes and Grand Canyon imagery. Generally, the system requires private businesses and corporations to compete for contracts through formal bids to the U.S. government. If awarded, these contracts allow private businesses to hold leases to buildings and operations in the park for a set number of years (varies by contract), but they must follow strict guidelines. Specifics for each contract may vary, but concessionaires are required to submit regular reports concerning their operations, follow all park natural and cultural resource protection rules, house and care for their service employees, and provide NPS the opportunity to review and set their prices for tourist services, hours of operation, and extent of services offered. In return, the concessionaire may claim a portion of their annual revenue and profits, after franchise fees and investments in park facilities. The contract also requires these private businesses to make substantial investments in maintenance and constructions projects for buildings and other facilities they operate (but do not own). If the contract is not approved for renewal by the NPS when it expires, then the company must vacate the park and all buildings and facilities they operate, handing these assets over to the next winner of the contract. An example of this arrangement, adjusted to ease financial burdens during the Great Depression, is the 1933 contract offered to the Fred Harvey Company. The NPS executed a twenty-year contract that "required payment of 22.5 percent of profits after allowing 6 percent for capital investment" (Anderson 2000, 26).

Private businesses operating at the Grand Canyon under concessionaire contracts from the 1930s to 1950s represented a mixture of corporations, railroad companies, and family or individual entrepreneurs. This was a time of economic transition for the canyon as the tide shifted from individual and family businesses to a corporate-government partnership between the NPS, Santa Fe Railroad, and Fred Harvey Company. For most of the twentieth century, Santa Fe Railroad and the FHC were the major concessionaires at the South Rim of Grand Canyon National Park. But there were also smaller operations there, including Verkamps Curios Stores, Kolb Studio, and the Babbitt Brothers Trading Company. The Union Pacific Railroad operated transportation and hospitality services for the North Rim. This transition was not smooth as smaller businesses fought to maintain their land claims and their slice of the Grand Canyon's increasing profitability.

Along the South Rim, scenic viewpoints often held economic privilege as well. This transition is captured in postcards of the canyon from this era, especially ones that featured scenic rim-side viewpoints that also hosted economic enterprises situated just out of view in the postcard scenes. Many of the named viewpoints represented in these postcards, such as Grand View Point, O'Neil's Point, Rowe's Point, and Hance Cove, refer to the people or their business behind the scenes of these images (Youngs 2019). For example, a protracted battle between canyon pioneers and photographers Emery and Ellsworth Kolb, the NPS, and the Santa Fe Railroad played out over decades. The brothers arrived at the canyon between 1901 and 1902, started a business of selling photographs of tourists riding mule into the canyon, and soon built a small home and photo studio on a South Rim site they gained from Ralph Cameron, a miner turned tourist guide (Anderson 2001, 28–29). Their home studio was perched on the edge of the South Rim within walking distance to the Grand Canyon Village. They marketed themselves as the "view hunters" of the Grand Canyon, building a small business into a profitable enterprise by performing daredevil stunts, such as hanging off cliffs, to capture dramatic views of the canyon. The Kolb brothers also created the first film of running boats down the Colorado River on an ambitious yearlong journey starting in 1911. They later turned the experience into a lecture tour and book. It became the longest running film in the United States with daily screenings in their studio on the South Rim narrated by the brothers from 1915 to 1976 (fig. 76).

The Santa Fe Railroad and the Fred Harvey Company did not like the competition from the Kolb Brothers for tourist dollars on the South Rim. For years they attempted to squeeze the brothers out of business or press the NPS to revoke their concession permit (Kolb 1914; Naylor 2017; Anderson 2000). Unsuccessful, they engaged a contentious spatial strategy instead. The Santa Fe Railroad constructed Lookout Studio on the South Rim, completed in 1914, just a short distance from the Kolb brothers' studio (fig. 77). It was strategically set on the rim path between the tourist entry point at the SFRR depot and El Tovar Hotel, capturing tourist traffic walking from the depot to the Kolb studio. The SFRR studio offered competition to the Kolbs with similar offerings of rim-side views from balconies, an interior lounge with a fireplace, and a small store selling postcards, photographs, and paintings. The 1936 Frasher Foto postcard captures Lookout Studio on the left side of the frame and the vast canyon views on the right, well into this protracted

Fig. 76. Kolb Brothers' home and studio, ca. 1912. Courtesy Grand Canyon National Park Museum Collection, image GRCA #07731.

battle with the Kolb brothers and the construction boom years of Grand Canyon Village expansion.

Midcentury postcard imagery captures the Grand Canyon during a tremendous period of development and constructions in the 1930s through the surge in visitation after World War II. Together, the Santa Fe and Union Pacific Railroads and the Fred Harvey Company, constructed, improved, and maintained extensive building projects including hospitality structures, utilities, employee residences, and transportation. A 1939 CTC postcard of Bright Angel Lodge presents a scene of this modern tourism development in motion (fig. 78). A large, smooth driveway takes center stage here, flanked on either side by a steady stream of passenger cars, a neat border of shrubs and stones hemming the lodge entrance, and a background of bright green trees, blue sky, and rising clouds. The National Park Service also expanded their operations and structures. The agency constructed administrative buildings, roads, trails, residential buildings, and visitor campgrounds. In terms of spatial distribution of territory and investment, the Santa Fe Railroad and Fred Harvey Company operated services at Grand Canyon Village on the

Fig. 77. Lookout Studio, South Rim, Grand Canyon Village, Frasher Foto postcard 1936. Courtesy Frasher Foto Collection/HJG and Pomona Public Library, Pomona, California. Frasher Foto Postcard Collection, index #B3861. Title: "Grand Canyon from the Lookout, Grand Canyon National Park, Arizona."

South Rim along with inner canyon trails and facilities, while the Union Pacific Railroad focused their efforts on the North Rim village.

Park superintendent Miner Raymond Tillotson noted that 1931 was the "biggest building construction program in the history of the park" (qtd. in Anderson 2000, 28). This growth spurt may seem surprising during the Great Depression. Visitation to Grand Canyon National Park (GRCA) declined from 184,093 people in 1929 to a low of 105,475 in 1933 before steadily rising again (appendix A). But for Grand Canyon National Park and many other national parks in the American West., the 1930s offered a reprieve from the impacts of visitation and a boom for new construction. At the Grand Canyon, the Civilian Conservation Corps was particularly influential in reshaping the canyon's cultural landscape through construction projects such as building roads, trails, structures, a trans-canyon telephone line, planting trees landscaping for erosion control, and razing older structures. A 1939 CTC postcard of Bright Angel Lodge represents a well-tended and verdant canyon scene with a pruned juniper tree in the left foreground, a traffic island in the center of the image decorated with manicured shrubs,

Fig. 78. Entrance to Bright Angel Lodge, 1939 postcard. Curt Teich and Fred Harvey used postcard imagery to highlight their modern visitor services boosted by 1930s investment and infrastructure expansions. Author's collection.

and a sandstone border lining the road leading up to the lodge (fig. 79). This is not a scene of a drought-prone desert landscape.

NPS managers took advantage of the influx of labor and federal dollars to carry out a series of planned construction programs in coordination with private companies and government contractors. This construction not only transformed the Grand Canyon's tourism villages at the South and North Rim. It spurred a growing network of roads that connected the Greater Grand Canyon Region to other tourism sites in the Southwest and the rest of the nation. Frasher Foto Postcard Company excelled at capturing these scenes of new road construction, especially on the corridors along the north and northeast areas of the canyon. A 1936 postcard titled *Aspen Trees on the Road to North Rim of Grand Canyon, Arizona* presents a thick stand of aspens and ponderosa pines bordering a wide, smooth dirt road open to a lone car driving toward the viewer (fig. 80). The postcard is equal parts photographic artistry and advertisement for the expanding road network of Arizona State Highway 67, connecting the North Rim tourist village to Jacob Lake and Kanab, Utah.

Fig. 79. *Bright Angel Lodge on the Canyon's Rim, Grand Canyon National Park, Arizona postcard.* Curt Teich Company postcard H-4470. Author's collection.

Fig. 80. *Aspen Trees on the Road to North Rim of Grand Canyon, Arizona*, 1936 postcard. Courtesy Frasher Foto Collection/HJG and Pomona Public Library, Pomona, California. Frasher Foto Postcard Collection, index # B3929.

Two other factors distinguish the construction and development of the 1930s from other eras and provide additional context for CTC and FFPC postcards. First, starting in 1930 and spurred by the second NPS director Horace Albright's direction, Grand Canyon NPS managers initiated the first master plan that kept the Grand Canyon Village on the South Rim as a key component. This plan influenced lasting effects on the spatial distribution of visitor services in the Grand Canyon and, eventually, on the locations depicted in the postcards and later *Arizona Highways* magazine images. The NPS plan focused tourist and commercial services along the rim while locating employee housing and utilities in the forest to the south. The Santa Fe Railroad paid for and built the tourism structures, while the Fred Harvey Company ran the day-to-day operations and hospitality services, including the hotels, dining rooms, and gift shops. The partnership between Santa Fe Railroad and Fred Harvey continued until Santa Fe railroad bowed out of the Grand Canyon in 1954 due to waning business and the decline in railroad travel; it sold most of its tourism structures to Fred Harvey for a song and donated its utility structures to the NPS (Anderson 2000, 2001).

Through various revisions and evolutions, the NPS master plan focused tourism development on a centralized corridor that ran from Grand Canyon Village on the South Rim to the tourism village on the North Rim near Bright Angel Point, connected through the inner gorge by a system of trails that lead into and out of the canyon. The inner canyon and the Colorado River corridor were less developed than the rims for tourism; nevertheless the Santa Fe Railroad and Fred Harvey established facilities there at Phantom Ranch and Havasupai Gardens (formerly Indian Garden). The decision by NPS to focus development in concentrated areas in their master plan while leaving other parts of the park as remote and undeveloped presages later environmental science and management ideas. Historian Michael Anderson suggests that a "hazy, incomplete, yet emerging sense of the value of wild ecosystems" may have influenced the plan's design (Anderson 2000, 40).

Buildings featured in Curt Teich postcard imagery from this time spotlight South Rim sites including El Tovar Hotel, Bright Angel Lodge and Cabins, Desert View Watchtower, Hopi House, Phantom Ranch cabins and complex, Lookout Studio, Hermit's Rest, Navajo Hogans (built as an attraction and housing near El Tovar Hotel), Tusayan Wayside Museum, and Yavapai Observation Station. On the North Rim, the Grand Canyon Lodge and cabins were the only buildings represented. Frasher Foto postcards featured Desert View Watchtower, Lookout Studio, and Moqui Camp on or near the South Rim and Grand Canyon Lodge and cabins on the North Rim.

Both the CTC and FFPC focused their efforts on a select and fragmentary view of park infrastructure, in terms of a narrow set of buildings, trails, and roads that corresponded with the centralized corridor plan for development. For example, at Grand Canyon Village some buildings, such as El Tovar Hotel, were common subjects in the Curt Teich postcard universe, while other prominent, centrally located and popular tourist destinations, such as Kolb Studio, did not appear in any of the postcard imagery. Many structures, trails, and roads that were essential in keeping Grand Canyon Village's service industry humming along were also overlooked. Employee housing, mule barns, the post office, railroad depot, maintenance buildings—all present as hubs of activity during this early and mid-twentieth century—did not appear in any of the postcards sampled. In a striking contrast to other forms of popular media, CTC and FFPC postcards did not include representations of proposed or constructed dam sites in any of their locations. Large-scale dam projects in process throughout the 1930s along the Colorado River, such as the Hoover Dam (1931–36) and discussions of new dams at Marble Canyon and Bridge Canyon were prominent in the *Arizona Highways* magazines but were absent from CTC and FFPC postcards. This may be explained, at least for CTC, by the geographic range of their customers. CTC maintained contracts with Fred Harvey Company that constrained their operations to sites in the national park, not a nearby dam sites outside of park boundaries. But it is curious that FFPC with its dedication to good roads and auto tour routes, did not include images of the engineering feats unfolding just to the west and north of Grand Canyon National Park.

The second factor of this era left an indelible impression on the canyon's iconographic arc and cultural landscapes while reinforcing or intensifying enduring environmental justice issues at Grand Canyon National Park, and more broadly, the Greater Grand Canyon Region. The NPS master plan focused tourism development on a centralized corridor while removing or diminishing historical and sometimes scattered sites of lodges, camps, trails, and other features used by early Anglo residents and American Indian tribes. These changes were framed through the lens of race and class that shaped development and equitable use and access of the canyon's resources while marginalizing social and cultural groups at the canyon. These issues are not limited to the Grand Canyon; they are present throughout the NPS system in the United States. At the Grand Canyon, however, the challenge to the egalitarian idea of public lands and national parks reveals its flaws in the dispossession of American Indians from their traditional homelands, appropriation of natural resources and locations for tourism services at the expense of traditional Indigenous cultural uses, and the removal of Indigenous housing and structures. In addition, the class and privilege shifted tourism economies of the Grand Canyon from the previous era's base of wealthy visitors with ample time and money, traveling by train and stagecoach, to middle class tourists traveling on shorter schedules with auto tours or in their personal vehicles.

Social and Cultural Landscapes Reconfigured

This former issue, removing Indigenous residential areas and discouraging traditional uses of lands in the park boundaries, played out in the NPS's 1930s Grand Canyon master development plan. Postcard visual representations of the cultural landscape reinforced these inequities. For example, a curious gap in the postcard imagery from this era is that no Havasupai peoples or their built landscapes appear in any of the CTC or FFPC postcards sampled for this study. Grand Canyon National Park is situated on the traditional lands of American Indian tribes of the Southwest including the eleven tribes that are now recognized by the NPS as Traditionally Associate Tribes. The Havasupai are one of these groups that hold strong ties to the land and waters that are now part of Grand Canyon National Park. They maintain a cultural history of living, working, and accessing those lands that precedes U.S. territorial claims to the area. The contested history of native land dispossession, discrimination, and forced removal from their traditional homelands is a theme that runs throughout US national park history across the United States (Hirst 2006, 2016; Shepherd 2010; Watahomigie-Corliss 2020).

Through treaties and negotiations that resulted in the dispossession of those lands and the forceful removal of Havasupai peoples from many of their traditional use areas in the Grand Canyon, the NPS and other government entities moved and centralized the tribe into an area around Havasu Canyon and Havasu Falls (to the west of Grand Canyon Village). Further limiting Havasupais' land rights, in just two years in the 1880s the federal government reduced the Havasupai Tribe's reservation from 38,400 acres to 518 (Keiter 2013, 127). It was not until the 1970s that they regained some of these lost acres through protracted legal disputes with the U.S. government.

Despite this situation, the Havasupai continued to live and work throughout the 1930s on the South Rim at a site then known as Supai Camp near Grand Canyon Village and within walking distance of the Santa Fe Railroad tracks. But with development and construction plans underway later that decade and under direction from the NPS, the "CCC recruits cleaned up the tiny community called Supai Camp west of Rowe Well Road in 1935 and 1939, demolishing shacks and building fourteen-by twenty-foot two-room cabins to house Havasupais with regular village jobs" (Anderson 2000, 27). The six cabins were completed by 1937, but an extended stalemate between the NPS, the Bureau of Indian Affairs, and the Havasupai over the transition from the old housing to the new resulted in a delay; the Havasupai did not move into the cabins until 1939 (Rothman 1998, 76). The Havasupai also engaged in the tourism economy of the Grand Canyon through guided horse and private auto tours from Grand Canyon Village along the west-running Havasupai Road to the Havasupai villages in Havasu Canyon of Supai and Hilltop. In the WPA guide that opened this chapter, the maps and tour descriptions include roads connecting the NPS Grand Canyon Village with Supai as well as descriptions and costs of these tours (1940, 471–95). Also, near Grand Canyon Village but down the Bright Angel Trail, they continued to use their traditional camps at about 3,800 feet on the south side of the inner canyon at the recently renamed to Havasupai Gardens. In 2022 the name of this site was changed to Havasupai Gardens to recognize the traditional Havasupai camp there and the long-standing use and habitation of the site (NPS 2022a). Indeed, even Bright Angel Trail was a well-used Havasupai path that they cut into the walls of the canyon following a natural geologic fault line.

In the 1930s, the Havasupai faced more challenges to their use of and access to Supai Camp and Havasupai Gardens. The NPS and CCC constructed new structures and removed older ones at Havasupai Gardens. From 1930 to 1932, "alarming trends in water consumption" spurred the Santa Fe Railroad to appropriate the "ample springs at Indian Garden for rim-side use" and build an extensive water pump and distribution system that delivered over a million gallons of water from Indian Springs up to the South Rim, eliminating the need for the "steady stream of water trains" that were required to supply the water demands of the growing tourism development at Grand Canyon Village (Anderson 2000, 27). Postcards tracked earlier iterations of this landscape. In a DPC postcard titled *A Stop at the Indian Gardens, Grand*

Fig. 81. *A Stop at the Indian Gardens, Grand Canyon National Park, Arizona, postcard.* This Detroit Publishing Company Phostint postcard was printed for Fred Harvey between 1910 and 1919. Newberry Library, Curt Teich Postcard Archives Collection, production # DPCH2831.

Canyon National Park, Arizona, a group of mule-riding tourists and their guides taking a midcanyon break about four and half miles down Bright Angel Trail. The location is nestled in a blanket of green vegetation. The red rock walls of the canyon create a focal dividing line midway through the image and stand in contrast to the green scene below. Although they are out of view, the presence of the springs nurtures this midcanyon oasis (fig. 81). The card provides no written or visual reference to the contested social and cultural history of the site (alternately referred to as "Garden" and "Gardens" in the postcards).

Ophelia Watahomigie-Corliss, a Havasupai tribal councilwoman, described the significance of Indian Garden to the tribe and their forced removal from the area by the NPS in the 1920s. "And it was truly a garden, once: Our Havasupai relatives, the Tilousi family, lived and gardened there a century ago, until the National Park Service kicked them out. The Bright Angel Trail hikers use to reach this area today is an old Havasupai trail" (2020). In another account, *I Am the Grand Canyon: The Story of The Havasupai People*, a brief glimpse into the complex and interwoven relationship between the Havasupai and the NPS is told through the experiences of a couple and their connection to Indian Garden: "During the winter of 1942–1943, Clark and Ethel Jack became the last Havasupais to spend a winter at Indian Garden. The National Park Service had hired Clark to maintain the Bright Angel Trail, and he decided to take his wife and winter next to the spring, where she herself had grown up. She remembers most of all feeling lonely at the place where once her grandfather, Burro, had farmed and laughed with his family" (Hirst 2006, 177). Ophelia Watahomigie-Corliss continues her description,

> In the early 1930s, the Park Service burned Supai Camp to the ground, and our people, including elders and children, were loaded into covered wagons in the snow, taken to the canyon's rim and forced to walk down a grueling 17-mile trail to Supai Village. That is where the Havasupai Reservation was created in 1880. Before that, however, Supai Village was used as our summer home. Our longtime winter home had always been the newly designated park, but now we had lost it forever. Inside what you call Grand Canyon National Park, the Havasupai have lived since time immemorial. We still live here.
>
> Billy Burro was the last Havasupai to live in Indian Garden, a place that had been enjoyed by our people for centuries. But industry began to dictate where Indians could and couldn't be, and public areas were forbidden because it was considered bad for business. Discrimination was rampant. At the Grand Canyon, we Havasupais were no longer welcome on our own land, because now it was reserved for tourists. Eventually, it was taken away altogether. Grand Canyon became a national park in 1919, and Billy, together with all Havasupais, were kicked out of Indian Garden. The people were relocated to the Indian work camp, with little option but to work for the railway. These were heartbreaking times for us, as our home became a tourist attraction. We had to endure constant racism; people like Billy were given the last name "Burro," for example, as if we were no more than pack animals. (2020)

The relationships between the NPS and the Traditionally Associated Tribes is an evolving and complex topic. The NPS is actively working with the tribes to form partnerships and co-create interpretation of park history. For this chapter, however, some of the NPS and concessionaire decisions—such as removing housing, camps, trails, and other elements—are pertinent as we trace the meanings and ideas invested in the canyon's cultural landscapes. But the NPS, concessionaires, and tribes also worked together in some capacity to co-create Grand Canyon's tourism landscape in ways that challenge easy interpretation. For example, Havasupai worked for the Fred Harvey Company, the Santa Fe Railroad, and the NPS. Havasupai tribal council members recount that by "1930, Havasupai workers had upgraded their trails for use by the park, laid the pipeline that brought water from Indian Garden to the South Rim, installed the park sewage line, helped build park roadways and buildings, and hand-carried the cables down the South Kaibab Trail for the suspension bridge to Phantom Ranch in 1926" (Kaska et al. 2016).

The NPS expanded public campgrounds in the Grand Canyon throughout the 1930s, and these sites proved highly popular with auto tourists. The NPS also invested in extensive new or refurbished essential infrastructure that remained "hidden landscapes" of waterpipes, garbage disposal, water treatment, and sewage to support the canyon's growing tourism base (Colten and Dilsaver 2009). Yet, no CTC or FFPC postcards depict campgrounds or other essential but hidden infrastructure.

Cultural landscapes such as those pictured in postcards—the hotels, restaurants, roads, camps, trails, and museums—are more than just buildings. They are visible markers of the social and political landscape. As geographer Richard Schein writes: "Each seemingly individual decision behind any particular U.S. landscape is embedded within a discourse. When the action results in a tangible landscape element, or total ensemble, the cultural landscape becomes the discourse materialized" (1997, 663). At the Grand Canyon, examples of such discourses might include NPS master plans, Santa Fe Railroad architectural design trends, tourist economic consumption patterns, and CCC investment of time and labor. We can see these discourses in the postcard imagery as a visible ensemble of new structures, infrastructure, roads, and trails and the removal of other structures that can be conceptualized as the visible intersection of several competing discourses.

Shifting Environmental Management Policies

The final theme that runs through the postcard representations from this era is the shifting NPS environmental management policies that reflected national debates and regional concerns about native vegetation, wildlife management, water supply and distribution, and tourism impacts on the environment. For example, when Curt Teich Company shifted its printing and production styles to photorealistic postcards in the 1950s, the representations of the canyon's environment changed too. Gone are embellished colors and editing that augmented the canyon's environment into the Astroturf green lawns in front of some of the lodges, the sapphire blue water of the Colorado River, the brilliant red and orange hues of the canyon's walls and strata. Compare representations of vegetation in two very different postcards of buildings that are within a short walking distance of one another in the Grand Canyon Village: El Tovar Hotel and Bright Angel Lodge. These postcards reveal the type of vegetation encouraged, maintained, and represented at these heavily visited tourist spots through NPS and concessionaire environmental management strategies and landscape aesthetics that bookend this era. Dense, green vegetation cultivated by the CCC's landscaping efforts are featured in the Bright Angel Lodge scene from the 1930s (see fig. 79). By the 1950s emerging ideas about ecology and environmental management provided an impetus for park managers to a shift to more drought-tolerant and native species that took center stage, such as succulents and juniper. In a 1955 CTC photorealistic postcard, gone are the dense stands of bright green trees and bushes crowding El Tovar Hotel's front entrance; instead native yucca pierce into the foreground with a few thin juniper trees standing behind (fig. 82).

Water, always an important element in an arid desert landscape, took on additional significance during this era. Almost all of the postcards sampled for this study portrayed water at the Grand Canyon in a singular form: the Colorado River as seen from the canyon's South Rim. At first glance, the postcards manufactured by CTC and FFPC present a disarmingly simple and consistent view of water at the canyon in the form of the Colorado River, as seen from the rim looking down into the canyon. Curt Teich postcards depicted the Colorado River as a brilliant blue stream coursing through the red contours of the Grand Canyon (see figure 70b). The Colorado River represented in these postcards from 1936 to 1955 was not yet controlled by the enormous Glen Canyon Dam (completed in 1966), not yet measured and released from the cold depths of Lake Powell. Instead, the Colorado River flowed with far more fluctuation, carrying warm, silt-laden water toward the Gulf of California. Although Frasher Foto postcards were not colorized, these postcards framed the Colorado River from similar angles and locations as the Curt Teich postcards in terms of depicting the river's winding course through the canyon (see fig. 70). The trend of representing

Fig. 82. A less lush Grand Canyon, 1955 postcard. Curt Teich Postcard production #5CK-248, 1955. Author's collection.

the Colorado River's colors as bright blue instead of the more accurate dusty shades of brown and dark green continued well into and beyond 1950s.

But while the postcard manufacturers focused on the Colorado River as a scenic attraction, the NPS and park concessionaires focused their attentions and efforts on water as an essential element for tourism and life in the Grand Canyon's expanding tourism villages. The NPS revitalized and refocused campaigns for investment in and construction of water redistribution systems to support the growing tourism economy in the canyon's arid environment. During the 1930s, NPS managers leveraged their access to the CCC to build an ambitious water distribution system in the Grand Canyon, an essential but often overlooked piece of infrastructure. The Utah Parks Company (UPC) installed a top-rate water and power system in the late 1920s on the North Rim, tapping into the source of Roaring Springs and then moving that water four thousand feet up to the rim via an extensive pipeline supported by a holding tank, a hydroelectric plant, and a pump house. The Santa Fe Railroad followed UPC's lead by installing additional hydrological infrastructure in 1932 to meet growing water consumption demands at Grand Canyon Village. The railroad appropriated the water from springs at Indian Garden, then built a pumping plant with turbine pumps, a seventy-thousand-gallon reservoir, extensive pipeline, and rim-side tanks to hold and control the flow of water from the canyon's interior to the South Rim (Anderson 2000, 27–29). Although water conservation measures were put into place at the Grand Canyon, demand continued to grow. The investment by SFRR in a new water distribution system decreased the cost of water and eliminated the need for a "steady stream of water trains" to supply Grand Canyon Village (Anderson 2000, 27).

Meanwhile, the nonhuman actors at the Grand Canyon—the plethora of animals, birds, and plants that called this canyon home—were increasingly divided along native and exotic species in postcard representations. Postcard manufacturers focused all their attention on representing only two species of animals in the park—deer and mules. Postcard producers overlooked the Grand Canyon's many carnivores such as black bears, mountain lions, coyotes, and foxes. They also dismissed many of the animals frequently seen at popular tourist sites along the south and North Rims; smaller species of mammals such as desert cottontail, black-tailed jackrabbits, and red- and golden-mantled squirrels are readily seen darting along the canyon trails near the park's developed areas. There are also a number of birds that surely occupied the skies and air above tourists during this era. Ravens and smaller birds such as swifts and swallows, red-tailed hawks, and vultures are frequent fliers around the canyon's rim and inner recesses. Along the Colorado River corridor, beaver, ducks, and several varieties of fish are regular residents. Finally, there are a number of hoofed herbivores in the Grand Canyon related to deer and mules. If CTC and FFPC creators wished to focus their creative gazes only on these animals, they could have found models in bighorn sheep or pronghorn. Such was not the case.

Instead, CTC and FFPC featured only deer and mules in their postcards from 1936 to 1955. The reasoning behind this choice is unclear from the postcard manufacturing records. However, for Curt Teich Company imagery, wild animals were more commonly illustrated than domestic ones. In particular, deer were featured more often than mules. Although wild, the native mule deer of the canyon were represented as a nonthreatening, even tame species. Curt Teich postcards represented these animals as gentle as pets, taking handouts of food from tourists or nursing young fawns (fig. 83). Frasher Foto postcards from this era did not include animals as frequent subjects; indeed, only one postcard shows an image of a mule deer, at an unspecified site, on the South Rim (fig. 84). Mules were not repre-

Fig. 83. *Native Deer on Steps of Bright Angel Lodge, Grand Canyon National Park, Arizona postcard.* A 1938 Curt Teich postcard showing canyon visitors on the steps of Bright Angel Lodge feeding mule deer. Curt Teich Postcard, production #8AH1584. Author's collection.

sented in the Frasher Foto postcards, however they frequently appeared in CTC cards, particularly as companions to tourists on the inner canyon trail rides. Mules became an iconic species for the Grand Canyon through popular visual representations that singled out this species as a symbol of the canyon. In *Kickapoo, a Veteran of the Trails*, CTC fuses the images of a mule with the canyon scenery. The 1941 postcard combines a portrait of an eerily decapitated mule's head floating above a background of the canyon's orange-and-tan-colored mesas, buttes, and plateaus (fig. 85). CTC's detailed documentation and records again provide a peek into the process and labor involved in creating this image. A CTC work schedule for this image indicates hours of retouching, blueprint stripping, opaquing, and hand-color proof to transform a "retouched photo" into the final postcard with color.

Although ecological science and environmental regulation were in the early stages of development and not yet woven into national park management and popular awareness in the 1940s and 1950s, the NPS and USFS engaged in various strategies and policies to control and manage wildlife on public lands. In 1929 an NPS biologist named George Meléndez Wright pro-

Fig. 84. *Deer in the Kaibab Forest near the South Rim of the Grand Canyon, Arizona.* A 1936 Frasher Foto postcard of a mule deer shows a lone animal standing near some possibly recently cut tress. Courtesy Frasher Foto Collection/HJG and Pomona Public Library, Pomona, California. Frasher Foto Postcard Collection, index #B3876.

posed the first wildlife survey project for the National Park Service (Sellars 1997). In the coming years he oversaw the project that resulted in the 1932 survey results and policy recommendations in a report titled "Fauna of the National Parks of the United States" (Dilsaver 1994, 104). This pathbreaking work suggested conservation strategies for a cohesive national park wildlife management strategy, emphasized the value of native species and the challenges of exotics, and encouraged a holistic view of wildlife and their park habitats. The report also emphasized the role of wildlife in tourism and park visitation, including that "the observation of animals in the wild state contributes so much to the enjoyment derived by visitors that this is becoming a park attraction of steadily increasing rank" (Dilsaver 1994, 105). When CTC represented deer as docile, native wildlife taking food handouts from tourists or mules as exotic but iconic and trusty companions on the trail, these images paralleled larger national debates and discussions about America's evolving wildlife policies and management decisions, the role of animals in national park visitor experiences, and native and exotic species.

Fig. 85. *Kickapoo, a Veteran of the Trails.* The CTC work schedule for this image from January 20, 1941, documents a white border and "art colortone" for retouching, blueprint stripping, opaquing, and hand color proofing as the work completed to transform this retouched photo (*opposite*) to the final postcard with color (*above*). Photo: Newberry Library, Curt Teich Postcard Archives Collection, production record for #h-3628 and 85b; postcard: Newberry Library, Curt Teich Postcard Archives Collection, postcard #h-3628.

Public opinion weighed heavily on the matter of natural resource management, notably in cases where appealing species, such as deer, were concerned. A case at Grand Canyon National Park rose to national prominence as a particularly thorny issue. Here the species in question was the exotic and domesticated mule, the vital link to the Grand Canyon's transportation between the rim and river and the engine of economy that promoted the allure of riding a mule along the canyon's steep trails. Mules occupy a complex but not entirely unique niche in Grand Canyon environmental history. In the late nineteenth and early twentieth centuries, miners used mules to haul their loads in and out of the canyon. Later, as the canyon economy shifted from mining to tourism, pioneer canyon entrepreneurs and later corporate interests heavily promoted mule riding as recreation and an iconic way to see the depths of the canyon's trails. However, some mules were cut loose from the miner's corrals as canyon pioneers left or transitioned to other businesses. The sure-footed ungulates roamed freely throughout the canyon and proliferated. Problems ensued. They trampled vegetation and overgrazed the fragile range along the rim and inner canyon areas. As a nonnative species, the mules qualified for a one-way ticket out of the canyon's ecosystem by new resource management guidelines. National Park Service staff thinned herds by shooting many of the animals, ultimately removing 2,800 mules from the park (Bolen and Sayre 1998, 392–93).

Public outcry over this method of eradication rose for an animal that many people associated more easily with family vacations and adventurous rides into the canyon than a threatening species to the canyon's "natural" habitat. Pressured by media coverage and politics, the federal government reacted in 1969 by passing the Wild Horse and Burro Act that outlawed killing these animals. The environmental impacts of the mules continued, however, putting the National Park Service in a compromising position. The controversy continued over the subject until a private organization launched an "Adopt a Burro" program that corralled and distributed the animals through adoption as pets (Sellars 1997; Bolen and Sayre 1998).

When Curt Teich Company and Frasher Foto postcards from the 1930s and 1950s were circulating, the story of Grand Canyon's burros had not yet reached its more controversial phase. It is worthwhile to consider, however, the cumulative effects of this postcard catalog on the iconographic arc of Grand Canyon wildlife and its potential influence on public opinion. After decades of colorful visual representations of mules and horses as friendly, sure-footed, and vital elements to any Grand Canyon visit, many tourists may have felt these animals were essential to a park tour and indeed the Grand Canyon itself.

Looking Back, Looking Ahead

Curt Teich artists, postcard printers, and the companies that ordered these postcards such as Fred Harvey Company selected certain parts of the canyon's environment and, through careful editing and application of color, built a visual catalog of symbols that came to represent the Grand Canyon. Although they may not have intended to build an arc of iconography custom tailored to the canyon, that is one of the aftereffects of their creation process. The formula for selecting certain elements of the Grand Canyon's environment—such as the Colorado River, scenic rim viewpoints, verdant vegetation, mules and deer—and then repeatedly representing these subjects in a growing catalog of postcard imagery served to commodify the canyon's scenery.

In this bustling era of park construction and development, it is striking how much of the Grand Canyon's cultural landscape is missing from the CTC and FFPC postcards. The postcards reflect many of these early twentieth century changes in construction and building projects at the Grand Canyon. But the CTC and FFPC postcards are limited to representing lodges, hotels, restaurants, shops, mule and horse trails, roads, and bridges. These are important landscape elements for any tourist development. But there are no campgrounds, no housing for NPS or concessionaire workers, no water or electric systems. Yet these are exactly the types of infrastructure and structures that the NPS and concessionaires heavily invested in and built during this era. They are also in demand as train travel waned and auto travel increased throughout this era. More visitors arrived at the Grand Canyon to auto camp, drive the park roads, and enjoy a picnic along a rim-side viewpoint. But they also performed the more mundane but necessary daily tasks of washing their camp dishes, flushing toilets, and throwing away garbage.

Of course, postcards of water lines and pump stations may not offer the visual appeal as Dutton's View from Point Sublime. It is feasible that the viewmakers of postcards—CTC, FFPC, Fred Harvey Company, Santa Fe Railroad, and other private companies—did not believe these infrastructure scenes would sell well or offered a fetching landscape scene. But the selection of subject matter and locations by these companies influenced popular geographic imaginations about the canyon and ultimately shaped environmental management and policy at the Grand Canyon. While private concessionaires invested heavily in state-of-the-art water and power infrastructure during the early 1930s to match the quickly growing demands for water and power on the South and North rim tourist developments, these infrastructure elements remained hidden landscapes, obscured behind trees or fences and rarely shared in public information or interpretation about the park. How could water use and the delicate balance of canyon environmental resources be tangible to park visitors and the general public if they remained unknown to visitors? Yet in the mid-twentieth century, ideas of sustainability, ecosystem health, ecology, environmental management were not yet established in the scientific or popular realms. But there was a growing awareness of the delicate balance of limited water and other natural resources in a dry, high desert environment such as the Grand Canyon, at least by NPS managers and park concessionaires who strived to meet the growing demands of park visitors.

By 1955, the Colorado River emerged as a common theme of visual representations of the Grand Canyon. It was the ideological centerpiece of environmental politics throughout the Greater Grand Canyon Region. Ideas about nature and culture clashed at the canyon. Some people believed the canyon, and more specifically its water, to be a powerful natural resource that should be harnessed, controlled, and guided towards utilitarian uses. Clashing with these sentiments, a growing number of individuals found a different version of nature to believe in. These people viewed nature as solace from urban stress, as a preserve for species diversity, as a counterbalance to human population growth, an entity with an intrinsic worth, as a nail-biting adventure that knocked you out of (or into) your senses. Taking cues from early wilderness advocates such as John Muir, Henry David Thoreau, and Ralph Waldo Emerson, those people sharing such sentiments in the mid-twentieth century believed in an environmental canyon defined by nature's intrinsic worth and ecological balance. World War II not only marked a shift in global political powers, it also acted as a dividing line between human reactions to the environment. After the war, environmental quality, human health, and ecological system balance gained increasing priority. These tensions were felt in environmental battles fought across the United States. Conflict over the fate of the Grand Canyon erupted between these powerful social and political tensions coursing through America's veins in the mid-twentieth century. Resource conservationists fought for nature as economic resource; emerging environmentalists fought for nature as wilderness and ecosystem. Both sides used images of the Grand Canyon to forge their visual rhetoric. The Grand Canyon was caught in the crosshairs of this debate, singled out of the American pantheon of public protected areas and wielded as a tool for garnering public opinion. Both sides manipulated images of the Canyon to make their arguments. As we turn to magazine images of the Grand Canyon in the Chapter 8, an entirely different view of the Grand Canyon emerges from the subject matter and locations featured in *Arizona Highways*.

7 People In (and Out of) Place

> Visitors looking for mementos to take home,
> that will remind them of the curiously
> silent Indians, wrapped tightly in colorful
> shawls, just like in the postcards.
>
> —Nora Narajano-Morse, "The Living Exhibit Under the Museum's Portal"

People were an important part of the formula for postcard representations during the era from 1936 to 1955. Visitation to Grand Canyon National Park vacillated during these years, due in part to global economic, social, and political pressures from the Great Depression and World War II. In 1936 park visitation hit 268,412 people, but by 1941 that number rose to 436,566 tourists. By 1944, at the height of the war, only 64,568 visitors came to Grand Canyon National Park, a nadir before steadily rising to 622,363 in 1947 and 892,400 in 1955 (appendix A). The park was a beneficiary of Americans with increased leisure time, financial resources, and a motivation to explore the nation's parks in the postwar years.

As more people visited the Grand Canyon, toured its attractions, and brought stories and mementoes home from their trips, the canyon's identity shifted from an idea in the popular geographic imagination of America to a factual and well-trodden tourist destination. Postcard representations informed this iconographic transition and popular understanding of the canyon. Tourists could purchase postcards at shops at the Grand Canyon Village run by Fred Harvey Company or Verkamps, at the North Rim village, and shops along the train, and later, auto routes to Grand Canyon National Park. As noted earlier, postcard collecting was a popular activity, too, especially from the early 1900s to the 1950s. Armchair travelers could purchase postcards in shops dedicated to postcard sales such as the ones that Detroit Publishing Company ran in Michigan or Frasher Foto Postcard Company in California. Curt Teich Postcard Company was a major player in this midcentury market, manufacturing thousands of postcards of the Grand

Canyon each year. As a numerical estimate of the volume of this activity, the Newberry Library, the public archive in Chicago that now houses the Curt Teich Company and Detroit Publishing Company postcard collections and digital archives, estimates that the Curt Teich Postcard Archives Collection includes "over 360,000 images produced by the company from 1898 and 1978 and over 110,000 production files documenting the creation of the company's postcards, and additional company records" (Newberry Library n.d.).

From 1936 to 1955, auto tourism and the number of visitors making the journey to the Grand Canyon generally rose as park access expanded. Much of the Grand Canyon's rugged inner recess was inaccessible by road. But the South Rim from El Tovar Hotel to Hermit's Rest could be viewed in an afternoon's drive. The South Rim was where most Grand Canyon visitors spent their time, and this seems to be the view that postcard manufacturers sought to reproduce and sell to visitors. As the Grand Canyon's popularity and iconic status rose, so, too, did visitors perceive the Grand Canyon as a South Rim attraction.

People representing park tourists and concessionaire employees appeared in many of the Curt Teich Company postcards from 1936 to 1955 but were absent from all the Frasher Foto postcards sampled for this era (see appendix C). Visual representations of white adult tourists engaged in leisure activities such as mule riding, auto touring, or standing near a scenic viewpoint were the most common subjects. The postcards represented Fred Harvey Company and Santa Fe Railroad employees as Hopi and Navajo adults and children in domestic scenes of childcare often while creating rugs, jewelry, pottery and other crafts; performing dances in front of crowds of park tourists; standing near scenic viewpoints; or standing in or near concessionaire hotels and other structures. In almost all of these postcards, a visual segregation of American Indian people and white people prevailed; representations of white and American Indian people were not shown together in the same frame. The most notable exception to this pattern may be found in postcards depicting Hopi dancers performing for tourists in front of Hopi House in the Grand Canyon Village on the South Rim (fig. 86). Postcards depicted the dances outside of the Hopi House, positioning the American Indian dancers as the object of tourists' gazes and as commodities to be consumed along with the canyon's scenery (Evans-Pritchard 1989; Weigle 1989).

The performance was part of a larger ecosystem of Fred Harvey Company and Santa Fe Railroad's commodification of American Indian cultures

Fig. 86. *Dance of the Hopi Indians, Grand Canyon National Park, Arizona*. In this 1937 Curt Teich Company postcard printed using the C. T. Art-Colortone process on linen stock card, Hopi dancers are shown performing in front of a crowd of white tourists near the South Rim, in front of Hopi House. This is one of the very few postcards that show white and American Indian people in the same frame (including white children) from the hundreds of images analyzed for this project. Curt Teich Postcard, H-3630. Author's collection.

throughout the Southwest through auto tours, performances, selling of crafts, and buildings such as Hopi House. As English scholar and historian Leah Dilworth contends, the "Fred Harvey Company and the AT&SF crated and coordinated touristic desires by rendering southwestern Indian life as a 'spectacle,' a cultural discourse that constructed epistemological and social relations between tourists and Indians as primarily visual; subjectivity resided with the touristic gaze, and Indians were objectified as culturally 'blind' and static, available for tourist consumption" (2001, 144). American Indians were shown in traditional clothes (fig. 87) and many times in family scenes with women, men, and children together. These postcards views, such as "Hopi Basket Weavers, Arizona" especially favored scenes of women crafting rugs, baskets, or pottery while the children played nearby (fig. 88). Overall, CTC featured American Indian artisans identified in the postcard captions as Hopi or Navajo at work either in Hopi House or nearby as basket weavers, rug weavers, pottery makers, and silversmiths.

Fig. 87. *Navajo and Hopi Indians on the Rim of the Grand Canyon*. In this 1936 Curt Teich linen postcard, people identified in the postcard identified as Navajos and Hopis are shown at the rim of the canyon, outfitted in brightly colored, detailed traditional dress. This is an uncommon postcard representation of a person looking directly at the camera (*far right*) from the Grand Canyon postcard sample set. Newberry Library, Curt Teich Postcard Archives Collection, production #D4349.

As such, Hopi and Navajo were the only people represented as working and living at the canyon, relegating white people to roles as tourists and voyeurs watching resident American Indians live their daily lives at the canyon. These CTC postcards supported and promoted a national park identity and an image of American Indians that was fueled, in part, by corporate interests (Blodgett 2007). Part of the cultural context of the Curt Teich Company postcards includes the popular culture influence of the short-lived "Indian Detours." Starting in the 1920s and fading by the 1930s, Fred Harvey Company and the Santa Fe Railroad contrived these auto tours of the Southwest as a way to capture a new tourism market as railroad travel waned and auto touring rose. Santa Fe Railroad arranged for Fred Harvey auto tour cars to meet passengers at railroad stops, then take them on journeys of several days to pueblos, ruins, and artists' studios before returning them to the stations to resume their train journey (Dilworth 1996, 90–93).

Fig. 88. *Hopi Basket Weavers, Arizona.* This Curt Teich postcard features two Hopi women crafting baskets with a young child playing nearby. American Indian artisans in scenes such as this were common subjects depicted in Curt Teich postcards. Courtesy Grand Canyon National Park Museum Collection, image GRCA #22321.

There is much missing from these images, and this line of visual reasoning expands and continues as the iconographic arc of Grand Canyon imagery grows. The postcards represent a limited view of the social and multicultural Southwest of the Greater Grand Canyon Region, failing to capture a more inclusive peoples, cultures, and traditions of the region. For example, no Curt Teich Company or Frasher Foto postcard depicted Havasupai, who were also employed by Fred Harvey and living in Grand Canyon Village at Supai Camp or, starting in 1939, at government-issued and -built cabins nearby (Rothman 1998, 76). As related by Havasupai tribal councilwoman Ophelia Watahomigie-Corliss: "When the Fred Harvey Company set up its hospitality industry on the South Rim near the turn of the 20th century, they hired Havasupai and created a work camp for them called Supai Camp" (2020). Historian Hal Rothman contends that "Havasupai labor offered none of the mythic characteristics of Hopi crafts, Indian dancing, or other kinds of ceremonial activities. The Havasupai performed ordinary jobs, the men laboring at construction and building, the women undertaking domestic and kitchen work" (1998, 74–75). Hispanos are also missing from the postcard imagery. As Dilworth asserts, Hispanos, like many American Indians, "participated in the area's economy as wage laborers; the railroads were built and maintained with Hispanic labor, and Hispanic workers were in high demand as agricultural laborers beginning in about 1900, when big irrigation projects were underway" (2001, 155–56). Dilworth observes how race and class shaped ideas of the exotic and spectacle and influenced the developing tourist economy of the GGCR. "But Hispanic . . . peasants defined by their labor, were not exotic. Unlike Indians, Hispanos did not qualify as a primitive folks worth preserving. . . . Their presence in the tourist spectacle threatened to reveal the actual infrastructure of massive capital and exploited labor that lay behind the spectacle. . . . As a result of these stereotypes and prejudices . . . Hispanos have found themselves . . . caught between hegemonic Anglo economic and political power" and the "Anglo glorification of Indian culture" (Dilworth 2001, 155–56).

The postcards also overlook the Hualapai living about thirty miles west of Grand Canyon Village in the Greater Grand Canyon Region. As active participants in regional hydropolitics, their protracted battle with the National Park Service and other U.S. agencies for access to the Colorado River that bordered the reservation deepened from the 1930s to 1970s in an effort to provide vital water for the community. As historian Jeffrey Shepherd notes, the "park had always opposed Haulapais' claim to the river" with "repeated claims the interests of the states and the general public, which relied on the river, vastly outweighed the needs of the Haulapais" (2010, 169). The Haulapais water access challenges present an alternative reality of visual representations of people working and living at the Grand Canyon. At Grand Canyon Village, water supply challenges were met with corporate investment, government management, and expanding tourism economies during the same era. These elements combined to create different outcomes in a parallel reality that favored increased water supply and access instead of legal challenges and prolonged battles.

Some postcards altered the social landscape of the Grand Canyon in more overt ways. Many postcard manufacturers, including Curt Teich, manipulated the image of the postcard by adding, removing, or altering the subject matter depicted in the card. Several postcards sampled revealed altered social scenes through the various printings of each card. For example, in a CTC postcard from 1937 titled *El Tovar, Grand Canyon National Park, Arizona*, the El Tovar Hotel is prominently displayed but not the center of attention (fig. 89). The postcard depicts the front entrance and extensive facade to El Tovar Hotel, a driveway and dense stands of trees in front of the hotel, and the rooftop of Hopi House. The viewpoint of the card is unusual for CTC imagery; the perspective is from an onlooker standing on top of Hopi House. People in the foreground are sitting and wrapped in blankets and or standing on the rooftop dressed in colorful shirts, pants, and headbands, all with their backs to the postcard viewer as they too look down on the scene in front of El Tovar Hotel. On the ground, near the driveway, another group of people—also dressed in colorful clothes—stand close together near a thick stand of iridescent green trees. The figures are too small to discern where their gaze lands, perhaps up at Hopi House or maybe downward and looking at each other as they converse about their day at the canyon. Interpretation of the action of the scene is open, but one scenario might be that it is an image taken of Hopi craftspeople standing on the roof of Hopi House, looking down at a group of tourists waiting for their group tour or perhaps just returning from a recent trip. This postcard was one of Curt Teich's most popular views with multiple reprintings over the course of several years. Such reprintings of this postcard reveal frequent but small changes to create new products. Some of the most noticeable changes included the color of people's clothing on the roof of Hopi House, the removal or addition of cars and trucks in the road and the reduction in numbers or changes in the color of the trees in the center of the image, or different shades of orange or brown paint on El Tovar Hotel's exterior.

At first glance, the postcard seems ordinary. CTC manufactured many postcards of El Tovar Hotel and Hopi House. However, a closer look reveals the touch of CTC postcard editing. At the center of the Hopi House onlookers' attention and in the center of the image, a small group of well-dressed of people stand near the trees and along the edge of a pathway connecting Hopi House to El Tovar through the stand of dense trees. Although the events being depicted are not clear, the image of the two groups of people separated across the courtyard are easily visible.

Now, compare the 1937 CTC postcard representing this scene at El Tovar Hotel with a later printing of this card from 1952 (fig. 90). In the 1952 card we see many of the same subjects: El Tovar Hotel, the stand of trees, the pathway, Hopi House rooftop, and small groups of people standing near the pathway while another group on the rooftop looks down on the scene below. But differences between the two cards are evident. CTC manufacturers and printers altered the sky over El Tovar Hotel from a deep blue with clouds in the 1937 image to a lighter shade of blue and a cloudless sky. The colors of the two images are quite different too. El Tovar Hotel's façade and the canyon cliffs in the background shifted from orange in 1937 to a darker brown and pink in 1952. The color of the Hopi House onlookers' clothes changed too; from vibrant yellow, green, and orange in 1937 to a more subdued pink, white, and dark green in 1952. The clothes and location of the rooftop viewers suggests Hopi men, women, and children. But such assumptions can be problematic. Historian Hal Rothman notes the complexity of Hopi roles and identities at Grand Canyon National Park, particularly when their labor and appearance is in play. "Hopi who worked at labor or service jobs were invisible as Indians: only in the regalia or in the Hopi House did they connect with tourists' perception of what an Indian should be" (Rothman 1998, 73).

But the surprising alteration between the cards is the object of attention for both the people on the roof and the group standing near the pathway. What was an open space in the driveway between El Tovar Hotel and Hopi House in 1937, CTC later revised to include a small tour bus and more people. The center of attention for the Hopi House onlookers is now evident. Instead of looking down onto an empty lawn, they may have been watching the tour bus scene. The group of people standing near the footpath and stand of trees now have a clear purpose as they seem to assemble for their tour or perhaps have recently disembarked from a bus.

CTC postcard manufacturing records reveal the directives behind some of these changes. The Photo Ticket and Estimate and Work Schedule forms that accompanied the image through the manufacturing stages documents the Fred Harvey Company's customer request with a hand-written note to update the image with "new colors" and to "put back people that were taken out of photo[,] see card" (fig. 91). Comparing figures 89 and 90 further illustrates that the tour bus and people were present in the earlier image, then removed in subsequent printings. The working version of this photo editing process is the black-and-white photograph that formed the basis of the image. Along the edges of the retouched photo, the handwritten notes and marks of the production crew reveal the image in process, just after the sky was painted over to remove the clouds but before the bus and additional people were added to the scene. (fig. 92). The CTC records, though detailed in their technical procedures, leave us to guess at the intentions of Fred Harvey Company and CTC in making this decision to remove the bus and

Fig. 89. (*top*) Editing the social landscape at the Grand Canyon. *Hotel El Tovar, Grand Canyon National Park, Arizona*, 1937 postcard. Look closely at this view of El Tovar Hotel to see the group of people standing near the trees at the pathway's end (center of image). Curt Teich Postcard production #7AH648, author's collection. Annotated by the author.

Fig. 90. (*bottom*) *Hotel El Tovar, Grand Canyon National Park, Arizona*, 1952 postcard. Newberry Library, Curt Teich Postcard Archives Collection, production #d10064, 1952.

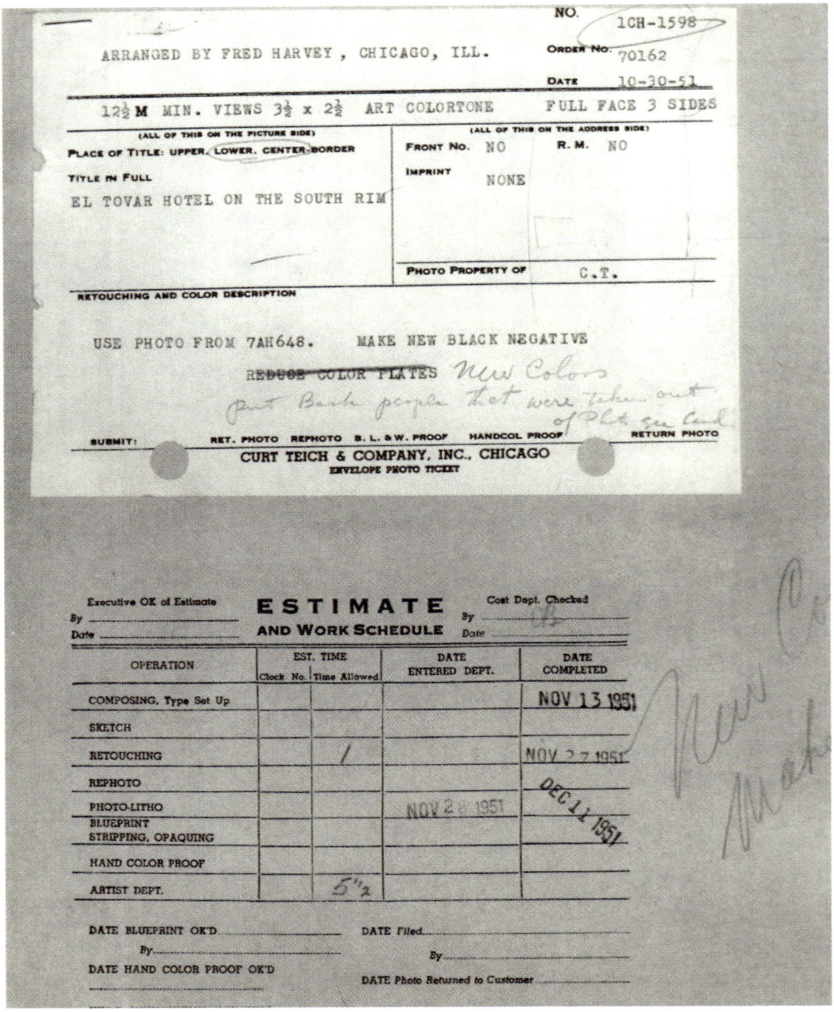

NO. 1CH-1598
ARRANGED BY FRED HARVEY, CHICAGO, ILL. ORDER NO. 70162
DATE 10-30-51
12½ M MIN. VIEWS 3½ x 2½ ART COLORTONE FULL FACE 3 SIDES
(ALL OF THIS ON THE PICTURE SIDE)
PLACE OF TITLE: UPPER. LOWER. CENTER-BORDER
TITLE IN FULL
EL TOVAR HOTEL ON THE SOUTH RIM
(ALL OF THIS ON THE ADDRESS SIDE)
FRONT NO. NO R. M. NO
IMPRINT NONE
PHOTO PROPERTY OF C.T.
RETOUCHING AND COLOR DESCRIPTION
USE PHOTO FROM 7AH648. MAKE NEW BLACK NEGATIVE
~~REDUCE COLOR PLATES~~ New Colors
put Back people that were taken out of Photo see Card
SUBMIT: RET. PHOTO REPHOTO B. L. & W. PROOF HANDCOL PROOF RETURN PHOTO
CURT TEICH & COMPANY, INC., CHICAGO
ENVELOPE PHOTO TICKET

Executive OK of Estimate
By
Date
ESTIMATE
AND WORK SCHEDULE
Cost Dept. Checked
By
Date

OPERATION	EST. TIME Clock No.	Time Allowed	DATE ENTERED DEPT.	DATE COMPLETED
COMPOSING, Type Set Up				NOV 13 1951
SKETCH				
RETOUCHING		/		NOV 27 1951
REPHOTO				DEC 11 1951
PHOTO-LITHO			NOV 28 1951	
BLUEPRINT STRIPPING, OPAQUING				
HAND COLOR PROOF				
ARTIST DEPT.		5½		

DATE BLUEPRINT OK'D
By
DATE HAND COLOR PROOF OK'D
DATE Filed
By
DATE Photo Returned to Customer

Fig. 91. Photo ticket and work estimate documentation for an El Tovar Hotel postcard, 1951. The work order, dated October 30, 1951 (*top*) advises using "new colors" and to "put back people that were taken out of photo." Newberry Library, Curt Teich Postcard Archives Collection, production records for #1CH-1598.

people from the photograph for the 1937 printing, then to add them back in for the 1952 image. However, based on my research with the CTC archives and other similar requests for editing and production, the reason may have simply been to create a new product using the same photograph but altered to include different colors and additional subject matter.

Fig. 92. Retouched photo of *El Tovar Hotel*. A postcard in production. Newberry Library, Curt Teich Postcard Archives Collection, production records #1CH-1598.

Building Canyon Culture

Construction and expansion of the Grand Canyon's South Rim and North Rim villages boomed during the 1930s with investment of capital and labor from the NPS, Fred Harvey Company, and Santa Fe Railroad. These cultural landscape changes brought more than just shelter, entertainment, or transportation to the Grand Canyon; they also created new social spaces and venues for a cross-cultural discourse that was unfolding across the Greater Grand Canyon Region from the 1930s to 1950s. An example of this discourse materialized may be seen in the Desert View Watchtower.

Fred Harvey Company constructed Desert View Watchtower, a stone tower and visitor service site on the southeast rim of the Grand Canyon in 1932. The building was part of the wave of concessionaire-financed construction and development taking place along the South Rim in the 1930s. FHC's chief architect and interior designer of forty years, Mary Elizabeth

Jane Colter, designed the structure and drew inspiration from the architecture of the Ancestral Puebloan ruins of the Colorado Plateau, particularly Hovenweep and Mesa Verde (Colter [1933] 2015). There was no previous tower or other major stone structure at that location before Colter's, but she designed the building a meticulous observation to detail so it appeared as a historic structure "naturally" in its place. "Colter wanted only natural surface stone so that the color and texture would naturally match the surrounding terrain, reinforcing the idea that the tower was growing out of the earth" (McQuaid and Bartlett 1996, 31). The building is panopticon situated at the very edge of the South Rim overlooking the canyon and the Colorado River. Colter insisted on design elements that increased the viewing potential from the aptly named Watchtower, including many small windows and several viewing decks affording dramatic views looking north into Marble Canyon, the Painted Desert, and into the canyon's depths along the Colorado River. She also installed reflectoscopes on the roof, an artist's invention that used a thin, convex, and highly polished slab of black onyx that reflects light and projects a condensed and simplified view of the Grand Canyon. The Desert Watchtower's survey of the canyon scene is immense; it is one of the few buildings on the South Rim that is visible to river runners a mile below on the Colorado River.

The building is the source of more written documentation than any other project pursued by Colter. Not surprisingly, then, the Watchtower was a common subject of CTC and FFPC postcards. A Frasher Foto postcard titled *Indian Watchtower at Desert View, Grand Canyon Nat'l Park Arizona* positions the frame of view on the tower as a central figure. The scene is tight and focused on the building, only hinting at the sweeping views of the canyon with the rim in the distance (fig. 93).

Desert View Watchtower is a blending of multiple cultures in its construction and design including some with active participation in the creation of this structure—Anglo in Colter and some of the construction workers—and others, such as the ancestral Puebloan, reappropriated. As other scholars have observed, "Colter was not reproducing a particular historical style but creating one of her own with roots in Native American culture: 'We tried to understand how a building suited to our purpose would have been built by Indians of the best Pueblo period. We adapted and combined'" (McQuaid and Bartlett 1996, 32; Colter [1933], 13). Colter's Desert View Watchtower also adapted and combined materials using local stone and wood as well as

Fig. 93. Desert View Watchtower, 1934. Courtesy Frasher Foto Collection/HJG and Pomona Public Library, Pomona, California. Frasher Foto Postcard Collection, "Indian Watchtower at Desert View, Grand Canyon National Park, Arizona," index #A7932.

Fig. 94. Hopi artist Fred Kabotie in the Desert View Watchtower, 1932. In this image, Kabotie is painting the Snake Legend onto the inner walls of the watchtower. Courtesy Grand Canyon National Park Museum Collection, image #GRCA 22671A.

the remains of former independent rim-side businesses pushed out by Fred Harvey Company and the Santa Fe Railroad. The log ceiling in the kiva, the large room on the first floor of the Watchtower, integrates logs from one of the earliest hotels at the South Rim, Grand View Hotel run by the Anglo husband and wife team of Peter and Martha Berry.

The Watchtower also includes elements contributed directly by a Hopi artist. As visitors climb the interior stairs up through the tower, they encounter several levels of paintings and artwork. The walls in the first main gallery were painted by Fred Kabotie, a Hopi artist from the Second Mesa, who Colter employed to decorate the interior walls of the tower (fig. 94). The paintings depict scenes and stories of Hopi life through it physical and spiritual origins. A 1940 Curt Teich Company postcard depicts a man, two women, and two children wrapped in colorful blankets and clothes looking up at Kabotie's Snake Legend painting (fig. 95). The postcard does not identify the group. This may be a family group or a staged scene orchestrated by Fred

Fig. 95. *Hopi Paintings in the Watchtower at Desert View.* Newberry Library, Curt Teich Postcard Archives Collection, production #1BH773.

Harvey Company and photographed by CTC artists. In any case, the postcard reinforces other CTC imagery that emphasized representations of American Indian men, women, and children in interior locations of Fred Harvey Company buildings, such as Hopi House, and often used as a visual strategy to confirm the authenticity of the location in the exotic desert Southwest.

The representation of American Indian cultures and traditions through the Watchtower's physical structure and interior design represents the discourses of concessionaire development strategies, NPS cultural resource management, and tribal connections to the Greater Grand Canyon Region. The tribes are deeply invested in the Grand Canyon as a living landscape and maintain physical connections to the canyon through traditions, ceremonies, and shared geographic knowledge. As geographer Barbara Morehouse argues in *A Place Called the Grand Canyon*, geography is central to understanding Indigenous land claims as territorial anchors and "specific landscapes serve as both moral guides and reminders of tribal connections" (1996, 14). Further, Morehouse asserts that "geographically specific places are indispensable to the cultures of the greater Grand Canyon peoples" who identified "specific natural features to mark the outer extent of their territory or to designate localities they associate with specific traditions, beliefs, and practices" (1996, 14). As the "ancestral homelands of many American Indian tribes, parks protect resources, sites, and vistas" that are "highly significant for the tribes" (Hirst 2016, vi). Archaeological and ethnographic research continues to evolve on the topic, but newer work confirms that the Grand Canyon—at times considered a barrier to travel and human settlement for its dry climate, steep vertical terrain, and limited water sources—may have been less of a challenge to human travel and agriculture in prehistoric times than previously understood (Smiley, Downum, and Smiley 2017). For example, the Hopi live east of the canyon and believe that they are the descents of Ancestral Puebloans who emerged from the Grand Canyon at the *Sipapuni* near the confluence of the Little Colorado and Colorado Rivers. Making a pilgrimage to this sacred space of origin is an essential part of tribal tradition. Several well-traveled trails from the Hopi Mesas to the Grand Canyon persist, including one to *Öonga*, the sacred site of the salt deposits near the confluence of the Colorado and Little Colorado Rivers and another trail that connects Hopi to the Havasupai. The Navajo and Zuni also trace their origin stories to the Grand Canyon, the Colorado River, and the landscapes around these areas. The Pai people (modern Hualapai, Yavapai Apache, and Havasupai tribes) and the Southern Paiute hold that their origins are in or near the Grand Canyon.

Take a Ride

The experiences and activities of tourists at the Grand Canyon shifted during the mid-twentieth century and CTC and FFPC imagery reflected that transition in recreation at the Grand Canyon. Stagecoaches, trains, and dirt roads gave way to automobiles and improved roads as popular forms of getting to and around the park. Inside Grand Canyon National Park, auto touring along the rim and mule riding into its depths topped the list of outdoor pursuits. Our modern view of exploring the Grand Canyon through river rafting the Colorado River, hiking the canyon trails, camping overnight at backcountry sites, or even running "rim to rim" (from the South Rim to North Rim or vice versa) was soon to emerge on the post–World War II scene.

Curt Teich postcards featured recreation as a popular theme for Grand Canyon imagery from 1936 to 1955. Conversely, Frasher Foto postcards did not include any representations of recreation, except scenic driving (although driving was not included as a recreational activity in this book's analysis). Also worth noting, the spatial division of specific locations and themes by each of the media types and production companies is much more visible as Grand Canyon National Park visitation and recreational activities increased throughout the twentieth century. For example, Curt Teich Company followed in the steps of Detroit Publishing Company by focusing their imagery primarily at Grand Canyon Village, southeast rim, midcanyon trails leading from the South Rim, and the river level near Phantom Ranch—all popular sites with tourist services and development. A majority of Frasher Foto imagery also featured South Rim scenes but included more North Rim locations than Curt Teich Company.

Curt Teich Company's predilection for featuring mules and their riders in postcards during this era no doubt contributed to the rise of this activity as iconic symbol of an authentic Grand Canyon experience. Mule riding into and out of the inner canyon, particularly along the Bright Angel or Kaibab Trail, was a unique experience for tourists to the Grand Canyon and one that concessionaires and the growing tourist industry heavily promoted. No doubt, sitting on a mule, peering over the edge of the seemingly bottomless canyon as one sways back and forth down the trail, is not for the faint of heart. This is also not a solo activity. As with so much of the national park tourism experience before World War II after the rise of the individual motorist, mule riding was and continues to be a group activity that shapes transportation corridors into cultural landscapes (Youngs, White, and Wodrich 2008, 798–800). Riders follow a lead wrangler in a long train of sure-footed animals that are well-versed and trained in the contours and perils of canyon trails (fig. 96). Mule wrangling and riding is a deeply woven part of the Grand Canyon's recreational landscape. These

Fig. 96. *On Kaibab Trail, Grand Canyon National Park, Arizona*, 1937. Newberry Library, Curt Teich Postcard Archives Collection, production #7AH688.

activities have distinct historical roots in the nineteenth century mining era that expanded as canyon pioneers developed business models that both accommodated and attracted early canyon tourists. The people in this scene are not identified as a group or even individually but they are represented as tourists dressed in muted shades of brown and green with white or tan shirts and large sun-shading hats. The mule train pausing on the inner canyon trail is pointing toward the great expanse of the canyon ahead and below, emphasizing the size of the Grand Canyon and its brilliantly colored red, orange, and tan strata.

Touring the Grand Canyon in the Auto Age

The 1930s were a major road-building era for the park and surrounding areas. The federal government upgraded or realigned much of the road system that is still used in the park today. A good deal of this work was accomplished through the Bureau of Public Roads (now known as the Federal Highway Administration). Regional, or "approach," roads to the park, however, were a different matter. Multiple agencies, corporate interests, and American Indian reservations bonded together in a begrudging collabo-

Fig. 97. *Near Mohave Point on the Grand Canyon Rim Drive, Grand Canyon National Park.* Curt Teich Company postcard, H-3996. Author's collection.

ration to build and maintain roads that brought auto travelers to Grand Canyon National Park. By the 1930s, however, many of these arrangements were wearing thin as the National Park Service felt more pressure to take over maintenance of these routes, such as the Navahopi Road (supported by the Santa Fe Railroad) and the south entrance approach road (supported by the State of Arizona). During the 1930s several park and regional road corridors were built or realigned.

As a reflection of the growing popularity of auto touring and routes to visit national parks in the American West, auto touring and tourists were common subjects of CTC and FFPC postcards in this era. These cards featured tourists gathered at a stop along a road on an auto tour, with lines of buses or large tour cars. Curt Teich Company's *Near Mohave Point on the Grand Canyon Rim Drive, Grand Canyon National Park, Arizona* is standard fare for this subject matter. A group of well-dressed people—men in jackets and ties, ladies in dresses and long jackets—stand near two group touring cars in the foreground with the expansive canyon and the Colorado River view behind them (fig. 97). Non-motorized travel also had its fair share of imagery with trails, mostly dirt walking paths or mule trails, as a key element here. These trail images provided a visual confirmation of visitors' access to the depths of the canyon and were depicted more often in CTC postcards.

Frasher Foto postcards, on the other hand, did not show people or animals on the trails but instead featured unpopulated views or simply those of cars moving along roads. CTC postcards featured Hermit Road (Grand Canyon Village to Hermit's Rest, South Rim) and the North Rim Entrance Road (today's Arizona State Route 67). The Kaibab Suspension Bridge was the only bridge shown in CTC postcards from this era. Frasher Foto postcards featured many roads and routes, including the North Rim Entrance Road and U.S. Highway 89 (between Flagstaff and Marble Canyon/North Rim of the Grand Canyon).

Shifting Visions: Select Locations in Imagery

Cumulatively, mid-twentieth century postcards represented South Rim scenes as the most common view of the Grand Canyon. As noted earlier in this study, this pattern may be attributed to CTC's contracts with the Fred Harvey Company, the profusion of cards manufactured by CTC, and FHC's focus of operations on the South Rim Grand Canyon Village. This imagery builds upon previous eras of imagery. Connecting back to Dutton's 1882 expansive and detailed depiction of Grand Canyon scenery from a rim-side perch, Curt Teich and Frasher Foto only added another layer to this dominant idea of what the canyon environment looked like and where one should see it from. Indeed, the most common location for both the Curt Teich postcards and the Frasher Foto postcards of this era, 1936 to 1955, was a rim-side view from the South Rim (see appendix C).

That both postcard manufacturers during this era relied so heavily on South Rim representations of the Grand Canyon may come as no surprise. Seeing the Grand Canyon through windshields quickly became the standard. From 1936 to 1955, auto tourism grew in popularity at a steady pace, park and access roads were gaining in their extent, and the number of visitors making the journey to the Grand Canyon generally rose. Much of the Grand Canyon's rugged inner recess was inaccessible by road, but the South Rim from El Tovar Hotel to Hermit's Rest could be viewed in an afternoon's drive. The South Rim was where most Grand Canyon visitors spent their time, and this seems to be the view that postcard manufacturers sought to reproduce and sell. As the Grand Canyon's popularity and iconic status rose, so, too, did visitors perceive the Grand Canyon as a South Rim attraction.

8 Canyon Be Dammed

> Why wilderness? Ask the men who have known it and who have made it part of their lives. . . . Wilderness to them is real and this they do know: when the pressure becomes more than they can stand, somewhere back of beyond . . . they will find release.
>
> —Sigurd Olsen, quoted in Callicott and Nelson, *The Great New Wilderness Debate*

Long viewed as a positive and appropriate form of development for national parks, the construction of roads, trails, bridges, public camping, and water and sewer systems to support tourism came under fire between 1936 and 1970. As the first director of the National Park Service, Stephen Mather vigorously pushed to develop the national parks for tourism, in an egalitarian approach to make scenery accessible to more people. However, the tide changed as environmentalists questioned the push for development and natural resource extraction. One influential group during this era was the Wilderness Society, formed in 1935 by Robert Marshall, Olaus Murie, Aldo Leopold, and Benton MacKaye to create and protect "wilderness areas and to preserve public lands" (Merchant 2007, 242–43). In the first issue of *Living Wilderness*, a magazine published by the society, editor Robert Sterling Yard wrote that the "Wilderness Society is born of an emergency in conservation which admits of no delay. The craze is to build all the highways possible everywhere while billions may yet be borrowed from the unlucky future" (qtd. in Fox 1986, 211). What was near to heresy in the 1930s with the push to build and expand infrastructure into and around the parks was now seen as something to limit, to control for the sake of nature as wilderness. Arizona's road and highway advocates were in for a bumpy ride.

After World War II, the Grand Canyon increasingly rose to the top of environmental agendas and national attention. It was not the scenic rimside viewpoints, the mule rides, the hotel hospitality, or the miles of paved roads that drew this recognition; instead it was the Colorado River and the inner canyon area. The inner canyon was becoming more than a mecca for outdoor enthusiasts; it was becoming a battleground.

There is magnetism about rivers and their rapids, an attraction felt by people even on opposites sides of environmental debates. As historian and whitewater boater Roderick Nash writes, "Dam builders eye whitewater with as much enthusiasm as boatmen" (1989, 8). Both see potential in those churning waves. For river runners it is the thrill of the ride, the challenge of a successful run that drives their attraction. Dam builders measure their attraction in the kinetic energy and economic potential of that rapid, the chance to power industrial aspirations and quench the thirst of some of the nation's largest western metropolitan areas (Fedarko 2014a, 2014b).

Arizona Highways framed the popular view of these environmental contests by portraying both the emerging wilderness ethic of backcountry and inner canyon travel and its counterpoint of modernism through development and massive dam engineering projects. The popular magazine continued to highlight scenic drives and rim-side viewpoints popular in its earlier issues, but editors and photographers also encouraged readers to leave their cars and walk or row their way into the Grand Canyon, down its trails and along its waterways. Imagery left the pavement behind thereby showing magazine readers another Grand Canyon, an environmental canyon.

Edward Abbey, author, activist, and desert curmudgeon once argued that "everybody has to go down the river some time" (1988, 107). Since the birth of commercial river rafting in the Grand Canyon in the 1950s, many people have taken his advice. Of all the words of praise and critique, observation and reflection that have been penned by cultural critic and art writer Lucy Lippard, these may surprise her audience the most: "I was lulled by being guided" (2001, 2). Yet that is just what Lippard confesses, connecting her ideas with the reality of Grand Canyon tourism experience. Her experience was that of so many other visitors who have floated through the canyon on the Colorado River, knowing it from the river up, instead of the rim down. Lippard was looking for a middle ground between theory and practice, an intellectual space as well as a physical place to experience the Grand Canyon beyond the layers of "human constructions" and instead in a world of individual experience and cold, wet water. She wrote that the "relations between doing and seeing, action and vision, construction and perception, lie at the core of the Grand Canyon experience" (2001, 2). It was the Colorado River and the experience of a river trip through the canyon that spurred her to write those words.

Lippard shares many similarities with other Grand Canyon visitors who came to the canyon for the Colorado River. At first the canyon was of little interest to her "beyond its obdurate identity as spectacle, a melodramatic aesthetic, and an academic cliché" (2001, 2). Her expectations were turned upside down in the canyon during that river trip, an experience that more and more park visitors would have from 1930s to the 1970s as commercial river running came to the canyon.

Promoting Grand Canyon—Magazine Representations and Visual Culture

The period of 1936 to 1970 was a pivotal time in the institutional history of *Arizona Highways*. During these years, photographic styles and equipment, the routes and methods that photographers used to reach their subjects, and the funding of the magazine all changed. As photographic technology advanced and cameras became smaller and lighter, photographers could wander farther away from Arizona's roads and farther into its wilderness. This process was evident in the transition of subject matter. Gradually, the landscape scenes of the magazine began to feature more hiking adventures, river trips, and motorboating excursions, all activities that required the photographer get out of the car and explore afield.

Color photography became a hallmark of the magazine and an important characteristic that set *Arizona Highways* apart from its competitors. By the late 1930s, the magazine included issues with color covers and color images interspersed throughout the magazine (Carlson 1951; Arizona Department of Transportation Research Center 2020). The December 1946 issue was "the first all-color issue of a nationally circulated consumer magazine" (Carlson 1951, no page).

The Grand Canyon was an often-repeated and prominent location pictured in *Arizona Highways*. Indeed, the status of the Grand Canyon as a significant Arizona tourism site is reflected in the subject matter of the first color issue in December 1946 featuring a snow-clad Grand Canyon. Color formatting elevated the magazine to national attention. Photographer and author Stephen Trimble observed that "*Arizona Highways* became synonymous with quality color printing and splashy landscape photography—and a powerful force in shaping public awareness of the Grand Canyon in the second half of the twentieth century" (2006, 27).

The shift to color photography is central to the impact of *Arizona Highways* photographs on popular understandings of the Grand Canyon. Anthropologists Catherine A. Lutz and sociologist Jane L. Collins assert in their study of *National Geographic* magazine images, "Color photography inevitably changes the nature of representation" (1993, 31). The decision to reproduce color photographs invokes other related choices, notably the mood of the photograph and the subjects to include in the image. In addition, color photography distinguished *Arizona Highways* from other magazines that continued to rely on black-and-white photographs. By 1955 the editor of *Arizona Highways*, Raymond Carlson, noted that the Grand Canyon accounted for thirty-one feature articles in the magazine, a subject only surpassed by features about Navajo Indians, of which there were thirty-three (Carlson 1951).

Arizona Highways' funding changed during the late 1930s. The State of Arizona's Department of Transportation—the same agency that is responsible for grading roads and installing mile markers across the state—funded the magazine's first issue in April 1925 and subsequent early issues through a combination of Arizona State Legislature annual appropriations, publication sales, and advertisements. That funding formula changed in 1938, when the Arizona Highway Commission put an end to advertisements in the magazine, a policy that persists to this day. As noted in earlier chapters, *Arizona Highways* expanded from a base of sales in newsstands, bookstores, and other retail outlets that also included individual, corporate, hotel, and library subscriptions. More recently, the magazine extended its reach through the associated *Arizona Highways Television* program, a Facebook page, and product sales such as the highly popular calendars (Arizona Department of Transportation Research Center 2020, 9). The magazine's audience—readers across Arizona, the United States, and internationally—grew over the years to a peak of 507,133 subscribers in 1977 (Wagner 2007), but the magazine's circulation has fallen over the years due to competition from other magazines and increases in subscription charges.

Dominant Images—Magazine Views of the Canyon

The results of a content analysis of 664 images found in *Arizona Highways* from 1936 to 1970 reveal differences in themes and locations (see appendix

C). Visual representations of the canyon that appeared in *Arizona Highways* were predominately photographs; however, maps, sketches, and reproductions of paintings also surface now and then in the publication. Of the 664 visual representations sampled, the most common subject was scenic views of the canyon (384 images). In descending order, the next most common subjects were white people (230), the Colorado River (103), and recreation (117). To a lesser degree, other subjects included in the *Arizona Highways* image set include water as lakes, streams, and waterfalls (93); mules and horses (42), dams (38), building exteriors (33), trails (32), American Indians (29), automobiles (28), roads and bridges (27), building interiors (20), miscellaneous (11), and children (5). Overall the trend during this period was to represent more scenic views, the Colorado River, white people, and recreation than in previous eras.

The locations of the illustrations sampled reveal a geographical bias. The Grand Canyon is a place that has been and continues to be experienced both horizontally via latitude and longitude coordinates, as well as vertically at rim, trail, or river locations (see appendix B). The most common horizontal locations were along the South Rim (159), followed by Lake Mead (111), northeast (98), midcanyon (93), North Rim (69), west (65), Havasupai (58), and images depicting the entirety of the canyon, found in maps or captured from aerial, or satellite perspectives (11).

Although representations of the South Rim and midcanyon locations were common during this period, there were some variations in the geographical locations represented. For instance, from the later 1930s and into the 1940s, images of Lake Mead, Havasupai, and west areas were quite common. By the 1950s and 1960s, the geographical focus of magazine images shifted to locations at the North Rim and northeast areas of the canyon. This shift may be tied to development and hydropolitics in the the Greater Grand Canyon Region. The 1930s and 1940s brought a boom of recreation and development to the western Grand Canyon with the completion of Hoover Dam and Lake Mead. Later in the century, Grand Canyon National Park expanded to include Marble Canyon and the construction and completion of Lake Powell and Glen Canyon Dam drew media attention and tourism dollars to the north and northeast GGCR.

The Colorado River was the most common vertical location represented in *Arizona Highways* during this period (348 instances), followed by rim locations (234) and, to a much lesser degree, representations of the canyon from aerial perspectives (42) or midcanyon locations (40). Unlike the postcard imagery that may have obscured the canyon or focused on building interiors, all Grand Canyon photographs in *Arizona Highways* included a clear view of the canyon. Representations that featured multiple views of the canyon, a somewhat common style for postcards, were absent from the *Arizona Highways* imagery. This may be due to the artistic focus on the magazine to feature original photographs or simply editorial decisions about page layouts and format.

Beyond the Pavement, into the Wilderness

As with the postcard imagery from Curt Teich and Frasher Foto, the most common subject of visual representations sampled from *Arizona Highways* issues were scenic views of the canyon. When discussing the imagery set, however, it is important to note that there was a distinct shift in the subject frequency and locations represented in the magazine from 1936 to 1970. While representations of scenic views and white people were common throughout this era, other subjects—such as the Colorado River, dams and water—increased during this period, especially views featuring impounded lakes such as Lake Powell and Lake Mead. Compared to earlier *Arizona Highways* images, there is less of an emphasis on automobiles, roads and bridges, and building interiors. During this era, *Arizona Highways* shifted its focus to new subjects as it left the pavement behind for wilderness and recreational activities such as backpacking, hiking, and river rafting that grew increasingly popular and accessible for more tourists.

Additionally, locations featured in *Arizona Highways* were not evenly represented over this period. During the first part of this era, images of the South Rim, Lake Mead, the west canyon area, and Havasupai were common. However, as the 1940s gave way to the 1950s (and plans for dam building in the Grand Canyon moved forward), *Arizona Highways* featured more representations of the North Rim, northeast, and midcanyon areas. The vertical locations featured in this era's imagery set may be the most telling of broader social and political discussions brewing. The two most common vertical locations were the Colorado River—increasingly framed as an inner canyon sanctuary of wilderness—and the south and North Rims—the perches from which people who favored cars, roads, and natural resource conservation looked down into the Grand Canyon. Although midcanyon and aerial views were well-used angles for photographers, it was river or rim locations that received the most press. Visual representations of the river in previous eras from Powell's famous exploits and the rim-side scenic viewpoints popularized by entrepreneurs and corporations eager to attract tourist dollars took on new meaning.

Reformulated for modern tastes, the rim-river visual dialect increasingly came to signify more than geographic locations or a choice between a hotel stay and a mule ride. Visual representations shaped popular geographic understanding about these locations and their connections to broader environmental debates. Lines were drawn and battles were fought. By 1970 the river corridor was the territory of wilderness advocates. Representations of the river corridor frequently featured recreational activities such as river rafting, hiking, and mule riding that were associated with wilderness ideals as the terms "backcountry" or "inner canyon" gained greater currency. Through striking oblique views of massive dam or bridge construction sites in the depths of the Grand Canyon, *Arizona Highways* photographers framed rim-side locations, on the other hand, as the domain of people with a different agenda for the Grand Canyon. With this insistent and repetitive focus of automobiles, roads, bridges, and dams, *Arizona Highways* editors and photographers positioned nature as either a scenic background or renewable resource for the modern twentieth-century desert economy. Certainly, dam proposals and threats to the natural flow cycles of the Colorado River were not new to Grand Canyon in the twentieth century (Pearson 2012). However, the tenor of the conversation shifted during the mid- and late twentieth century. Magazine photography, at least in *Arizona Highways*, became a vehicle to communicate the modern social construction of the Grand Canyon and the Colorado River as natural resources to be consumed, commodified, and controlled. Although Glen Canyon Dam and Lake Powell were certainly at river level in terms of elevation and included physical landscape features such as rocks and water, these features were framed in a different and separate way from ideas about nature held dear to environmental advocates. This was nature harnessed, nature corked, nature controlled.

A distinct trend during this period, however, was the growing frequency of representations that featured white people recreating on water. Class and ethnicity shaped tourist experiences at the Grand Canyon whereby white, affluent, middle- and upper-class tourists with more leisure time and money could afford the equipment and travel to the Grand Canyon for extended periods of time required for these longer trips into the river and trail backcountry. *Arizona Highways* may have been catering to these readers. Images of white people on auto tours of the canyon or mule rides into the canyon's depths—scenes common to earlier eras—gave way to other subjects. The magazine featured image after image of white people on motorized or oar-powered river trips and this same demographic in motorboats on Lake Mead and Lake Powell. Alternatively, while the magazine represented white people playing in the Grand Canyon, imagery focused on American Indians working and living in the canyon. Hand in hand with this trend, the magazine featured dams, particularly Glen Canyon, and construction scenes more frequently than images of El Tovar, Hopi House, or other icons of previous eras. Hiking and camping were increasingly popular activities during the postwar recreation boom in the United States fueled by increased leisure time, affluence, and greater access to war surplus equipment, such as tents, ropes, and inflatable rafts (Youngs 2014). At the Grand Canyon, hiking started to edge out mule riding as a popular activity.

This shift in magazine subjects also signals a shift in prevalent attitudes and perceptions about nature in America. Especially in the postwar era, nature was increasingly seen as a natural resource with value in economic, not aesthetic or spiritual, terms. Opposing this view, wilderness advocates pressed for the protection of nature for its intrinsic value, a limit to road and construction projects, and a wildlife matrix in parks and protected areas that privileged native species over exotic species. These broader social, cultural, and political discourses about nature had tremendous impact on the Grand Canyon as powerful social forces fought for their version of nature and conservation in this protected area.

Such was the case with the Grand Canyon throughout the 1950s and beyond as national debates about wilderness versus natural resource values took center stage with the Glen Canyon Dam project. Indeed, the impact of the Glen Canyon Dam controversy overshadowed almost every discussion about nature in the Grand Canyon during this period. Begun in 1956 and completed a decade later, this massive construction and water allocation project would steer Grand Canyon politics and the American environmentalism campaign onto a new course. *Arizona Highways* represented many of the subjects and locations that were central to this debate over the environmental canyon (see appendix C). Looking back at this imagery set, we glimpse a visual snapshot of some of the places and subjects that shaped popular imaginations about the Grand Canyon.

"This Is the Grand Canyon"

Scenic representations of the Grand Canyon were very common in *Arizona Highways* from 1936 to 1970, frequently featuring rim-side viewpoints boldly titled as "this is the Grand Canyon" (fig. 98). Several *Arizona Highways* scenic views sampled featured many canyon views, often captured from rim-side locations. Repercussions of this practice shaped popular geographic and environmental perceptions that proved a hurdle to Sierra Club and other wilderness advocates and preservationists as they fought Bureau of Reclamation and conservationists' plans over the future of Grand Canyon. Sierra Club leaders found that part of the challenge of their arguments against building the Glen Canyon Dam included convincing American audiences about where and what was worth protecting. Popular media such as *Arizona Highways* proved to be a useful tool in this campaign by creating a steady stream of high-quality photographs and engaging essays that featured the Colorado River and inner canyon as American scenic treasures worthy of preservation.

Unfortunately for wilderness advocates and preservationists fighting against the construction of Glen Canyon Dam, this select and often-repeated visual catalog of scenery at the rarely featured inner canyon and Colorado River scenes. Instead, popular visual representations of the Grand Canyon more often than not were located at specific and selected rim-side locations, places where "scenic" descriptions were firmly attached. In my analysis of the imagery, it is apparent that the central canyon area—near the South and North rim between Grand Canyon Village and Bright Angel Point—was the most often represented. These images functioned as visual and textual signposts for magazine readers, marking the scenic view of the canyon from the rim (more than any other subject or locations) as *the* Grand Canyon.

"River Adventure" Meets "Where the Lake and the Canyon Hold Hands"

Water plays a large part in the story of the Grand Canyon's iconographic arc. In an arid landscape dependent on limited water supplies, hydropolitics—the

"Watched the changing splendors from ledge to ledge . . ."
ESTHER HENDERSON

"Twixt iron walls thou rollest turbid waves . . ."
ESTHER HENDERSON

People from all over the world agree that Nature's most sublime spectacle is the Grand Canyon of Arizona. All who visit it are thrilled by its majestic mystery and those who have not yet seen it are eager to know more about it.

But it seems to be beyond the power of most of us ordinary mortals to describe Grand Canyon and the emotions it arouses. Visitors' comments vary in feeling from "Just rocks —what the 'ell!" to "Now I have seen God's face!" They also vary in length from President Howard Taft's concise "Golly, what a gully!" to purple passages of page-long paragraphs—which still leave much to be desired. No wonder someone said, "When the Creator made Grand Canyon, He forgot to make any adjectives to go with it!" We are likely to fumble for words and finally remark helplessly, "Well, it's beyond me!"

Many people, of course, have been more successful in expressing themselves. Volume after volume has been published about Grand Canyon. A whole library can be filled with books about different facets of this one fascinating subject. Explorers, historians, scientists, novelists are among those who have recorded certain aspects of the Canyon. But in most cases they have merely given us facts or vague but wordy descriptions. Interesting as these records often are, we are still unsatisfied. We realize there is more to our experience at Grand Canyon than they have expressed.

However, a survey of all that has been written about Grand Canyon does bring at last what we have been seeking. There are poets who have written about Grand Canyon with the skill and imaginative insight to express effectively the unique beauty of the Canyon, the feelings it arouses, and the thoughts it inspires.

For those of us who have visited the Canyon, such poetry keeps vivid our recollections, puts into words what we long in vain to express, and deepens our understanding of the experience we have had. For those who have not yet been there, this poetry gives glimpses through many eyes of Grand Canyon and its profound effect upon man.

No single poet has ever—or perhaps *can* ever—adequately express the Canyon's infinite variety and man's varied reactions to it. But from the best of the poetry, interpretations can be chosen which like bits in a mosaic finally form a complete word-picture of Grand Canyon.

"This," we can say with satisfaction, "*is* Grand Canyon!"

The amazement of our first look at Grand Canyon can never be forgotten. Modern man learns much about the Canyon before seeing it. Still we share the incredulous wonder felt by the first to view it:

PAGE TWELVE • ARIZONA HIGHWAYS • MARCH 1954

Fig. 98. "This Is the Grand Canyon," in *Arizona Highways*, 1954. Echoing historic Detroit Publishing Company postcards that affixed labels and place-names on their images, here *Arizona Highways* makes a clear statement about where and what is the Grand Canyon and adds another layer to imagery of those claims. Yet again, this iconic view of the canyon is from the rim looking into the canyon's depths, with clouds floating above. State of Arizona, Arizona Memory Project, *Arizona Highways* 30, no. 3 (March 1954): 12.

political and social battles of water access and use—shape human settlement and contests for ownership through the Greater Grand Canyon Region. Indeed, an excursion into the catalog of water representations at the Grand Canyon leads to some unexpected destinations. In the early part of this sampling period, Lake Mead was a commonly represented water source in *Arizona Highways*. Many of the captions and articles that accompanied Lake Mead photographs from this time unflinchingly noted that this area was part of the Grand Canyon. This may be surprising to readers today. Lake Mead is far from what one might define as the Grand Canyon. Yet looking at image after image of happy motorboating enthusiasts, water skiers, and fisherman at this location that was touted as "where the lake and the canyon hold hands," I had to reconsider my position (*Arizona Highways* caption for April 1940 feature article on the Grand Canyon). Wasn't this the same section of the Grand Canyon that John Wesley Powell braved in the 1890s? During his first trip through the Grand Canyon down the Colorado River in 1869, Powell took his leave of the canyon at the Virgin River near the Grand Wash Cliffs, well within Lake Mead's current terrain. Much of the Colorado River that Powell floated down is now under Lake Mead or its upstream sibling, Lake Powell. To inscribe this shift in hydrological landscapes to that of popular geographic imaginations, after 1950, *Arizona Highways* features Lake Powell as a more common subject and location.

Lakes are not the only water form to flood the pages of *Arizona Highways* during this time. Creeks and waterfalls are also common subjects, especially Havasu Falls (fig. 99) and Mooney Falls. But the most common vertical location—drawn from the rim, to the midcanyon trails, to the bottom of the Grand Canyon—during this period is also the most common: the Colorado River. As social forces clashed over the use and control of the Colorado River, its image rose to prominence in *Arizona Highways* with photographs featuring river runners in motorized rubber rafts or wooden human-powered oar dories (fig. 100). Starting in the 1960s, these Colorado River rafter representations were juxtaposed with images of tourists fishing, sailing, or motorboating on Lake Mead (fig. 101) and motorboating or waterskiing on Lake Powell (fig. 102).

Even within the group of river rafters floating down the Colorado River, tensions brewed. Motorized and nonmotorized rafters crowded the Colorado River during this time, irritating each other and proving that the method of transport could define different cultures of outdoor recreationalists. Commercial rafting was pioneered in the Grand Canyon by Norm Nevills and his Mexican Hat Expeditions. An expert oarsman, he was a believer in the scenic beauty of the canyon without the noise of motors (fig. 103). However, this mode of river transport was challenged by later river runners, notably Georgie White Clark, known to river runners as simply Georgie White, was an enterprising woman who used World War II surplus boats and large outboard motors to plow through the canyon's most challenging rapids while hauling enormous flotillas of tourists down the Colorado River through the Grand Canyon. While other river runners may have pioneered the use of rubber rafts for floating the Colorado River, Georgie introduced distinct technical and economical innovations to the burgeoning rafting scene in the canyon. She lashed large rafts together into a "G-rig" for greater flexibility and stability through the tempestuous rapids and her "share the expense" trips that proved immensely popular for tourists wishing to float the river but limited by their tight budgets (figs. 104 and 105). While Georgie's trips may have made the inner canyon more accessible to middle class Americans, the influx of inner-canyon tourists from her trips and as well as from other river runner created challenging impacts on the Colorado River's sandbars and camping spots. By 1979, the National Park Service developed River Management Plans to that limited the number of recreational users on the Colorado River and provided guidelines to dimmish their impacts on the environment.

Taming the Canyon

As noted earlier, the nonhuman actors at the Grand Canyon—the multitude of animals, birds, and plants that called this place home—were divided along native and exotic species lines in popular representations. This was a formative period for ecological science and environmental regulation, and the genesis and development of these ideas and values about nature can be seen in the popular imagery. From the 1930s through much of the 1940s, many National Park Service management and planning decisions focused on improving tourists' experiences and access to the parks. However, after World War II, National Park Service officials acknowledged the scientific potential of national parks for research (Sellars 1997, 258–261). This discussion came to the forefront in 1963 with the release of the Leopold Report. It was the first natural resource management document prepared by scientific experts *outside* of the National Park Service. Among other

Swimming below Havasu Falls

Fig. 99. Swimming below Havasu Falls, 1954. State of Arizona, Arizona Memory Project, *Arizona Highways* 35, no. 8 (August 1959): 26.

recommendations, the report called for the distinction between native and exotic species in national parks and a new wildlife management style for the park service that privileged native species habitat and survival over that of exotic (Sellars 1997, 214–15).

Mules and horses were the only animals represented in *Arizona Highways from 1936 to 1970* (fig. 106). This focus on domesticated, introduced exotic species, to the exclusion of native species is curious indeed. *Arizona High-*

Fig. 100. The Colorado River before Glen Canyon Dam (*above and opposite*). In 1954, as Glen Canyon Dam's construction date loomed, *Arizona Highways* ran a series of articles contrasting the various uses of water in the region. These images are from an article about Glen Canyon (*above*) and Marble Canyon (*opposite*), areas of the Grand Canyon that were threatened by the construction of Glen Canyon Dam and Lake Powell. Note the small inflatable raft and boaters dwarfed by the canyon's walls in the image above. In contrast to the postcards, the Colorado River in both of these images is a silt-laden brown. The dam projects cooled the river's temperature and decreased the sediment load of this textbook exotic stream in the desert Southwest. State of Arizona, Arizona Memory Project, *Arizona Highways* 30, no. 5 (May 1954): 41, 21.

Fig. 101. Breezing along on Lake Mead, 1939. State of Arizona, Arizona Memory Project, *Arizona Highways* 15, no. 10 (October 1939): 23.

Fig. 102. Lake Powell, America's Newest Playground, 1964. State of Arizona, Arizona Memory Project, *Arizona Highways* 40, no. 1 (January 1964).

Fig. 103. Rest in Marble Canyon, 1954. This image recasts the Grand Canyon as a place of leisure and quiet contemplation, in contrast to the dam construction photographs in other parts of Marble Canyon that highlighted the Grand Canyon as a construction site and source of hydroelectric power. The boats pictured here are part of Mexican Hat Expeditions, a company run by two boatmen who formerly worked with Norm Nevills and later bought his pioneering commercial river trip business known as Nevills Exepeditions. Compare this scene with the earlier *Noonday Rest at Marble Canyon* by Thomas Moran. State of Arizona, Arizona Memory Project, *Arizona Highways* 30, no. 5 (May 1954): 16.

"White-Water Party — Marble Canyon"
"Soap Creek Rapids — Marble Canyon"

Fig. 104. Commercial rafting in inflatable boats through the Grand Canyon. Georgie White Clark, with her makeshift, military surplus rubber rafts and "share the expense" trips introduced hundreds of people to the inner Grand Canyon along the Colorado River corridor. Her trips offered access for more people to see and experience this difficult to reach part of the inner canyon. State of Arizona, Arizona Memory Project, *Arizona Highways* 41, no. 4 (April 1965): 14.

PHOTOGRAPHS BY JOSEF MUENCH

Running Soap Creek Rapids in Marble Canyon

A White Water Adventure

RIVER TRIP through the MARBLE and GRAND CANYONS

BY JOSEF MUENCH
AS TOLD TO
JOYCE ROCKWOOD MUENCH

Adventure was spelled in my mind for many years, as DARKEST AFRICA. Each letter of it, in that private dictionary, stood for personal thrills in a primeval wilderness, unconquered, unspoiled. That is all changed now. The jungles of the distant continent could not wait for me to travel halfway around the world. My revised dictionary notes that game is disappearing there, and that now, ADVENTURE waits in America's own backyard, through the "Grand Run." Between the lines describing the canyons of our third longest river, excitement is highlighted by the warm Arizona sun. Instead of humid jungle, where unknown danger lurks, I will take the open challenge of the mighty Rio Colorado, the Red River, which Spanish explorers were the first to see. Above, and below the chasms of the Marble Gorge and Grand Canyon, man has throttled the current, turned the turbulent, master-force of the Southwest into placid lakes of sky blue. I can, however, personally vouch for the fact that between Lake Powell and Lake Mead, Big Red has kept his rollicking, boisterous way, for some 315 miles of pure, undiluted big ADVENTURE.

The water is still brown, "too thick to drink, too thin to plough." The coyote's voice is heard. Stars are as bright as neon lights, and the world of men and telephones, TV and income taxes, is farther away than the Dark Continent itself. Starkly written on cliffs, sometimes in 3,000-foot pages, the history of the earth's crust is plainly legible. Compromising with danger, the modern white water explorer is carried past on a magic carpet of neoprene. Youngsters from eight to eighty now have the time of their lives on the stream so widely advertised as "the world's most dangerous river."

The big game they bag is some of the globe's most flamboyantly colored rock architecture, their weapon a camera. Leading the safari, instead of a hard-bitten hunter, is Georgie White, "Queen of the Rivers." Former Ferry Command pilot in the last war, she has conducted, without a single casualty, more people through the Grand Canyon than about all the other guides put together.

PAGE TEN Arizona Highways APRIL 1965

PAGE ELEVEN Arizona Highways APRIL 1965

Fig. 105. River trip through Marble and Grand Canyons, 1965. With powerful motors and shortened trip times, Georgie White Clark's river trips became a popular way to see the Grand Canyon and Colorado River. A war of aesthetics and class simmered throughout the 1960s and 1970s in the inner canyon, as motorized, inexpensive river trips with short float times and large groups opened the canyon to more tourists and challenged the slower, quieter, small group, nonmotorized trips. State of Arizona, Arizona Memory Project, *Arizona Highways* 41, no. 4 (April 1965): 10–11.

ways portrayed the wilderness setting of the inner canyon and Colorado River with visual representations of its frothy rapids and waves, big sandy beaches, and isolated side canyons. Yet, the array of wild animals along the river corridor did not capture the attention of the magazine's editorial staff or photographic freelancers. Common sights such as bighorn sheep, ravens, fish, deer, and the many snakes and lizards did not find their way into the pages of the magazine during this era. This approach effectively sanitized the canyon to emphasize the safe and controlled aspects of domesticated nature represented as the mules and horses of the trail. Simplifying the animal, reptile, and bird diversity of the canyon in these popular images misinformed the magazine's readership and created a social and cultural climate that did not allow space for these wilder parts of the canyon's environment.

Landscapes of Labor and Leisure

The dichotomy between white and American Indian racial roles at the Grand Canyon shifted during this period. In previous eras and popular visual representations of the canyon, American Indians were firmly attached to ideas of home, work, craftsmanship, and spectacle as an "other." Postcards, for example, featured Hopi and Navajo weavers and pot makers with their families nestled in the close quarters of hogans or at Hopi House. Hopi and Navajo peoples made frequent appearances in these representations yet, many American Indian groups with enduring traditional connections to the canyon such as the Havasupai, Hualapai, and Paiute were excluded from these images. *Arizona Highways* photographs from 1936 to 1970 both supported and presented a counternarrative to this structure by featuring a multitude of representations of American Indian domestic life, craftsmanship, and racial stereotyping but expanded their range to locations throughout Arizona, not just at the Grand Canyon.

In the western Grand Canyon, American Indian representations featured Havasupai working and living as farmers, ranchers, and horse guides in and around Supai (fig. 107). They were shown as hardy western denizens, often cast as a spectacle for their agricultural and low technology lives in a time when mainstream culture in America was racing toward an urban postwar era marked by freeways, TV sitcoms, and space age technology. While *Arizona Highways* represented some American Indians as working and living in the Grand Canyon, white people were represented as playing in the Grand Canyon in a majority of images that included people as subjects. Typical images from this time period showed white people recreating in motorboats on Lake Mead or Lake Powell, on mule rides into the midcanyon area, on river rafting trips along the inner canyon and Colorado River, and on horseback rides into Supai (fig. 108). Children and families were rarely highlighted during this time period.

Damming the Canyon

Battles over dam proposals and construction played a large role in environmental debates and discussions throughout the mid- and late twentieth century as southwestern populations in towns and cities grew and demands for water increased. As Phoenix, Los Angeles, and Las Vegas looked for new sources of water and hydroelectric power, the mighty Colorado River

Fig. 106. (*above and opposite*) Mule riders on North Rim trails, 1947 and 1965. Note the very different use of color in these two images of the same place: the North Rim trails of the Grand Canyon. The photo on the left reveals a verdant scene of trees and shrubs crowding the riders; the photo on the right plays up the canyon's red, orange, and buff hues and the steep cliffs of the canyon. The magazine images, just like the postcards, use the tools of their artists to construct specific views and emphasize certain elements of the canyon's environment. Here are seen color, framing, and location selection at play. State of Arizona, Arizona Memory Project, *Arizona Highways* 23, no. 9 (August 1947): 24; and *Arizona Highways* 40, no. 4 (April 1965): 1.

Patriarch of the Tribe. This venerable old man is one of the patriarchs of the tribe, and on occasion goes to Grand Canyon to greet some visiting dignitary. (Carlos Elmer.)

Havasupai Chief. Over 100 winters have passed him by—this chief of the Havasupais. Like all Indians, this tribe venerates the aged. His are the words of wisdom, gathered by long years of experience. (Carlos Elmer.)

Tilling the Soil. From the rich floor of Cataract Canyon comes food and sustenance for the Havasupais. The tribe farms extensively in their limited domain. In the distance are the massive walls of Cataract Canyon, part of the Grand Canyon, whose steepness has been a source of protection to the tribe for centuries. (Josef Muench.)

JUNE, 1940 33

Fig. 107. Farming at Supai, 1940. Agriculture and subsistence farming were also part of the Grand Canyon experience. In the lower images a Havasupai man pauses his work as he tends the crops. Representations of American Indians at or in the Grand Canyon were more common in the prewar era of *Arizona Highways* than in the later 1940s and 1950s. State of Arizona, Arizona Memory Project, *Arizona Highways* 16, no. 6 (June 1940): 33.

Fig. 108. Motorboating on Lake Mead, 1959. In contrast to the Havasupai farmer in fig. 107 or the basket weavers in the DPC postcards of Hopi House, white people in *Arizona Highways* magazine were consistently depicted in leisure and recreation activities such as this motor boating scene at Lake Mead. The use of color and framing here focus the center of the image on the boat and passengers as red and orange high cliffs just above the green and placid waters of the new Lake Mead, formed from the dammed waters of the Colorado River. State of Arizona, Arizona Memory Project, *Arizona Highways* 35, no. 2 (February 1959): 42.

moved into the spotlight. Hoover Dam (initially called Boulder Dam), which controls the flow of the Colorado River and created Lake Mead, was constructed between 1928 and 1936 on the Arizona-Nevada border. The closing of Hoover Dam's floodgates eventually filled the reservoir, which, at full capacity, is the largest reservoir in the United States by volume (National Park Service 2022b). Lake Mead is 65 miles from Hoover Dam to Pearce Ferry, with 550 miles of shoreline and 9.3 miles at its largest width. The Boulder Canyon Project Act of 1928 authorized the construction of the dam in Black Canyon, about thirty miles east of Las Vegas, Nevada, and the same Black Canyon that confounded Lieutenant Ives and his steamboat crew in 1857. Hoover Dam was built by the federal government for flood control, agricultural irrigation in the Colorado Basin and Imperial Valley, water-based recreation, and municipal water supply for Los Angeles (National Park Service 2022b). But commercial hydropower was a primary driver for the construction of the dam. The U.S. Bureau of Reclamation manages water and power deliveries while the National Park Service manages the recreation and natural and cultural resource protection.

Upstream, the massive Glen Canyon Dam impounds Colorado River water that creates Lake Powell. The dam was constructed between 1956 and 1963 to support municipal and agricultural water and hydroelectric power demands as communities grew after World War II. It took seventeen years for the reservoir to fill and become the second-largest human-made lake in the United States. Water is released from the dam to match the fluctuating demands for hydroelectric power and water use by agriculture, recreation, and urban communities in the West (Worster 1985; Carothers and Brown 1991; Reisner 1993; Sneddon 2015; Owen 2017; Sadler 2018). The construction of Glen Canyon Dam ignited national debates about water use, the environmental impacts of dams, and the value of free-flowing rivers for scenic, recreational, and spiritual uses. A public outcry against the dam cited the flooding and loss of Navajo sacred sites as well as Glen Canyon and its side canyons. Supporters of the dam celebrated new boating and recreational opportunities at the lake, hydropower, flood control, and irrigation for agriculture. These debates played out in the pages of *Arizona Highways* as the magazine featured articles both in favor of and critical of Glen Canyon Dam and its uses.

Hoover Dam and Glen Canyon Dam were not the only water allocation and construction projects on the minds of the U.S. Bureau of Reclamation. The agency set to work building and maintaining canals, power plants, and other dams across the West. In the western Grand Canyon, proposals surfaced in the 1920s and continued to be discussed through the 1960s for dam to be built at Colorado River mile 238, near the Hualapai Indian Reservation. Another proposal, for a dam at Marble Canyon in the northeastern Grand Canyon, also surfaced in the 1960s but was extinguished when President Gerald R. Ford signed the Grand Canyon Enlargement Act in 1975. The legislation incorporated Marble Canyon into Grand Canyon National Park, thus extending the park northeast, doubling the park's size, and subduing plans for additional dams.

There is a tremendous amount of scholarly and popular writing and research about Colorado River dam projects, controversies, and uses. *Arizona Highways* featured photographs and essays that actively engaged in some of the dam construction debates throughout the 1960s and 1970s. Although it did not feature as prominently or directly in the magazine imagery, it is the 1956 Colorado River Storage Project Act that shaped Greater Grand Canyon Region water battles in extinguishing the proposals for dams at Marble Canyon and Bridge Canyon and establishing one of the "most complex and extensive river resource developments in the world" (Bureau of Reclamation 2021). The act provided structure for the development and management of water resources in the Upper Colorado River Basin states of Colorado, New Mexico, Utah, and Wyoming for the purposes of water storage, flood control, hydroelectric power, and regulating flows of the Colorado River.

The political and social side effects of representing the Grand Canyon as aesthetically valuable for its rim-side "scenic" locations were numerous. Decades of popular media representations of the canyon focused almost singularly on rim-side locations, not inner canyon river sites. Vision, and visibility, became key aspects of this heated debate about nature at the Grand Canyon. These inner canyon locations, on the periphery of popular geographic and environmental perceptions of the Grand Canyon, later became pivotal sites in a battle between the Bureau of Reclamation and the Sierra Club for the future of the Grand Canyon and regional water allocation schemes. Tensions flared in 1963 when the gates of the Glen Canyon Dam closed, initiating the flooding of Glen Canyon and the creation of Lake Powell. The National Park Service accepted the responsibility of managing Lake Powell as a park unit and recreational site, further blurring the lines between conservation and preservation (Sellars 1997, 180–81).

Visual representations of the Colorado River and Glen Canyon played an important part in this argument and launched the Sierra Club's efforts to promote wilderness preservation through publicity campaigns, visual representations of wilderness, and popular media. When the Bureau of Reclamation announced the Pacific Southwest Water Plan in 1963 that included two dam sites in the Grand Canyon, the Sierra Club was prepared for a fight. As part of this regional water allocation scheme, one dam would be located in Marble Canyon that would flood fifty-three river miles, and another would be positioned in Bridge Canyon flooding ninety-three miles upstream (Nash 2001, 228). The dams seemed inevitable. While engineering crews tested the inner canyon's walls for stability and surveyed the dam sites (blasting deep tunnels into the canyon's walls that are still visible from river level today), wilderness advocates pursued more public and popular means for their protests against inner canyon development. The passage of the Wilderness Act in 1964 bolstered environmental agendas by declaring some federal lands as wilderness areas "where the earth and its community of life are untrammeled by man, where man himself is a visitor who does not remain" (Wilderness Act 1964).

Seeing is believing, or in this case, seeing is preserving. The Bureau of Reclamation argued that the canyon sites were well out of sight of most tourist locations and views into the Grand Canyon. Preservationists did not relent. These sites, they argued, must be preserved for the idea of wilderness. The war between these two powerful social forces raged onward, becoming increasingly complex. Other agencies and activist groups became involved, including the Department of the Interior through the National Park Service, the Army Corps of Engineers, the Wilderness Society, the Havasupai Nation and the Navajo Nation. Even the Internal Revenue Service played a role in this drama. Neither the Bridge Canyon nor Marble Canyon dams were built, but they both served as friction points in water policy and environmental management in the American West.

Each side in this pivotal debate in American environmental politics used visual representations and vision to make their case. The twists and turns, challenges and negotiations of this prolonged battle between preservationists and conservationists have been well documented in a number of historical accounts (Reisner 1993; Sellars 1997; Nash 2001; Dunaway 2005). The debate over damming the Grand Canyon jettisoned this place into the national spotlight. Environmental historian Finis Dunaway details the Sierra Club's use of Elliott Porter's Glen Canyon and Grand Canyon photographs in coffee table books to promote wilderness values in the face of the dam-building debates of the 1960s (2005, 170–93). Dunaway notes that the Sierra Club argued against additional dams in the Grand Canyon by asserting that a free-flowing Colorado River would ensure that the canyon remained a sacred American space (172). The images of the 1960s Grand Canyon did not stand alone in their ability to shape this debate over the environmental canyon; they were shaped by decades of visual representations of the Grand Canyon that preceded them.

To their credit, or perhaps chagrin, *Arizona Highways* editors chose to feature stories about Glen Canyon from both sides of the debate with articles and photographs portraying both preservationist and conservationist ideas about natures—although perhaps a bit too late to have an impact on dam construction. In the 1930s and 1940s, for example, the magazine featured several issues with photographs of motorboating, sailboating, and fishing on Lake Mead. The accompanying articles celebrated the engineering feat of the Hoover Dam that created the lake and the economic and recreational benefits of the dam. In 1954, on the other hand, several issues portrayed hiking in the canyon, Colorado River rafting trips, swimming in the canyon's waterfalls, and other low-impact wilderness-oriented activities. Once construction on the Glen Canyon Dam began, however, *Arizona Highways* presented photograph after photograph at locations around the construction site, portraying it from almost every angle, including aerial images before the river was dammed (fig. 109), rim-side images of the site (fig. 110), an aerial view of the construction site detailing the total cost of the project (fig. 111), and representations of workers erecting the dam. The images and essay are supportive of the dam project, praising the engineering feat as "An American Triumph." For example, figure 110 features a man standing on the edge of a cliff looking into the depths of the dam construction site with his back to the viewer. His stance and windswept tie give the sense that he is proudly overlooking the scene of heroic engineering feats below. Other images, such as figure 111 from January 1964, followed suit.

The prevalence of Glen Canyon Dam construction images in *Arizona Highways* entirely eclipsed the representation of almost all the other buildings and structures at the Grand Canyon. However, images of building exteriors along the South Rim did make it into the magazine before the Glen Canyon Dam controversy flared up.

Fig. 109. Glen Canyon Dam construction site from an aerial perspective, 1959. State of Arizona, Arizona Memory Project, *Arizona Highways* 25, no. 9 (August 1959): 1.

grew longer, reaching out over the deep chasm until at last they joined and were crowned with the American Flag. It was a sight to be remembered. A few months later, on a warm February day in 1959, the bridge was dedicated and opened to public travel. From that moment on the bridge has provided a superb viewing point from which to watch the construction of Glen Canyon Dam, just upstream. Guides are now stationed on the bridge for safety and to answer the questions of visitors, who have been coming in ever-increasing numbers – 134,000 in 1959; 182,000 in 1960; 251,000 in 1961; 310,000 in 1962; and about 400,000 in 1963.

Outside of a myriad other problems, among them the complications of setting up the town of Page, Lem Wylie's main concern in 1956 was to actually start working on the dam. The first objective was to divert the river away from the damsite. This job alone took a year and a half. Two 41-foot wide tunnels – one in each of the canyon walls – were drilled through a half mile of sandstone and were lined with concrete. Then, out of the broken rock and sand taken from the tunnels and from other excavation, a cofferdam slowly began to take shape. The purpose of the cofferdam was, of course, to direct the river into the tunnels and to permit dewatering of the dam's foundation area.

In early February, 1959, when the river flows were normally low, officials of the prime contracting firm, Merritt-Chapman and Scott Corporation, declared that they were ready to close the cofferdam. Although there was no emergency, there was concern, for the cofferdam could not be closed in times of high river flow, and the erratic Colorado River had been known to flood even in February.

As power shovels and bulldozers narrowed the channel with boulder after boulder, the river countered with increasing velocity. It soon reached the point where boulders weighing many tons were rolled downstream by the swift water. Steel frames and concrete forms were then lowered into the gap and held by cables. Finally, on February 11th, after three days and nights of fighting, the cofferdam was closed; the river had been moved from its ancient bed and was flowing through the diversion tunnels. During the months ahead the cofferdam was raised to a height of 140 feet – actually a good-sized earth fill dam in itself.

With phase one, diversion of the river, completed, heavy equipment then began moving in for phase two, excavation of the foundation. From early drilling reports, Lem knew just about how far down they would have to go to reach bedrock. At maximum depth it was 137 feet. The digging was slow and methodical, yet at the same time interesting. A short distance below the river bed the men began to uncover stratified gravel beds, and below that a narrow, steep-walled "inner gorge," where the river had flowed thousands of years ago. The walls of this inner gorge were weirdly eroded into "pots and flutes" that suggested to geologists much turbulence, even cataracts, in this stretch of the river, a condition far different from that of modern times.

Placement of the first bucket of concrete on June 17,

Graceful arch of steel joins canyon walls

Fig. 110. Man vs. the Dam, 1964. In this 1964 photograph (*lower right*), the image is framed and the subject matter arranged around a man standing on a windswept, high cliff overlooking the building site of Glen Canyon Dam. State of Arizona, Arizona Memory Project, *Arizona Highways* 40, no. 1 (January 1964): 11.

TOTAL COST OF PROJECT WHEN FINISHED (INCLUDING BRIDGE AND TOWN OF PAGE): APPROXIMATELY $300,000,000

PHYSICAL DATA — GLEN CANYON STORAGE UNIT

DAM		
Type: Concrete arch.		
Height above river bed	ft.	580
Height above lowest point in foundation	ft.	710
Crest length	ft.	1,550
Crest width	ft.	25
Base width	ft.	340
Concrete	cu. yds. (dam)	4,830,000
	(powerplant)	275,000
There are 3¼ million cu. yds in Hoover Dam, and 10½ million in Grand Coulee.		
Crest elevation	ft.	3,715
Maximum discharge through spillways	sec. ft.	276,000
RESERVOIR		
Capacity	ac. ft.	28,040,000
Area	acres	162,700
Elevation reservoir water surface	ft.	3,700
The river elevation at Glen Canyon is 3,142 ft.		
Length	miles	186
POWERPLANT		
Capacity	kw.	900,000
Number of units		8
Capacity of each generator	kw.	112,500
Capacity of each turbine	hp.	155,500

An American Triumph

River Storage Project, being built by the Bureau of Reclamation of the Department of the Interior.

Glen Canyon Dam now appears virtually complete. The last mass concrete was placed in September of 1963. Workmen are applying finishing touches to the elevator shafts and to the abutment approaches. Generators and turbines are being installed in the powerplant. To the casual visitor, the work is all but finished. He can only wonder about events that took place here in years past, or about the almost fantastic amount of knowledge, planning, and careful execution that were required to bring the dam into being.

More than any other man, L. F. "Lem" Wylie has called the shots at Glen Canyon Dam. As the Project Construction Engineer, he alone has had final responsibility for the quality of everything built at Glen Canyon. Of course, Lem has had a staff of inspectors and engineers working out of the Bureau of Reclamation office in Page, checking each detail of the contractor's work. But Wylie made the big decisions.

FOLLOWING PANEL

"GLEN CANYON DAM – POETRY IN STEEL AND CONCRETE" BY W. L. RUSHO. This photograph of Glen Canyon Dam was taken from a helicopter last September, a few days after the last bucket of concrete was poured in the dam. The dam rises 580 feet above the river bed. The maximum thickness of the dam at the foundation is 340 feet, at the crest 25 feet. 4x5 Speed Graphic camera; Ektachrome; f. 10 at 1/400th second; turbulent, stormy day.

• PAGE SEVEN *Arizona Highways* JANUARY 1964 •

Fig. 111. "An American Triumph" at the Grand Canyon. State of Arizona, Arizona Memory Project, *Arizona Highways* 40, no. 1 (January 1964): 7.

Water Play

From 1936 to 1970, *Arizona Highways* representations of the Grand Canyon featured an increasing number of images of inner canyon recreation, especially water sports. Early in the time period, Lake Mead activities such as motorboating, sailboating, fishing, picnicking, and waterskiing were common subjects in the magazine. Later, similar activities were shown at Lake Powell. Commercial river trips emerged in the United States during this postwar era, building on the availability of cheap military surplus boats and gear, an outdoor recreation boom across the country, increased incomes, and more leisure time. *Arizona Highways* documents key scenes and pivots as this outdoor recreation industry develops into a major source of economic and social influence in the American West. Hiking also grew in popularity during this era, taking advantage of many of the same trends and technical developments as river running. Hikers and campers benefitted from outdoor equipment technology advances from World War II, such as lighter aluminum poles for tents, stronger synthetic cloths and ropes, and new backpack and boot designs. *Arizona Highways* editors and photographers captured hikers on trails along the canyon's rim and midcanyon sections, as well as deep in the inner canyon (fig. 112). River rafting overshadowed all other recreation by the end of this period.

Autos, Bridges, Trails, and Roads

The Colorado River courses through 277 river miles in the Grand Canyon, a distance roughly equivalent to the drive from Grand Canyon Village on the South Rim to Las Vegas, Nevada (National Park Service 2022). Until the 1930s and the road-building projects undertaken by the National Park Service, the State of Arizona, and the Arizona Department of Transportation (formerly the Highway Bureau) that trip would have taken much longer. From 1936 to 1970, *Arizona Highways* returned, at least briefly, to its highway engineer roots. In multiple issues, representations of the Glen Canyon Dam construction site included trucks, heavy machinery, cement mixing, steel cables, and hard-hat-wearing construction crews. Although cars and auto tours fell by the wayside in photographs during this time, bridges, or at least one bridge, was a common subject: the Glen Canyon Dam bridge over the Colorado River near Page, Arizona (fig. 113). Images such as a 1959 color cover photo positioned engineering projects, such as this bridge in a heroic light. The image includes a man with a hard helmet standing on the edge

In Twilight Canyon

Cliff dwelling in Lake Canyon

Water sports!

line? Why that is as much as two-thirds across the continent!" A brief review of geography may be in place.

The Colorado River, master stream of the Southwest, third longest river in the United States, has been called variously, pioneer-delayer, rock sculptor, trouble-maker (if you can blame it for lengthy interstate legal battles over who shall have its water to use). Its water comes down out of the Rocky Mountains of Wyoming and Colorado into Utah, nicks off a corner of northwestern Arizona before making the border with Nevada and then California, finally emptying into the Gulf of California under the Mexican flag. The Green River, actually larger but still considered a tributary and headwaters, wriggles through eastern Utah south from Wyoming. In Southeastern Utah the two join forces in the presence of cliffs almost two thousand feet high, right in the heart of the proposed Canyonlands National Park. Cataract Canyon carries the joint stream southwest and the lower part of its tumultuous white-water run will be smoothed by the extreme head of the new lake, with many side canyons fingering from the main body in Glen Canyon. New Mexico contributes the San Juan River, already tamed by Navajo Dam, east of Farmington, and Utah makes its principal addition through the Escalante River.

Until the model town of Page sprang into being as construction town, operation headquarters, and tourist center, overlooking Glen Canyon Dam, there was no real settlement the length of Glen, and more. There was one highway, at Hite where a small ferry made a link in Utah State 95. Boats could put in the water there or at Lees Ferry, an historic site now fourteen miles below the dam.

People can be excused for not knowing where and what Glen Canyon was. Expecting a million annual visitors to change that, the Glen Canyon National Recreation Area was established and is being developed as rapidly as such an immense project can practicably be. Visitors need not, however, wait on full development of facilities. From the moment the Bureau of Reclamation plugged the lower diversion tunnel on January 21, 1963, Lake Powell was in business. It continues to stretch its arms, lazily when the run-off from above is at its minimum, flexing muscles when snow or rainfall feeds it faster.

Long before the water began to back up, other changes in the landscape were apparent. U.S. Highway 89 left the tinted plateau through which the Colorado River's Marble Gorge runs, switchbacked the steep Echo Cliffs and piercing the crest by a dramatically engineered "V" arrived topside at the site of Page on

• PAGE EIGHTEEN *Arizona Highways* JANUARY 1964 •

Fig. 112. In Twilight Canyon. In this 1964 *Arizona Highways* representation of hikers in the inner canyon (*upper left*), this quiet scene reveals the side channels and slot canyons of the Grand Canyon. Many of these small alcoves were soon to be lost to flooding from the dam projects underway. State of Arizona, Arizona Memory Project, *Arizona Highways* 40, no. 1 (January 1964): 18.

of the Colorado River with his back to the viewer as he gazes at the Glen Canyon Dam Bridge looming over his head. The red rock canyon walls and deep blue sky stand out dramatically. Extending U.S. Highway 89 over this part of the canyon in 1964 allowed the dam construction crews to have better access to the site from their homes in the newly established community of Page. Without the bridge, dam construction crews would have had to drive a considerable distance around the canyon. The only automobiles seen in the magazine during this time were at the construction site.

The 1930s were a peak time for road construction in and around the Grand Canyon. While many of the roadways accessing the Grand Canyon from the north, south, and east were constructed, realigned, or repaired by the 1940s, the Glen Canyon Dam had a distinct impact on regional transportation networks (fig. 114). Before the Glen Canyon Dam Bridge was constructed in 1964, crews had to cross the Colorado River and the Grand Canyon over Marble Canyon, south of the dam construction site, using U.S. 89 and the Navajo Bridge. By the 1940s, inner park roads (through Grand Canyon National Park) were well used by auto tourists and organized auto touring groups to access the South Rim from Flagstaff. Plans to extend the road from Grand Canyon Village to Supai were dropped; however, Hermit Road was still used as a popular auto-touring route along the South Rim.

Park Expansion and Shifting Locations of Imagery

Although representations of the South Rim and midcanyon were common throughout this period, there were some variations in the geography of locations represented (fig. 115). For instance, throughout the later 1930s and into the 1940s, Lake Mead, Havasupai, and west area images were quite common. During the 1950s and 1960s, the geographical focus of the magazine shifted so that locations at the North Rim and northeast areas of the canyon were more commonly represented. The Grand Canyon National Park Enlargement Act of 1975 may have influenced this geographical trend in representation. In 1975 the largest expansion of park lands since 1927 occurred, adding Grand Canyon National Monument, Marble Canyon, and some Tusayan National Forest lands to double the park's size to over 1.2 million acres (Anderson 2000, 67). The most common horizontal locations were along the South Rim followed by the Lake Mead, northeast, midcanyon North Rim, west, Havasupai, and images depicting all of the canyon (such as maps and aerial or satellite perspectives; see appendix C).

Fig. 113. Glen Canyon Bridge over the Colorado River, near Page, Arizona. State of Arizona, Arizona Memory Project, *Arizona Highways* 35, no. 9 (August 1959).

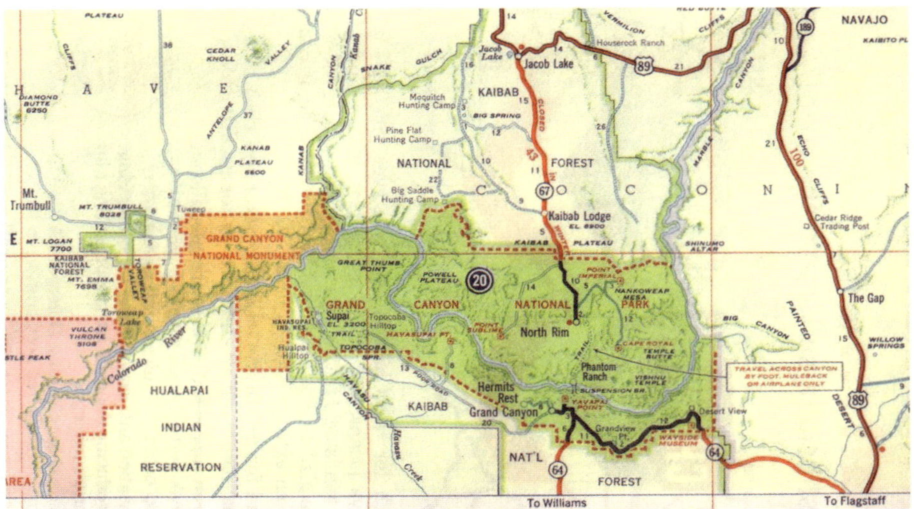

Fig. 114. Road map of Arizona, 1958. This detail captures the context of the Greater Grand Canyon Region as the construction of Glen Canyon Dam and Lake Powell progressed from 1955 to 1965. The map also captures the region before Grand Canyon National Park was expanded and extended to include Marble Canyon. Detail from "Utah: Points of Interest and Touring Map" by the H. M. Gousha Company for Standard Oil Company of California, 1958. Source: Author's collection.

The Colorado River was the most common vertical location represented in *Arizona Highways* during this period, followed by rim locations and, to a much lesser degree, representations of the canyon from aerial perspectives or midcanyon locations. There were no representations of the Grand Canyon in *Arizona Highways* during this period that did not include a clear view of the canyon itself. Representations that featured multiple views of the canyon, a somewhat common style for postcards, was absent from the *Arizona Highways* imagery.

The repetitive Colorado River views that *Arizona Highways* presented its readers throughout this era reinforces the power and importance of this particular river and location in the wide-ranging expanse of the Grand Canyon. Magazine editors and photographers may have been motivated by construction activity and park road expansion, but their images also speak to larger ideas about water, power, technology, and industry (Summit 2013; White 2011; Dunaway 2005; Grusin 2004). With each sweeping rim or inner canyon view of active dam building, with each image that pro-

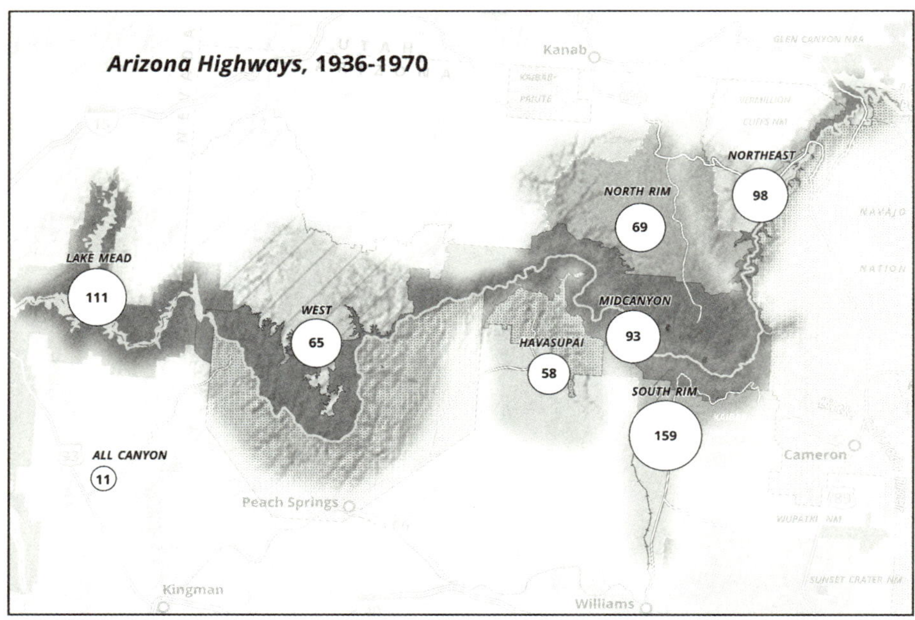

Fig. 115. Map of horizontal locations represented in *Arizona Highways*, 1936–70. The white circles in each horizontal region note the number of magazine representations for that area during this period. Cartography by Robert M. Edsall. Based on data from the U.S. Geological Survey, National Park Service, and author's content analysis results from archival research.

claimed an "American Triumph" or showed a heroic view of a person with their back to the camera overlooking the expansive canyon construction scene of Glen Canyon Dam Bridge, these photographs added another layer to the complex meanings that people associated with the Grand Canyon. Dam building was another way of representing ideas about industry, the triumphs of American engineering technology, and efficient use (or so it seemed) of water to quench the thirst of rapidly growing desert cities such as Phoenix and Tucson. These images fortified the idea that through the control of nature, humans could potentially have it both ways, enjoying outdoor recreation such as motorboating on Lake Mead and hiking in the solitude of Twilight Canyon, while also ensuring that desert cities bloomed and crops flourished from the water in carefully regulated and managed reservoirs and large-scale dams.

9 Where Is the "Real" Grand Canyon?

> This place will always challenge those who think of it as one place, *the* Grand Canyon, to be captured in its entirety in a single picture—a daunting notion, a fool's errand.
>
> —Stephen Trimble, *Lasting Light*

Contemporary visitors to the Grand Canyon often have a difficult time trying to find the place they traveled to see. Grand Canyon National Park encompasses over 1.2 million acres, 277 river miles, and a canyon a mile deep and 10 miles wide. How could a contemporary canyon visitor not find this immense landscape feature?

The culprit, it seems, is competing publicity and historic geographic associations for valuable (visual) resources. A 2008 *Arizona Republic* article titled "Which Grand Canyon Is the Real Grand Canyon?" illuminates some of the contests for visitor dollars associated with authentic canyon experiences, place-based tourism, and reclaimed or reappropriated geographic locations (fig. 116). Notably, both viewpoints are situated on the rim looking *into* the Grand Canyon with spectacular panoramic views of the canyon's depths and extent. One rim view is located inside the administrative boundaries of Grand Canyon National Park, at Grand Canyon Village, managed by the National Park Service. The "other" rim view is at a place known as Grand Canyon West, on the Hualapai Indian Reservation, owned and operated by the Hualapai Tribe. Following the historic arc of popular Grand Canyon images over time from postcards through photographs, tourists have been trained to seek out the iconic rim-side views of the Grand Canyon from NPS sites within Grand Canyon National Park, specifically along the South Rim trail near El Tovar Hotel in Grand Canyon Village or the North Rim view near Grand Canyon Lodge at Bright Angel Point.

JACK KURTZ /THE ARIZONA REPUBLIC

Which Grand Canyon is the real Grand Canyon?

The South and North rims?

JOHN STANLEY/THE ARIZONA REPUBLIC

Visitors enjoy the patio overlooking the North Rim at Grand Canyon Lodge. Purists say the North and South rims offer the true and better canyon experience.

Or the west rim?

TOM TINGLE/THE ARIZONA REPUBLIC

Tourists enjoy the Skywalk. The Hualapai Tribe says its Grand Canyon West is less commercialized than amenities near the Grand Canyon National Park.

As popularity of Hualapai's Skywalk grows, so, too, does its rivalry with the national park

By Dawn Gilbertson
THE ARIZONA REPUBLIC

LAS VEGAS — Clare Cornick and Pat Pascale boarded the Sweet-Tours charter bus from the Marriott Grand Chateau time-share just after sunrise, bound for their first peek into the Grand Canyon.

The childhood friends from New Jersey, now living on opposite coasts, opened their free breakfast packs and settled in for the three-hour drive to Grand Canyon West, the isolated, internationally known home to the new glass Skywalk.

They picked it over Grand Canyon National Park because it was less than half the distance and put them back in Las Vegas before dark. The trip to the park would have meant three more hours on the road.

"I didn't want to mess with that," said Pascale, a retired educator.

Their rationale is marketing gold to the Native Americans behind Grand Canyon West and heresy to Canyon purists at the government-run park to the east, a fixture of family vacations and outdoor adventures for decades.

In the 14 months since the Skywalk opened and tripled visitor counts at 20-year-old Grand Canyon West, the rivalry and rhetoric between the "two" canyons has widened beyond the 250 miles that separate them.

See CANYON Page A8

Fig. 116. "Which Grand Canyon Is the Real Grand Canyon?" In this June 8, 2008, feature story the *Arizona Republic* explores differ perceptions of the Grand Canyon's identity and core location. Note the image on the left is from the North Rim near Grand Canyon Lodge and the image on the right features the Skywalk. The lower images titled "The South and North Rims?" and "Or the west rim?" pose a misleading juxtaposition, since both Grand Canyon Village and Grand Canyon West, the primary locations cited in the article as the two places in contention for the real Grand Canyon title, are on the South Rim of the canyon. Clipping from the author's collection.

The Hualapai's development of Grand Canyon West, however, offers an "alternative to the Grand Canyon National Park" (Hualapai Tribe n.d.). Grand Canyon West is located on the southwest rim of the canyon about 250 miles west of Grand Canyon Village. Geographically, it is closer to Las Vegas (about a two-hour drive). Grand Canyon Village, on the other hand, is about a four-hour drive to Las Vegas and twice as far away. The tribe is keenly aware of this geographic advantage. They use their proximity to Las Vegas to promote Grand Canyon West as a similar, scenic rim-side view of the Grand Canyon and Colorado River as what is available at the NPS Grand Canyon Village. On the tribe's website, the allure is clear: "Grand Canyon West has features you just won't find at the South or North Rims. Get an aerial view of the Canyon through a glass bridge on the Skywalk, take a white-water rafting tour with Hualapai River Runners, take a helicopter & boat tour, soar over cliffs on a zip line, and explore the area's history at the Native American Village and Guano Point" (Grand Canyon Resort Corporation 2023).

The Hualapai Tribe's Grand Canyon West offers a familiar mixture of tourist activities including hiking, camping, and horseback tours along with more modernized adventures via helicopter or one-day whitewater trips on motorized rafts Grand Canyon Resort Corporation in 2023. In a relatively short time since 2007, the Hualapai developed opportunities for tourists to see the canyon from a variety of geographic viewpoints—from the rim, from the depths along the Colorado River, and even from the sky above on board a helicopter. What makes this canyon business venture stand out, however, is a clever and subtle reformulation of authenticity and place-based tourism. At Grand Canyon West, the Hualapai Tribe plays upon tourist expectations and desires for a "Wild West" experience of horseback riding, camping, "cowboy entertainment," and campfire cookouts. At the same time, the tribe reclaims these activities and reappropriates them for the Grand Canyon West experience. Here tribal members can control the medium *and* the message. The website for the Hualapai Ranch at Grand Canyon West, for example, offers tourists a robust list of "ranch amenities" including:

> Spend the Night [*sic*] at the Hualapai Ranch in our rustic cabins facing the Canyon Rim!
> Hot lunches served at the Dancehall
> Enjoy live entertainment while having your meal
> Join the cowboys making S'mores and telling stories around an open fire in the evening.

Learn how to rope and quick draw during the day.
Enjoy western hospitality, cowboy entertainment,
  wagon rides and more.
Photo opportunities with Hualapai Members
A choice . . . of hot breakfasts
Gift Shop with western merchandise
Free Wi-fi

Note the inclusion of "photo opportunities with Hualapai Members" mixed in with the "western hospitality" and "cowboy entertainment." These activities are not new to the canyon scene or to the tourism experiences in the American West, but they are an appropriation and reformulation of western tropes that reflect American Indian agency.

The history of American Indian land dispossession and removal often went hand in hand with American Indians as entertainment, tracing back to at least the nineteenth century and the creation of the national park system in the United States (Dilworth 2001; Jacoby 2001; Spence 1999; and Morehouse 1996). Cultural historian Leah Dilworth notes that Fred Harvey's "Indian Tours of the Southwest" "spectacle represented the Southwest as a peaceful and fully domesticated region. It was not the wild, manly cowboys-and-Indians West represented by Frederic Remington's mounted Plains warriors" (2001, 152). The Santa Fe Railroad and Fred Harvey played key roles in the massive political, social, and cultural transformation of the American West that shifted these lands and the people who lived there toward a tourism economy driven by mobility, affluence, and the consumption of western landscapes and people as entertainment. This process also included a "classification" of tribes and a privileging of certain tribes over others (Rothman 1998, 70–71). Historian Hal Rothman wryly noted that to the "disadvantage of the peoples of the canyon region, the railroad and the Harvey Company engaged in a clear mythification process that mirrored their combined efforts elsewhere in the Southwest. This mythic southwestern overlay privileged Hopi and pueblo culture above Navajo, and Navajo above Havasupai, Yavapai, and Hualapai" (1998, 70). The Hualapai Ranch at Grand Canyon West engages this mythification head-on, by reappropriating the process and repositioning the tribe as an active participant in the creation of the tourism experience in the Grand Canyon without SFRR's and Fred Harvey's imposed privileging of other tribes above theirs.

At Grand Canyon West, Hualapai tribal members play the role of cowboys, who entertain tourists during the day with roping and quick drawing and by night by making S'mores and "telling stories." As the website says, a visitor's "adventure on the West Rim of the Grand Canyon" at Hualapai Ranch "provides western flavor with many cowboy activities that can be enjoyed by all. There is a dining hall where you will be able to enjoy western type cuisine and watch our entertainers during your meal." All this for the price of a Hualapai Legacy ticket that is required for all visitors to the Hualapai Ranch. This all-inclusive ranch provides rustic comfort and western flavor that fulfills tourists' cravings for that mythical Wild West of the Grand Canyon but shaped by the Hualapai tribal narrative instead of by the Santa Fe Railroad's or Fred Harvey's. For example, at the west rim, visitors can learn about the Hualapai traditions through storytelling, song, dance, and regalia as performed by the Hualapai Bird Singers or take a self-guided tour of a Native American village set up with interpretation provided by the tribe, or join a Smooth Float Tour on the Colorado River run by Native guides of the Hualapai River Runners. The tribe also offers programs, classes, and public education at the Hualapai Cultural Center in Peach Springs, Arizona.

The Hualapai's appeal for their version of the real Grand Canyon also rests heavily on the visual appeal of the canyon and a specific series of colors to portray the canyon, perhaps following the historic visual arc formulated and replicated in postcards and photographs. "Yellow, blue, pink, red, and purple: these are the colors of the Grand Canyon. Get a taste of the Old West and strengthen your relationship with nature on horseback." Here horseback rides down into the canyon—just as we've seen in many images of the canyon from Detroit Publishing Company to Curt Teich to Frasher Foto—is also still a staple of the "real" canyon experience.

The centerpiece of Grand Canyon West is Skywalk, a glass bridge that juts out of the canyon's walls while suspending tourists four thousand feet above the canyon's depths with dramatic views of the Colorado River below (fig. 117). In a June 8, 2008, article in the *Arizona Republic*, Dawn Gilbertson reported that many visitors to Grand Canyon National Park "mistakenly believe" the Skywalk is located at a National Park Service–managed site. When they realize their mistake, they are 250 miles from their destination. The National Park Service has taken to posting flyers on the windows of entrance fee stations to the park that advise visitors that the Skywalk is "not here" with directions to turn around and drive west for a few hours to reach that location.

GRAND CANYON West

Explore EVEN MORE AT THE WEST RIM

Fig. 117. Grand Canyon West Skywalk at the Hualapai Indian Reservation. Grand Canyon Resort Corporation, https://grandcanyonwest.com/explore/west-rim/.

The Skywalk is a somewhat recent and controversial addition to Grand Canyon's cultural landscape. Completed in 2007, its construction dismayed some Grand Canyon National Park fans who protested the development along the canyon's walls and its safety. Some visitors loyal to the national park found different reasons to object to the glass bridge. A woman quoted in the *Arizona Republic* article expressed her concern for visitors who chose the Skywalk: "They won't ever know that's not the real Grand Canyon." The article cites that "purists" such as this woman "say the North and South rims offer the true and better canyon experience"; while the Hualapai contend that the Skywalk, offers less development than its national park rival. In the article critics, noting the proximity of Grand Canyon West to Las Vegas, call the Hualapai visitor center "Grand Canyon lite or Vegas-style."

The Grand Canyon debate involves a number of issues. The National Park Service rim locations have been a center of Grand Canyon visitation since the turn of the twentieth century. Tourists rarely visit the Hualapai site; instead, it is relegated to the periphery of conventional tour operators. Access to the park service site is along paved highways and well-marked regional road connections; the entrance to the Hualapai site was along fourteen miles of dirt road until, in 2014, the entire roadway was finally paved. At the center of this debate is a contest over how we frame nature. These developments offer the chance to experience a visual-cultural landscape steeped in different histories, cultures, and political contexts. When exploring the visual-cultural Grand Canyon, there is more than one real Grand Canyon.

National park landscapes are produced through complex social, cultural, and economic interactions between the National Park Service, concessionaires, park visitors, and interest groups. As each of these groups endeavors to exert a specific identity upon a certain landscape, a complex and interwoven process is set in motion and guided by an ever-shifting agenda of negotiation, contestation, and revision. Cultural landscapes in national parks are not static landscapes confined to their material elements; instead they are dynamic places better understood as mediums through which multiple representations, practices, and performances of power, wielded by individuals and stakeholders, stream through an ongoing project to create and constrict how the material landscape looks and functions.

The Grand Canyon authenticity disputes are rooted in a larger question: where is the real American West? Geographer Donald Meinig notes that the West "is a powerful symbol within the national mythology, but as soon as we attempt to connect symbol with substance, to assess the relationships between the West as Place in the imagination and the West as a piece of the American continent, we are confronted with great variation from place to place" (qtd. in Hauslauden 2003, 19). Indeed, this study's review of visual representations of the Grand Canyon supports Meinig's claim. There is a great deal of variation from place to place in the Grand Canyon.

But where is the *real* Grand Canyon? From this research and review of visual representations in popular media, one thing seems clear: there are many Grand Canyons. It can be a rim-side scenic overlook. It can be a mule ride down a steep trail into the canyon's depths. It can be a pulse-quickening ride down a rapid full of cold, clear Colorado River water. There are many variations and iterations. I have explored several factors that shape place imagery of the Grand Canyon in popular media; but visual representations of the Grand Canyon in popular media are often a primary source of information for visitors to the canyon, and their imaginations have, no doubt, been shaped by images in magazines, newspapers, and films, and on postcards and websites.

Finding the real Grand Canyon is a question of vertical as well as horizontal locations. For John Wesley Powell and his crew, the Grand Canyon was an inner canyon experience, a place defined by towering rock walls, dangerous rapids, and long days spent wondering what was around the next bend. Powell's words focused on the Colorado River corridor and the landscapes he encountered. Clarence Dutton's view from the rim, on the other hand, established a spatial discipline for understanding the canyon not from the river but from the overlooks. "With few exceptions, those who came to the Canyon saw it, as Dutton did, from the rim" (Pyne 1998, 71). Turn-of-the-twentieth-century tourists knew the canyon from the rim and inner canyon trails, visiting the south and North Rim scenic viewpoints and taking mule rides into the canyon after jostling along dirt wagon roads to reach their destination. Auto tourists also visited the canyon's rim-side viewpoints. River rafters and inner canyon hikers came to know the canyon from the river up instead of the rim down. Editors, photographers, and postcard manufacturers shaped popular perceptions of these areas by created visual representations of the landscapes and locations. Visual representations of material landscapes are "not just innocent documents of the built environment"; instead they are "constructed images of constructed places" that convey the cultural ideals and changing values of the society that creates and propagates these images (Schein 1993, 8).

Finding the real Grand Canyon is a task laden with hard political and environmental realities. The Grand Canyon has undergone a tremendous cultural metamorphosis from a place once known as an "altogether valueless" location (Ives 1861, 110) to a national park that attracts over four million visitors a year. It is a story that weaves together many miles, many people, and many canyons. It is a story that traces what may be seen and what may be read. Visual representations of the Grand Canyon are embedded in social, cultural, economic, and political discussions that change over time. The Grand Canyon encompasses an area of immense environmental diversity within the Colorado Plateau. Although much of the development and popular imagery of the canyon focused on rims, inner canyon, or river locations, the forested lands that stretch beyond the rims were also fought over locations.

A 2009 newspaper article in the *Northern Arizona News* described the reintroduction of a Grand Canyon bill that sought to protect some of the canyon's environment from uranium mining. The initiator of that bill invoked the canyon's enduring power: "It is the icon of our National Park System and our forest, and as such has a different status in the history of public lands and the value of public lands." The congressman continued: "We're making a distinction, and maybe it's an unfair distinction to other areas, but at some point you need to draw a line in the sand." Visual representations of the canyon are not innocent documents but are instead value-laden materials crafted by a network of promoters, managers, users, and others over time. The Grand Canyon is fought over, and the best viewing spots are in competition because there is a substantial cultural inheritance at the Grand Canyon. As the canyon shifted from idea to fact to symbol, it gained in cultural significance and environmental protection.

Protecting the Greater Grand Canyon Region's Visual Legacy

How we see the canyon has real political, social, and cultural consequences. The places that we have come to know and recognize as the Grand Canyon are preserved; the areas that have not been represented as the Grand Canyon in popular media are facing challenges to preservation, environmental quality, and visitation. Quite often, rim and river locations have been privileged and burned into the popular imagination for this place through selective and repetitive visual representations. However, much of the Grand Canyon is not seen in these images. These areas have been historically and visually relegated to the back lot of national park productions, much to the detriment of wildlife and ecosystem protection.

Commenting on this trend, historian J. Donald Hughes noted that the park enlargement act of 1975 nearly doubled the size to 1,892 square miles, "but the idea that the national park was intended to protect scenery was implicit in the fact that the new boundaries primarily ran along the rims, putting the interior of the canyon within the national park and leaving most areas back from the rims, with their wildlife habitats, in other jurisdictions"

(Hughes 2005, 107). It is these areas, back beyond the rim, that face some of the greatest environmental protection challenges today. Clarence Dutton's view from the rim had lasting consequences for wildlife policy.

Grand Canyon in *Arizona Highways*, 1971–85

Arizona Highways representations of the Grand Canyon sampled from 1971 to 1985 revealed a range of themes and locations. The most common subjects in this set of magazine representations included scenic views of the canyon, white people, and the Colorado River (fig. 118). The most common horizontal locations were the north and South Rims, with trailing counts of representations of northeast, west, and Havasupai categories. Rim and river locations were the most common categories noted for images of vertical spaces as well as a few midcanyon representations. In a marked shift from the 1936–70 magazine sample set, representations of dams diminished quite a bit during this latter sample. In this study sample of *Arizona Highways* imagery, few automobiles and roads appear. For a magazine founded by highway engineers, funded and managed through Arizona's Department of Transportation, one might expect more representations of these subjects. Author Charles Bowden, however, notes that *Arizona Highways* "has thrived for most of this century by seldom, if ever, printing the photograph of an actual highway" (Bowden qtd. in Lippard 1999b, 138). This pattern can be attributed to the strong mission of the magazine and its editors to promote tourism in Arizona by emphasizing landscape photography and Arizona's rural locations, sometimes beyond the pavement's end.

Magazine representations of the Grand Canyon from 1971 to 1985 emphasize a variety of canyon subjects and locations (fig. 119). Indeed, as the Grand Canyon transformed into a scenic icon, the accumulated imagery merged together and shifted social, cultural, political, economic themes and spatial patterns. The editors decided to feature not only the South and North Rims favored in previous representations but also locations such as Grand Canyon West and northeast areas. In part, this selection can be attributed to the Grand Canyon's popularity as a tourist attraction and the increasing use and accessibility of high-quality cameras by the general public. As more people visited the Grand Canyon and became familiar with the visual representations of it, amateur as well as professional photographers ventured into the canyon to capture their own pictures. Some of

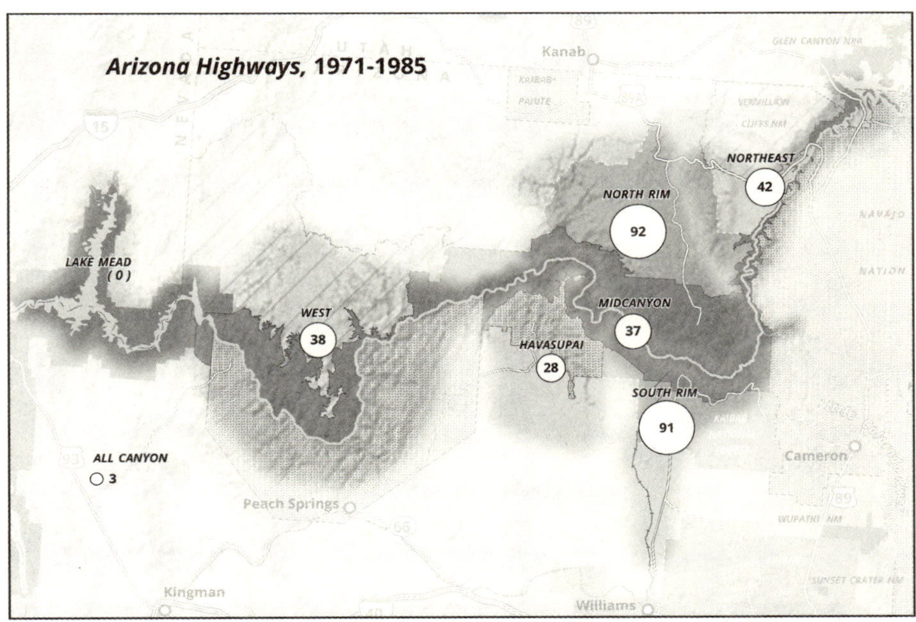

Fig. 118. Map of horizontal locations represented in *Arizona Highways*, 1971–85. Cartography by Robert M. Edsall. Based on data from the U.S. Geological Survey, National Park Service, and author's content analysis results from archival research.

these avid photographers submitted their work to *Arizona Highways*, which was nourished exclusively by freelance photographic submissions. Stephen Trimble, a canyon photographer, notes this fact as individuals mesmerized with the image of the canyon and familiar with its contours through hiking, rafting, and other adventures expressed a preference for these views. The effects of *Arizona Highways* photography cascaded through aspiring canyoneers. "Hikers enamored with *Arizona Highways* bought themselves 4x5s and began taking photography workshops" (Trimble 2006, 68–69). The pattern that begins to emerge from this sample illustrates how more contemporary viewmakers started to expand their representational reach. Increasingly, postcard and magazine viewers could see that the Grand Canyon contains a vast array of environments and experiences. This makes the task of finding the real Grand Canyon more reliant on our perceptions of this majestic landscape than political boundaries may reveal. Indeed, there is more than one canyon.

Fig. 119. *Arizona Highways*: Grand Canyon outdoor recreation boom. In the 1970s and 1980s the magazine featured more images of adventure outdoor recreation, such as whitewater rafting (*above*) and family hiking (*opposite*) in the Grand Canyon, as demand rose for these activities and equipment became less expensive as well as more readily available. State of Arizona, Arizona Memory Project, *Arizona Highways* 52, no. 5 (May 1976): 20, and *Arizona Highways* 60, no. 9 (September 1984): 19.

I cannot see the colors: the reds seem faint, the greens bleak smudges.

By 2:20, the lip of the Inner Gorge reveals the Colorado River, a green ribbon thrown carelessly against dark rock. A bighorn crosses the trail five minutes ahead of me, and a high school girl from Oklahoma shakes with excitement.

"I'd like to spend a day," she confides, "as each of the animals in the Grand Canyon."

By 3:40 I am at the bottom and in camp.

The air temperature is seventy degrees, and women lie on the beach drinking the sun.

I am 4600 feet below the Rim.

I stretch out and sip Scotch from my Sierra cup and look at the stone wall across Bright Angel Creek.

One world falls away and sleep coaxes me toward another one.

JACK DYKINGA PHOTO

NAME: *Jack Huppler*
HOME: *Midland, Texas*
PROFESSION: *Oil industry*
"I came to the South Rim twenty years ago and looked. You walk down it because it's there to walk down. It's the bigness."

The second day takes me through gigantic walls 2000 million years old: Vishnu schist. The creek rips along as if the stone were butter. Then the Canyon widens, and the trail wanders through thickets of sawgrass and cottonwoods. The ground turns to muck and canyon wrens trill on all sides. I look back and see the South Rim rising up like the wallpaper of the day before. Except now, I am in the wallpaper, and it is no longer flat. The bands of color become stone, and the stone is texture rubbing across my fingers. The air sags with scent off the meadow and lizards dart. From time to time, a red squirrel watches my progress.

Off the stream a desert of blackbrush, agave, prickly pear cactus, and mesquite hems in the thread of water racing from the melting snows of the North Rim.

Postcards of the Grand Canyon, 2009

What does a twenty-first-century sample of postcard and magazine representations reveal about the visual and cultural landscapes of the Grand Canyon? A sampling from two gift shop locations in the Grand Canyon region present another glimpse at the canyon's iconographic arc as it shifted from fact to symbol, from a known location to the abstract wild, from environmental canyon to cosmic canyon (Pyne 1998). For this part of the study, I gathered postcard "rack samples" from gift shops in Williams, Arizona, and Flagstaff, Arizona. In Williams I visited the historic Santa Fe Railroad depot and purchased all the postcards on display that presented images of the Grand Canyon. At Flagstaff, I visited another Santa Fe Railroad depot located in downtown and now home to the city's official visitor's center and purchased all the postcards for sale. The Williams postcard rack sample includes postcards from one manufacturer, Impact Photographics (figs. 120, 121, and 122). All of the Flagstaff postcards were manufactured by Smith-Southwestern, Inc. (fig. 123).

These sets of postcards reveal a pattern of rim-side locations featuring scenic canyon views (see appendix C). Both the Impact Photographics and the Smith-Southwestern postcards include scenic views from the rim, the Colorado River, maps, and Havasu Falls. The Impact Photographics postcards vary by including one snow scene taken from a rim-side location looking into the canyon and several scenes of people standing along rim-side viewpoints looking at the canyon. The Smith-Southwestern postcards detour by including images of trail scenes, a train steaming along the tracks in front of El Tovar Hotel on the South Rim, Grand Canyon West, and a whitewater rafters. An Impact Photographics postcard features a collage of many images, including a Route 66 logo framing a scenic view of the Colorado River from the rim. Oddly, the postcard does not include any images of roads, but the logo implies that perhaps the river is the new iconic highway of the West. The printing and manufacturing of the postcards also veer from the historical examples and each other. The Impact Photographics postcards are printed in Korea and include details not found in other postcards sampled for this study (such as glitter glued onto the front of the card and a cutout for a hiking boot stencil).

Both postcard sample sets featured a variety of Grand Canyon locations (fig. 124). Impact Photographics postcards favored South Rim horizontal and

Fig. 120. Postcard rack sample, Impact Photographics, 2009. Note the emphasis on purple as the interior color for the canyon. This is a diversion from earlier imagery that focused only on red, orange, and yellow shades. Author's collection.

Fig. 121. Postcard photo collage, Impact Photographics, 2009. In this photo collage two iconic American landscapes are fused together: the Grand Canyon and Route 66. Although Route 66 does not connect to the Grand Canyon (only to the town of Flagstaff, south of the canyon), these places and the Colorado River are fused together. Author's collection.

GRAND CANYON
NATIONAL PARK

GRAND CANYON
GRAND CANYON
RAILWAY
GRAND CANYON
Colorado River
Grand
Canyon

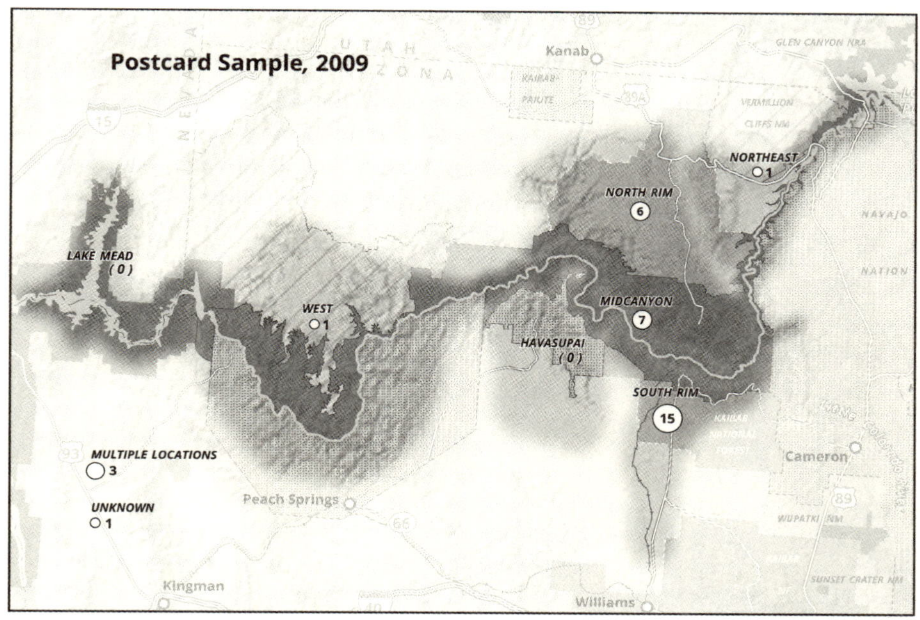

Fig. 122. (*opposite top*) Postcard pastiche, Impact Photographics, 2009. In what may be the strangest and most geographically disorienting interpretation of Grand Canyon landscapes, this postcard overlaps several very different locations at the canyon: the inner canyon trail with mule riders, the Desert Watchtower on the South Rim, the Colorado River at the bottom of the canyon, and a lightning storm from the rim. The subtle boundary between each of the images may fool the casual viewer into thinking the Desert Watchtower rises from the depths of the canyon alongside the sandbars of the Colorado River. Author's collection.

Fig. 123. (*opposite bottom*) Postcard rack samples, Smith-Southwestern Inc., 2009. Note the shift in colors for the canyon toward a more realistic dark green Colorado River and an emphasis on purple shades for the inner canyon views. Recent imagery also emphasizes adventure outdoor recreation such as hiking and whitewater rafting. The historic Santa Fe Railroad has been revitalized to offer a short scenic train ride for tourists from Williams, Arizona, to the South Rim of Grand Canyon Village and a depot near El Tovar Hotel. Author's collection.

Fig. 124. (*above*) Map of horizontal locations represented in 2009 postcard sample. Note that this map includes combined totals for both postcard manufacturers (Impact Photographics and Smith-Southwestern) and representations of a "west" and a "northeast" rim viewpoint. Cartography by Robert M. Edsall. Based on data from the U.S. Geological Survey, National Park Service, and author's content analysis results from archival research.

vertical locations, while the Smith-Southwestern postcards showed North Rim, South Rim, midcanyon horizontal locations, and rim vertical locations (see appendix). The Impact Photographics postcards included Yavapai Point, Navajo Point, and Toroweap Overlook; the Smith-Southwestern postcards featured Guano Point at Grand Canyon West, Cape Solitude, Moran Point, Yavapai Point, and Navajo Point. Impact postcards represented two views the Smith-Southwestern postcards did not: one featured a scenic view from Cape Solitude in the eastern canyon and another postcard focused on the Grand Canyon West from the rim. Many of the Impact and Smith-Southwestern postcards also noted (on their backs) that the Grand Canyon is a World Heritage Site and one of the so-called seven natural wonders of the world.

Conclusion

From Rim to River and Beyond

> Once again, the political and private have been marked by the plots of the symbolic, which, as always happens, has proven the producer of reality.
>
> —Umberto Eco, *Travels in Hyperreality*

As we trace popular imagery of the Grand Canyon through accumulating layers, the location of the "real" Grand Canyon becomes more obscure. Consider, for example, the shifts in knowing where the Grand Canyon was as its political boundaries waxed and waned from a forest reserve in 1893 to national monument in 1908 to national park in 1919. Add to this the wide range and diversity of popular imagery that represented the canyon's environment from mule trails, to El Tovar Hotel dining rooms, rim-side overlooks, to whitewater thrills along the Colorado River. Each image built the Grand Canyon's cultural capital from a place sidestepped by Spanish explorers to one of America's premier nature sites. Its supersized iconic status as a nature park, its use and management as one of the most visited national parks in America, and its cultural, historical, and visual heritage proves too much to contain with rigid boundaries.

Instead, the Grand Canyon is a region, a place with permeable boundaries and shifting ecotones that change over time as different locations and subjects strike a chord in American popular and environmental culture. Similar to an ecosystem, the Grand Canyon region is a large system comprised of many smaller yet interconnected areas that are healthiest when networks and migration patterns are functioning. Our appreciation of ecological boundaries shifts with our understanding of environmental perception. The boundary between nature and culture is not exact; instead, it is like an ecotone, a fuzzy boundary that indicates a change in environment or, in the case of the Grand Canyon, a change in ideas about nature and culture as one migrates between these epistemological areas. This, I would argue, is the real Grand Canyon. It is larger than any one era or one location. It is an iconographic region.

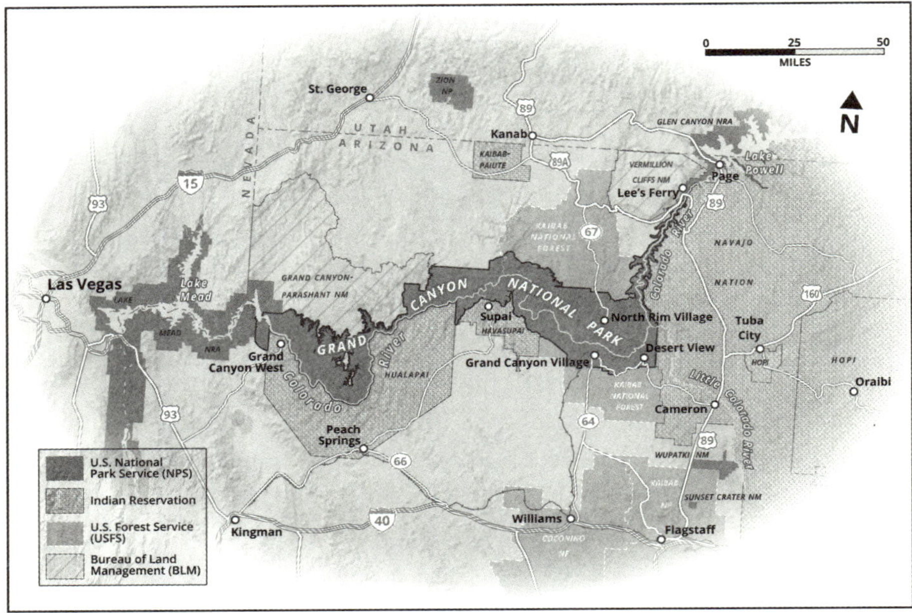

Fig. 125. Map of the Greater Grand Canyon Region. Cartography by Robert M. Edsall. Design by Yolonda Youngs. Based on data from the National Park Service, U.S. Geological Survey, ESRI, and the author's research.

With this new approach and appreciation for varied visual, cultural, and historical ideas, we can consider a Greater Grand Canyon Region that encompasses a large expanse of northern Arizona (fig. 125) The regional approach allows for a more inclusive cultural Grand Canyon that can cross historical land division and political boundaries to create stronger ecological and social connections to the complex networks and transboundary migrations that bind this area together. It includes lands managed by multiple agencies (National Forest Service, National Park Service, Bureau of Land Management, Bureau of Reclamation), eleven Traditionally Associated tribes, and expanding towns and cities.

If there is to be a more culturally and socially inclusive Greater Grand Canyon Region, then the diverse historical actors who played parts in its social construction must be equally included in accounts of the region. A multicultural GGCR includes first-person interpretation, active partnerships, and open dialogue across state and municipal groups and agencies from

American Indian, Anglo, Hispanic, Latinx, African American, and Asian American inhabitants.

As a step in that direction, the National Park Service recognizes the tribes as an active, contemporary presence in park policy and management and is working collaboratively with them to recognize tribal self-determination and long-standing historical, cultural, and spiritual connections to the Grand Canyon. This work moves toward healing wounds inflicted from almost a century of federal government policies of assimilation and termination. As a part of this effort, tribal members are calling on the NPS to commit to programs and policies that educate park visitors about American Indian cultures and peoples and emphasizing first-voice narratives from tribal members that discuss the contested history of Indigenous land dispossession, discrimination, and forced removal from lands that are now national park units (Hirst 2006, 2016; Shepherd 2010; Watahomigie-Corliss 2020). Although the NPS is making new and reinvigorated efforts to pursue an open and collaborative relationship with the Traditionally Affiliated Tribes, tensions still remain about access for tribal members to park resources and locations for "cultural and spiritual practices," interpretation of their history and its significance to the human footprint in the Grand Canyon, and managing lands to be respective and inclusive of "tribal interests and concerns." (Hirst 2016, vi). Through new and evolving collaborations and consultations between the NPS and the Traditional Affiliated Tribes, tribal involvement at the Grand Canyon now includes "first-voice interpretation, cultural demonstrations, youth education and employment, and economic development" (Hirst 2016, ix).

Revisiting the conceptual diagram of the Grand Canyon's iconographic arc discussed in the introduction is a productive starting point for scholars to organize the historical and visual history of seeing nature at the Grand Canyon (fig. 126). This conceptual diagram—modeled after Arthur Krim's 2005 Route 66 study, then adapted for the Grand Canyon context—visually summarizes the cumulative findings of this research. Although the cultural-iconographic arc diagram assesses how visual representations work at the Greater Grand Canyon Region, it may be modified for use with other protected and public lands or any iconic location with an archive of visual imagery. Consider how this might work for a study of the Monument Valley, the Eiffel Tower, Saint Mark's Square in Venice, or the Taj Mahal. Each of

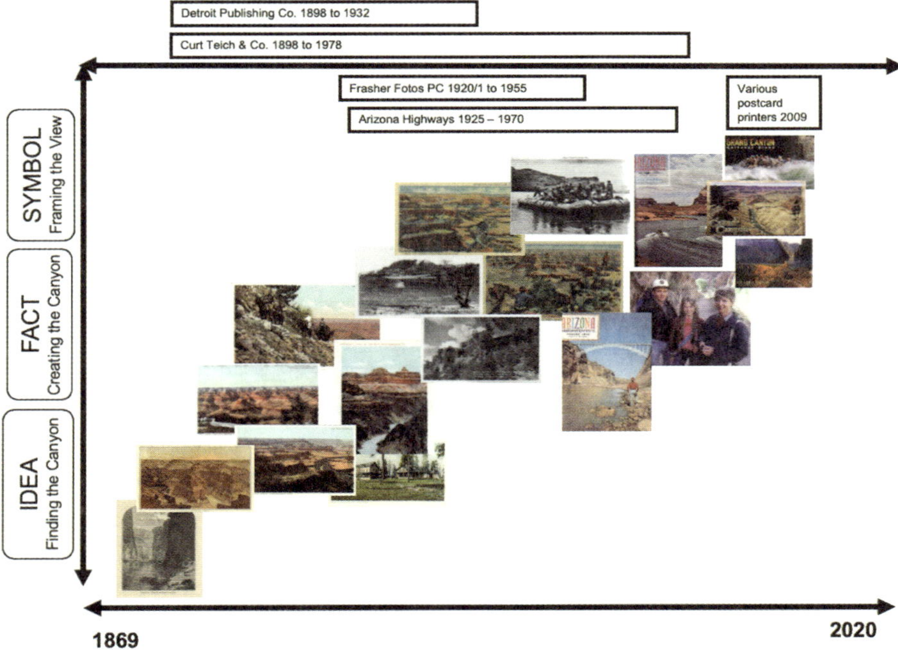

Fig. 126. The iconographic arc of the Grand Canyon. Created by the author and inspired by Arther Krim's Route 66 study (2005).

these locations is known to us through the lens of environmental perception and shaped by an accumulating arc of visual representations in postcards, magazine photographs, films, and other popular media.

Applications for Landscape Interpretation

Throughout this book, I have explored changing visual representations of the environment through popular media sources, analyzed the content and discussions of these visual representations, and ground-truthed these representations in an effort to expand our understanding and interpretation of scenic quality, environmental integrity, and cultural resources in national parks. This research developed in cooperation with the National Park Service Interpretive and Cultural Resource staff at Grand Canyon National Park and with the Grand Canyon Association; both groups supported applied aspects of the project. My intention here is to take the lessons that I learned from the theoretical and historical research of this project and apply it in a grounded application that may benefit National Park Service interpretation and educational programs and the communities they serve.

While this book builds on some aspects of the NPS cultural landscape program for historical landscapes, it also challenges the program to expand current practices and approaches and offer an alternative model to understanding and interpreting visual cultural landscapes. While historical context is important if the NPS could embrace a definition of cultural landscapes that moves beyond the narrow bounds of "significance in American history and authenticity to a historic time period" (National Park Service 2021), new doors could open for better understanding and interpreting national park landscapes as active, contemporary places shaped by ongoing socially and politically evolving processes by diverse actors. This could encourage new interpretations of national parks that challenge hegemonic ideas of authenticity or historical significance. Do we need to categorize helicopter rides in Grand Canyon National Park and the flight corridors they use by their significance in American history and their authenticity to a specific time period in order to interpret them as cultural landscapes? Are there other ways we could understand this recreational activity and its soundscape?

Framing Nature offers a new model for understanding and interpreting visual cultural landscapes and viewsheds (fig. 127). Under the NPS Cultural Landscape Program, there are thirteen types of "landscape characteristics" that are found in cultural landscapes. The primary category that directly connects with the visual representations of cultural landscapes is "views and vistas," defined as "the composition of other landscape characteristics, such as lookout structure or a view framed by vegetation" (National Park Service 2021). While these are important elements, this category overlooks the process of socially constructing a cultural landscape and the important work of "representing, structuring or symbolizing surroundings." Expanding NPS categories beyond views and viewsheds could embrace broader concepts of visual cultural landscapes that include the social process of representing and symbolizing places and may offer appealing interpretation to an increasingly diverse American public. For example, what places in the Grand Canyon are important for Hopi tribal members, how are those places depicted in popular imagery, and how does that influence cultural heritage preservation at the Grand Canyon? The concept of visibility is a cultural artifact worthy of preservation (Machlis et al. 2000; National Park Service 2021). Previous research concerning visibility in national parks centered on

Fig. 127. Framing the view. This image of the Grand Canyon was captured in October 2020 inside the Desert View Watchtower, looking out across the Grand Canyon. Photograph by the author.

the environmental impacts of increasing air pollution but overlooked the role that viewsheds play in the social and historical fabric of national parks (Cahn 1982; Prichard 1982; Davis, Graber, Acker 2003).

My research offers NPS cultural resource managers an alternative approach to expanding its programs by interpreting and documenting how the Grand Canyon was socially constructed as an iconic American landscape through popular images and how those images shaped environmental management, cultural heritage preservation, and tourism at the canyon.

This study also offers an alternative guide for developing interpretive and educational products and programs for the Grand Canyon as national park managers, visitors, and concerned citizens work collaboratively to protect this vast landscape for future generations. This book goes behind the scenes of some of the most iconic viewsheds in Grand Canyon National Park to better understand their role in shaping ideas about U.S. environmental management and policy. I encourage a shift to new approaches in the National Park Service definition of cultural and historic resources, one that explicitly includes the concept of view and visibility as a cultural artifact worthy of preserving. Few would argue that clean air is important. Seeing the Grand Canyon and protecting that visibility, an attribute wrapped up in clean and clear air protection, is also a key ingredient to seeing and appreciating this vast landscape.

Previous research concerning visibility in national parks centered on the environmental impacts of increasing air pollution but overlooked the role that these viewsheds play in the social and historical fabric of national parks. How we frame nature has long-term effects on the social, cultural, and environmental health of the Grand Canyon. The Greater Grand Canyon Region must be addressed. This region is bound together by common environmental conditions, shared histories and cultures, and deeply felt political and social convictions. It is bound by nature, vision, and history. As the author Barry Lopez observes, "to keep landscapes intact and the memory of them, our history in them alive, seems as imperative a task in modern time" (2004, 97).

Appendix A

Annual Visitation Statistics for GRCA

Note: For updated annual visitation statistics for Grand Canyon National Park beyond this table, visit the U.S. National Park Service Visitor Use Statistics website at https://irma.nps.gov/Stats/Reports/Park/GRCA. Annual visitation statistics are posted with a delay of one year (e.g., 2019 statistics were not available until 2020).

Table 1. Annual Visits to GRCA, 1919–2022

Year	*Number of Visits*
1919	37,745
1920	67,315
1921	67,485
1922	84,700
1923	102,166
1924	108,256
1925	134,053
1926	140,252
1927	162,356
1928	167,226
1929	184,093
1930	172,763
1931	156,964
1932	121,267
1933	105,475
1934	140,220
1935	206,018
1936	268,412
1937	297,876
1938	336,557
1939	395,940
1940	371,613
1941	436,566
1942	132,584
1943	71,650
1944	64,568
1945	169,960
1946	486,834
1947	622,363
1948	618,033
1949	600,690
1950	665,039
1951	682,152
1952	737,159
1953	836,878
1954	814,700

1955	892,400	1985	2,711,529
1956	1,033,700	1986	3,035,787
1957	1,102,400	1987	3,513,030
1958	1,064,000	1988	3,859,886
1959	1,169,400	1989	3,966,209
1960	1,187,700	1990	3,776,685
1961	1,253,000	1991	3,886,031
1962	1,447,400	1992	4,203,545
1963	1,539,500	1993	4,575,602
1964	1,576,600	1994	4,364,316
1965	1,689,200	1995	4,557,645
1966	1,806,000	1996	4,537,703
1967	1,804,900	1997	4,791,668
1968	1,986,300	1998	4,239,682
1969	2,192,600	1999	4,575,124
1970	2,258,200	2000	4,460,228
1971	2,402,100	2001	4,104,809
1972	2,698,300	2002	4,001,974
1973	1,909,700	2003	4,124,900
1974	1,888,600	2004	4,326,234
1975	2,625,100	2005	4,401,522
1976	2,791,600	2006	4,279,439
1977	2,627,200	2007	4,413,668
1978	2,748,642	2008	4,425,314
1979	2,131,716	2009	4,348,068
1980	2,304,973	2010	4,388,386
1981	2,472,270	2011	4,298,178
1982	2,293,127	2012	4,421,352
1983	2,248,082	2013	4,564,840
1984	2,173,584	2014	4,756,771

2015	5,520,736
2016	5,969,811
2017	6,254,238
2018	6,380,495
2019	5,974,411
2020	2,897,098
2021	4,532,677
2022	4,732,101
Total	**236,257,914**

Note: Data for 2022 is the most recent year available. *Source*: NPS Grand Canyon National Park Total Recreation Visitation, 1919–2019, accessed May 28, 2020, https://irma.nps.gov/Stats/ssrsreports/Park%20specific%20reports/Annual%20park%20recreation%20visitation%20graph%20-1904%20-%20last%20calendar%20year.

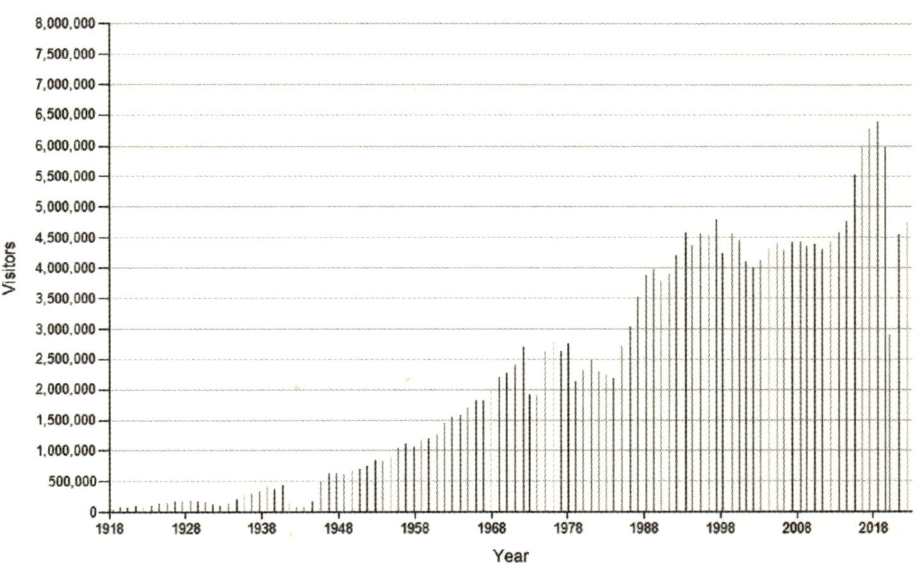

Fig. 128. Total Grand Canyon recreation visits, 1918–2022.

Appendix B

Content Analysis Decoded

As a guide to readers interested in a more detailed accounting of the quantitative data and analysis that informs the findings of this book, this appendix section describes my rationale for selecting and naming the major thematic and spatial categories that I used for the content analysis of all the postcard and magazine photographs. This is a mixed-method study that employs both quantitative and qualitative analysis. In many ways interpretive and qualitative research is a subjective enterprise. The description, selection, and definition of the categories of analysis (themes and spatial locations) and the interpretations I draw from an assessment of these images for their meanings and values about nature and its relationship to culture made throughout this work are my contrivances. As a researcher, I am adding my own layer of interpretation and visualization to the Grand Canyon. Throughout the data collection, analysis, and interpretation stages, my goal has been to create a research structure that is based on previous work on visual content analysis in cultural geography and visual culture and media scholarship. The analysis section of this study cross-references all categories to illuminate and discuss dominant patterns in the data through the themes and locations shown in the imagery. My focus for this analysis was on every postcard and photograph of the Grand Canyon produced by Detroit Publishing Company (DPC), Curt Teich Company (CTC), Frasher Foto Postcard Company (FFPC), and *Arizona Highways*.

At the start of this process, I discovered thousands of images found in postcards and photographs of the Grand Canyon in archives and libraries across the United States. Initially, I was overwhelmed by the number and variety of subjects and locations depicted in the imagery. I needed to prune this massive data set down to a manageable size. To begin, I focused my research on the three postcard manufacturers that were the most prolific for their day. Combined, these companies manufactured postcards from roughly 1900 to the late 1970s, well within the target time period I explore in this study.

Another important consideration for this study was the accessibility of the image collections. Some postcard collections found at libraries and archives are incomplete sets, while others reside in private collections. Each of the sets that I chose for this study are in public archives and libraries, and many of them are increasingly digitized and available online. Over the fifteen years of my research, the extensive Curt Teich Postcard Archives and the Detroit Publishing Archives moved in 2016 from the Illinois Digital Archives at the Lake Country Discovery Museum in Wauconda, Illinois, to the Newberry Library in Chicago. The move expanded the holdings in the collections, added new collections, and expanded digital and online access to this archive. I draw on both the Illinois Digital Archives and Newberry Library collections. These are tremendous resources for postcard scholars and others interested in this form of popular media. The Newberry's Curt Teich Postcard Archives Collection's home page describes the extent of the collection:

> The Curt Teich Postcard Archives Collection was transferred in December 2016 to the Newberry from the Lake County Discovery Museum in Wauconda, Illinois, which served as its home since 1982. The Collection is widely regarded as the largest public collection of postcards and related materials in the United States. When received at the Newberry Library it was estimated at 2.5 million total items and over 500,000 unique postcard images.
>
> The core of the collection is the Records of the Curt Teich Company, which includes over 360,000 images produced by the company from 1898 [to] 1978, over 110,000 production files documenting the creation of the company's postcards, and additional company records.
>
> Several additional postcard collections and archives have been added to the Teich Archives Collection over the past 35 years, including the Detroit Publishing Company Collection, the Dexter Press Records, the John High Collection, the V. O. Hammon Company Collection, the Leonard A. Lauder Raphael Tuck Collection, and many others.

Sorting through the complex, overlapping histories and manufacturing timelines of some of the postcard manufacturers can be confusing for newcomers to postcard history, especially when it comes to Detroit Publishing Company and Curt Teich Company. The postcards and records for these companies now mingle together in public and digital archives. The closing of business for DPC and the growth of CTC from the 1920s onward, combined with the transition of Fred Harvey Company contracts for manufacturing postcards from DPC to CTC also obscures the issue. Therefore, identifying Curt Teich postcards can require close observation at times. Over the years, Curt Teich manufactured postcards for several publishers and distributors and did not always print its logo on the cards. After Detroit Publishing Company went out of business, Fred Harvey opened a direct account with Curt Teich. Under this agreement, Curt Teich manufactured postcards that Fred Harvey Company then published and distributed. This arrangement can be traced through the diligently placed code numbers on all Curt Teich postcards, which reveal that Curt Teich was the manufacturer of the Fred Harvey cards even though the cards were printed without Curt Teich's name, only crediting Fred Harvey on the postcard. A similar arrangement was made by Curt Teich with Verkamps, another Grand Canyon concessionaire on the South Rim. Indeed, careful inspection of the backs of many postcards from this era verify that Curt Teich manufactured postcards for other companies that acted as publishers and distributors for the cards. The postcard set discussed in this appendix consists of all of the Grand Canyon postcards that were manufactured by Curt Teich Company from 1936 to 1955.

In terms of my selection of postcards from these vast collections, I removed some images from my sample set due to the locations they represented. Detroit Publishing and Curt Teich, with their large collections of images from around the United States, included Grand Canyon of the Yellowstone River (in Yellowstone National Park) with searches for "Grand Canyon." After requesting all images produced by each manufacturer by the subject and geographic location of "Grand Canyon, Arizona," I sorted through them and removed the images of Yellowstone. The 1,473 images analyzed for this study is the final data set after this sorting process. This includes 86 DPC postcards, 86 FFPC postcards, 259 CTC postcards, and 34 postcards from two manufacturers in 2009. It also includes 1,008 *Arizona Highways* photographs.

The public archival access to *Arizona Highways* magazine also transferred and digitized during the course of my research and writing. My goal in seeking out *Arizona Highways* magazine photographs was to cross-reference images published in the magazine during roughly the same time frame as the postcards but in a different medium. That led me to seek out *Arizona Highways*, a publication produced by the State of Arizona and an incredible visual archive of photographs and images for Arizona, generally, and the Grand Canyon, in particular. It is one of the most notable magazines for its promotion of both of these places. I initially consulted issues of the print magazine through Arizona State University's Hayden Library government documents reading room in Tempe, Arizona. The collection included most but not all issues of the magazine (1925–61, 1967–71, 1972–96). However, a few years ago *Arizona Highways* partnered with the Arizona State Library and the Arizona Memory Project to digitize and make publicly available all the issues of the magazine. Entire issues of *Arizona Highways* from 1931 to the 2020s are now accessible as free digitized files through the Arizona Memory Project (http://azmemory.azlibrary.gov/cdm/landingpage/collection/aho). The project team continues to digitize with a goal to upload all back to the first issue in 1925.

In terms of themes, I eventually whittled down a large list of twenty-eight thematic categories to a more concise list of eleven: scenic, people, buildings, dams, water, recreation, animals, automobiles, trails, roads and/or bridges, and miscellaneous, with a few subcategories under these. In addition, I decided upon vertical spatial categories (river, rim, midcanyon, and aerial) to analyze the cards for their locations and cross-reference this information with the historic timeline of production and thematic differences.

The thematic categories vary slightly between the postcards and magazine based on differences found in the media types. These variations are due to differences in manufacturing each medium, technology (the process used to capture and edit images), prevalence of themes (e.g., the postcards depicted far more American Indian children than did the magazine), and the time periods (most of the postcards were created before Glen Canyon Dam, so it follows that none of this imagery includes dams as subjects or themes). Through the data analysis stages of this work, I refined these categories to be as consistent as possible across media types; the postcards and magazine representations were evaluated using relatively similar categories. My model for this type of matrix derives from similar content analysis projects that assess the thematic and spatial contents of popular media sources depicting historic national park scenes (Wyckoff and Nash 1994; Wyckoff and Dilsaver 1997). Although I strive to be consistent in my categorization of the visual images, there are some variations on the themes across the media sources.

All the postcards are catalogued according to eighteen thematic categories, five horizontal categories (spatial), and six vertical categories (spatial). The thematic categories include scenic (vegetation/green), scenic (vegetation/brown), scenic (canyon layers view), people (Anglo), people (American

Indian), people (children), buildings (interior), buildings (exterior), dams, water (Colorado River), water (lakes, streams, waterfalls), recreation (mules with riders, only), animals (mules and horses), animals (wildlife), automobiles, trails, roads and/or bridges, and miscellaneous. Note that because the images usually contained multiple subjects, some postcards may be examined for several themes. Table 2 lists the thematic categories used to assess all postcards. It is provided here to assist in understanding this shorthand for thematic commonalities found in the images.

Table 2. Thematic categories of postcards

Thematic category	*Subject matter*
Scenic: vegetation/green	Broad scenic vistas usually showing the canyon's geological layering, the Colorado River corridor with cliffs and river as dominant subjects, emphasizing green vegetation
Scenic: vegetation/brown	Broad scenic vistas usually showing the canyon's geological layering, the Colorado River corridor with cliffs and river as dominant subjects, emphasizing brown or lack of vegetation
Scenic: canyon layers view	Broad scenic vistas usually showing the canyon's geological layering
People: white	Representations of white people
People: American Indian	Representations of American Indian people
People: children	Representations of Children
Buildings: interior	Interior spaces of buildings
Buildings: exterior	A depiction of the exterior of a building
Dams	Glen Canyon Dam
Water: Colorado River	Scenes depicting activities on the river, on the riverside, or view along the river corridor
Water: lakes/streams/ waterfalls	Other water features in the Grand Canyon, excluding the Colorado River
Recreation: mules with riders (only)	Scenes depicting people riding mules

Animals: mules and horses	Mules or horses only
Animals: wildlife (deer)	Deer, squirrels, other canyon wildlife
Automobiles	Cars and trucks
Trails	Hiking and mule trails, usually dirt
Roads and/or bridges	Highways, interstates, or park roads
Miscellaneous	Various scenes that do not fit into any of the above categories

Note: Data from 2019 is the most recent year available. *Source*: NPS Grand Canyon National Park Total Recreation Visitation, 1919–2019, accessed May 28, 2020, https://irma.nps.gov/Stats/ssrsreports/Park%20specific%20reports/Annual%20park%20recreation%20visitation%20graph%20-1904%20-%20last%20calendar%20year.

Thematic categories listed as scenic refer to postcards that depict broad vistas usually showing the canyon's geological layering and the Colorado River corridor with cliffs and river as dominant subjects. The variations—vegetation/green or vegetation/brown and canyon layers view—refer to the colors in the postcard representations. This curious case grabbed my attention as I sorted through the Curt Teich and Detroit Publishing Company cards. The brightly colored trees and shrubs in these scenes grabbed my attention. Based on my many field work visits and research stays at the Grand Canyon and knowledge of its ecology, I realized that this unusual display of greenery at this high desert and arid location was artificial. This finding was supported by my repeat photography fieldwork that included ground-truthing historical postcard images with the locations they depict and then capturing repeat photographs of them. Ground truthing is a geography and cartography method of checking data collected remotely or at a distance with measurements made at a specific location. In the context of repeat photography, this involved taking a postcard with visual data created historically by artists or photographers working remotely (in Chicago, for example) and checking the veracity of that information by visiting the specific location of the image and gathering photographs of the contemporary scene (as a type of measurement, if you will). Through the process of revising and augmenting these images in the transition from photographs to postcards, many elements of the postcard representations went through a process analogous to contemporary photo editing programs that enhance or change images (photoshopping). These changes were often repeated and recreated as plates were used over and over to produce popular postcards.

Scenic views of the Grand Canyon accounted for a majority of the Curt Teich postcards from 1936 to 1955. Many of these postcards featured views from the south or North Rim with certain locations identified as named viewpoints. South Rim scenic viewpoints represented in Curt Teich postcards from this time period included Hopi Point, Desert View/"The Watchtower," Grand View, Mohave Point, Powell Point/Powell Memorial, Lipan Point, Yavapai Point, Pima Point, from or near El Tovar, Hermit's Rest, Moran Point, Yaki Point, Maricopa Point, and Breeze Point. The North Rim, with its lack of early investment by a private corporation like the Santa Fe Railroad fell behind the South Rim in commercial development. The North Rim also had a less developed road system guiding auto tours and private motorists along a choreographed route with scenic stops along the way. North Rim viewpoints featured in Curt Teich postcards included Angel's Window, Point Imperial, Cape Royal, Point Sublime, Bright Angel Point, and View from Grand Canyon Lodge.

A Note on Thematic Categories and Representations of People

People figure prominently in many of the postcards. At times their faces are well defined, while other times the viewer sees only the subject's back or a blurred face in a crowd. Categorizing people depicted in these postcard and photographs was one of the most difficult tasks of this project. The process was riddled with issues of identity, authenticity, and social and cultural misrepresentation. Ultimately, I chose to rely upon the context of the images provided. When the postcard or photograph captions described the people in the scene as Hopi or Navajo, these postcards were noted under the thematic category as People: American Indian. Children are also represented in the postcard imagery as People: Children.

All of these categories of people, of course, are up for debate as the postcard company or the business that hired it may have provided the wording for the captions to meet the business's ideas of how it would like the canyon's denizens portrayed. It does not mean those words matched the reality of the canyon, just as the postcard images themselves could easily be edited and distorted. At other times, the captions were missing any sort of description of the people. For these instances, I based the interpretation of the scene on the shading of their skin tones. People represented as white in the postcards were noted in my thematic categories as People: white. I realize that this is a less than satisfying solution as I am categorizing people by the color that postcard manufacturers applied to their images, without knowledge about who those people actually were in the images. In addition, as I discuss in the text of this book, people represented as white in these postcards were almost always engaged in leisure or recreational activities such as mule riding or relaxing by a fireplace and dressed like tourists. It would be simple enough to wear any clothes one wished, like an actor in disguise, in order to appear as a member of one group or another. With those complex choices in mind, I accepted that all decisions about these categories of people would be tentative and partial, up for debate by future scholars who may wish to replicate or revise my analysis. There is ample opportunity to improve upon my method here. I look forward to other researchers performing a similar content analysis on postcards and photographs of the Grand Canyon with the intent of critically evaluating and improving the accuracy of the identities portrayed in these images.

Additional Categories and Themes

Buildings and other structures were grouped into three categories: postcards that depicted the interior of buildings (such as the dining room of El Tovar Hotel), the exterior of buildings (Historic Verkamps from the South Rim), and dams (Glen Canyon Dam). Water featured prominently in many postcards. I divided this category into two listings—Colorado River and a more general listing for all other water features.

A distinct difference between the postcard and magazine representations may be seen in the different recreational scenes each medium depicts. The only recreational activities that the postcards depict are scenes with tourists riding mules and auto touring. The magazine highlighted a greater variety of recreational activities.

Animals are limited in the postcard appearances as either domestic (mules and horses) or wild (deer and squirrels). Material cultural landscape features include automobiles, trails (mule or hiking trails into or out of or along the rim of the canyon), and bridges (e.g., Kaibab Suspension Bridge). Finally, there were a few subjects that eluded easy or consistent categorization. These subjects were noted in the miscellaneous thematic category.

Spatial Categories of Vertical and Horizonal Locations

The spatial categories used to assess the postcards included both horizontal and vertical elements. As a geographer, I am keenly interested in *where* these postcard scenes are located and, throughout the book, I suggest why postcard manufacturers selected these places. The Grand Canyon is a place that has been and continues to be experienced both horizontally—latitude and longitude coordinates—and vertically—rim, trail, or river locations (Fig. 129 and Fig. 130). My use of vertical and horizontal categories is intended as a way to decipher and map the locations depicted in the postcards. This method of assessing the many locations of images both horizontally and vertically is also directed as a critique of the dominant narrative about the Grand Canyon as a rim *or* river experience. One of the arguments of this book is that there are multiple "grand canyons"; that is, multiple places that are experienced, portrayed, and recognized in a visual mosaic we recognize as *the* Grand Canyon.

With this cross-section in mind, I developed categories for vertical and for horizontal locations. This information is particularly useful for the mapping analysis undertaken in this study. The vertical categories that I used for all postcard assessments include the following: river, midcanyon, rim, aerial, no view, and multiple views. The horizontal categories referred to in my assessment of all the postcards include North Rim, South rim, midcanyon, unknown, multiple. These categories vary slightly from the horizontal mapping categories represented in fig. 129. In other words, the shaded areas of the map represent the subregions of the Grand Canyon from a horizontal "slice" of the canyon perspective including the North Rim, South Rim, and midcanyon areas. Due to the difficulty of representing the horizontal postcard categories of "unknown" and "multiple" as a discrete location on the map, they are instead noted in a subtle text box inserted into the left bottom corner of each map. Also note that the horizontal categories used for the magazine representations include additional categories of Lake Mead, Havasupai, west, northeast, and all canyon (discussed in the following paragraphs about the magazine imagery). A table noting the locations assigned to the six vertical categories (Table 3) and one describing the five horizontal categories (Table 4) and their corresponding locations are provided below as a reference for this study's results.

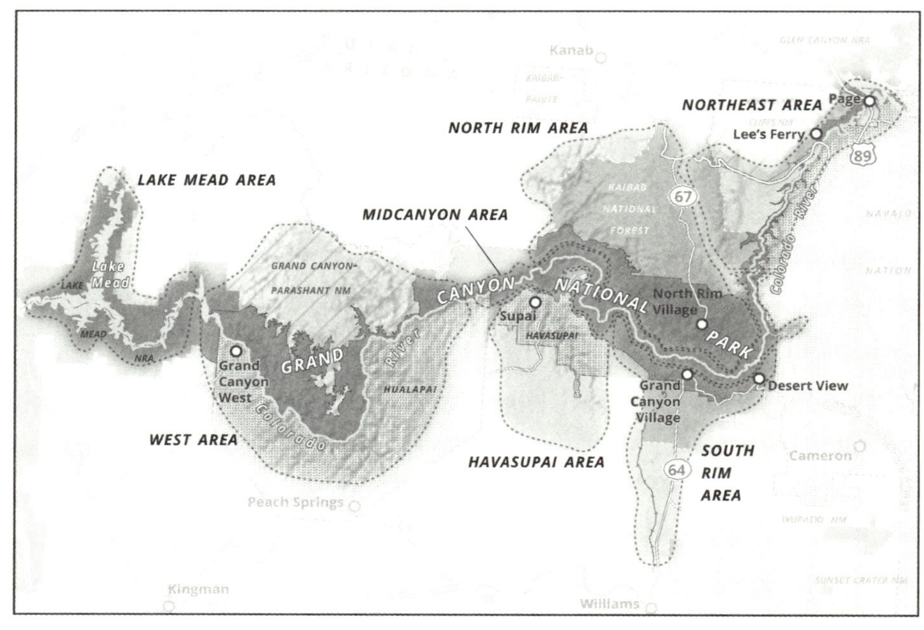

Fig. 129. Horizontal categories base map. Subregions, such as midcanyon and northeast, are designated to relate the locations represented in the postcards and photographs in this study. Cartography by Robert M. Edsall. Design by Yolonda Youngs. Based on data from the National Park Service, U.S. Geological Society, ESRI, and the author's research.

Fig. 130. Vertical categories of the Grand Canyon rim-to-river transect. Photograph by author.

Table 3. Vertical categories: Postcards and magazines

Vertical category	*Location*
River	Along the Colorado River corridor
Midcanyon	Along the trails and camps between the river and the rim
Rim	Images taken at or facing toward the north or South Rim of the canyon
Aerial	Views taken from helicopters, planes, or satellites
No view	No visible signs of canyon scenery (taken indoors or outdoors of focused subject matter with no scenic view of the canyon visible in the frame)
Multiple views	Some postcards presented multiple images and locations

Table 4. Horizontal categories: Postcards

Category	*Named features within boundaries of category*
North Rim	Kaibab National Forest (north), North Rim Lodge, Vishnu Temple, Zoroaster, North Rim Village (Grand Canyon Lodge), Roaring Springs, Deer Creek
South Rim	South Rim Village, Kaibab National Forest (south), Tusayan, entrance gate (old) to canyon, Scenes along Arizona State Highway 64
Midcanyon	Inner canyon and Colorado River corridor areas between the North and South Rims (from confluence of the Little Colorado River and the Colorado River downstream to the border of Havasupai and Hualapai Indian Reservations). Includes Phantom Ranch, popular mule and hiking trails into and out of the canyon (NPS designation of "corridor trails"), Hermit Rapid, Crystal Rapid, Granite Rapid
Unknown	Unable to locate geographically; no features or descriptions marking the location
Multiple	Some postcards presented multiple images and locations of the canyon on one postcard

Thematic and Spatial Categories of Magazine Imagery

In my assessment of *Arizona Highways* visual representations of the Grand Canyon, the thematic and spatial categories that I employed to analyze and categorize the images varied slightly from the parameters used to evaluate the postcards. All the magazine images are catalogued according to sixteen thematic categories, eight horizontal categories (spatial), and four vertical categories (spatial). Note that the thematic categories vary slightly between the postcards and magazines based on differences found in the media types. These variations are due to differences in manufacturing each medium, technology differences, and prevalence of themes, and the time periods.

The list of thematic categories assigned to the magazine imagery is slightly shorter than the same categories for the postcards. For example, the categories for scenic-vegetation/green and scenic-vegetation/brown are not used to assess the magazine images, because they do not apply. The creation, production, manufacturing, and distribution of the magazine imagery created a different set of visual representations than the postcards. Although the photographs and other images in *Arizona Highways* were edited and reformatted through this process, the dramatic augmentation of the images to emphasize the color of the vegetation (or lack thereof) was not evident in the images that I sampled for this study. Another difference is the expansion of the recreation category to include a greater diversity of activities, including hiking and river rafting (two activities not in evidence in the postcard imagery). Aside from this, the thematic categories assigned to the magazine imagery are similar to the postcard thematic categories (table 5).

Table 5. Thematic categories: Magazine

Thematic category	*Subject matter*
Scenic: canyon layers view	Depict scenes of broad scenic vistas usually showing the canyon's geological layering
People: American Indian	Representations of American Indian people
People: white	Representations of white people
People: children	Children
Buildings: interior	Interior spaces of buildings
Buildings: exterior	A depiction of the exterior of a building

Dams	Glen Canyon Dam
Water: Colorado River	Scenes depicting activities on the river, on the riverside, or view along the river corridor
Water: lakes, streams, waterfalls	Other water features in the Grand Canyon, excluding the Colorado River
Recreation: mule riding, hiking, raft	Scenes depicting people riding mules, hiking, or riding in a boat, or participating in water activities
Animals: mules and horses	Mules or horses only
Animals: wildlife	Deer, squirrels, other canyon wildlife
Automobiles	Cars and trucks
Trails	Hiking and mule trails, usually dirt
Roads and bridges	Highways, interstates, or park roads
Miscellaneous	Various scenes that do not fit into any of the above categories

The spatial categories used to assess the *Arizona Highways* image, on the other hand, vary slightly from the ones employed in the assessment of postcards. The vertical categories are the same categories used to assess the postcard images (see table 3). However, the horizontal categories include a few additions (table 6). Note that the "unknown" and "multiple locations" categories are not included in the magazine assessment, because the magazine imagery always included a caption, subject matter, or other referencing material so I could locate the image geographically. I also assessed the postcard images so each postcard was counted as one visual representation but multiple locations could be shown in that one postcard. Notably, the magazine imagery did not allow such strict dissection. I counted each magazine image as one visual representation. There were no cases that showed multiple locations in one image. Horizontal categories added to the magazine assessment include Lake Mead, Havasupai, west, northeast, and all-canyon. The postcard images, either by limits of technology or by their historical moment of production (e.g., before Glen Canyon Dam was built) do not include some of these categories.

Table 6. Horizontal categories: Magazine

Horizontal category	*Location*
North Rim	Kaibab National Forest (north), North Rim Lodge, Vishnu Temple, Zoroaster, North Rim Village (Grand Canyon Lodge), Roaring Springs, Deer Creek
South Rim	Kaibab National Forest (south), South Rim Village, Tusayan, entrance gate (old) to canyon, scenes along U.S. Highway 180 and State Highway 64
Midcanyon	Inner canyon and Colorado River corridor areas between the North and South Rims (from confluence of the Little Colorado River and the Colorado River downstream to the border of Havasupai and Hualapai Indian Reservations). Includes Phantom Ranch, popular mule and hike trails into and out of the canyon (NPS designation of "corridor trails"), Hermit Rapid, Crystal Rapid, Granite Rapid
Lake Mead	Lake Mead, Pearce Ferry, take-out for Powell in 1872 and at Grand Wash cliffs in 1869; in the 1930s before it was dammed, it was the Grand Canyon, then faded out of Grand Canyon into Mead
Havasupai	Havasupai Indian Reservation, Havasu Falls, Mooney Falls
West	Hualapai Indian Reservation, Tuweep/Toroweap, Diamond Creek, Havasupai Skywalk, Lava Falls, Kanab Creek
Northeast	Lee's Ferry, Marble Canyon, Lake Powell, Nankoweap, Navajo Indian Reservation, Vasey's Paradise, Red Wall Cavern, scenes along U.S. Highway 89. Confluence of Little Colorado River and Colorado River is the dividing line between North Rim, south rim, and midcanyon sections
All-canyon	Maps and other imagery showing multiple locations at the canyon in one frame

Appendix C

Data Tables

Postcard and Magazine Content Analysis Results

The following tables provide specific counts of locations and subjects represented in Grand Canyon postcard and magazine imagery discussed in Chapters 3 to 9. Note that the percentage refers to the subject's representation in the total image set.

Table 7. Subjects represented in postcards, 1900–1935

	Detroit, 1900–1909		***Frasher, 1929–1935***		***Detroit and Frasher***
Subject	*Total number (n=86)*	*Total percentage (%)*	*Total number (n=65)*	*Total percentage (%)*	*Total number*
Scenic	58	67%	45	69	103
Vegetation: green shades	38	44%	46	71	84
Vegetation: brown shades	0	0%	5	8	5
People: white	15	17%	2	3%	17
People: American Indian	10	12%	0	0%	10
People: children	6	7%	0	0%	6
Buildings: interior	16	19%	0	0%	16
Buildings: exterior	13	15%	18	28%	31
Dams	0	0%	0	0%	0

Water: Colorado River	13	15%	11	17%	24
Water: lakes, streams, falls	0	0%	2	3%	2
Animals: mules with riders	12	14%	0	0%	12
Animals: mules and horses	1	1%	0	0%	1
Animals: deer	0	0%	1	2%	1
Automobiles	0	0%	4	6%	4
Trails	11	13%	2	3%	13
Roads and/or bridges	1	1%	11	17%	12
Miscellaneous	7	8%	2	3%	9
Total	**201***		**149***		**350***

Note: Some of the 86 Detroit cards and 65 Frasher cards contained multiple subjects.

Table 8. Horizontal locations in postcards, 1900–1935

	Detroit, 1900–1909		***Frasher, 1929–1935***		***Detroit and Frasher***
Location	*Total number (n=86)*	*Total percentage (%)*	*Total number (n=65)*	*Total percentage (%)*	*Total number*
North Rim	0	0%	23	35%	23
South Rim	62	72%	36	55%	98
Midcanyon	17	20%	0	0%	17
Unknown	7	8%	5	8%	12
Multiple	0	0%	1	2%	1
Total	**86**		**65**		**151**

Table 9. Vertical locations in postcards, 1900–1935

	Detroit, 1900–1909		*Frasher, 1929–1935*		*Detroit and Frasher*
Location	*Total number (n=86)*	*Total percentage (%)*	*Total number (n=65)*	*Total percentage (%)*	*Total number*
River	8	9%	0	0%	8
Midcanyon	11	13%	0	0%	11
Rim	42	49%	43	66%	85
Aerial	0	0%	0	0%	0
No view	25	29%	22	34%	47
Multiple views	0	0%	0	0%	0
Total	**86**		**65**		**151**

Table 10. Subjects in *Arizona Highways*, 1925–1935

Subject	*Total Number (n=13)*	*Total percentage (%)*
Scenic	6	35%
People: American Indian	0	0%
People: white	1	6%
People: children	0	0%
Buildings: interior	0	0%
Buildings: exterior	4	24%
Dams	0	0%
Water: Colorado River	2	12%

Water: lakes, streams, waterfalls	0	0%
Recreation: mule riding, hiking, rafting	0	0%
Animals: mules and horses	0	0%
Animals: deer	0	0%
Automobiles	0	0%
Trails	2	12%
Roads and bridges	2	12%
Miscellaneous	0	0%
Total	**17***	

**Note*: Some of the 13 *Arizona Highways* visual representations contained multiple subjects.

Table 11. Horizontal locations in *Arizona Highways*, 1925–1935

Location	*Total Number (n=13)*	*Total percentage (%)*
North Rim	2	15%
South Rim	9	69%
Midcanyon	0	0%
Lake Mead	0	0%
Havasupai	0	0%
West	0	0%
Northeast	1	8%
All-canyon	1	8%
Total	**13**	

Table 12. **Vertical locations in *Arizona Highways*, 1925–1935**

Location	***Total Number (n=13)***	***Total percentage (%)***
River	0	0%
Midcanyon	1	8%
Rim	9	69%
Aerial	3	23%
No view	0	0%
Multiple views	0	0%
Total	**13**	

Table 13. **Subjects in postcards, 1936–1955**

	Curt Teich, 1936–1955		***Frasher, 1936–1937***		***Curt Teich and Frasher***
Subject	*Total number (n=259)*	*Total percentage (%)*	*Total number (n=21)*	*Total percentage (%)*	*Total number*
Scenic	194	28%	12	29%	206
Vegetation: green shades	178	25%	11	27%	189
Vegetation: brown shades	9	1%	2	5%	11
People: white	51	7%	0	0%	51
People: American Indian	31	4%	0	0%	31
People: children	13	2%	0	0%	13

Buildings: interior	21	3%	0	0%	21
Buildings: exterior	55	8%	5	12%	60
Dam	0	0%	0	0%	0
Water: Colorado River	45	6%	5	12%	50
Water: lakes, streams, waterfalls	4	1%	0	0%	4
Animals: mules with riders	25	4%	0	0%	25
Animals: mules and horses	1	0%	0	0%	1
Animals: deer	6	1%	1	2%	7
Automobiles	6	1%	1	2%	7
Trails	38	5%	1	2%	39
Roads and/or bridges	14	2%	3	7%	17
Miscellaneous	10	1%	0	0%	10
Total	**701***		**41***		**742***

**Note*: Some of the 259 Curt Teich cards and 21 Frasher cards contained multiple subjects.

Table 14. **Horizontal locations in postcards, 1936–1955**

	Curt Teich, 1936–1955		*Frasher, 1936–1937*		*Curt Teich and Frasher*
Location	*Total number (n=259)*	*Total percentage (%)*	*Total number (n=21)*	*Total percentage (%)*	*Total number*
North Rim	25	10%	7	33%	32
South Rim	162	63%	13	62%	175
Midcanyon	39	15%	0	0%	39
Unknown	26	10%	1	5%	27
Multiple	7	3%	0	0%	7
Total	**259**		**21**		**280**

Table 15. **Vertical locations in postcards, 1936–1955**

	Curt Teich, 1936–1955		*Frasher, 1936–1937*		*Curt Teich and Frasher*
Location	*Total number (n=259)*	*Total percentage (%)*	*Total number (n=21)*	*Total percentage (%)*	*Total number*
River	43	17%	0	0%	43
Midcanyon	9	9%	0	0%	1
Rim	164	63%	13	62%	177
Aerial	4	2%	0	0%	4
No view	42	16%	8	38%	50
Multiple views	5	2%	0	0%	5
Total	**259**		**21**		**280**

Table 16. **Subjects represented in *Arizona Highways*, 1936 to 1970**

Subject	*Total number (n=664)*	*Total percentage (%)*
Scenic	384	58%
People: American Indian	29	4%
People: white	230	35%
People: children	5	1%
Buildings: interior	20	3%
Buildings: exterior	33	5%
Dams	38	6%
Water: Colorado River	103	16%
Water: lakes, streams, waterfalls	93	14%
Recreation: mule riding, hiking, rafting	117	18%
Animals: wildlife	5	1%
Animals: mules and horses	42	6%
Automobiles	28	4%
Trails	32	5%
Roads and bridges	27	4%
Miscellaneous	11	2%
Total	**1,197***	

**Note*: Some of the 664 magazine representations contained multiple subjects.

Table 17. Horizontal locations, *Arizona Highways*, 1936–1970

Location	*Total number (n=664)*	*Total percentage (%)*
North rim	69	10%
South Rim	159	24%
Midcanyon	93	14%
Lake Mead	111	17%
Havasupai	58	9%
West	65	10%
Northeast	98	15%
All-canyon	11	2%
Total	**664**	

Table 18. Vertical locations, *Arizona Highways*, 1936–1970

Location	*Total number (n=664)*	*Total percentage (%)*
River	348	52%
Midcanyon	40	6%
Rim	234	35%
Aerial	42	6%
No view	0	0%
Multiple views	0	0%
Total	**664**	

Table 19. Subjects represented in a twenty-first century postcard set, 2009

	Impact Photographics		*Smith-Southwestern*	
Subject	*Total number (n=20)*	*Total percentage (%)*	*Total number (n=14)*	*Total percentage (%)*
Scenic	7	35%	1	7%
Vegetation: green shades	10	50%	6	43%
Vegetation: brown shades	0	0%	4	29%
People: white	3	15%	1	7%
People: American Indian	0	0%	0	0%
People: children	0	0%	0	0%
Buildings: interior	0	0%	0	0%
Buildings: exterior	1	5%	1	7%
Dams	0	0%	0	0%
Water: Colorado River	3	15%	4	29%
Water: lakes, streams, waterfalls	2	10%	2	14%
Recreation: mules with riders, river rafting	1	5%	2	14%
Animals: mules and horses	0	0%	0	0%
Animals: deer	0	0%	0	0%
Automobiles	0	0%	1	7%

Trails	0	0%	0	0%
Roads and/or bridges	0	0%	0	0%
Miscellaneous	2	10%	1	7%
Total	**29**		**23**	

Note: Some of the 14 Smith-Southwestern postcards and 20 Impact Photographics postcards contain multiple subjects.

Table 20. Horizontal locations, twenty-first century postcard set, 2009

	Impact Photographics		***Smith-Southwestern***	
Location	*Total number (n=20)*	*Total percentage (%)*	*Total number (n=14)*	*Total percentage (%)*
North rim	3	15%	3	21%
South rim	13	65%	4	29%
Midcanyon	2	10%	5	36%
Unknown	0	0%	1	7%
Multiple	2	10%	1	7%
Total	**20**		**14**	

Table 21. Vertical locations, twenty-first century postcard set, 2009

	Impact Photographics		***Smith-Southwestern***	
Location	*Total number (n=20)*	*Total percentage (%)*	*Total number (n=14)*	*Total percentage (%)*
River	1	5%	3	21%
Midcanyon	1	5%	1	7%
Rim	14	70%	8	57%
Aerial	0	0%	0	0%
No view	1	5%	2	14%
Multiple views	3	15%	0	0%
Total	**20**		**14**	

Summary Tables of All Visual Content Analysis Data

Table 22. Subjects represented in all postcards, 1900–2009

	Detroit, 1900–1909		*Frasher, 1929–1935*		*Curt Teich, 1936–1953*		*Frasher, 1936–1937*		*Impact and Smith-Southwestern, 2009*	
Subject	*Frequency*	*Percentage of representations (n=86)*	*Frequency*	*Percentage of representations (n=65)*	*Frequency*	*Percentage of representations (n=259)*	*Frequency*	*Percentage of representations (n=21)*	*Frequency*	*Percentage of representations (n=34)*
Scenic: vegetation/green	38	44%	46	71%	178	67%	11	52%	16	47%
Scenic: vegetation/brown	0	0%	5	8%	9	3%	2	10%	4	12%
Scenic: canyon layers view	58	67%	45	69%	194	74%	12	57%	8	24%
People: white	15	17%	2	3%	51	19%	0	0%	4	12%
People: American Indian	10	12%	0	0%	31	12%	0	0%	0	0%
People: children	6	7%	0	0%	13	5%	0	0%	0	0%
Buildings: interior	16	19%	0	0%	21	8%	0	0%	0	0%
Buildings: exterior	13	15%	18	28%	55	21%	5	24%	2	6%

Dam	0	0%	0	0%	0	0%	0	0%	0	0%
Water: Colorado River	13	15%	11	17%	45	17%	5	24%	7	21%
Water: lakes, streams, waterfalls	0	0%	2	3%	4	1%	0	0%	4	12%
Recreation: mules with riders	12	14%	0	0%	25	9%	0	0%	3	9%
Animals: mules and horses	1	1%	0	0%	1	0%	0	0%	0	0%
Animals: deer	0	0%	1	2%	6	2%	1	5%	0	0%
Automobiles	0	0%	4	6%	6	2%	1	5%	1	3%
Trails	11	13%	2	3%	38	14%	1	5%	0	0%
Roads and/or bridges	1	1%	11	17%	14	5%	3	14%	0	0%
Miscellaneous	7	8%	2	3%	10	4%	0	0%	3	9%
Total	**201**		**149**		**701**		**41**		**52**	

Table 23. All postcard representations, horizontal locations, 1900–2009

	Detroit, 1900–1909		***Frasher, 1929–35***		***Curt Teich, 1936–55***		***Frasher, 1936–37***		***Impact and Smith-Southwestern, 2009***	
Location	*Frequency*	*Percentage of representations (n=86)*	*Frequency*	*Percentage of representations (n=65)*	*Frequency*	*Percentage of representations (n=259)*	*Frequency*	*Percentage of representations (n=21)*	*Frequency*	*Percentage of representations (n=34)*
North Rim	0	0%	23	35%	25	10%	7	33%	6	18%
South Rim	62	72%	36	55%	162	63%	13	62%	17	50%
Midcanyon	17	20%	0	0%	39	15%	0	0%	7	21%
Unknown	7	8%	5	8%	26	10%	1	5%	1	3%
Multiple	0	0%	1	2%	7	3%	0	0%	3	9%
Total	**86**		**65**		**259**		**21**		**34**	

Table 24. All postcard representations, vertical locations, 1900–2009

	Detroit, 1900–1909		***Frasher, 1929–1935***		***Curt Teich, 1936–1955***		***Frasher, 1936–1937***		***Impact and Smith-Southwestern 2009***	
Location	*Frequency*	*Percentage of Representations (n=86)*	*Frequency*	*Percentage of Representations (n=65)*	*Frequency*	*Percentage of Representations (n=259)*	*Frequency*	*Percentage of Representations (n=21)*	*Frequency*	*Percentage of Representations (n=34)*
River	8	9%	0	0%	43	17%	0	0%	43	126%
Midcanyon	11	13%	0	0%	9	9%	0	0%	9	26%
Rim	42	49%	43	66%	164	63%	13	62%	177	521%
Aerial	0	0%	0	0%	4	2%	0	0%	4	12%
No view	25	29%	22	34%	42	16%	8	38%	50	147%
Multiple views	0	0%	0	0%	5	2%	0	0%	5	15%
Total	**86**		**65**		**267**		**21**		**288**	

Table 25. Subjects represented in *Arizona Highways*, 1923–1985

	1925–1935		1936–1970		1971–1985		
Subject	*Frequency*	*Percentage of representations (n=13)*	*Frequency*	*Percentage of representations (n=664)*	*Frequency*	*Percentage of representations (n=331)*	*Total frequency*
Scenic: Canyon layers view	6	46%	384	58%	234	71%	624
People: American Indian	0	0%	29	4%	2	1%	31
People: white	1	8%	230	35%	97	29%	328
People: children	0	0%	5	1%	1	0%	6
Buildings: interior	0	0%	20	3%	2	1%	22
Buildings: exterior	4	31%	33	5%	16	5%	53
Dams	0	0%	38	6%	2	1%	40
Water: Colorado River	2	15%	103	16%	82	25%	187
Water: lakes, streams, waterfalls	0	0%	93	14%	36	11%	129

Recreation: hiking, mule riding, raft	0	0%	117	18%	41	12%	158
Animals: wildlife	0	0%	5	1%	2	1%	7
Animals: mules and horses	0	0%	42	6%	10	3%	52
Automobiles	0	0%	28	4%	2	1%	30
Trails	2	15%	32	5%	12	4%	46
Roads and bridges	2	15%	27	4%	3	1%	32
Miscellaneous	0	0%	11	2%	0	0%	11
Total	**17**		**1,197**		**542**		**1,756**

Table 26. Horizontal locations in *Arizona Highways*, 1925–1985

	1925–1935		***1936–1970***		***1971–1985***		
Location	*Frequency*	*Percentage of representations (n=13)*	*Frequency*	*Percentage of representations (n=664)*	*Frequency*	*Percentage of representations (n=331)*	*Total frequency*
North Rim	2	15%	69	10%	92	28%	163
South Rim	9	69%	159	24%	91	27%	259
Midcanyon	0	0%	93	14%	37	11%	130
Mead	0	0%	111	17%	0	0%	111
Havasupai	0	0%	58	9%	28	8%	86
West	0	0%	65	10%	38	11%	103
Northeast	1	8%	98	15%	42	13%	141
All-canyon	1	8%	11	2%	3	1%	15
Total	**13**		**664**		**331**		**1,008**

Table 27. Vertical locations in *Arizona Highways*, 1925–1985

	1925–1935		***1936–1970***		***1971–1985***		
Location	*Frequency*	*Percentage of representations (n=13)*	*Frequency*	*Percentage of representations (n=664)*	*Frequency*	*Percentage of representations (n=331)*	*Total frequency*
River	0	0%	348	52%	114	34%	462
Midcanyon	1	8%	40	6%	63	19%	104
Rim	9	69%	234	35%	131	40%	374
Aerial	3	23%	42	6%	23	7%	68
No view	0	0%	0	0%	0	0%	0
Multiple views	0	0%	0	0%	0	0%	0
Total	**13**		**664**		**331**		**1,008**

References

Archives and Manuscript Collections

Arizona State University, Hayden Library, Tempe, Arizona

Arizona Government Documents. *Arizona Highways* Magazine. Call # TRT 40.3: A64 (1972–96); HGY 1.3: A64 Index (1925–61 and 1967–71).

Benson Ford Research Center, The Henry Ford Museum, Dearborn, Michigan

Detroit Publishing Company, online exhibit and collections https://www.thehenryford.org/collections-and-research/digital-collections/archival-collections/420246/.

David Rumsey Map Collection, Cartography Associates, Hayden Arizona

Grand Canyon maps (digitized collection, online). F806.A87 Index (1925–1966) http://www.davidrumsey.com/search?utf8=%E2%9C%93&term=grand+canyon.

Library of Congress, Washington DC

Online collections: Geography and Map Division. American Memory: Mapping the National Parks; Prints & Photographs Reading Room Online; Detroit Publishing Company Photograph Collection; Catalog. Search: Grand Canyon, Detroit Publishing Co. http://www.loc.gov/pictures/search/?q=grand%20canyon%20detroit%20publishing%20company.

National Park Service, Grand Canyon National Park, Arizona

Grand Canyon Museum Collections (postcards, maps, photographs).

Newberry Library, Chicago, Online and Digital Collections

Curt Teich Postcard Archives Digital Collection.

Detroit Publishing Company Collection is also housed in the Curt Teich Postcard Archives Digital Collections. https://www.newberry.org/collection/research-guide/curt-teich-postcard-archives-collection.

New York Public Library Digital Collections

Miriam and Ira D. Wallach Division of Art, Prints, and Photographs: Photography Collection. Grand Canyon, Arizona. Detroit Publishing Company postcards. http://digitalcollections.nypl.org.

Northern Arizona University, Flagstaff. Online and Digital Collections

Cline Library, Special Collections & Archives, Colorado Plateau Archives. https://archive.library.nau.edu/digital/collection/cpa.

Pomona Public Library, Pomona, California

The Frasher Foto Postcard Collection, Special Collections. https://calisphere.org/collections/7781/. Digitized postcard collection, partially available online. Note that the library collection is titled Frasher Foto Postcard Collection, though the company published some postcards as Frashers Fotos Postcards.

University of New Mexico, Albuquerque

Center for Southwest Research and Special Collections and the Map and Geographic Information Center (MAGIC). Historic maps of Spanish colonial period, historic postcards and stereoview cards, rare books, and pamphlets.

Published Works

Abbey, E. 1988. *One Life at a Time, Please.* New York: Henry Holt.

Alcoze, T. A., and M. Hurteau. 2001. "Implementing the Archaeo-Environmental Reconstruction Technique: Rediscovering the Historic Ground Layer of Three Plant Communities in the Greater Grand Canyon Region." In *The Historical Ecology Handbook: A Restorationist's Guide to Reference Ecosystems*, edited by D. Egan and E. A. Howell, 413–24. Washington DC: Island.

Anderson, M. F. 1998. *Living at the Edge: Explorers, Exploiters, and Settlers of the Grand Canyon Region.* Grand Canyon AZ: Grand Canyon Association.

———. 2000. *Polishing the Jewel: An Administrative History of the Grand Canyon National Park.* Grand Canyon AZ: Grand Canyon Association.

———. 2001. *Along the Rim: A Guide to Grand Canyon's South Rim from Hermit's Rest to Desert View.* Grand Canyon AZ: Grand Canyon Association.

Anthamatten, P., and H. Hazen. 2014. "Changes in the Global Distribution of Protected Areas, 2003–2012." *Professional Geographer* 67 (2): 195–203.

Arreola, D. 2013. *Postcards from the Rio Bravo Border: Picturing the Place, Placing the Picture, 1900s–1950s.* Austin: University of Texas Press.

———. 2017. *Postcards from the Sonora Border: Visualizing Place through a Popular Lens, 1900s–1950s.* Tucson: University of Arizona Press.

________. 2019. *Postcards from the Chihuahua Border: Revisiting a Pictoral Past, 1900s–1950s.* Tucson: University of Arizona Press.

______. 2021. *Postcards from the Baja California Border: Portraying Townscape and Place, 1900s–1950s.* Tucson, University of Arizona Press.

Arrigo, A. 2014. *Imaging Hoover Dam: The Making of a Cultural Icon.* Reno: University of Nevada Press.

Arizona Department of Transportation Research Center. 2020. *Economic Impact and Contribution of "Arizona Highways Magazine" to State Tourism.* Phoenix: Arizona Department of Transportation. https://apps.azdot.gov/files/ADOTLibrary/publications/project_reports/pdf/spr764.pdf.

Arizona Hospitality Research and Resource Center, School of Hotel and Restaurant Management. 2005. *Grand Canyon National Park Northern Arizona Tourism Study (Executive Summary)*. Flagstaff: Northern Arizona University.

Baldwin, B. 1998. "On the Verso: Postcard Messages as a Key to Popular Prejudices." *Journal of Popular Culture* 22 (3): 15–28.

Balenquah, L. 2016. "Hopi Kyaptsi 'Respect' for Ancestral Connections." In *We Call the Canyon Home: American Indians of the Grand Canyon Region*, edited by S. Hirst, 1–8. Grand Canyon AZ: Grand Canyon Conservancy.

Barringer, M. 2002. *Selling Yellowstone: Capitalism and the Construction of Nature*. Lawrence: University Press of Kansas.

Bassett, F. 2021. "Postcard Collection–Appendix C. Wish You Were Here: The Story of the Golden Age of Picture Postcards in the United States." New York State Library. Accessed July 27, 2023. http://www.nysl.nysed.gov/msscfa/qc16510ess.htm.

Begay, R. M. 2016. "Grand Canyon in the Navajo Lifeway: Creation of the People, the World, and the Ceremonies." In *We Call the Canyon Home: American Indians of the Grand Canyon Region*, edited by S. Hirst, [page nos]. Grand Canyon AZ: Grand Canyon Conservancy.

Belknap, B., and L. Belknap Evans. 2007. *Grand Canyon River Guide*. 3rd ed. Evergreen CO: Westwater.

Bell, C., and J. Lyall. 2002. *The Accelerated Sublime: Landscape, Tourism, and Identity*. Westport CT: Praeger.

Benton-Short, L. 2016. *The National Mall: No Ordinary Public Space*. Toronto: University of Toronto Press.

Berger, A. 2008. *Manufacturing Desire: Media, Popular Culture, and Everyday Life*. New Brunswick NJ: Transaction.

Blake, K. S. 2003. "Colorado Fourteeners and the Nature of Place Identity." *Geographical Review* 92 (2): 155–79.

———. 2004. "Great Plains Native American Representations along the Lewis and Clark Trail." *Great Plains Quarterly* 24 (4): 263–82.

———. 2014. "Making Mythic Landscapes." In *North American Odyssey: Historical Geographies for the Twenty-first Century*, edited by Craig Colten and Geoffrey L. Buckley, [page nos]. Lanham MD: Rowman and Littlefield.

Blodgett, P. 2007. "Defining Uncle Sam's Playgrounds: Railroad Advertising and the National Parks, 1917–1941." *Historical Geography* 35 (1): 80–113.

Bolen, E., and T. Sayre. 1998. *Ecology of North America*. New York: John Wiley.

Booth, D. 2002. *Searching for Paradise: Economic Development and Environmental Change in the Mountain West*. Lanham MD: Rowman & Littlefield.

Booth, P. 2005. "The Civilian Conservation Corps' Role in Tourism: The CCC's Retooling of Arizona's Natural Resources." In *A Gathering of Grand Canyon Historians:*

Ideas, Arguments, and First-Person Accounts, edited by Michael Anderson, 81–86. Grand Canyon AZ: Grand Canyon Association.

Brooks, K. B. 2006. *Public Power, Private Dams: The Hells Canyon High Dam Controversy*. Seattle: University of Washington Press.

Buckley, G. L. 2004. *Extracting Appalachia: Images of the Consolidation Coal Company 1910–1945*. Athens: Ohio University Press.

Bureau of Reclamation. 2021. "Upper Colorado Region." Last updated August 19, 2021. https://www.usbr.gov/uc/rm/crsp/index.html.

Burroughs, J. 1908. *Leaf and Tendril*. Boston: Houghton, Mifflin.

Cahn, R. 1982. "The Conservation Challenge of the '80s." In *National Parks in Crisis*, edited by E. Horstman. Washington DC: National Parks and Conservation Association.

Callicott, J., and M. Nelson. 1998. *The Great New Wilderness Debate*. Athens: University of Georgia Press.

Carlson, R. 1951. "The Years of *Arizona Highways*." Preface to the *Cumulative Index of Issues Vols. 1–27, 1925–51*. Phoenix: Arizona Department of Transportation. No. F806 A87, Index Arizona Collection, Hayden Library, Arizona State University, Tempe.

Carothers, S. W., and B. T. Brown. 1991. *The Colorado River through Grand Canyon: Natural History and Human Change*. Tucson: University of Arizona Press.

Carr, E. 1999. *Wilderness by Design: Landscape Architecture and the National Park Service*. Lincoln: University of Nebraska Press.

———. 2007. *Mission 66: Modernism and the National Park Dilemma*. Amherst: University of Massachusetts Press.

Carruthers, J. 2014. "Environmental History with an African Edge." In *The Edges of Environmental History: Honouring Jane Carruthers*, edited by C. Mauch and L. Robin. *Rachel Carson Center Perspectives*, vol. 1:9–16. doi.org/10.5282/rcc/6255.

Chesher, C. K. 2003. *Moviemaking: Canyon Country Chronicles*. Moab UT: Canyonlands Natural History Association.

Clark, A. H. 1975. "First Things First." In *Pattern and Process: Research in Historical Geography*, edited by R. Ehrenberg, 9–21. Washington DC: Howard University Press.

Clean Air Task Force. 2000. *Out of Sight: Haze in our National Parks, A Clear the Air Report*. Boston MA: Clean Air Task Force.

Cole, K., and D. Maxwell. 2019. "Cultural Resource Management and Repeat Photography." In *Long Exposures: Repeat Photography and Parks as Portals to Learning*, edited by the Public Lands History Center at Colorado State University. Fort Collins: Colorado State University, the Center for Literary Publishing.

Coleman, A. 2015. "River Rats in the Archive: The Nature of Texts." In *Rendering Nature: Animals, Bodies, Places, Politics*, edited by M. S. Schaffer and P.S. K. Young, [page nos]. Philadelphia: University of Pennsylvania Press.

Colten, C., and L. Dilsaver. 2009. "The Hidden Landscape of Yosemite National Park." *Journal of Cultural Geography* 22 (2): 27–50.

Colter, M. (1933) 2015. *The Manual for Drivers and Guide Descriptive of the Indian Watchtower at Desert View and its Relation, Architecturally, to the Prehistoric Ruins of the Southwest. Fred Harvey Company*. Grand Canyon AZ: Grand Canyon Association.

Conzen, M. P. 1990. *The Making of the American Landscape*. 2nd ed. London: Routledge.

Cosgrove, D. 2008. *Geography and Vision: Seeing, Imaging, and Representing the World*. London: I. B. Tauris.

Cosgrove, D., and S. Daniels. 1988. *The Iconography of Landscape: Essays on the Symbolic Representation, Design and Use of Past Environments*. Cambridge: Cambridge University Press.

Cresswell, T. 2013. *Geographic Thought: A Critical Introduction*. Chichester, West Sussex: Wiley-Blackwell.

Cronin, J. K. 2011. *Manufacturing National Park Nature: Photography, Ecology, and the Wilderness Industry of Jasper*. Vancouver: University of British Columbia Press.

Cronon, W., ed. 1996. *Uncommon Ground: Rethinking the Human Place in Nature*. New York: W. W. Norton.

———. 2003. "The Riddle of the Apostle Islands: How Do You Manage a Wilderness Full of Human Stories?" *Orion* (May–June): 36–42.

Crouch, D., and N. Lubbren. 2003. Introduction to *Visual Culture and Tourism*, edited by D. Crouch and N. Lubbren, 1–22. Oxford: Berg.

Culver, L. 2010. *The Frontier of Leisure: Southern California and the Shaping of Modern America*. New York: Oxford University Press.

Dahlberg, A., R. Rohde, and K. Sandell. 2010. "National Parks and Environmental Justice: Comparing Access Rights and Ideological Legacies in Three Countries." *Conservation and Society* 8 (3): 209–24.

Daniels, S., and D. Cosgrove. 1988. "Introduction: Iconography and Landscape." In *The Iconography of Landscape: Essays on the Symbolic Representation, Design, and Use of Past Environments*, edited by S. Daniels and D. Cosgrove, 1–11. Cambridge: Cambridge University Press.

Davis, G., D. Graber, S. Acker. 2003. "National Parks as Scientific Benchmark Standards for the Biosphere: Or, How are You Going to Tell How It Used To Be, When There's Nothing Left to See?" In *The Full Value of Parks: From Economics to the Intangible*, edited by D. Harmon and A. Putney, 129–40. Lanham MD: Rowman and Littlefield.

DeBres, K., and J. Sowers. 2009. "The Emergence of Standardized, Idealized, and Placeless Landscapes in Midwestern Main Street Postcards." *Professional Geographer* 61 (2): 216–30.

Dellenbaugh, F. 1962 [1908]. *A Canyon Voyage: The Narrative of the Second Powell Expedition*. Tucson: University of Arizona Press.
DeLyser, D. 2005. *Ramona Memories: Tourism and the Shaping of Southern California*. Minneapolis: University of Minnesota Press.
Dilsaver, L. 1994. *America's National Park System: The Critical Documents*. Lanham MD: Rowman and Littlefield.
———. 2004. *Cumberland Island National Seashore: A History of Conservation Conflict*. Charlottesville: University of Virginia Press.
———. 2009. "Research Perspectives on National Parks." *Geographical Review* 99 (2): 268–78.
Dilsaver, L., and C. Colten, eds. 1992. *The American Environment: Interpretations of Past Geographies*. Lanham MD: Rowman & Littlefield.
Dilsaver, L., and W. Wyckoff. 2005. "The Political Geography of National Parks." *Pacific Historical Review* 74 (2): 237–66.
———. 2009. "Failed National Parks in the Last Best Place." *Montana: The Magazine of Western History* 59 (3): 3–93.
Dilworth, L. 1996. *Imagining Indians in the Southwest*. Washington DC: Smithsonian Institution Press.
———. 2001. "Tourists and Indians in Fred Harvey's Southwest." In *Seeing and Being Seen: Tourism in the American West*, edited by D. Wrobel and P. Long, 142–64. Lawrence: For the Center for the American West, University of Colorado at Boulder, by the University Press of Kansas.
Dora, V. 2009. "Traveling Landscape-Objects." *Progress in Human Geography* 33 (3): 334–54.
Dorst, J. 1999. *Looking West*. Philadelphia: University of Pennsylvania Press.
Dumbarton Oaks. 2023. "Curt Teich Co./Curteich-Chicago/C.T. American Art/C.T. Art-Colortone." Accessed on July 28, 2023. https://www.doaks.org/research/library-archives/dumbarton-oaks-archives/collections/ephemera/names/c-t-american-art.
Duncan, J. 1993. "Sites of Representation: Place, Time and the Discourse of the Other." In *Place, Culture, Representation*, edited by J. Duncan and D. Ley, 39–56. London: Routledge.
Dunaway, F. 2005. *Natural Visions: The Power of Images in American Environmental Reform*. Chicago: University of Chicago Press.
Dutton, C. 1882. *Atlas to Accompany the Monograph on the Tertiary History of the Grand Canõn District, Department of the Interior, United States Geological Survey, J. W. Powell Director. U.S.A. Washington 1882*. New York: Julius Bien.
Eco, U. 1986. *Travels in Hyperreality*. San Diego: Harcourt.
Endalman, J. 2002. "Detroit Publishing Company Exhibit Online: DPC History." The Henry Ford Museum. Accessed December 20, 2014. http://www.thehenryford.org/exhibits/dpc/history/retail.asp.

Ensenberger, P. 2009. Personal Communication. March 5, 2009. *Arizona Highways* Director of Photography. Phoenix AZ.

Evans-Pritchard, D. 1989. "How 'They' See 'Us': Native American Images of Tourists." *Annals of Tourism Research* 16 (1): 89–105.

Farrell, R. 1997. "Arizona Highways: The People Who Shaped a Southwestern Magazine, 1925–1990." Master's thesis, Prescott College.

Fedarko, K. 2014a. *The Emerald Mile: The Epic Story of the Fastest Ride in History through the Heart of the Grand Canyon*. New York: Simon and Schuster.

———. 2014b. "A Cathedral Under Siege: Development Threatens the Grand Canyon." *New York Times*. August 10, 2014.

Feldman, J. W. 2011. *A Storied Wilderness: Rewilding the Apostle Islands*. Seattle: University of Washington Press.

Fiege, M. 2005. *The Republic of Nature: An Environmental History of the United States*. Seattle: University of Washington Press.

Finney, C. 2014. *Black Faces, White Spaces: Reimagining the Relationship of African American to the Great Outdoors*. Chapel Hill: University of North Carolina Press.

Fox, S. 1986. *The American Conservation Movement: John Muir and His Legacy*. Madison: University of Wisconsin.

Frank, J. 2013. *Making Rocky Mountain National Park: The Environmental History of an American Treasure*. Lawrence: University Press of Kansas.

Francaviglia, R. 1994. "Elusive Land: Changing Geographic Images of the Southwest." In *Essays on the Changing Images of the Southwest*, edited by R. Francaviglia, D. Narrett, and B. Narramore, 8–39. College Station: Texas A&M University Press.

———. 2005. *Mapping and Imagination in the Great Basin: A Cartographic History*. Reno: University of Nevada Press.

Francesconi, S. 2011. "Multimodally Expressed Humor Shaping Scottishness in Tourist Postcards." *Journal of Tourism and Cultural Change* 9 (1): 1–7.

Fried, S. 2011. *Appetite for America: Fred Harvey and the Business of Civilizing the Wild West, One Meal at a Time*. New York: Bantam.

Germic, S. 2001. *American Green: Class, Crisis, and the Deployment of Nature in Central Park, Yosemite, and Yellowstone*. Lanham MD: Lexington.

Gober, P. 2018. *Building Resilience for Uncertain Water Futures*. New York: Springer.

Goin, P. 2001. "Visual Literacy." *Geographical Review* 91 (1–2): 363–69.

Goldman-Rivera, D. 2003. "Touring *Arizona Highways*: The State's Best Known Magazine as Tourist Site." PhD diss., Arizona State University.

Goodwin, R. 2019. *América: The Epic Story of Spanish North America, 1493–1898*. New York: Bloomsbury.

Gottfried, H. 2013. *Landscape in American Guides and View Books: Visual History of Touring and Travel*. Lanham MD: Lexington.

Grand Canyon Association. 2012. *The Amazing Kolb Brothers: A Grand Life at Grand Canyon*. Pamphlet that accompanied the exhibit at the Historical Kolb Studio, South Rim Village, Grand Canyon National Park. Grand Canyon AZ: Grand Canyon Association, Grand Canyon National Park Service, Northern Arizona University Cline Library.

Grand Canyon National Park. 2021. Grand Canyon in Depth Video Series. Episode 1: "More Than a View." Last accessed June 20, 2023. Available at https://www.nps.gov/grca/learn/photosmultimedia/grand-canyon-in-depth.htm.

Grand Canyon National Park. 2023. Park Statistics. Accessed July 17, 2023. https://www.nps.gov/grca/learn/management/statistics.htm.

Grand Canyon Resort Corporation. 2023. "Experience Grand Canyon West." Accessed July 28, 2023. https://grandcanyonwest.com/.

Grand Canyon Trust. 2016. "Proposal Brief: The Greater Grand Canyon Heritage National Monument." Accessed June 7, 2023. https://www.grandcanyontrust.org/sites/default/files/resources/GGCHNM_Proposal_Brief.pdf.

Graf, W. 1985. *The Colorado River: Instability and Basin Management*. Washington DC: Association of American Geographers.

Gratton, V. 1992. *Mary Colter: Builder Upon the Red Earth*. Grand Canyon AZ: Grand Canyon Natural History Association.

Grebowicz, M. 2015. *The National Parks to Come*. Stanford: Stanford University Press.

Grusin, R. 2004. *Culture, Technology, and the Creation of America's National Parks*. Cambridge: Cambridge University Press.

Gumprecht, B. 2001. *The Los Angeles River: Its Life, Death, and Possible Rebirth*. Baltimore: Johns Hopkins University Press.

Hanna, S. P., and V. J. Del Casino Jr., eds. 2003. *Mapping Tourism*. Minneapolis: University of Minnesota Press.

Harris, C. 1978. "The Historical Mind and the Practice of Geography." In *Humanistic Geography: Prospects and Problems*, edited by D. Samuels and Marwyn, 123–37. Chicago: Maaroufa.

Hales, P. 1988. *William Henry Jackson and the Transformation of the American Landscape*. Philadelphia: Temple University Press.

Harvey, M. 2000. *A Symbol of Wilderness: Echo Park and the American Conservation Movement*. Seattle: University of Washington Press.

Hasyn, J. 2004. "Namibia's Grand Canyon." *Globe and Mail*, January 17, 2004. Accessed March 22, 2009. http://www.theglobeandmail.com/servlet/story/LAC.20040117.NAMIBIA17/TPStory/Travel.

Hausladen, G. J., ed. 2003. *Western Places American Myths*. Reno: University of Nevada Press.

Havlick, D. G. 2018. *Bombs Away: Militarization, Conservation, and Ecological Restoration*. Chicago: University of Chicago Press.

Heacox, K. 2001. *The Making of the National Parks*. Washington DC: National Geographic.
Hirst, S. 2006. *I Am the Grand Canyon: The Story of the Havasupai People*. Grand Canyon AZ: Grand Canyon Association.
———, ed. 2016. *We Call the Canyon Home: American Indians of the Grand Canyon Region*. Grand Canyon AZ: Grand Canyon Conservancy.
Hoelscher, S. D. 1999. "The Photographic Construction of Tourist Space in Victorian America." *Geographical Review* 88 (4): 548–70.
———. 2008. *Picturing Indians: Photographic Encounters and Tourist Fantasies in H. H. Bennett's Wisconsin Dells*. Madison: University of Wisconsin Press.
Holt, R. M. 1959. "Frashers Fotos—Postcard King of the West." *Pomona Valley Historian*. 71–78. Accessed July 28, 2023. https://content.ci.pomona.ca.us/digital/collection/Frasher/id/8038/.
Howard, K., and D. Pardue. 1996. *Inventing the Southwest: The Fred Harvey Company and Native American Art*. Flagstaff AZ: Northland Publishing.
Hualapai Tribe. n.d. "About Hualapai." Accessed July 27, 2023. http://hualapai-nsn.gov/about-2/.
Hughes, J. 1978. *In the House of Stone and Light: A Human History of the Grand Canyon*. Grand Canyon National Park AZ: Grand Canyon Natural History Association.
———. 2005. [check mention of this source in chapter 4]
Hyde, A. 1990. *An American Vision: Far Western Landscape and National Culture*. New York: New York University Press.
Isenberg, A. 2004. *Downtown America: A History of the Place and People Who Made It*. Chicago: University of Chicago Press.
Ives, J. 1861. "Report Upon The Colorado River of the West, Explored in 1857 and 1858 By Lieutenant Joseph C. Ives, Corps Of Topographical Engineers, Under The Direction Of The Office Of Explorations And Surveys, A. A. Humphreys, Captain Topographical Engineers, In Charge. By Order Of The Secretary Of War." Senate. 36th Congress, 1st Session. Ex. Doc. Washington DC: Government Printing Office.
Jackson, D. C. 2013. *Pastoral and Monumental: Dams, Postcards, and American Landscape*. Pittsburgh: University of Pittsburgh Press.
Jackson, J. B. 1972. *American Space: The Centennial Years 1865–1876*. New York: W. W. Norton.
Jacoby, K. 2001. *Crimes against Nature: Squatters, Poachers, Thieves, and the Hidden History of American Conservation*. Berkeley: University of California Press.
Jakle, J. A. 2003. *Postcards of the Night: Views of American Cities*. Santa Fe: Museum of New Mexico Press.
James, G. W. 1900. *In and Around the Grand Canyon*. Boston: Little, Brown.
Jenkins, J. 2016. *Celluloid Pueblo: Western Ways Film and the Invention of the Postwar Southwest*. Tucson: University of Arizona Press.

Kantor, I. 2007. "Ethnic Cleansing and America's Creation of National Parks." *Public Lands and Resources Law Review* 28 (1): 40–64.

Kaska, D. J. Uqualla, A. Hanna, R. Tilousi, C. Tilousi, and S. Hirst. 2016. "The Havasupai." In *We Call the Canyon Home: American Indians of the Grand Canyon Region*, edited by S. Hirst. Grand Canyon AZ: Grand Canyon Conservancy.

Keiter, R. B. 2013. *To Conserve Unimpaired: The Evolution of the National Park Idea.* Washington DC: Island Press.

King, A. 1997. "The Politics of Vision." In *Understanding Ordinary Landscapes*, edited by P. Groth and T. Bressi, 134–44. New Haven CT: Yale University Press.

Kinsey, J. 1992. *Thomas Moran and the Surveying of the American West.* Washington DC: Smithsonian Institution.

Klett, M. 2019. "Repeat Photography in Landscape Research." In *The SAGE Handbook of Visual Research Methods*, 2nd ed., edited by L. Pauwles and D. Mannay, 114–131. London, UK: Sage Publications.

Krim, A. 2005. *Route 66: Iconography of the American Highway*, edited by D. Wood. Santa Fe NM: Center for American Places.

Kolb, E. L. 1914. *Through the Grand Canyon from Wyoming to Mexico.* New York: Macmillan.

Lake County Discovery Museum. n.d. "Guide to Dating Curt Teich Postcards." Accessed September 21, 2020. https://www.newberry.org/sites/default/files/researchguide-attachments/Teich_Postcard_Dating_Guide_2016.pdf (page discontinued).

Langlois, K. 2016. "State of the Grand: Development Proposals Look to Cash in on the Park's Growing Popularity." *High Country News.* April 4, 2016.

Lane, K. M. D. 2013. "Reading Boulder Dam: Landscape Alteration as National Transformation in 1930s America." *Aether: The Journal of Media Geography* 11 (1): 102–26.

———. 2018. "Commentary: Old and New." *Historical Geography* 46 (1): 151–59.

Larson, L., and L. Swanbrow. 2006. "Postcards of Phoenix: Images of Desert Ambivalence and Homogeneity." *Landscape Journal* 25 (2): 205–17.

Larsen, S. C., and T. J. Brock. 2006. "Great Basin Imagery in Newspaper Coverage of Yucca Mountain." *Geographical Review* 95 (4): 517–36.

Lavender, D. 1982. *Colorado River Country.* New York: E. P. Dutton.

Lewis, P. F. 1979. "Axioms for Reading the Landscape." In *The Interpretation of Ordinary Landscapes*, edited by D. Meinig, 11-32. New York: Oxford University Press.

Library of Congress. n.d. *Detroit Publishing Company: About this Collection.* Accessed August 24, 2020. https://www.loc.gov/collections/detroit-publishing-company/about-this-collection/.

Limerick, P. 2000. *Something in the Soil: Legacies and Reckoning in the New West.* New York: W. W. Norton.

———. 2001. “Seeing and Being Seen: Tourism in the American West.” In *Seeing and Being Seen: Tourism in the American West*, edited by D. M. Wrobel and P. T. Long, 39–58. Lawrence: University Press of Kansas.

Lippard, L. 1999a. *The Lure of the Local: Senses of Place in a Multicentered Society*. New York: The New Press.

———. 1999b. *On the Beaten Track: Tourism, Art, and Place*. New York: The New Press.

———. 2001. “Too Much: The Grand Canyon(s).” *Harvard Design Magazine* 10 (Winter/Spring): 1–6.

Lopez, B. 2004. *Vintage Lopez*. New York: Vintage Books.

Louter, D. 2006. *Windshield Wilderness: Cars, Roads, and Nature in Washington's National Parks*. Seattle: University of Washington Press.

Lowenthal, D. 1975. “The Place of the Past in the American Landscape.” In *Geographies of the Mind: Essays in Historical Geosophy in Honor of John Kirtland Wright*, edited by D. Lowenthal and M. J. Bowden, 000–000. London: Oxford University Press.

———. 2015. *The Past Is a Foreign Country: Revisited*. Cambridge: Cambridge University Press.

Lutz, C., and J. Collins. 1993. *Reading National Geographic*. Chicago: University of Chicago Press.

Machlis, G., J. Rogers, D. Bray, J. Cinner, and B. Forist. 2000. *A Look Ahead: Key Social and Environmental Forecasts Relevant to the National Park Service*. (Federal Report) Prepared for Discovery 2000. The National Park Service General Conference. September 11–15, 2000. St. Louis MO.

Machlis, G. E., and J. B. Jarvis. 2018. *The Future of Conservation in America: A Chart for Rough Water*. Chicago: University of Chicago Press.

Machlis, G., and D. Tichnell. 1985. *The State of the World's Parks: An International Assessment for Resource Management, Policy, and Research*. Boulder CO: Westview Press.

Marston, O. R. D. 2014. *From Powell to Power: A Recounting of the First One Hundred River Runners through the Grand Canyon*. Flagstaff AZ: Vishnu Temple Press.

Martin, T., and D. Whitis. 2021. *Guide to the Colorado River in the Grand Canyon: Lees Ferry to South Cove*. 8th ed. Flagstaff AZ: Vishnu Temple Press.

Mason, K. 2004. *Natural Museums: U.S. National Parks, 1872–1916*. East Lansing: Michigan State University Press.

McClelland, L. 1998. *Building the National Parks: Historic Landscape Design and Construction*. Baltimore: Johns Hopkins University Press.

McCloud, S. 1993. *Understanding Comics: The Invisible Art*. New York: Harper Collins.

McGreevy, P. 1994. *Imagining Niagara: The Meaning and Making of Niagara Falls*. Amherst: University of Massachusetts Press.

McLuhan, E., and F. Zingrone, eds. 1995. *Essential McLuhan*. Concord ON: House of Anansi.

McNamee, G. 1997. *Grand Canyon Place Names*. Boulder CO: Johnson Books.

McPhee, J. 1971. *Encounters with the Archdruid*. New York: Farrar, Straus, and Giroux.

McQuaid, M. and K. Bartlett. 1996. "Building an Image of the Southwest: Mary Colter, Fred Harvey Company Architect." In *The Great Southwest of the Fred Harvey Company and the Santa Fe Railway*, 24-35, edited by M. Weigle and B. Babcock. Phoenix: Heard Museum.

Meagher, M., and D. B. Houston. 1998. *Yellowstone and the Biology of Time: Photographs across a Century*. Norman: University of Oklahoma Press.

Meikle, J. 2015. *Postcard America: Curt Teich and the Imaging of a Nation, 1931–1950*. Austin: University of Texas Press.

Meinig, D. 1971. *Southwest: Three Peoples in Geographical Change 1600–1970*. London: Oxford University Press.

———. 1979. "Symbolic Landscapes: Models of American Community." In *The Interpretation of Ordinary Landscapes*, edited by D. Meinig, 164–94. New York: Oxford University Press.

Merchant, C. 2007. *American Environmental History: An Introduction*. New York: Columbia University Press.

Meléndez, A. G., M. J. Young, P. Moore, and P. Pynes, eds. 2001. *The Multicultural Southwest: A Reader*. Tucson: The University of Arizona Press.

Miller, C. 2012. *Public Lands, Public Debates: A Century of Controversy*. Corvallis: Oregon State University Press.

Miller, J. 2012. "The Long Draw: On the Trail of an Artistic Mystery in the American West." *Harper's Magazine* (January).

Miller, G., and D. Miller, D. 1976. *Picture Postcards in the United States, 1893–1918*. New York: Clarkson N. Potter.

Mitman, G. 2013. *Reel Nature: America's Romance with Wildlife on Film*. Seattle: University of Washington Press.

Monmonier, M. 2018. *How to Lie with Maps*. 3rd ed. Chicago: University of Chicago Press.

Montesino Pouzols, F., T. Toivonen, E. Di Minin, A. S. Kukkala, P. Kullberg, J. Kuustera, J. Lehtomaki, H. Tenkanen, P. H. Verburg, and A. Moilanen. 2014. "Global Protected Area Expansion Is Compromised by Projected Land-Use and Parochialism." *Nature*, no. 516: 383–86.

Morehouse, B. 1996. *A Place Called Grand Canyon: Contested Geographies*. Tucson: University of Arizona Press.

Narajano-Morse, N. 1996. "The Living Exhibit under the Museum's Portal from Mud Woman: Poems from the Clay." In *The Great Southwest of the Fred Harvey*

Company and the Santa Fe Railway, edited by M. Weigle and B. Babcock, 197–200. Phoenix: Heard Museum.

Nash, R., ed. 1968. *The American Environment: Readings in the History of Conservation*. Menlo Park CA: Addison-Wesley.

———. 1989. *The Big Drops: Ten Legendary Rapids of the American West*. Boulder CO: Johnson Books.

———. 2001. *Wilderness and the American Mind*. 4th ed. New Haven CT: Yale University Press.

Nash, S. 2017. *Grand Canyon for Sale: Public Lands Versus Private Interests in the Era of Climate Change*. Oakland: University of California Press.

National Park Service. 2002. *Air Quality in National Parks*. 2nd ed. Air Resources Division, Lakewood, Colorado. Washington DC: U.S. Department of the Interior.

———. 2021. "Get to Know Us, What are Cultural Landscapes?" Updated July 9, 2021. Accessed July 11, 2023. https://www.nps.gov/orgs/1557/pclp_orginfo.htm.

______. 2022. "Frequently Asked Questions." Updated March 10, 2022. Accessed July 27, 2023. https://www.nps.gov/grca/faqs.htm#:~:text=But%20most%20people%20measure%20the,277%20miles%20%2F%20446%20km%20long.

______. 2022a. "Indian Garden Now Officially Called Havasupai Gardens." Updated December 27, 2022. Accessed July 28, 2023. https://www.nps.gov/grca/learn/news/indian-garden-officially-renamed-to-havasupai-gardens.htm.

———. 2022b. "Overview of Lake Mead." Updated December 13, 2022. https://www.nps.gov/lake/learn/nature/overview-of-lake-mead.htm.

———. 2023. "Cultural Landscapes 101." Updated July 12, 2023. Accessed July 31, 2023. https://www.nps.gov/articles/cultural-landscapes-101.htm.

———. 2023a. Annual Park Ranking Report for Recreation Visits in 2022. Park Type: National Park. Updated July 22, 2023. Accessed July 26, 2023. Note that search must include only national parks. Table updated annually. https://irma.nps.gov/Stats/SSRSReports/National%20Reports/Annual%20Park%20Ranking%20Report%20(1979%20-%20Last%20Calendar%20Year).

———. 2023b. "Visitor Use Statistics. Grand Canyon NP." Updated May 6, 2023. Accessed June 9, 2020. https://irma.nps.gov/Stats/SSRSReports/Park%20Specific%20Reports/Annual%20Park%20Recreation%20Visitation%20Graph%20(1904%20-%20Last%20Calendar%20Year)?Park=GRCA.

———. n.d. "A Living Canyon: Discovering Life at the Grand Canyon." Accessed June 24, 2023. https://www.nps.gov/grca/planyourvisit/upload/grca_ecology.pdf.

Naylor, R. 2017. *The Amazing Kolb Brothers of Grand Canyon: Photographers, Adventurers, Pioneers*. Flagstaff AZ: Grand Canyon Association.

Neumann, M. 1999. *On the Rim: Looking for the Grand Canyon*. Minneapolis: University of Minnesota Press.

———. 2002. "Making the Scene: The Poetics and Performances of Displacement at the Grand Canyon." In *Tourism: Between Place and Performance*, edited by S. Coleman and M. Crang, 38–53. New York: Berghahn Books.

Newberry Library. 2020. Curt Teich Postcard Archives Digital Collection. Description of collection and items. Accessed August 1, 2023. https://www.newberry.org/collection/research-guide/curt-teich-postcard-archives-collection.

Newhall, B. 1982. *The History of Photography from 1839 to the Present*. New York: Museum of Modern Art.

Nye, D. 2003. "Visualizing Eternity: Photographic Constructions of the Grand Canyon." In *Picturing Place: Photography and the Geographical Imagination*, edited by J. Schwartz and J. Ryan, 74–95. London: I. B. Tauris.

O'Brien, W. E., and W. N. Njambi. 2012. "Marginal Voices in 'Wild' America: Race, Ethnicity, Gender, and 'Nature.'" *The National Parks. The Journal of American Culture* 35 (1): 15–25.

Owen, D. 2017. *Where the Water Goes: Life and Death on the Colorado River*. New York: Riverhead Books.

Patin, T. 1999. "Exhibitions and Empire: National Parks and the Performance of Manifest Destiny." *Journal of American Culture* 22: 41–60.

———, ed. 2012. *Observation Points: The Visual Poetics of National Parks*. Minneapolis: University of Minnesota Press.

Pearson, B. 2012. "How the Forest Service Saved the Grand Canyon." *Forest History Today* 18 (1): 3–11.

Philpott, W. 2013. *Vacationland: Tourism and Environment in the Colorado High Country*. Seattle: University of Washington Press.

Pickles, J. 2004. *A History of Spaces: Cartographic Reason, Mapping, and the Geo-coded World*. London: Routledge.

Piper, K. 2002. *Cartographic Fictions: Maps, Race, and Identity*. New Brunswick NJ: Rutgers University Press.

Pisani, D. J. 1992. *To Reclaim a Divided West: Water, Law, and Public Policy, 1848–1902*. Albuquerque: University of New Mexico Press.

Powell, J. (1874) 2003. *The Exploration of the Colorado River and Its Canyons*. New York: Penguin.

———. 1875a. "The Canōns of the Colorado." *Scribner's Monthly*, [volumes/date missing] 293–310, 394–409, and 523–37.

———. (1895) 1961. *The Exploration of the Colorado River and Its Canyons*. Originally published as *The Canyons of the Colorado*. New York: Dover Publications Inc.

———. 1909. "The Scientific Explorer." In *The Grand Canyon of Arizona: Being a Book of Words from Many Pens, about the Grand Canyon of the Colorado River in Arizona*. Chicago: Passenger Department of the Santa Fe.

Pritchard, P. 1982. "Visibility in Our National Parks is Not Being Adequately Protected." In *National Parks in Crisis*, edited by E. Connally, 107–12. Washington DC: National Parks and Conservation Association.

Pritchard, J. 1999. *Preserving Yellowstone's Natural Conditions: Science and the Perception of Nature*. Lincoln: University of Nebraska Press.

Pyne, S. 1998. *How the Canyon Became Grand: A Short History*. New York: Viking Penguin.

———. 2012. "The Shock of the Old." In *Reconstructing the View: The Grand Canyon Photographs of Mark Klett and Byron Wolfe*. Berkley: University of California Press.

Reisner, M. 1993. *Cadillac Desert: The American West and Its Disappearing Water*. New York: Penguin Books.

Righter, R. 2005. *The Battle Over Hetch Hetchy: America's Most Controversial Dam and the Birth of Modern Environmentalism*. Oxford: Oxford University Press.

Roosevelt, T. 1903. "Address of President Roosevelt at Grand Canyon, Arizona, May 6, 1903." Theodore Roosevelt Papers. Library of Congress Manuscript Division. Accessed August 22, 2020. https://www.theodorerooseveltcenter.org/Research/Digital-Library/Record?libID=o289796. Theodore Roosevelt Digital Library Dickinson State University.

Rose, G. 2016. *Visual Methodologies: An Introduction to the Interpretation of Visual Materials*. 4th ed. London: Sage Publications.

Rothman, H. 1998. "The Tourism of Hegemony I: Railroads, Elites and the Grand Canyon." In *Devil's Bargains: Tourism in the 20th Century American West*, edited by H. Rothman, 50–80. Lawrence: University Press of Kansas.

———. 2001. "Shedding Skin and Shifting Shape: Tourism in the Modern West." In *Seeing and Being Seen: Tourism in the American West*. edited by D. M. Wrobel and P. T. Long, 100–120. Lawrence: University Press of Kansas.

Rothstein, E. 2003. *Visions of Utopia*. Oxford: Oxford University Press.

Rowe, J. 2006. *Arizona Real Photo Postcards: History and Portfolios*. Nevada City NV: Carl Mautz Publishing.

———. 2010. "Have Camera, Will Travel: Arizona Roadside Images by Burton Frasher." *Journal of Arizona History* 51 (4): 337–66.

Runte, A. 2010. *National Parks: The American Experience*. 4th ed. Langham MD: Rowman and Littlefield.

Sadler, C. 2018. *The Colorado*. Brooklyn: National Sawdust and This Earth Press.

Sandweiss, M. A. 2002. *Print the Legend: Photography and the American West*. New Haven CT: Yale University Press.

Sawyer, C. F., and D. R. Butler. 2006. "The Use of Historical Picture Postcards as Photographic Sources for Examining Environmental Change: Promises and Problems." *Geocarto International* 21 (September): 73–80.

Schein, R. 1993. "Representing Urban America: 19th-Century Views of Landscape, Space, and Power." *Environment and Planning D: Society and Space* 11: 7–21.

———. 1997. "The Place of Landscape: A Conceptual Framework for Interpreting an American Scene." *Annals of the Association of American Geographers* 87 (4): 660–80.

Schwartz, J. 2014. "Science and Sentiment: The Work of Photography in Nineteenth-Century North America." In *North American Odyssey: Historical Geographies for the Twenty-First Century*, edited by Craig Colten and Geoffrey L. Buckley, 227–50. Lanham MD: Rowman and Littlefield.

Schwartz, J., and J. Ryan. 2003. *Picturing Place: Photography and the Geographical Imagination*. London: I. B. Taurus.

Schullery, P. 1997. *Searching for Yellowstone: Ecology and Wonder in the Last Wilderness*. Boston: Houghton Mifflin Company.

Schulten, S. 2001. *The Geographical Imagination in American, 1880–1950*. Chicago: University of Chicago Press.

———. 2012. *Mapping the Nation: History and Cartography in Nineteenth-Century America*. Chicago: University of Chicago Press.

Schwantes, C. 2003. *Going Places: Transportation Redefines the Twentieth-Century West*. Bloomington: Indiana University Press.

Sears, J. 1989. *Sacred Places: American Tourist Attractions in the Nineteenth Century*. Amherst: University of Massachusetts Press.

Sellars, R. 1997. *Preserving Nature in the National Parks: A History*. New Haven CT: Yale University Press.

Senf, R., S. J. Pyne, M. Klett, M. and B. Wolfe. 2012. *Reconstructing the View: The Grand Canyon Photographs of Mark Klett and Byron Wolfe*. Berkeley: University of California Press.

Shaffer, M. 2001. *See America First: Tourism and National Identity, 1880–1940*. Washington: Smithsonian Institution Press.

Shepard, J. 2010. *We Are an Indian Nation: A History of the Hualapai People*. Tucson: University of Arizona Press.

Sitney, P. 1992. *Modernist Montage: The Obscurity of Vision in Cinema and Literature*. New York: Columbia University Press.

Smiley, F. E., C. Downum, and S. G. Smiley. 2017. *The Archaeology of Grand Canyon: Ancient Peoples, Ancient Places*. Grand Canyon AZ: Grand Canyon Association.

Smith, L. 2004. The Contested Landscape of Early Yellowstone. *Journal of Cultural Geography* 22 (1): 3–26.

Smith, L., L. Karosic, and E. Smith. 2015. "Greening U.S. National Parks: Expanding Traditional Roles to Address Climate Change." *Professional Geographer* 67 (3): 438–46.

Sneddon, C. 2015. *Concrete Revolution: Large Dams, Cold War Geopolitics, and the US Bureau of Reclamation*. Chicago: University of Chicago Press.

Sottile, C., and K. Dahlgren. 2015. "Grand Canyon Development Plan Sparks Dispute among Navajo" NBC Nightly News. February 8, 2015. http://www.nbcnews.com/nightly-news/grand-canyon-development-plan-sparks-dispute-among-navajo-n302521.

Spence, M. 1999. *Dispossessing the Wilderness: Indian Removal and the Making of the National Parks*. Oxford: Oxford University Press.

Staff, F. 1966. *The Picture Postcard and Its Origins*. New York: Praeger.

Stilgoe, J. R. 2005. *Landscape and Images*. Charlottesville: University of Virginia Press.

Starrs, P. 1988. "The Navel of California and Other Oranges: Images of California and the Orange Crate." *California Geographer* 28: 1–41.

Staveley, G. 2015. *The Rapids and the Roar. A Boating History of the Colorado River and Grand Canyon*. Flagstaff AZ: Fretwater Press.

Stechschulte, N. S. 1994. *The Detroit Publishing Company Postcards: A Handbook for Collectors of the Detroit Publishing Company Postcards Including Checklists of the Regular Numbers, Contracts, Harveys, Miscellaneous Art Cards, the 50,000 Series, Sets, Little Phostint Journeys, Mechanical Postcards, the Panoramas, and Many Others*. Big Rapids MI: N. S. Stechschulte.

Stegner, W. 1992. *Beyond the Hundredth Meridian: John Wesley Powell and the Second Opening of the West*. New York: Penguin.

Strand, G. 2008. *Inventing Niagara: Beauty, Power, and Lies*. New York: Simon and Schuster.

Summit, A. 2013. *Contested Waters: An Environmental History of the Colorado River*. Boulder: University of Colorado Press.

Sutter, P. 2009. *Driven Wild: How the Fight Against Automobiles Launched the Modern Wilderness Movement*. Seattle: University of Washington Press.

Sylvester, P. 2019. *A Nomad's Guide to Exploring Copper Canyon, Mexico*. Accessed June 27, 2023. https://www.worldnomads.com/explore/north-america/mexico/copper-canyon-guide.

Thornbush, M. J. 2008. "Postcards Used to Track Environmental History." *Environmental History* 13 (2): 360–65.

Trimble, S. 2006. *Lasting Light: 125 Years of Grand Canyon Photography*. Flagstaff AZ: Northland Publishing.

Tuan, Y.-F. 1974. *Topophilia: A Study of Environmental Perception, Attitudes, and Values*. University of Minnesota Press.

———. 1977. *Space and Place: The Perspective of Experience*. University of Minnesota Press.

Tweed, W. C. 2010. *Uncertain Path: A Search for the Future of National Parks*. Berkeley: University of California Press.

Vale, T. 2005. *The American Wilderness: Reflections on Nature Protection in the United States*. Charlottesville: University of Virginia Press.

Watahomigie-Corliss, O. 2020. "Uranium Mining Threatens Our Home, The Grand Canyon." *High Country News*, April 14, 2020. https://www.hcn.org/articles/indigenous-affairs-mining-uranium-mining-threatens-our-home-the-grand-canyon.

Watt, L. A. 2017. *The Paradox of Preservation: Wilderness and Working Landscape at Point Reyes National Seashore*. Oakland: University of California Press.

Weber, J., and S. Sultana. 2013. "Why Do So Few Minority People Visit National Parks? Visitation and the Accessibility of 'America's Best Idea.'" *Annals of the Association of American Geographers* 103 (3): 437–64.

Weber. 1992. *The Spanish Frontier in North America*. New Haven CT: Yale University Press.

Weber, R. 2012. *Lost Canyons of the Green River: The Story Before Flaming Gorge Dam*. Salt Lake City: University of Utah Press.

Weber, S., and D. Harmon, eds. 2008. *Rethinking Protected Areas in a Changing World: Proceedings of the 2007 George Wright Society Biennial Conference on Parks, Protected Areas, and Cultural Sites*. Hancock MI: George Wright Society.

Weigle, M. 1989. "From Desert to Disney World: The Santa Fe Railway and the Fred Harvey Company Display the Indian Southwest." *Journal of Anthropological Research* 45 (1) 115–37.

Weigle, M., and B. Babcock, eds. 1996. *The Great Southwest of the Fred Harvey Company and the Santa Fe Railway*. Phoenix: Heard Museum.

Wells, C. W. 2013. *Car Country: An Environmental History*. Seattle: University of Washington Press.

Werther, M., and L. Mott. 2002. *Linen Postcards: Images of the American Dream*. Wayne PA: Sentinel Publishing.

White, Richard. 2011. *The Organic Machine: The Remaking of the Columbia River*. New York: Macmillan Publishers.

Wilderness Act. 1964. (16 U.S.C. 1131–1136). Public Law 88-577. 88th Congress, Second Session. September 3, 1964. https://www.nps.gov/subjects/wilderness/upload/W-Act_508.pdf.

Williams, T. T. 2016. *The Hour of Land: A Personal Topography of America's National Parks*. New York: Sarah Crichton Books.

Wilson, A. 1992. *The Culture of Nature: North American Landscape from Disney to the Exxon Valdez*. Cambridge MA: Blackwell Publishers.

Wilson, R. 2020. *America's Public Lands: From Yellowstone to Smokey Bear and Beyond*. 2nd ed. Lanham MD: Rowman and Littlefield.

Work Projects Administration (WPA). 1940. *Arizona: A State Guide*. New York: Hastings House Publishers.

Worster, D. 1985. *Rivers of Empire: Water, Aridity, and the Growth of the American West*. New York: Pantheon Books.

———. 2001. *A River Running West: The Life of John Wesley Powell*. New York: Oxford University Press.

———. 2003. *Environmental History: The View at the Grand Canyon*. Modified January 16, 2003. Accessed July 22, 2020. http://www.nps.gov/parkhistory/hisnps/NPSHistory/environmentalhistory.htm.

Wright, R. G. 1996. *National Parks and Protected Areas: Their Role in Environmental Protection*. Cambridge: Blackwell Science Ltd.

Wyckoff, W. 2003. "Understanding Western Places: The Historical Geographer's View." In *Western Places American Myths: How We Think About the West*, edited by G. Hauslauden, 000–000. Reno: University of Nevada Press.

———. 2014. *How to Read the American West: A Field Guide*. Seattle: University of Washington Press.

———. 2020. *Riding Shotgun with Norman Wallace: Rephotographing the Arizona Landscape*. Albuquerque: University of New Mexico Press.

Wyckoff, W., and L. Dilsaver. 1997. "Promotional Imagery of Glacier National Park." *Geographical Review* 87(1): 1–26.

Wyckoff, W., and C. Nash. 1994. "Geographical Images of the American-West: The View from 'Harpers Monthly,' 1850–1900." *Journal of the West* 33 (3): 10–21.

Young, T. 2002. "Virtue and Irony in a U.S. National Park." In *Theme Park Landscapes: Antecedents and Variations*, edited by T. Young and R. Riley. Washington DC: Dumbarton Oaks Research Library Collection.

———. 2004. *Building San Francisco's Parks, 1850–1930*. Baltimore: Johns Hopkins University Press.

———. 2014. "The End of Camping: Coming Home to the City." *BOOM: The Journal of California* 4 (3): 70–75.

Young, T., and L. Dilsaver. 2011. "Collecting and Diffusing the World's Best Thought." *George Wright Forum* 28 (3): 269–78.

Youngs, Y. 2011. "On Grand Canyon Postcards." *Environmental History* 16 (1): 138–47.

———. 2012. "Editing Nature in Grand Canyon National Park Postcards." *Geographical Review* 102 (4): 486–509.

———. 2014. "Shaping Tourism." In *North American Odyssey: Historical Geographies for the Twenty-First Century*, edited by C. Colten and G. L. Buckley. Lanham MD: Rowman and Littlefield.

———. 2018. "Wild, Unpredictable, and Dangerous: A Historical Geography of Hazards and Risk in U.S. National Parks." In *The American Environment Revisited: Environmental Historical Geographies of the U.S.*, edited by G. Buckley and Y. Youngs, [000–000]. Lanham MD: Rowman and Littlefield.

———. 2019. "Viewing Power and Place at Grand Canyon: Grand View Point, 1880–1926". *Journal of Arizona History* 60 (4): 507–24.

———. 2020. "Danger Beyond This Point: Visual Representation, Cultural Landscapes, and the Geography of Environmental Hazards in U.S. National Parks." *GeoHumanities: Space, Place, and Humanities* 6, no. 2, 314–46.

Youngs, Y., D. White, and J. Wodrich. 2008. "Transportation Systems as Cultural Landscapes in National Parks: A Historical and Interpretive Study of Visitors' Transportation Behavior in Yosemite Valley." *Society and Natural Resources: An International Journal* 21 (9): 797–811.

Zelinsky, W. 1973. *The Cultural Geography of the United States*. Englewood Cliffs NJ: Prentice-Hall.

Zukin, S. 1991. *Landscapes of Power: From Detroit to Disney World*. Berkeley: University of California Press.

Index

Page numbers in italics indicate illustrations. Page numbers with t indicate tables.
AH = *Arizona Highways* magazine
GRCA = Grand Canyon National Park

IN THE AMERICA'S PUBLIC LANDS SERIES

The First Atomic Bomb: The Trinity Site in New Mexico
Janet Farrell Brodie

Restoring Nature: The Evolution of Channel Islands National Park
Lary M. Dilsaver and Timothy J. Babalis

Framing Nature: The Creation of an American Icon at the Grand Canyon
Yolonda Youngs

To order or obtain more information on these or other University of Nebraska Press titles, visit nebraskapress.unl.edu.